THIS FAR
BY FAITH

(fig. 1) Pictorial Quilt. Harriet Powers (1837–1911). Athens, Georgia, about 1895–1898. *Bequest of Maxim Karolik. Courtesy, Museum of Fine Arts, Boston.*

THIS FAR

BY FAITH

READINGS

IN

AFRICAN-AMERICAN

WOMEN'S

RELIGIOUS

BIOGRAPHY

EDITED BY

JUDITH WEISENFELD

AND

RICHARD NEWMAN

ROUTLEDGE NEW YORK AND LONDON

Published in 1996 by

Routledge
29 West 35th Street
New York, NY 10001

Published in Great Britain by

Routledge
11 New Fetter Lane
London EC4P 4EE

Library of Congress Cataloging-in-Publication Data

This far by faith : readings in African-American women's religious
  biography / edited by Judith Weisenfeld and Richard Newman.
      p.   cm.
    ISBN 0–415–91311–X. — ISBN 0–415–91312–8 (pbk.)
    1. Afro-Americans—Religion.   2. Afro-American women—Biography.
3. Religious biography—United States.   4. Women and religion—
United States—Biography.   I. Weisenfeld, Judith.   II. Newman,
Richard, 1930–   .
BR563.N4T463   1996
277.3'08'082—dc20   95–31000
                                                                 CIP

For Al Raboteau, Teacher, Colleague, Friend

CONTENTS

ACKNOWLEDGMENTS   ix

INTRODUCTION: WE HAVE BEEN BELIEVERS: PATTERNS
OF AFRICAN-AMERICAN WOMEN'S RELIGIOSITY   1
JUDITH WEISENFELD

PART 1   AFRICAN-AMERICAN WOMEN'S RELIGIOUS ARTS

1   THE HARRIET POWERS PICTORIAL QUILTS   21
     MARIE JEANNE ADAMS

2   WILLIE MAE FORD SMITH OF ST. LOUIS: A SHAPING
     INFLUENCE UPON BLACK GOSPEL SINGING STYLE   32
     WILLIAM THOMAS DARGAN AND KATHY WHITE BULLOCK

3   LUCIE E. CAMPBELL WILLIAMS:
     A CULTURAL BIOGRAPHY   56
     REVEREND CHARLES WALKER

PART 2   AFRICAN-AMERICAN WOMEN AND
          CHURCH INSTITUTIONS

4   PRAYING IN THE SHADOWS: THE OBLATE SISTERS
     OF PROVIDENCE, A LOOK AT NINETEENTH-CENTURY
     BLACK CATHOLIC SPIRITUALITY   73
     THADDEUS J. POSEY, O. F. M., CAP.

5   THE CONTROVERSY OVER WOMEN'S MINISTRY IN THE
     AFRICAN METHODIST EPISCOPAL CHURCH DURING
     THE 1880s: THE CASE OF SARAH ANN HUGHES   94
     STEPHEN WARD ANGELL

6   "WARRIOR MOTHER OF AFRICA'S WARRIORS OF THE
     MOST HIGH GOD": LAURA ADORKOR KOFEY AND THE
     AFRICAN UNIVERSAL CHURCH   110
     RICHARD NEWMAN

7 MARY MCLEOD BETHUNE AND THE METHODIST EPISCOPAL
   CHURCH NORTH: IN BUT OUT   124
   Clarence G. Newsome

8 RELIGION, POLITICS, AND GENDER: THE LEADERSHIP OF
   NANNIE HELEN BURROUGHS   140
   Evelyn Brooks Higginbotham

9 A BLACK WOMAN IN A WHITE MAN'S CHURCH:
   AMY E. ROBBINS AND THE REORGANIZATION   158
   Roger D. Launius

10 MINISTER AND FEMINIST REFORMER: THE LIFE OF
   FLORENCE SPEARING RANDOLPH   177
   Bettye Collier-Thomas

PART 3 AFRICAN-AMERICAN WOMEN AND
        CHRISTIAN MISSIONS

11 ELIZABETH MARS JOHNSON THOMSON (1807–1864):
   A RESEARCH NOTE   189
   Randall K. Burkett

12 "WHO IS SUFFICIENT FOR THESE THINGS?"
   SARA G. STANLEY AND THE AMERICAN MISSIONARY
   ASSOCIATION, 1864–1868   203
   Judith Weisenfeld

13 SPELMAN'S EMMA B. DELANEY AND THE AFRICAN MISSION   220
   Sandy D. Martin

PART 4 AFRICAN-AMERICAN WOMEN, RELIGION,
        AND ACTIVISM

14 IN SEARCH OF HARRIET TUBMAN'S SPIRITUAL AUOTIOBRAPHY   239
   Jean M. Humez

15 REPRESENTING TRUTH: SOJOURNER TRUTH'S KNOWING
   AND BECOMING KNOWN   262
   Nell Irvin Painter

16 SEPTIMA P. CLARK AND THE STRUGGLE FOR HUMAN RIGHTS   300
   Grace Jordan McFadden

   SELECTED BIBLIOGRAPHY FOR FURTHER READING   313

   INDEX   319

ACKNOWLEDGMENTS

We would like to thank Dr. Bettye Collier-Thomas of Temple University and Dr. Stephen Ward Angell of Florida A&M University for permission to include their previously unpublished articles in this collection. Thanks from Judith to Timea Szell, Celia Deutsch, Dick Newman, and Marlie Wasserman for their comments on the introduction. We are also grateful to our editor at Routledge, Marlie Wasserman, for the encouragement that moved this project from its planning stages to publication, to her assistant, Mary Carol DeZutter, for guidance in preparing the manuscript, and to our production editor, Kim Herald.

JUDITH WEISENFELD

WE HAVE BEEN BELIEVERS: PATTERNS OF AFRICAN-AMERICAN WOMEN'S RELIGIOSITY

We have been believers yielding substance for the world.
With our hands have we fed a people and out of our
    strength have they wrung the necessities of a nation.
Our song has filled the twilight and our hope has
    heralded the dawn.
——Margaret Walker, "We Have Been Believers,"
For My People 1942

The religious lives of African-American women loom as a substantial and yet largely undiscovered terrain in the study of religion in America. Despite the relative lack of scholarly attention to African-American women's personal spiritual experiences and expressions, both women's communities of faith, as well as their religiously based impulses to effect social change have constituted the core of the personal histories of many women of color. Even a cursory examination of the range of African-American women's experiences across the lines of class, region, time, sexuality, and particular religious affiliation reveals a stunning range of spiritual expressions for women as varied as Aretha Franklin, Sojourner Truth, Marie Laveau, Maya Angelou, and Mary McLeod Bethune. While these and many other women do not measure the value, duration, or depth of their religious experience against a uniform standard, they nevertheless indicate the influence of religion on their lives in some way. As Margaret Walker's powerful poem, excerpted above, emphasizes, religious belief systems have assisted African-American women in centering themselves and their communities in times of hardship, and they have provided a language for expressing the joy and hope of better times.

This volume approaches the large question of the character and function of religious experience and expression for African-American women through the telling of individual religious life stories. The essays included here do not seek to idealize black women's religious lives, but, rather, they attempt to understand the complexities of religion in America from the range of perspectives afforded by African-American women's experiences. Some of the women who appear in this collection were connected to or emerged from many Protestant denominations, including the African Methodist Episcopal, African Methodist Episcopal Zion, Methodist Episcopal, Presbyterian, Pentecostal, and Baptist. Others were committed to Roman Catholicism, Mormonism, the African Universal Church, or African-derived traditions, and yet others with no particular affiliation still grounded their lives in spiritual concerns. Some of the women had important relationships with men, some had families, and many sacrificed a great deal for their spiritual convictions. All of these women, together and as unique individuals, whether famous, of enduring influence in American society, or lost to the historical record save for these essays, provide a singular perspective on American and African-American religiosity. Nevertheless, it would do them a disservice to view each woman outside the context of larger issues concerning African-American women and religion.

◆ ◆ ◆

First, why have we separated out the particular case of African-American women for such a collection of essays? Central to our analysis of religion in America is an understanding of religious experience as embedded in social contexts. While the most intimate, direct, and personal religious experience can be examined productively as merely an individual event, no person fails to be influenced by the powerful social forces within which she finds herself. For African-American women, experiences and identities—religious and otherwise—necessarily emerge through their participation in a society built around particular constructions of race, gender, class, sexuality, and other such categories.[1] To speak of the socially constructed nature of race, for example, is to view it not as a biological fact inhering in genetics, but, rather, as a lens through which people recognize difference, exercise power, and enact community boundaries. To recognize race, gender, class, and sexuality as socially constructed expressions of power does not, however, negate the reality of these categories as means both of disempowering people and also of constructing positive communal and individual identities. Additionally, we must see the interaction of all of these categories with one another in ways that make the experiences of African-American women different from those of other women and of men. In this way, a thorough, critical examination of the specificity of African-American women's experiences becomes of serious importance.

Because Harriet Tubman, for example, lived as a woman whose gender and sexuality were understood through the prism of her race and class as an enslaved person, her experience of gender, racial, and class status necessarily differed from that of a white American woman or man, an African-American man, an Asian-American woman, and so on, in her same time. Moreover, her experience within these socially constructed categories differed from that of an African-American woman of free status. These essays probe the ways in which religious experience mediates and is mediated by the specific persons and contexts of a variety of African-American women.

The study of African-American women and religion is also critical to broader understandings of religion in America. Attention to the specificity of black women's religious experiences complicates and brings new dimensions to any discussion of questions of tradition, authority, and religious subjectivity—all of which have been traditionally positioned as male in black church studies. Scholarship that emphasizes the institution of "the black church"—an umbrella term for historically black denominations—as the only venue for religious experience and expression and that sees ordained positions within those churches as the primary means of authenticating leadership presents only a partial picture of African-American religious life. Such studies necessarily exclude women's experiences because they do not fully appreciate the range of approaches that African-American women have taken to participate as agents in their own religious lives and in the religious lives of their communities. As an introduction to the essays collected here, then, we take up broad themes that emerge from a consideration of the aggregate of individual religious lives of black women, using examples from the experiences of women not present in the articles included in this text. In collecting these essays we do not assume any norm for religious subjectivity established by whiteness or maleness, nor one through which African-American women *must* be evaluated. Instead, we place the women themselves at the center of the project.

POWER AND HOPE

The large degree to which personal religious experience, the bonds of communities of faith, and sacred traditions all afforded African-American women access to varieties of power should not be underestimated. While power is conventionally construed as derived from institutions and hierarchies, it is the case that African-American women most often created and utilized power in ways that do not appear significant according to traditional standards. As Jua-lynne Dodson has argued, despite the lack of access to formal positions of re-ligious leadership in most Christian churches, African-American women understood their power to rest *not* in those positions exclusively, but also in their overall impact on their communities, through their ability to mobilize people and financial resources, for example.[2] Dodson, then, emphasizes the social context of power, an issue to which we will return in discussing the ways in which religion served as a base for African-American women to challenge the prevailing social order. First, however, let us take note of the kinds of power African-American women derived from the most intimate of religious experiences—the direct encounter with the divine.

The conversion experience, so central in the Christian tradition, became yet more profound for African-American women in the context of the American system of chattel slavery. The conversion experience gave en-slaved African-American women—forced into the status of "natally alien-ated" people, as Orlando Patterson has termed it, and severed both from their ancestors and from their descendants—entry to a different realm of power from that of their masters and connected them to a different sort of lineage from the ones which had been denied them. Clifton H. Johnson's collection of the conversion narratives of ex-slaves makes it apparent that conversion provided, for some enslaved African-Americans, definitive proof of their divinely conferred humanity. Moreover, such powerful interactions with God and the revelations, through visions and voices, of their place in God's plan provided an important means of constructing ultimate meaning from the incomprehensible experience of slavery.[3]

One woman, interviewed over sixty years after the end of slavery, cata-logued the horrors of the institution and reflected on her childhood experi-ence with one especially brutal white slaveholder. She recalled, "Yes, in them days it was hell without fires. This is one reason why I believe in a hell. I don't believe a just God is going to take no such man as that into his king-dom."[4] For this woman, a divine order larger than her own suffering of beatings or the murder of babies by the slaveholder provided consolation and motivation to survive. Speaking of God, she continued:

He has taken fear out of me. He shows me things, but they are spiritual and come from his matchless wisdom, and the world can't see nor under-stand them. I profess to know nothing about the world nor its ways. I can't read a line either of the scriptures or any other kind of writing. . . . So I may not speak the words just like they are in his printed book, but I am right anyhow and know it. I often wish I did know how to read, but since I didn't have the chance to learn—being fearsome to be seen with a book when I was a slave—God has seen my need and made me satisfied. He has taken me, a fool—for sometimes my head was beat so I thought I was foolish—and hidden with me the secret of eternal life. He has made me to stand up on my feet and teach the world-wise out of his wisdom that comes from on high.[5]

Another woman articulated, in the bluntest terms, the assurance that her conversion experience provided, saying, "I have always been a sheep. I was never a goat. I was created and cut out and born in the world for heaven."[6]

For some African-American women, the power of direct encounters with God through prayer and visions not only illuminated their humanity, but also freed their voices. In perhaps the best-known African-American spiritual narrative, *The Life and Religious Experience of Jarena Lee, a Coloured Lady, Giving an Account of Her Call to Preach the Gospel*, first published in 1836, Lee devotes great attention to the ways in which her direct experiences with God following her conversion conferred on her the authority to speak as a religious leader as well as opened up possibilities for her life not previously available.

Reared in New Jersey and outside the context of slavery, Lee was sent from home early in life to work as a servant. Rather than emphasize the mundane biographical details of her life, Lee organized her narrative around her conversion experience—one much like those discussed above— and around her struggles to do what she saw as God's will revealed to her. Among the things she struggled with was a command to speak with religious authority in public. Lee wrote that a voice said to her, "Preach the Gospel; I will put words in your mouth, and will turn your enemies to become your friends."[7] The opposition she faced and the sacrifices that public preaching required of her, including leaving her children behind as she assumed her place as an evangelist, sometimes caused Lee to waver in her commitment. However, her narrative assures its readers that she felt that God remained with her in very personal ways and gave her the authority and power to preach.

Amanda Berry Smith, a well-known nineteenth-century traveling evangelist, also produced a narrative recounting her religious experiences. Born a slave in Maryland, Smith was bought out of slavery, along with the rest of her family, by her father. Smith asserted that it was her mother's Christian faith that helped to convert the daughter of their white owner, who then effected the agreement allowing the Berry family to purchase their freedom. Smith recounted her religious, personal, and work life in New York in a narrative rich with detail of continual interactions with God, as well as temptations and conversations with Satan. She asserted that it was in the context of a vivid struggle between God and Satan, as she sat in a Methodist church, that she experienced sanctification, an experience that she and others who hold to this doctrine see as separate from the conversion experience. Smith recalled:

> And somehow I seemed to sink down out of sight of myself, and then rise; it was all in a moment. I seemed to go two ways at once, down and up. Just then such a wave came over me, and such a welling up in my heart, and these words rang through me like a bell: "God in you, God in you," and I thought doing what? Ruling every ambition and desire and bringing every thought unto captivity and obedience to His will. How I have lived through it I cannot tell, but the blessedness of the love and the peace and power I can never describe. O, what glory filled my soul! The great vacuum in my soul began to fill up; it was like a pleasant draught of cool water, and I felt it.[8]

After this, Smith wrote that God directed her to preach, with a vision of the letters GO, and a voice telling her, "Go, preach."[9] Like Jarena Lee, Smith emphasized the hardships of a life as an African-American woman traveling the world and preaching in public at a time when women did not do such things without opposition. Smith's autobiography in particular places her experiences firmly in the context of religious communities suffering the profound impact of racism, and Smith underscores the degree to which constructions of race influence her sense of white and black Christian communities. In both Lee's and Smith's narratives, and those of other African-American women preachers in the nineteeth century, the authors attributed the power to preach, and their ability to withstand and thrive despite racism and sexism, to their direct experiences with God.[10]

In addition to the authority African-American women derived from their most personal and intimate spiritual experiences, many women also gained personal and social power through their role as moral exemplars in their communities. Cheryl Townsend Gilkes has explored this particular avenue to power in a discussion of the roles of church mothers as "older, venerated, Spirit-filled women who hold considerable power within *nearly* au-

tonomous and well-organized parallel women's worlds."[11] Given the historically significant gendering of religious leadership as male in both Christian and non-Christian contexts in America, the "dual-sex" system prevalent
in black churches, in which African-American women organized, directed,
and administered a range of church-based religious organizations, became
an important means through which they could assert their own agendas for
the church community. Evelyn Brooks Higginbotham's study of the
women's movement among black Baptists and, most notably, the Woman's
Convention, founded in 1900, of the National Baptist Convention, the
largest black Baptist denomination, trenchantly illustrates the ways in which
black Baptist women's organizations assisted women in developing a sense
of their own concerns as well as a mechanism through which to influence
their communities in positive ways.[12]

Sarah Rice relates the story of the conferring of the status of church
mother on her in a small Baptist church in Jacksonville, Florida in the early
1950s. Having recently joined this particular congregation at the age of
about forty-four, Rice expressed surprise at the honor. She reported, "The
pastor said, 'Sister Rice, do you know why they voted for you? They respect
you. It's not a matter of age; it's a matter of respect and the confidence the
people have in you.'" Rice went on to say that she "reluctantly accepted,"
but grew in confidence and in the esteem of the church over the years, and
came to be an important voice within the church and on behalf of women in
particular.[13]

Religious experience as a grounding for African-American women's
sense of self and ability to participate in the formulation of communal identities stands as a significant thread connecting the individual stories of religious African-American women. Through intimate spiritual experiences,
African-American women's stories often emphasize, they gained the assurance of a divine guidance and, as a result, found the power to speak, to organize, to lead, and to hope for all things possible.

FLEXIBILITY AND CREATIVITY

Without question, the Christian tradition stands out historically as central to
the experiences of a majority of African-American women involved in religious life. However, a number of issues bear mentioning here that serve to il-
luminate the finer contours of black women's religious experiences. While
African-American women have exhibited profound devotion to particular denominational or other religious structures that have, in turn, benefited from

their energy and talents, many African-American women, whether out of necessity or choice, have also demonstrated a flexibility in their religiosity.
Rather than a measure of inconsistency, some black women's adaptability in
religious contexts points to other significant meanings.

The flexibility revealed in the religious lives of some African-American
women arises in response to the constraints of context, including the impact
of racism, the pressures of family life, or their curtailed access to a particular religious form. In such circumstances, many women merely made the
most of what the situation offered them. Sara Brooks, born in 1911 to a
farming family in rural Alabama, described the family's typical Sunday:

> We lived in the country and we wasn't livin' really close around anyone, so
> we'd love to get out—we'd get out and go to church in order to go some-
> place. We'd go to Sunday school and we'd stay to church. Our church did-
> n't have a meeting but once a month, so we'd stay at our church those
> Sundays, and if our church didn't have a meeting that Sunday, we'd leave
> our Sunday school and go to another church. We'd go to Trimble first Sun-
> day, second Sunday we'd go to Horizon, third Sunday we'd go to Pleas-
> antville, and the fourth Sunday we'd go to the Methodist church. See?
> That's the way we went. But we went *every* Sunday. . . .[14]

Where Sara Brooks emphasizes the impact of scarce resources spread
out in a rural district as the motivating factor for her family's attendance at
a variety of church services, Frances "Frank" Rollin's diary reveals a different approach. Rollin, a nineteenth-century Boston abolitionist and author,
wrote in her diary on a Sunday in early January of 1868 that she had attended one church in the morning, visited with a family of former underground railroad organizers for tea, and had gone to a different church in the
afternoon. Neither congregation had been listed in her previous week's account of church attendance. Rollin's sojourns through Boston's religious
communities seems to have been primarily related to her thirst for powerful and moving sermons. Rollin often referred to an individual church as
"belonging" to the pastor whose sermon attracted her.[15] Yet, as committed
as Rollin remained to Protestant belief and practice, she made the following diary entry just two months later:

> March 1. Worked on my book in the morning. Later, there was a sitting for
> spiritual purposes. The table was clearly lifted and twisted about and the
> spirit answered to C. L. Felt as though it meant Grandma. I left the room.

I am no skeptic, "I thank God," as Goethe said, "that I do not doubt the possibility of anything."[16]

Like many other educated activist women of the nineteenth century, Rollin proved to be open to a variety of religious experiences and, again, as many in the same period, she was drawn to spiritualism. Rollin's attraction to spiritualism stemmed particularly from the answers she felt it provided to questions about physical health in this world, and life in the next.

Alice Dunbar-Nelson, known for her marriage to poet Paul Lawrence Dunbar, but also for her career in journalism and as a tireless activist in the black women's club movement, points to the diversity of religious expression among African-American women with her participation in the Unity movement throughout the 1920s. Related to Christian Science and other New Thought religious perspectives, Unity emphasizes the absolute goodness of God and the power of human consciousness—also seen as inherently divine—to effect positive outcomes. Dunbar-Nelson became attracted both to the healing and prayer aspects of this nondoctrinal form of Christianity, and her diary reveals her difficulties with faith, as well as the power she derived from prayer and contemplation.

Having struggled with her commitment to Unity prayer and mediation, Dunbar-Nelson's August 7, 1921 diary entry spoke of a failure to "put in practice what I've read." She continued, "I'm a dumb driven cattle and deserve all I get."[17] Yet on August 21 she had begun to find strength in her reading of Unity literature. She wrote:

> My head was stuffy after staying in the office until eight o'clock, so I went for a walk after coming home. Out 11th Street [in Wilmington, Delaware], quiet and broody under the trees, with pleasant homes; across 10th Street Park and up the stairs to the reservoir. It was heavenly up there—lovely water, soft grass, the clover leaves shut tight and shedding the dew; the moon big and red gold, hanging over the trees and matching the electric lights around the banks. Boys and girls enjoying themselves after the fashion of kids. I hungered, dreaming over the loveliness of it all. And I tried to think through this conception of the Infinite, Omnipotent Good, within me, around me, ME. I went downstairs and sat on a bench in the park near a weeping willow tree, bending over the skating pond. It was as still as if it had been painted.[18]

Dunbar-Nelson still felt despair many times throughout the year, and turned to Unity for guidance. In October of 1921 she wrote:

I fear I am slipping back. I am cross, pessimistic, bitter, things are going wrong with me generally; I am nervous and tired and irritable; I cannot seem to make any headway, and above all that, rheumatism! It is maddening! Both knees as bad as they were when I used to suffer so terribly in years gone by. The only consolation I have in the matter is that it is not a sign of age, since I have had it practically all my life, thirty years anyhow. Or more. But it is fearfully inconvenient and devastating. I want to invoke the aid of Silent Unity, but do not seem to be able to make the connection. I MUST GET MYSELF TOGETHER.[19]

Dunbar-Nelson's attraction to Unity and other New Thought movements clearly stemmed, in part, from her need to address issues of physical healing. She turned to Unity to seek relief from her own rheumatism, and she assisted family members in seeking healing through Unity's emphasis on the mind-body connection.

The openness of African-American women to the diversity of religious forms often becomes most visible with respect to issues of healing. Onnie Lee Logan, a midwife in Alabama from the 1930s through the 1980s, spoke of her sense of vocation, saying, "I do believe that it was meanted by God for me to deliver babies and to he'p the people that I have helped."[20] Because of her firm belief in the divine nature of her vocation, Logan often sought direct access to God to assist her during particularly difficult births. Describing one such case, she recalled:

I said, "Look here." I went on in and got her comfortable. I said, "Now you just stay right there and get a good rest and I'm gonna tend to you." I went in the bathroom, closed the do' after I got her comfortable, and I talked to God. When I talked to Him, He talks back to me. He told me what to do until I went in there. Got on my knees and consulted God and I come outa there knowin' what to do cause He just guided my hands. He guided those lil hands and this mind and I did it and it worked. That give to know there's a high power somewhere and all you got to do is believe.[21]

In addition to Logan's understanding of her own talents as derived from her relationship with God, she also argued that Southern African-American folk remedies were efficacious because of God's action to make them work. Thus, although a committed Christian, Logan saw no conflict with folk remedies, often derived from Native American or African traditions. For Logan, it was not of paramount importance that the individuals using the

folk remedy conform to orthodox belief, but rather that they believe in the
kind of divine power that Logan herself spoke of guiding her.[22]

Luisah Teish, an African-American practioner in the West African
Yoruba tradition, accords healing a prominent position in her attraction to
this African tradition and her turn to it from a Catholic upbringing. In an interview Teish described the importance of "talking, cleansing, and feeding"
in her healing sessions with others:

> Let's say somebody [an artist] came to me because her hands kept
> swelling or she kept cutting her hands. I would do a reading and ask,
> "Who is this person's personal deity?" Once I found this out, I would ask
> the deity, "Why are this person's hands swelling up?" More than likely, the
> answer would be, "This is happening because we need to call attention to
> the fact that this person is not doing something, not using the power in her
> hands the way it should be used." That's the talking part, you see.

After pursuing the question of the obstructions preventing the person from
releasing the creative power in her hands, Teish continued:

> The next thing I'd do is wash from her hands the tiredness, the sense of
> subordination, and so on that she had suffered by thinking of herself as
> only someone's secretary. . . . I'd put herbs and grain into her hands, feed-
> ing them and then instruct her to go get some paints and do it [begin work-
> ing]. Talking, cleansing, and feeding are very important. We do, literally and
> externally, what must be done symbolically and internally.[23]

The growing interest in traditional African religions currently demonstrated
by African-American women stems, in part, from a search for African roots
for African-American spirituality, but also from a desire to find what Teish
conveys in her account—a system that emphasizes a connection between
the spiritual and material, between body, mind, and action.

Finally, the use of the arts represents an important means through which
African-American women demonstrate their religious creativity. Through
music and poetry, for example, women like Mahalia Jackson and Josephine
Heard carved out space for their own brands of religious leadership, making significant contributions to the religious lives of others. Born a slave in
North Carolina in 1861, Josephine Heard went on to become active, along
with her minister husband, in the work of the African Methodist Episcopal

Church. In addition, in 1890 Heard published *Morning Glories*, a volume of poetry dealing with American racism, African-American leadership, love, and religious themes. She also became an occasional contributor to the *Christian Recorder*, an influential journal of the African Methodist Episcopal Church, as well as to other journals. Her 1890 poem, "I Will Look Up" reads, in part:

> I will look up to Thee
> With faith's ne'er-failing sight,
> My trust repose in thee,
> Through dark and chill earth's night.
>
> I will look up to Thee,
> Though rough and long the way,
> Still sure Thou leadest me
> Unto the perfect day.[24]

Although there is no evidence that Heard sought religious leadership in the ministry or that she experienced frustration in this area, she remains representative of many women, particularly in the nineteenth century, who entered religious discussions and theological debate by way of poetry.

Mahalia Jackson, among the best-known gospel singers, grew up in New Orleans, the daughter of a Baptist minister. There she became steeped in the city's great musical traditions of jazz and blues, as well as the church music of her own congregation and of the Holiness and Pentecostal churches in her neighborhood. Jackson began to receive public acclaim while singing in a church choir in Chicago in the late 1930s, then a center of the emerging and controversial musical form of gospel. She recalled:

> The more gospel singing took hold in Chicago and around the country, the more some of the colored ministers objected to it. They were cold to it. They didn't like the hand-clapping and the stomping and they said we were bringing jazz into the church and it wasn't dignified. Once at church one of the preachers got up in the pulpit and spoke out against me.
> I got right up, too. I told him I was born to sing gospel music. Nobody ever had to teach me. I was serving God. I told him I had been reading the Bible every day most of my life and there was a Psalm that said: "Oh, clap your hands, all ye people! Shout unto the Lord with the voice of a trumpet!" If it was undignified, it was what the Bible told me to do.[25]

For Mahalia Jackson and other women who participated in forms like
gospel music and poetry, not only did these arts provide an avenue for their
personal religious expression, but their creativity also expanded the possibilities for religious experience and meaning for everyone who came into
contact with their talents.

ACCOMMODATION AND CHALLENGE

The relationship between individual religious experience and the social context in which that experience is located has often emerged as a central concern of religiously oriented African-Americans. For black Christian women,
the question of what it means to share a religious tradition with white Americans who have so often brutalized, debased, and dominated African-Americans is a critical one. Is Christianity, so closely linked with whiteness and its
power and privileges in America, appropriate for African-Americans who re-
ject constructions of themselves as inferior by virtue of race? Harriet Jacobs,
in her 1861 autobiographical novel, *Incidents in the Life of a Slave Girl*, relates a chilling scene, illustrative of this issue, that she witnessed while attending a Methodist class meeting led by a brutal white slave trader and also
attended by "a poor, bereaved mother." Jacobs recalled:

> The class leader was the town constable—a man who bought and sold
> slaves, who whipped his brethren and sisters of the church at the public
> whipping post, in jail or out of jail. He was ready to perform that Christian
> office anywhere for fifty cents. This white-faced, black-hearted brother
> came near us, and said to the stricken woman, "Sister, can you tell us how
> the Lord deals with your soul? Do you love him as you did formerly?"
>
> She rose to her feet, and said, in piteous tones, "My Lord and Master,
> help me! My load is more than I can bear. God has hidden himself from
> me, and I am left in darkness and misery." Then, striking her breast, she
> continued, "I can't tell you what is in here! They've got all my children.
> Last week they took the last one. God only knows where they've sold her.
> They let me have her for sixteen years, and then—O! O! Pray for her
> brothers and sisters! I've got nothing to live for now. God make my time
> short!"
>
> She sat down, quivering in every limb.[26]

This particular woman took comfort from the power of her religious commitment and, at the same time, she felt the profound cruelty of understanding

herself to be a creature of the divine and yet held in bondage. In addition, the function of the slaveholder as mediator of the divine in this case amplifies the difficulties she faced. The kind of experience that Jacobs portrayed in the novel illuminates the degree to which constructions of race and gender in America shape the ways in which individuals approach religious life and understand religious community. For African-American Christian women under slavery, for example, notions of African-American inferiority and the negative valence of "blackness" caused them to view their experience of Christianity in sometimes radically different ways from white Americans. In addition, their situation required that they evaluate the relationship between the Christianity of the slaveholders and the reality of their oppression.

The double bind of African-American Christian experience has been that, while empowering some, Christian teaching has sometimes served to contain the desire of African-American women to challenge the social order that so constrains their lives. In summing up her perspective on her life and experiences, Onnie Lee Logan, for example, said,

> I would say to black people that are bitter to take yo' time. You caint hurry God. That was my point. There's a song that we sing. You caint hurry God. Wait on Him. Be patient and wait and that's what I got—patience and I wait. A midwife like me, they just take their time and let God work the plan.[27]

Precisely this aspect of the thought of some African-American Christians—patient endurance of suffering—has motivated a great deal of criticism of Christianity by African-Americans in other religious traditions. Aminah Beverly McCloud's study, *African American Islam*, includes a range of voices of African-American women who chose various forms of Islam, many because of their experience and perception of Christianity. Ayesha, one of the women interviewed by McCloud, put it most candidly:

> One thing is clear. Christianity is one of the roots of black folk's problems in this country. It's got black folk thinkin' that white folk are God. As long as black folk are singin' and shoutin' in church thinkin' that some white god is gonna save them they will not and can never fight to preserve their humanity.[28]

Despite the reality that religion has sometimes functioned as a force motivating African-American women to take an accommodationist stance towards American racism, religion has also served as an avenue for many women to challenge aspects of their social environment. Very real danger lay in religious protests against the dominant racial order from the period of slavery on. Susie King Taylor, born a slave in Georgia, escaped with her family during the Civil War and participated in the efforts of African-Americans to aid the war against the Confederacy. She recalled the great degree of threat that whites in the area felt from the religious gatherings of enslaved African-Americans. She wrote, "I remember, one night, my grandmother went out into the suburbs of the city to a church meeting, and they were fervently singing this old hymn—

> Yes, we all shall be free,
> Yes, we all shall be free,
> Yes, we all shall be free,
> When the Lord shall appear,—

when the police came in and arrested all who were there, saying they were planning freedom and sang 'the Lord,' in place of 'Yankee,' to blind any one who might be listening. Grandmother never forgot that night. . . ."[29]

As with Susie King Taylor's grandmother, religiously-motivated activism emerges as perhaps the single most prevalent theme in the essays collected here. This activism took a variety of forms, and through these forms African-American women confronted a range of enemies. By mounting challenges to the very structures of white supremacy in America, and by contesting gender constraints within black communities that denied them access to leadership and other opportunities, these religious women made contributions that place them among the most significant figures in American history.

THIS FAR BY FAITH

The essays gathered here represent the best available materials on African-American women's religious biography. In compiling the selections we sought to represent the broadest possible range of experiences, including women closely linked with both African-American and predominantly white mainstream Protestant institutions. In addition, we have sought geographical diversity, representation of non-institutionally-based religious figures, religious leaders and laywomen, as well as women representing a variety of time periods. We recognize, however, the limitations of the collection, imposed by the lack of availability of biographical profiles of African-American Muslim, Holiness, and Pentecostal women, for example. All these categories represent a significant sector of African-American women's religious experiences not fully portrayed here. Despite the shortcomings that arise from the current state of the field, it is our hope that this collection of essays in African-American women's religious biography, along with the growing body of scholarship on African-American women and religion, will chart new directions in the study of religion in America.

We have organized the essays around four themes that emerge from the selections. The first group of articles presents profiles of women who engage in religious arts such as music and visual arts. The second group focuses on the interactions between African-American women and a variety of institutional religious structures, while the essays in the third section examine missionary efforts on the part of African-American women. The fourth group of essays explores various forms of activist work in which African-American women have become involved and the religious underpinnings of such activism.

NOTES

1. Among the best introductions to discussions of race as a social construction are Anthony Appiah, "The Uncompleted Argument: DuBois and the Illusion of Race," in Henry Louis Gates, ed., *"Race," Writing, and Difference* (Chicago: University of Chicago Press, 1986), 21–37; Barbara J. Fields, "Ideology and Race in American History," in J. Morgan Kousser and James M. McPherson, eds., *Region, Race, and Reconstruction: Essays in Honor of C. Vann Woodward* (New York: Oxford University Press, 1982), 143–177; and Evelyn Brooks Higginbotham, "African-American Women's History and the Metalanguage of Race," *Signs* 17 (Winter 1992), 251–274.

2. Jualynne E. Dodson, "Power and Surrogate Leadership: Black Women and Organized Religion," *SAGE* V (Fall 1988), 37–42.

3. Clifton H. Johnson, ed., *God Struck Me Dead: Voices of Ex-Slaves* (1969; reprint, Cleveland, Ohio: The Pilgrim Press, 1993). These narratives, collected from 1927 to 1929 by a Fisk University graduate student, were in response to specifically asking former slaves to speak about their religious lives and conversion experiences. Edited by Clifton H. Johnson for publication in 1969, they are published without names or other biographical details, although information about gender, region, religious affiliation, and age are often included.

4. Johnson, 161.

5. Johnson, 156.

6. Johnson, 58. She refers to Matthew 25:31–46, which reads, in part, "When the Son of man comes in his glory and all the angels with him, then he will sit on his glorious throne. Before him will be gathered all the nations, and he will separate

them one from another as a shepherd separates the sheep from the goats, and he will place the sheep at his right hand, but the goats at the left. Then the King will say to those at his right hand, 'Come, O blessed of my Father, inherit the kingdom prepared for you from the foundation of the world'. . . ."

7. *The Life and Religious Experience of Jarena Lee, A Coloured Lady, Giving an Account of Her Call to Preach the Gospel* in William Andrews, ed., *Sisters of the Spirit: Three Black Women's Autobiographies of the Nineteenth Century* (Bloomington: Indiana University Press, 1986), 35.

8. Amanda Smith, *An Autobiography: The Story of the Lord's Dealings With Mrs. Amanda Smith The Colored Evangelist* (1893; reprint, New York: Oxford University Press, 1988), 76–77.

9. Smith, 148.

10. For other nineteenth-century black women's spiritual narratives, see the Schomburg Library of Nineteenth Century Black Women Writers, *Spiritual Narratives* (New York: Oxford University Press, 1988).

11. Cheryl Townsend Gilkes, "The Roles of Church and Community Mothers: Ambivalent American Sexism or Fragmented African Familyhood?" *Journal of Feminist Studies in Religion* 2 (Spring 1986), 50.

12. Evelyn Brooks Higginbotham, *Righteous Discontent: The Women's Movement in the Black Baptist Church, 1880–1920* (Cambridge: Harvard University Press, 1993).

13. Sarah Rice, *He Included Me: The Autobiography of Sarah Rice*, transcribed and edited by Louise Westling (Athens: University of Georgia Press, 1989), 157.

14. Thordis Simonsen, ed., *You May Plow Here: The Narrative of Sara Brooks* (New York: W.W. Norton and Co., 1986), 31.

15. Carol Ione, *Pride of Family: Four Generations of American Women of Color* (New York: Summit Books, 1991), 94.

16. Ione, 96. For more on spiritualism in this period and on women's involvement, see Ann Braude, *Radical Spirits: Spiritualism and Women's Rights in Nineteenth-Century America* (Boston: Beacon Press, 1989).

17. Gloria T. Hull, ed., *Give Us Each Day: The Diary of Alice Dunbar-Nelson* (New York: W.W. Norton and Co., 1984), 54.

18. Hull, 61.

19. Hull, 92.

20. Onnie Lee Logan, *Motherwit: An Alabama Midwife's Story*, as told to Katherine Clark (New York: Plume, 1989), 106.

21. Logan, 144.

22. Logan, 62. For a more general discussion of African-American folk healing, see Albert J. Raboteau, "The Afro-American Traditions," in Ronald L. Numbers and Darrel W. Amundsen, eds., *Caring and Curing: Health and Medicine in the Western Religious Traditions* (New York: Macmillan, 1986), 539–562.

23. Mimi Albert, "Out of Africa," *Yoga Journal* (January/February 1987), 63. See also Luisah Teish, *Jambalaya: The Natural Woman's Book of Personal Charms and Practical Rituals* (New York: Harper and Row, 1985).

24. Josephine Delphine Henderson Heard, *Morning Glories* (Philadelphia: n.p., 1890) in James Melvin Washington, ed., *Conversations With God: Two Centuries of Prayers by African Americans* (New York: HarperCollins, 1994), 63;

18

Renate Maria Simson, "Whoever Heard of Josephine Heard?" *College Language Association Journal* (December 1982), 256–261.

25. Mahalia Jackson with Evan McLeod Wylie, *Movin' on Up* (New York: Hawthorn Books, 1966) in Milton C. Sernett, ed., *Afro-American Religious History: A Documentary Witness* (Durham: Duke University Press, 1985), 451–452.

26. Harriet A. Jacobs, *Incidents in the Life of a Slave Girl Written by Herself* (1861; rev. ed., Jean Fagan Yellin, ed., Cambridge: Harvard University Press, 1987), 70.

27. Logan, 176.

28. Aminah Beverly McCloud, *African-American Islam* (New York: Routledge, 1995), 148.

29. Susie King Taylor, *Reminiscences of my Life in Camp with the 33rd U. S. Colored Troops, Late 1st South Carolina Volunteers* (1902; rev. ed., ed., Patricia W. Romero and Willie Lee Rose, New York: Markus Wiener Publishing, 1988), 32.

PART 1

AFRICAN-AMERICAN WOMEN'S RELIGIOUS ARTS

1

MARIE JEANNE ADAMS

THE HARRIET POWERS
PICTORIAL QUILTS

Only two quilts from the hand of Harriet Powers, a black American woman, are known, but each is in the possession of a major museum.
The artist, born (1837) a slave in Georgia, survived the Civil War, and with
her husband established a small farm on the outskirts of Athens, Georgia,
where she lived until her death in 1911. Both her quilts are "pictorials," de-
picting scenes from the Bible in appliqué technique. The exhibition of
Afro-American decorative arts, organized by the Cleveland Museum of Art,
brought these historic textile treasures together for a tour of several cities in
the eastern United States in 1978 and 1979.

Harriet Powers created these quilts at a time in the late nineteenth century when quilt-making had become, for the most part, the unimaginative
repetition of simple traditional designs or a garish mixture of commercial
patterns. Her Bible quilts are original, lively and subtly balanced statements
of her deeply felt spiritual life. Fortunately, the exceptional quality of Harriet Powers's work was sufficiently evident in her own time that an interested white woman, Jennie Smith, took the trouble of recording the artist's
interpretations of each of the scenes in the two quilts. Because few personal
records of black women from this period exist, the pictorial quilts and its
texts are precious documents.

Mrs. Powers exhibited her first Bible quilt (fig. 1) at the Cotton Fair of
1886 in Athens. It consisted of a large rectangular cotton cloth (88 x 73¾
inches) on which eleven scenes were arranged in three rows. By means of
small appliqué figures, the scenes represented the tempting of Eve in the

Garden, the killing of Abel, Jacob's dream, Judas at the Last Supper, and the Crucifixion. This showpiece, now in the possession of the Smithsonian Institution, captured the imagination of at least one of the town's residents, Jennie Smith. Most of what we know about the artist derives from an eighteen-page manuscript written by Ms. Smith and published by a scholar from the University of Maryland, Gladys-Marie Fry.[1] Ms. Smith, an artist and art teacher of considerable local reputation, was fascinated by the originality of the design. She tracked down the maker and recorded the encounter as follows:

> I found the owner, a negro woman who lived in the country on a little farm where she and her husband made a respectable living. She is about sixty-five years old (actually she was 49), of a clear ginger-cake color and is a very clean and interesting woman who loves to talk of her "old miss" and her life "befo de wah."

However, Mrs. Powers refused to sell the show quilt at any price.

About four years later, in need of money, she sent word to Ms. Smith that the quilt was now for sale. Ms. Smith's account gives a clear notion of how Mrs. Powers treasured the quilt and was reluctant to part with it.

> She arrived one afternoon in front of my door in an oxcart with the precious burden in her lap encased in a clean flour sack, which was still enveloped in a crocus sack. . . . After giving me a full description of each scene with great earnestness, she departed . . .

Mrs. Powers visited Ms. Smith several times to see again "the darling offspring of her brain," as she called the quilt, and in this way, her comments identifying the scenes on the first and ultimately on the second quilt were recorded.

It seems almost certain that Jennie Smith arranged the exhibit of the first Bible quilt in the Colored Building at the Cotton States Exposition in Atlanta in 1895 and that this resulted in a commission from the wives of professors at Atlanta University to create the second Bible quilt (fig. 1), as a commemorative gift in 1898 to a trustee.[2]

Mrs. Powers seems to have given much more thought to the arrangement and design of the figures in the commissioned work, because it is larger (69 x 105 inches) and more complex than the first quilt. This now-famous, much-exhibited quilt portrays fifteen scenes. Ten are drawn from familiar Bible stories which concern the threat of God's judgment inextricably fused with His mercy and man's redemption, among which are the Fall, Moses in the wilderness, Job's trials, Jonah and the whale, the Baptism of Christ and the Crucifixion. One scene refers to local events she knew from hearsay about a rich couple and a runaway pig. Four others depict astronomical or meteorological events, only one of which occurred in Mrs. Powers's adult life, an extremely cold spell of 1895 in the eastern United States. Given Mrs. Powers's intensely religious outlook, she interpreted these events in the celestial atmosphere as messages from God to mankind about punishment, apocalypse, and salvation.

Visually, one's first overall impression of the Boston quilt is of a melee of scattered figures on a crowded surface. Upon further viewing, individual scenes, defined by red polka-dot outlines, gradually emerge. The many small, rounded figures floating freely in space yield an impression of spontaneous gaiety and grace. In its liveliness and charm, Harriet Powers's quilt looks the epitome of folk art: the human figures in cut-out shapes, anachronistically costumed, make fanciful gestures and ignore the restraints of gravity; the animals look coy and harmless; and bits of color appear unrealistically over the surface. The contrast between the grand scale of the subject matter and the tiny simple forms with their concrete detail is enough to bring a smile to the viewer's face, as in such easily recognizable scenes as Adam and Eve (square 4), touching as they stand beside the huge snake in the garden under "God's all-seeing eye and God's merciful hand," and Jonah shown just at the vivid moment when his arm is seized by the whale (square 6).

Mrs. Powers could not read but committed the Bible stories to memory from sermons and folk tradition. The serpent in Eden is shown with feet which he had, according to legend, before he suffered God's curse at the Fall. She was fascinated by animals and may have known that large snakes can have tiny feet. The reality of the Bible stories to her shows in the wish she expressed to attend the Barnum and Bailey Circus to see the "Bible animals." In two of the non-Biblical scenes, she incorporates characters from traditional folk narratives: the hog named Betts (square 13) and the man frozen at his jug of liquor (square 11).

The work of Harriet Powers fits into the category of folk art narrowly defined as the product of unschooled craftspersons who incorporate elements of metropolitan traditions of style, technique or form as essential parts of their own work. In representations, the color is often arbitrary, proportions and spatial relations awry, shapes generalized and details emphasized. Harriet Powers's style of storytelling and composition belong to this folk tradition of image-making. Nevertheless, her subject matter draws on the world-church doctrines of Christianity and she has formed the quilt by piecing together milled cloth and applying the figures by sewing machine. This kind of artistic mixture is associated with rural populations who rely partially on urban society—for its markets, machinery, or social attitudes—to maintain their way of life.

The more one examines the style and the content of Harriet Powers's work, the more one sees that it projects a grand spiritual vision. Pondering the pictorial content of each scene and its relationships to the others leads one to realize the depth of her concern for and how well she grasped the apocalyptic yet redemptive vision of Christian doctrine.

The loving spirit in which Mrs. Powers handles the pictorial and decorative elements makes exploration of every part of the quilt a pleasurable and rewarding pursuit. For each square she invents a new composition. The scope of her interest shows in the many different kinds of motifs she introduces, representing men, women, children, large animals, birds and other small creatures, fantasy beasts of Revelations, trumpets and a bell, a house, a boat, a coffin and special symbols such as the hand of God, stars, comets and other cosmic bodies. Although small, these objects are defined as solid masses, and all are set at a variety of angles to each other. The human figures are visually arresting because of the pose of outspread arms or arms held away from the body. All the poses involve gestures of action: Job calling on God with arm outstretched (square 1), the figures on the 'weather' scene (squares 2, 8, 12) raising their arms in seeming alarm.

For each event, Mrs. Powers abstracts a few figures to convey the action and introduces informative detail: the frozen breath of the mule (square 11), the metallic thread used for the crown of the rich woman (square 13), blood and water streaming from the side of Christ, indicating an intense phase of His suffering (square 15). She carefully varies yet reuses patterned cloth pieces in the appliquéd figures and repeats types of motifs, such as the heavenly bodies, devices which subtly link the scenes together. The cosmic, stellarated designs appear in every square except the one in the lower left corner, which depicts the only recent (1895) event. She lavishes attention on these heavenly bodies; they give the scenes their scale and aura of importance. In contrast to the other figures, each of which is formed by one piece of appliqué, the cosmic motifs are composed of tiny pieces of cloth, painstakingly fitted into sharply pointed forms of contrasting color, and sewn together by hand.

Yet the vaguely whirling sequence of objects within each square, the multitude of directional lines which do not meet or correspond across the surface, the action stances and upraised arms of so many figures, and the choppy, changing colors arouse feelings of violent activity and alarming uncertainty. Mrs. Powers's greatest formal achievement lies in maneuvering the stylistic elements conveying the two extremes of effect—carefully tended arrangements and threatening chaos—into a dynamic equilibrium.

The strongest stabilization comes from the light-and-dark color contrast of the backgrounds of the squares which creates a visual checkerboard effect (See fig. 1). The darker tones of squares 2, 4, 8, 12, and 14 provide an underlying stable geometric order for the entire varied, crowded surface. At the right end, separated by a broad band of mottled pink, a dark, center square (square 10) marks the head of the bed.

If the squares are read from left to right as Ms. Smith did when recording Mrs. Powers's comments, the scenes seem to be simply strewn across the page not in any order, briefly as follows:

first row: Job praying for his enemies
His coffin
Black night of 1780
Moses with the brazen serpent
Adam and Eve
John the Baptist with Christ

second row: Jonah and the whale
Multiplying pairs of birds (last days of Noah)
Falling stars of 1833
Creation of pairs of animals, continued
Angels and beasts of Revelations

third row: Creatures frozen in the cold night of 1895
Red light night of 1846
Rich people who go to punishment and the independent
hog named Betts
Creation of pairs of animals continued
Crucifixion

Considering that Mrs. Powers was drawing on stories she had heard in various sermons and in oral tradition, it is unlikely that she would aim to follow events in the strict order that they are fixed in the Bible. Judging by what she selected, I think she recorded fateful events concerning people in her society, cataclysmic natural occurrences, and Biblical figures which demonstrated the Christian themes of her interest: threat, deliverance, and repose.

◆ ◆ ◆

The Old Testament heroes she chose, Moses, Noah, Jonah, and Job, are well-known examples of men who experienced not only God's harsh judgment but also His power to deliver them from frightening circumstances, and Christian doctrine interprets each as a foreshadowing of the eventual comprehensive salvation to be offered by Christ. Mrs. Powers shows each one at a different phase of his interaction with God's powers, and artistically contrasts action scenes for Moses and Jonah with the placid charm of the animal pairs (squares 7, 9, 14) who are to be saved from the Flood.

Her great originality, dramatic gifts, and thematic interest come to the fore in her remaining choices of subject matter: the spectacular happenings in the skies over the United States (squares 2, 8, 11, and 12), drawn from tales that circulated orally throughout the country. The remarkable part of her usage is that her references are so accurate that comparison with diaries and other contemporary accounts, done by Gladys-Marie Fry of the University of Maryland,[3] confirms and elaborates the specific occasions she records.

Mrs. Powers notes "the dark day of May 19, 1780" (square 2). Dark days, when the daytime atmosphere turns black with pollution from forest fires, have been known throughout history, but the most famous in her day was that Black Friday in May in New England when some observers were convinced the end of the world was at hand. Mrs. Powers indicates visually the ominous character of this event by the presence of seven stars and a trumpet, New Testament signals of Judgment Day.

Another spectacular event that she chose is the "falling of the stars on November 13, 1833" (square 8). This can be identified as the Leonid meteor storm which produced not an hour-long but an eight-hour long display of shooting stars. Eyewitness accounts believed that "the sky is on fire," and "Judgment Day is here." The impressive character of the storm is shown in a print by a contemporary artist. Common people attached great significance to the event, and it was used as a time-fixing device by which births and deaths were determined. In Jennie Smith's record, Mrs. Powers said of this day: "The people were frightened and thought the end of time had come. God's hand stayed the stars."

The events (square 11) that Mrs. Powers recalls from the "cold Thursday, 10 of February 1895," when people and animals froze in their tracks, also took place in New England. That cold spell was so severe that the temperature even in Athens, Georgia, fell to a minus one degree (F). The next scene (square 12) the "red light night of 1846" probably (Fry 1976:22) refers to the meteor showers on the tenth and eleventh of August that year, which seemed to set the sky aflame. Of her depiction, Mrs. Powers said, "Women, children and fowls were frightened but God's merciful hand caused no harm to them." It is evident that her interest focused on these events as displays of Divine threat and deliverance. As Reginia Perry (1976), a specialist in Afro-American art, observed, "The combination of religious and astrological subjects is a lesson of revelation and warning to the sinful of the power of God, which is demonstrated through eclipses, falling stars, 'red light nights' and extreme temperatures." In these pictorials Harriet Powers is not so much interested in recounting a narrative as she is in making a declaration of faith in a message.

Her variations on the theme of God's power to rescue appear more striking if we take a cue from the orientation of the designs. Usually quilt designs are arranged to be viewed from all angles or from the foot of the bed, that is, from the observer's point of view. However, the designs in this quilt are to be seen from one side only. This orientation suggests that the columns of images could also be read vertically. (The details of the stitching show that the squares were put together in vertical columns which is evidence that at some level of her thought, Mrs. Powers grouped the scenes in vertical order.).

Read this way, the first, third, and fifth columns seem to be more highly charged with meaning while the intervening columns offer weaker variations on the theme of punishment and remission.

In the first column on the left, all the squares depict persons upon whom the judgment of God fell unexpectedly. The action is not redemptive. These scenes show individuals confronting God's judgment: Job praying for his enemies and his coffin rising to the sky, and Jonah being seized by the whale. At the top of the lowest square (square 11), two figures—both of which represent the woman who on the cold night was "frozen at the gates"—wear the same white material as the angels of Judgment Day (square 10), thus pointedly conveying that these people, frozen where they stand, confront their ultimate fates.

The last column, at the right end of the quilt, displays both the very mechanics of judgment in the form of the angels, vials of wrath and beasts of Revelations that will destroy the wicked, and the means of salvation in the redemptive Baptism and Crucifixion scenes.

The center column reiterates the threat of God's judgment and deliverance by emphasizing sinners and release from bondage. In the only Biblical scene in the column (square 3), Moses, bringing the children of Israel out of slavery in Egypt, raises the brazen serpent as a form of healing (that is, a token of salvation) for those afflicted by fiery serpents as a result of having offended God. In the center square (square 8), the "falling stars" are released from their celestial places to provide a warning message of God's power and mercy to the worthless, lazy sinners, "the varmints," in Mrs. Powers's words, who then rush out of their beds.

The lowest square (square 13) presents two rich Southern persons (former slave owners?), sinners who did not know God and therefore go to eternal punishment. In the foreground stands the largest single figure on the quilt, the independent hog named Betts, clearly a female, who ran 500 miles from Georgia to Virginia. Her flight provides a scarcely veiled reference to the path of runaway slaves of pre-Civil War days. This image crimps together at this central point the grand meaning of the religious theme and the struggle for freedom from slavery and suggests a parallel between Mrs. Powers's faith in the Biblical stories of deliverance and her vision of her life experience as a freed slave. Viewed in this light, juxtaposing events within the first four columns from the Old Testament and from the skies over the United States makes sense as comparable old orders. The last column stands alone as a new message of lasting deliverance.

Efforts to trace information orally transmitted about Harriet Powers's life have not yet added any clues. As Dr. Gladys-Marie Fry notes (1976:19–20), the census data, tax rolls, and records of deeds in the counties where Mrs. Powers lived supply only sparse documentation. According to the 1870 census, Harriet Powers's husband is a "farm hand," and she lists her occupation as "keeping house." They had three children and their personal estate amounted to $300. Neither Harriet nor her husband could read or write. It seems they became successful small farmers with a stock of animals and tools and at one time they owned four acres of land. Their fortunes eventually declined: by 1895 Mr. Powers had left their domicile, and in 1901 the land was sold. As indicated by her yearly tax payments, Harriet maintained herself independently, probably by sewing for people in her community. When she died at age seventy-four in 1911, her personal effects amounted to $70.

More information about Harriet Powers would not only be interesting as her personal history but also might help solve a tantalizing issue about her work, that is, the question of its similarity to African design. John Vlach, a specialist in Afro-American art, reviews this comparison in the catalog of the Afro-American decorative arts show (1978:48–54). Mrs. Powers's work is closest in appearance to the appliquéd cotton cloths of the

Fon people of Dahomey. According to tradition, the kings who lived at
Abomey, the capital of Dahomey, and maintained a guild of tailors at the
court, claimed exclusive rights to the output of appliquéd cloths, but in fact
these cloths were used as costume, festival ornamentation, and wall hangings by the religious and secular elite in all the major towns. The large cotton wall hangings portray isolated figures or framed scenes referring to
events that took place in the Fon kingdom as well as depict various activities and insignia of the religious and secular elite. (The catalog of the
Afro-American decorative art show (Vlach 1978:50, Fig. 20) illustrates a
late nineteenth century example.)

In the nineteen sixties the most commonly known form of Fon appliqués
was smaller than the known court hangings and was designed for sale to foreign visitors and tourists. In a symbolic and pictorial manner, these cloths
show vignettes or motifs from the reigns of Fon kings from early seventeenth century to 1892 when the king was defeated by the French.[4] Usually on a black or gold (or more recently blue, white or red) background,
brightly colored figures are appliquéd in a seemingly haphazard manner. In
general, however, objects and persons associated with earlier kings are on
the upper portion of the hanging, while those connected with more recent
kings are mainly on the lower half. The men of the family guild at Abomey
who made the appliqué cloths identified each figure by the name of the
king to whose reign the design refers and usually by a saying of that king.
(See typescript of the Whydah Museum, 1964; and Kent, 1971: 73–78.)
These verbal referents are used to explain, often by means of word play, the
link between the visual motif and the king. Slightly varying interpretations
may be given by different tailors.

The degree of similarity between this style and Mrs. Powers's work is impressive. The general approach to depiction corresponds to her manner, using flat, colored, massive figures arranged at various angles to each other in
a nongeometric equilibrium. The images are also placed roughly in rows.
Both employ human figures, animals, and objects as motifs which are repeated in simple form. Perhaps the most consistent formal similarity is the
degree of curvature in the shaping of the images. Both obviously aim for a
comprehensive view of their subject.

The differences are, however, striking. The African figures are brighter
in hue and more complex in that the images are formed from several colored patches, red, blue, green, purple, and white, which indicate costume
and anatomical parts. The emotional tone is more variable in the African
works. Offensive weapons and scenes of battle and other physical violence
recur in the court cloths. Even in the cloth from the early 1960s, long af-

ter the last royal battles, the ferocious aspects of the lion and the shark, in the lower part of the cloth, are emphasized by the open mouths and large teeth.

How African influence may have reached Harriet Powers, who was born in Georgia, is problematic. By the time her parents' generation would have come to the South, most slaves were being imported from the Congo and Angola. Even if they came from West Africa and from Dahomey, they would not necessarily be knowledgeable about the appliqué techniques. The appliquéd cloths were made only in the capital city of Abomey by family guilds of tailors, all retainers of the monarch, and the guilds included only men and young boys. It seems most likely that she could have acquired a knowledge of African style by hearsay only from other, older house slaves of her "old miss" or from her parents or other older persons. However interesting this question of African influence and inspiration remains, there is no doubt that Harriet Powers transformed her American experience with religion and with freedom into a work of lasting art.

NOTES

I wish to thank S. B. Frost, Department of Religious Studies, McGill University, Montreal, and Mrs. Phyllis Morrison, textile specialist of Cambridge, Massachusetts, for helpful discussions on content and technique of the Boston Bible quilt.

1. The following account and quotations from Ms. Smith's manuscript are taken from the excellent study by Dr. Gladys-Marie Fry (1976).
2. The women at Atlanta University gave the quilt to Charles Cuthbert Hall (b. 1852, d. 1908) in gratitude for his help in establishing Emory College and because he was supportive of the blacks in the South and spoke out on their behalf. His granddaughter, Mrs. Katherine Hall Preston, remembers it hanging on a large wall in the family's summer residence, Synton House, in Westport. The family decided it should be in a museum and eventually Mr. Karolik, a collector of decorative arts and patron of the Boston Museum of Fine Arts, purchased it for $800 and gave it to the Museum. Pinned to the quilt was the handwritten note recording Mrs. Powers's comments on each of the squares.
3. Information on the four local events derives from Dr. Fry's detailed study (1976).
4. Some cloths also include the insignia of the subsequent puppet ruler. However, one usurper who ruled between 1797 and 1818 never appears. He is said to have sold the proper Queen Mother and many of her retainers into slavery to prevent their assisting the rightful heir to the throne. The earliest known appearance of this type of composition—a sequential display of insignia from the entire Alado-honu dynasty—is reported for the late 1950s. It may have been created as a response to the rising nationalist feeling that led to independence in 1960.

REFERENCES

Fry, Gladys-Marie 1976.   "Harriet Powers: Portrait of a Black Quilter" in *Missing Pieces: Georgia Folk Art*, Atlanta: Georgia Council for Arts and Humanities.

Kent, Kate P. 1971. Introducing West African Cloth. Denver: Museum of Natural History. pp. 73–78.

Museum of Fine Arts, Boston, Anony. n.d. A Pattern Book, Based on an Appliqué Quilt by Mrs. Harriet Powers, American, 19th Century.

Perry, Regenia A. 1976. Selections of Nineteenth Century Afro-American Art, "Harriet Powers (1837–1910)," n.p. New York: Metropolitan Museum of Art.

Smithsonian Institution, Anony. n.d. Information Sheet on Harriet Powers' Bible Quilt, T14713. Washington D.C.: The National Museum of History and Technology, Textile Division.

Vlach, John M. 1978. *The Afro-American Tradition in Decorative Arts*. Exhibition Catalog. Cleveland: Museum of Art.

Whydah Museum, Anony. 1964. Les noms et les symboles royaux. Typescript. Whydah, Dahomey (Now People's Republic of Benin).

2

WILLIAM THOMAS DARGAN
AND KATHY WHITE BULLOCK

WILLIE MAE FORD SMITH OF ST. LOUIS: A SHAPING INFLUENCE UPON BLACK GOSPEL SINGING STYLE

This writing describes and analyzes the singing style of Willie Mae Ford Smith as a major influence upon gospel music performance practice. We take this approach because Smith's contributions, especially during the peak of her career in the 1940s, are not widely available and are preserved on a few 78 rpm recordings from the late 1940s and perhaps the early 1950s. Through the work of producer-author Anthony Heilbut, some of her songs have been re-recorded and some early releases are to be reissued.[1] But for now, many questions remain about the nature and significance of her contributions to the form. Through the recordings and publications of Heilbut and through George Nierenberg's celebrated film *Say Amen, Somebody,* Mother Smith,[2] as she is called in church and organizational circles, has become more visible to us. But who is she, really, and what is the substance of her lasting contributions? Much work remains before either of these questions can receive a definitive answer. The present study begins the process of reconstructing and assessing her legacy as a seminal force in the development of gospel music.

Willie Mae Ford Smith seems to have exerted both musical and philosophical influence on the lives of major gospel artists and groups that flowered during gospel's golden age in the 1950s. Her daughter, Jackie Jackson, remembers from her childhood and teenage years visits to the Smith home by the Simmons-Akers Singers, the Ward Singers, the Roberta Martin Singers, the Caravans, Inez Andrews, Rev. and Mrs. Dorsey, and Rev.

Clarence Cobb of First Deliverance Church in Chicago. Another group of singers, such as national artists Mahalia Jackson, Brother Joe May, Martha Bass, and the O'Neal Twins, in addition to local singers Fannie Foster, Fletcher and Elizabeth Higgins, Genesser Smith, Geneva Gentry, and Lucy Fletcher, either studied with or received occasional coaching from Mother Smith (Jackson 1988a). Why were these and other important persons drawn to Mother Smith? How did she propose to teach what was then considered far from academic? These questions suggest the need for careful attention to the family and personal background that produced the booming contralto diva, whose voice Dorsey likened to that of blues queen Bessie Smith.

◆ ◆ ◆

Willie Mae Ford Smith was born June 23, 1904, in Rolling Fork, Mississippi, as the seventh of fourteen children of Clarence Ford and the former Mary Williams. Soon thereafter, in connection with the father's work on the railroad, the family moved to Memphis, Tennessee. Mother Smith remembers attending church with her sisters, being converted, and also hearing the blues in Memphis.

> There was a clubhouse in back of our house where men would gamble and do other bad things, and they would throw money down out of the window for me to sing the "Boll Weevil." . . . I was a kid, I didn't know anything 'bout the blues, but I thought I knew, and the Lord got me outta that. When I got saved, I had no more desire to sing the blues, but I had the spirituals in my mind.
>
> My mother used to stand me up on a table and I'd sing in church. I could sing a long meter and a spiritual, we didn't know anything about classics (Willie J. Smith 1988).

Clarence and Mary Ford were devout Christians with an active interest in singing. The Ford sisters remember that their parents sang well enough to perform as a duo in area churches. It must have been after the family moved to St. Louis in 1917 that the Ford Sisters, encouraged by their father, organized a female quartet featuring Mary, Emma, Willie Mae, and Geneva.

Mother Smith and her sister, Mrs. Geneva Ford Clark, remembered that:

> My father would line us up together on the floor and get us to singing. We enjoyed it and kept on doing it. We went to the National Baptist Convention

to perform as the Ford Sisters. They accepted us halfheartedly. They hadn't really accepted gospel. When Thomas Dorsey heard us singing in Louisville, he was still playing for Ma Rainey at the tent shows (Ford Family 1988).

As the Ford sisters married and bore children during the 1920s, the quartet gradually became inactive, and the sisters encouraged Willie Mae as a soloist by sending her to represent the group when everyone could not be present. In 1924 Willie Mae married James Peter Smith, a small-businessman, who had come to St. Louis from New Orleans. Two children, Willie James and Jacquelyn, were born to this union.

In 1937 Smith won wide recognition at the National Baptist Convention for her performance of "If You Just Keep Still," a song of her own composition (Southern 1982, 350). Also during the later 1930s—probably in 1938—she underwent the Pentecostal experience of Holy Spirit baptism, with speaking in tongues. She remembers that:

> When the Lord filled me with the Holy Ghost . . . I was in Ohio singing, and Mrs. [Artelia] Hutchins was [there] singing "Let it breathe on me, Let the Holy Ghost breathe on me." When the Holy Ghost hit me, I hit the floor. On the train coming back to St. Louis, I kept everybody up all night long, trying to talk, speaking in tongues. . . . Honey, this child got soused good. The Lord had to fix me up, because you see I was a wild person, just like a wild buck. I made fun of holiness people. I laughed at 'em and tried to do the holy dance. I would just cut up (Willie Mae Ford Smith 1988).

Following this experience, the spiritual fervor and sense of calling long associated with Smith's personal and musical reputation became more pronounced. This new zeal seems to have emboldened her propensity for testifying, witnessing, or just philosophizing between selections in performance. Also in the late 1930s and 1940s Smith acknowledged a calling to the ministry and was ordained by the African Methodist Episcopal Zion church. In that time, the very thought of a woman aspiring to the pulpit attracted the chagrin of ministers in many quarters. Nevertheless, because of her performances before national audiences—both at the Baptist Convention and in 'he Convention of Gospel Choirs and Choruses—the calls continued to come for her to travel.

An organizational role for Smith in gospel music was cast in 1939 when she began her work as supervisor of the Soloists' Bureau of Dorsey's Convention (National Convention 1983, 35). A wave of growing popularity as a performer along with these affiliations kept her traveling during the 1940s. Her daughter, Jackie, remembers that she was home only a week or so per month at the peak of her travel during the 1940s. She performed frequently at churches in places like Buffalo, Detroit, Cleveland, and Chicago, and small towns around the Midwest, and she appeared less frequently in other towns and cities throughout the United States.[3]

Extended-family arrangements carried the Smith family through these years, as relatives and friends saw to the rearing of the Smith children. Jackie remembers growing up under wings of her aunts, Geneva Clark and Emma Stewart, while her brother, Billy, remained at home under the care of his father and a friend who had come with him to St. Louis from New Orleans, Jerry Pratt. Another key element in the Willie Mae Ford Smith story was put in place during the early 1930s when she and her husband adopted Bertha, the accompanist who traveled and performed with her for more than twenty years. It is said that:

> [Mother] and Bertha were like pig and pork. [She] augmented what mother was doing. She would start talking and Bertha would know what she was gonna sing. . . . It was almost as if Bertha had radar (Jackson 1988a).

Indications are that perhaps the late 1930s and clearly the 1940s were a time of intense activity for Mother Smith, who must have been away from St. Louis for as much as three weeks per month over a ten-year period (Jackson 1988b). Toward the end of the 1940s Mother Smith and Mahalia Jackson sang for an Easter Sunrise service at the Hollywood Bowl in California, where a company arranged to record several selections and offered each a contract. The Smith son, Billy, who was attending Tennessee A&I State College in Nashville at the time, remembers what followed from that performance this way:

> This man heard both her and Mahalia and wanted to sign 'em up. [But] Mother never did anything without the advice of my father and my grandfather. . . . They . . . said, "Naw, don't sign up with this." . . . They thought it was something slick. They didn't even want to be associated with anything that was supposed to be slick. So she didn't sign up (Willie J. Smith 1988).

After these events, Mother Smith's life and her career as a gospel performer took unexpected turns. Familiar and trusted pillars of family and musical support fell away, as her husband died in 1950, and soon thereafter Bertha, the adopted daughter who accompanied her from the early 1930s, became far less dependable. Billy Smith remembers that:

> When Dad died, [Mother] didn't quite have that freedom, because, though we were older children in college by that time, she still felt like she had to kind of hang around there and watch us. . . . She didn't go as much as she did when Dad was living. She began to taper off. Then Bertha got sort of dissatisfied with the traveling. She had to get new people to play for her, and it just wasn't the charisma she had before. It wasn't in sync anymore (Willie J. Smith 1988).

Later, during the mid-1950s, Mother Smith joined and was ordained a minister in Lively Stone Apostolic Church in St. Louis, an affiliate of the Pentecostal Assemblies of the World, the largest of several Pentecostal-Apostolic denominations. From that period to the present local performances, community involvement, and a fiery zeal for ministry and church affairs, have occupied her. Several recordings on the Savoy label during the 1970s, a 1983 featured role in *Say Amen, Somebody,* and the coveted Heritage Award from the National Endowment for the Arts in 1988 have signaled her re-emergence and kept before us as a gentle refrain, the four-word name, Willie Mae Ford Smith until her death in 1994.

Real comprehension of the person is far beyond the scope of this study. But we can turn here to a brief examination of the music Smith made and the sense of aura she projected, especially during her peak popularity in the 1940s. Our approach to the music and personal style that was Willie Mae Ford Smith grows from analysis of her recordings and from accounts of her singing by those closely associated with her. From this approach follows the question of how analysis can support and clarify the perceptions of Mother Smith, her relatives, and her friends about her performance style and the unique qualities that fashion her contributions to the gospel community at large.

From the performance accounts that predate the present analysis there emerges a singer who used her repertoire to leave deep and lasting impressions on her audiences. St. Louis singer-songwriter Doris Fidmont Frazier (1988) remembers:

> [I] felt really lifted when Willie Mae Ford Smith or the O'Neal Twins were in services. . . . The way she put the song over was special. She was always kind of stout and robust, and she just came across like she knew what she

was singing about. That's what thrilled my heart. I've loved the Lord a long time and you really know when people are for real and when they're not. As you go around a lot, you meet . . . singers that do not do anything for you, but Willie Mae Ford Smith . . . just really had a big impact on my life.

Singer and radio announcer Zella Jackson Price, whose mother served as road manager to Mother Smith during a period in the 1940s, remembers:

Mother Smith was dramatic and . . . she was Holy-Ghost filled. . . . She was dramatic. When she said she felt like flying away, in your mind's eye, you could visualize this. . . . She had power in her voice [and] in her expression. She was a *singer*. I've seen her walk out singing . . . on the way to her next appearance . . . and folks is just shoutin' everywhere, hats flyin' and carryin' on, just somethin' terrible. She'd come in and just wreck all them buildings. That was Mother Smith, and she loved it (Price 1988).

Obviously fans of Mother Smith, these singers were clearly inspired by what they heard and saw of her in local St. Louis performances. For Jackie Jackson, however, because she traveled with her mother during summers away from school, the recollections of pictures her mother drew in sound as well as sight are etched into her memory. As a girl, Mrs. Jackson also sang in a family group, simply called the Trio, that also included her first cousins Violet Stewart and Mary Geneva Clark. In addition, she and her brother were at home with Mother Smith and also traveled in the car as her father chauffeured her mother to in-town performances. Daughter Jackie and son Billy remember those times this way:

If the program was supposed to start at seven or seven-thirty, . . . she'd leave home at 8:30. . . . [But] nobody would leave . . . they'd just sit there and wait. . . . Mother perspired quite freely, so she'd carry this cape. When she'd leave home, she wasn't perspiring, so she'd throw [the cape] back and the kids in the neighborhood used to call her Superman. She'd break out the door with that cape kind of leaning in the back (Willie J. Smith 1988).

And they'd say "It's a bird—." They used to tease us, [but] it was a lot of fun. They called her performances "programs." [But] it was an evangelistic service, . . . a revival in song, because sometimes they would stop and actually open the doors of the church. The preachers resented her and she could not stand in the pulpit, but the people would come from miles around to hear her sing (Jackson 1988a).

They didn't have . . . microphones, but they could hear the resonance in her voice (Willie J. Smith 1988).

The program would open with a devotional service, the trio might sing, then she'd always begin . . . with "King of My Life, I Crown Thee Now." If the trio was around, we would continue to sing and Mother would pray this fervent prayer. She would always end the prayer by saying, "and when I've come to the end of my time, may I look behind me and see a well-spent life, and on before me a joyful day. I'll give Thy name the praise better there than I can here. These and all other blessings we ask in the name of Thy Son, Amen" (Jackson 1988a).

◆ ◆ ◆

What she would sing after prayer would all depend on the mood of the crowd as well as her own mood. She sometimes started off with a slow song, or it might be a fast song. It would just depend on the circumstances. She never wrote anything down that I recall. As she began to talk, and I guess pick up vibrations or circumstances, . . . how she felt when she got there is how that program would go. It would never be a slump because she comes alive with the crowd. Then sometimes there would be people saying, "Sister Smith, Mother Smith, Aunt Willie Mae, would you sing such and such?" It was always an impromptu type of thing. People would write requests and it would [also] be according to her mood. Like she said, it was by divine dictation. There was nothing structured about it except the beginning and the end. She would always open up with "Lest I Forget" and end up with her arrangement of "God Be with You Till We Meet Again."

I used to watch her sing and in my mind I'd sing along with her. She was a dramatic singer, and her gestures were always on time with what she was singing. For instance, one of my very favorites that I remember from way back is "Give Me Wings."

It was like she was talking to an audience as one would stand before a podium and say, "let me tell you something." She would have her hands in front of her in, shall I say, soloist style, and her facial expression would be . . . And her head . . . She would say,

"Every [sic] since I found the Christ . . ."

Then her eyes would get bigger and there would be a happy expression.

"There's been something in my life . . ."

and there would be a nod of her head like, "Okay now, there's something in my life that makes me . . ." and she'd stick her chest out and then . . . take her arms out to the side just briefly, just slightly [and sing],

"Flying away . . ."

As a boxer, [she would have her] fist[s] together, and just slightly move her elbows away from her body; she would lean forward . . .

"Flying away to be at rest."

"I'm feelin' lonely" came across like an anecdotal phrase to what she was saying.

"I've found the Christ and there's been something in my life,
Makes me feel like flyin' away."

[She was saying that] they don't want me to verbalize or to act out, because I've found the Christ. The people around me don't seem to understand where I am. That's why I'm feelin' lonely. People don't understand me now; I wanna get away. That's what I perceived, even as a youngster.
As she'd say,

"Wolves of hell are all around"

it would seem as though she was looking all around—they're here, they're there, they're every place. Then she'd sorta throw her head back and look up and her arms would go out a little more [this time] as she'd sing,

"Makes me feel like flyin' away to be at rest."

She would gesture up toward the sky or toward the ceiling, close her eyes and throw her head back as she said,

"to be at rest."

Then she would throw her head back and say,

"*Lord,* give me wings,
please give me wings."

Then she would lean forward and say,

"Wings of faith"

then she would step back and say,

"to fly away"

Then she would kinda come to a restful position [and sing],

"to be at rest."

She could do that and it would be just so picturesque. You know how one looks up when something's on your mind and you're trying to recall it? She'd have that kind of [far away] expression on her face as she did the verse that says,

"Late some nights when I recline,
Something moves upon my mind"

When she did the verse that says,

"As I go from door to door,
Loved ones are gone to come no more."

It was as though she was knocking on doors. She was so graceful. If you could have seen the way she . . . You could imagine her going, not running, but her movements would be very graceful—as though she were knocking first with one hand and then with the other hand. Then she would go into

"Lord, give me wings,
Please give me wings."

[She would] hover over the pulpit and lean forward to say,

"Wings of faith"

Then she would step back when she got to

"Fly away."

Then her arms would come [down and cross when she sang],

"To be at rest."

And the church would go up. They really would.

She would sing five or six songs on a program before the break, [then] she would lift her own offering. The people would pass and shake her hand as they put money in the collection. As the people counting the money told her what was raised, she would say something like "I need twenty more dimes to make up what I need," not ever giving a figure. . . . And she would walk in the audience and they would put it in her hand. She always asked for a certain number of coins, I never recall her asking for ten more people to give me a dollar.

She would pray . . . over the offering and then she'd talk. Sometimes if there were guests—people who wanted to sing—she'd let them sing then. . . . Then she would come on after these people and sing about the same number of pieces she sang in the first half. Sometimes near the end, there would be an altar call when people came for prayer.

Local singers really wanted to be on her programs, because she had an audience. People would be hanging out the windows. In the summer it would be so hot in those churches, and they would stay there. There would be standing room only.

Because she was always sweating profusely at the end, everybody was very concerned about her not catching cold. There was a scarf that was put around her neck, and the cape, and there was always these beautiful white handkerchiefs that Bertha kept laundered. There was a stack of handkerchiefs that would always accompany her to her programs. . . .

Back in the late thirties and forties it was stylish to wear a flower in the hair. And I can't remember in those days when she didn't wear the flower.

Like the older people would say, she always primped, you know. She always fixed her face up and always tried to be as pretty as she could be.

She's always been on stage. Mother's 84. If my father had lived he would have been 103. That's the age deficit. She handled and manipulated him as I look back. That's why I say she's always on stage, she just had a way about her. She was always grand. When she was home, her bedroom was a sanctuary, . . . everybody creeped around the house, because she was resting. . . . My father would say, "your mother's resting." Then when she would get up about noon—[and] put on these beautiful housecoats, always long. She was a prima donna. And as often as she went out of town, whenever she came home it was an occasion for my dad. He would do something special—special meal, a gift . . . The housekeeper would come in and get that house together because Bill [as he called her] was coming home (Jackson 1989).

◆ ◆ ◆

Distinct musical implications and personal features are identifiable in her daughter's picture of Mother Smith. She has hurried through neither her life nor her songs. Neither clock nor metronome having guided her movement, she has cultivated an uncanny feel for intuitive reality that has told her where to be and when in quite specific, if relative, terms. Simply put, the irreverent might say she has been lucky, and her brethren would call her blessed with an uncanny sense of timing.

Her programs projected a sense of ministry and solemn worship. What she did not find in these settings, she imperceptibly fashioned from the raw materials of her experience. But she always began with the intangibles of what she found.

Singing has been for Willie Mae Ford Smith a world in which she lives, rather than a mere phase of life she has picked up and put down. This ideal is apparent in the attention to detail with which she fashioned each part of the whole story, play, or mood that unfolded in her singing as well as in her movement. While her voice seems nearly as strong in some recent recordings as it must have been in the 1930s and 1940s, her movements and the sense of the music conveyed in live performances have undoubtedly changed with the maturation process.

The ease and self-assurance, the spiritual fervor, the power and depth of her expression, and the sheer energy of her voice were apparent gifts which Mother Smith has shared freely with those around her. Yet she has also been the center of attention, the star of the show, the prima donna. Somewhat before the age of celebrity gospel singers, she held star status. While she worshiped God in and through the songs, some nearly worshiped her. She was likely the first St. Louis gospel figure to attain superstar status. Yet she never achieved the popularity attributed to protégés Mahalia Jackson and Brother Joe May. Her status and sense of herself was largely founded upon the family structure she relied upon for support. When this bastion began to fall, her audience appeal began to decline.

Musical analysis of Smith's recordings lends further support to the foregoing observations. Twenty-seven recorded performances have been considered in this study, with attention given to harmony, text, pitch, and rhythm, the latter as the dominant structural element. The model for this analysis was developed during a study of the singing style of Mahalia Jackson by one of the authors (White 1982), wherein conventional methods proved inadequate for demonstrating the complexities and sense of energy generated by such performances. (Similarities in structure, style, and vocal timbre between the singing styles of Smith and Jackson suggest the need for a comparative analysis of their recorded performances.)

Although the greatest number of her recorded selections were composed gospel songs, hymns and traditional songs have also been prominent in Smith's repertoire. Depending upon the given range of the melody, most of her performances span an octave or more. Projecting with great power a deep, rich, timbre, her tenor range is especially evident on recordings made in the 1970s and 1980s. In these late recordings, drums and, later, saxophone were added to the piano and organ heard on early records from the late 1940s and early 1950s.

The scale structures most frequently heard in Smith's recordings vary from the five-note pentatonic scale to the seven-note major scale, with the lowered third and seventh degrees idiomatic to black vocal style. These "blue notes" are most often heard in major tonalities, with minor keys being used more sparingly.

The tempo and rhythmic structure of her performances fall into two broad categories: metered and non-metered songs. In the metered songs, the tempos range from slow $\frac{12}{8}$ or $\frac{9}{8}$ to fast $\frac{4}{4}$ tempos, with most being paced in a medium or walking $\frac{12}{8}$ meter. As a likely carry-over from the lining-out hymn style, in which the Ford Sisters were well-grounded, most of Smith's hymn performances utilize free or non-metered form. Such performances move in very slow tempos and make extended use of both melismas and sustained melody tones. In the absence of a periodic metric substructure, the songs are formed and structured from points of emphasis in the accentuation of harmony, melody, and text.

Several important characteristics of Smith's performances emerge from this study. First, vocal lines constantly alternate between avoidance of and coincidence with the downbeat formed by meter, text, and/or harmony, thus generating a floating, unhindered, dance-like quality. Second, upbeat phrases are frequently prolonged or extended, especially at points of cadence. Third, cadences are continuously interrupted or overlapped by new material, preventing any sense of resolution until the very end of the piece. These characteristics, which help to generate the tremendous intensity of the performances, result from the interaction of vocal lines with text, harmony, meter, phrasing, and accompaniment.

Within the vocal lines, each pitch seems to have its own weight or function, the low tonic being unequal to its octave. The farther away the pitch from the low tonic, the more tension and stress it seems to create. The octave is thus heard as almost "dissonant," requiring resolution through an often gradual descent to the final. Such descending patterns can be quite stylized and specifically identified with certain performers.

Two songs closely associated with Willie Mae Ford Smith, "Give Me Wings" and "The Lifeboat Is Coming," provide respective examples of Smith's metered and non-metered singing. Set in $\frac{4}{4}$ meter, "Give Me Wings" is accompanied by piano, organ, and drums. Likely recorded about 1950, the earlier of two recorded versions of the song is transcribed in Appendix

A. Smith's performance may be heard as a broad AB structure, in which verses one, two, and three (A) are followed by three repetitions of the chorus (B). Each verse and chorus consists of sixteen measures, subdivided into two eight-measure phrases. In turn, each eight-measure phrase consists of two two-measure statements, followed by a four-measure response. In a broader sense, the text of each verse and each chorus is divided into four parts: the first and third sections generate the arsis, or unresolved, sections; while the second and fourth parts, being the same (abcb), create the thesis or resolving sections. By contrast, the order of melodic-harmonic sections is reversed: parts one and three are the same, while the second and fourth parts differ (abac). This contrast between levels of expression in the forms accounts in some measure for the high level of intensity heard throughout the performance.

Also enhancing the performance is the upbeat, swing feeling that is accentuated by overlapping cadences. For example, the verbal aside "Ah, feelin' lonely" is accompanied each time by the half cadence that ends the first eight measures of both the chorus and verse sections of "Give Me Wings." Thus, implicit in the function of both text and harmony is the upbeat to the next passage. The same sense of growing intensity is achieved harmonically by an increase in the rate of harmonic change (from one to two chords per measure) at the end of each verse and chorus.

The vocal line is marked by frequent use of rhythmic variation and anticipation. Upbeat, progressively more syncopated phrases introduce the verses and subsequent choruses. In Example 1 we can see that, by the final chorus, the recurring A has been replaced by the high C.

Example 1. Cadences from "Give Me Wings," as performed by Willie Mae Ford Smith

Each time the chorus begins with "wings, Lord," Smith creates a different variation that returns to the final. Over the downbeat, she articulates the first beat of the chorus with the word "wings," then anticipates beat one in the following measure with the word "Lord" (see Ex. 2).

Example 2. Chorus openings from "Give Me Wings," as performed by Willie Mae Ford Smith

The interaction of these means of generating tension and release accounts for the power and distinctive urgency that Smith and her accompanists have poured into the performance. This sense of inspired alternation between expected and unexpected rhythms, between stasis and change in the harmonies, and between worried melody notes and those occurring within the given scale lend a delicacy and charm to the performance bespeaking the essential Willie Mae Ford Smith. The tempo of this incessantly dancing song is placed deftly between that of gospel songs in moderate compound meter and up-tempo shout songs. It is a bounce rhythm that spends much more time springing and soaring upward than hovering for a place to land.

Sometimes called "gospel blues" (because of its use of phrasing and harmonic patterns similar to twelve-bar blues), the sixteen-bar structure of "Give Me Wings" identifies the performance both with the congregational singing tradition in black holiness churches and with the works of Dorsey, W. Herbert Brewster, Alex Bradford, and other gospel song composers. Fortuitous is the coincidence between the sense of movement that characterizes this gospel bounce and the notion of flight, as evoked by the text. While the overriding message of the song conveys buoyancy and joy, the ever-present second thought, "I'm feelin' lonely," effectively communicates the longing of a spirit not yet released from mortality.

Perhaps Smith's best-known performance in the free or nonmetered style, "The Lifeboat Is Coming," is a two-part form, with each section comprised of four text lines. The most striking characteristic of this style is the vast expanse of expressive structure that is created from limited poetic, harmonic, and textual means. At the beginning the verse suggests a $\frac{6}{8}$ meter with extended cadences. As the song progresses, however, not only is each cadential passage prolonged but, within certain phrases, specific beats are emphasized by prolongation (see Appendix B, measure 9). This extreme liberty with given rhythms enables Smith to sing with the sense of personal testimony that underlies the gospel aesthetic.

The pitches in "The Lifeboat" form the G major scale with the addition of the lowered seventh substituted in the final descending melodic line of the song. Sustained pitches are frequently re-energized by the addition of recurrent, descending pitch-rhythm patterns. Among the most common of these is the four-note pattern indicated in Example 3, which occurs at the end of a long-held pitch. By descending one step and returning to the accentuated pitch before the final descent, a broad arsis gesture is subdivided into two smaller upbeats, which together generate greater intensity.

Example 3. Motive from "The Lifeboat Is Coming," as performed by Willie Mae Ford Smith

As in the metered song, the vocal line generates conflict by avoiding downbeats and by interpolating dissonant pitches against the underlying harmony. The vocal line often reaches beyond, then returns to, its cadential target and, in so doing, delays the point of arrival until after the downbeat (see measures 9–10). In other instances, dissonant pitches are sustained as a means of emphasis, thus extending the sense of completion before a low final (see measure 8, beat 1).

One of the most powerful passages in the piece occurs in the second part of the chorus, where Smith implores, "the light, light, light." Tension is extended to a remarkable degree, as each pitch generates an arsis gesture which is overlapped by the following one. In the first repetition of the word, the melody overshoots the octave G, moving to the high B (measure 14), which creates a strong tension. The four-note motive that follows adds energy to the line by subdividing the second arsis into two smaller gestures. However, as the pattern ends on the G, Smith ascends again to the high B. Each time the word "light" is sung, the melodic line is varied, each repetition being more insistent than the previous one. These gestures propel the music to the next passage introduced by the upbeat "can't you hear."

Leaping from low A to the octave G (see measure 16), Smith empowers the penultimate measure with still more energy, as the high G seeks downward resolution. The passage slowly descends, pausing first on the D and again at the upbeat before the last measure on low G, set against the dominant harmony, thus maintaining the tremendous tension up to the final measure. All elements finally merge, as the melody moves slowly through the delaying passage, scale steps 3-2-1, to the final over the tonic chord. Smith ends the song with the almost spoken words "take hold."

Like "Give Me Wings" and other Smith performances, "The Lifeboat" has always been a highly dramatic visual experience. Eyewitnesses generally agree that, with Bertha's help, Mother Smith had a way of making you feel, hear, and see the tense urgency of both the Master Himself calling the repentant sinner and the metaphor of the rescue boat on the dark and raging sea.

In the contrasts between dark and light, sadness and joy, action and repose, and other possible opposites one might isolate in Willie Mae Ford Smith performances, one finds the sense of balance and completeness that marks her singing as a seminal stylistic influence. Many gospel performers can exhibit vocal power and agility within a limited expressive range, but few demonstrate equal profundity of insight in both reflection and release.

In one Smith performance, dancing melodies seem to soar and glide easily over underlying harmonies; in another, extended melodic range and prolonged pitches push the sense of dramatic tension to the breaking point. In some cases coinciding, in others conflicting, with an underlying rhythmic and/or harmonic substructure, her artistry is revealed in the uncanny balance one finds between surprise and expectation.

In one sense Willie Mae Ford Smith was and is the unsung heroine whose life and music is of seminal importance to any history of style and performance practice in black gospel music. In another sense her story is representative of so many would-be gospel divas who have retained their grounding in the context of a local church community. By constantly stepping out of character during the various phases of her life, Smith represents a pioneering force in black gospel, one who has affected the history of this tradition in at least three important ways.

First, in the late 1930s and 1940s she defined the important role that female solo singers have come to play in gospel music by striking out on her own against the odds that she could earn either respect or admiration from her audiences. Second, she did for gospel singing what Dorsey did for gospel piano and songwriting, when she effected the transfer of worried notes, bends, scoops, growls, and melismas from the blues and spirituals to the gospel idiom. Finally, her profile as a preacher-singer cannot be ignored, as it indicates what has long been controversial about gospel music as a religious form. In our time it has become common for male or female gospel singers to acknowledge a calling to the ministry. However, the idea was not generally accepted during the 1930s and 1940s, and the issue of women in the ministry was far less accepted among mainline Protestant black churches. During the 1940s this sense of calling, as well as the quest for "more of God," as she put it, moved Mother Smith away from Baptist circles and toward Pentecostal and holiness churches. This factor may also provide a clue to the puzzle of why Smith's popularity never matched that of those protégés who succeeded her during the golden age of gospel in the 1950s.[4]

For the researcher the legacy of Willie Mae Ford Smith is both a gift and an awesome challenge. Because what we know of her does not conform to the mold, as it were, of the gospel artist, further study of her life and work may effect a redefinition of the essential elements of black gospel music history. In turn, we may come to understand the musical world of the black church as infinitely varied, complex, and interrelated with the range of social, cultural, and economic forces that play upon the destiny of black Americans in our century.

NOTES

We are indebted to the following persons for their assistance and contributions: Horace Boyer, Nicholas John Basson, George Holloway, and Anthony Heilbut.

1. According to Heilbut (1985, 187), three of Willie Mae Ford Smith's recordings were issued during the period ca. 1949–1950, as listed in the discography included here. While we have not found evidence that brings into question his statement, no documentation has been found to date for the recordings of "Give Me Wings" and "What Manner of Man" that were issued about 1950. Several selections from this period are to be re-released on Spirit Feel 1001. Later in the 1970s and 1980s Heilbut produced the several other recorded performances

cited in the discography. However, this output of recorded performances is far disproportionate to the significance generally accorded Smith by performers and researchers of gospel music.

2. The sobriquet "Mother" is a title of honorary status generally given to well-respected elderly women in black church circles. Certain Holiness and Pentecostal churches have developed a more formal role and function for mothers, but in general, the term carries a status roughly equivalent to that of deacons or deaconesses.

3. Cities described by Jackson (1988a; 1988b) as places where Mother Smith went "very often" included Cincinnati; Kansas City; Atlanta; New York City; Philadelphia; Washington, D.C.; Reidville, Massachusetts, near Boston; Pittsburgh; Milwaukee; Minneapolis; Tulsa; New Orleans; Norfolk, Virginia; and Hartford. Cities where she performed on a less frequent basis included Los Angeles; Seattle; Memphis; Charlotte, North Carolina; Nashville; Denver; Witchita; Oklahoma City; and Houston.

4. While certain holiness churches and Apostolic denominations in particular do constitute a highly sectarian world in themselves, Sister Rosetta Tharpe, Ernestine B. Washington, and others since have emerged from such bodies to receive national acclaim. However, Smith's life experience carried her into rather than brought her out of the Apostolic church world. For additional information concerning black Apostolic church music and traditions, see Dargan (1983).

REFERENCES

Boyer, Horace Clarence. 1986. Black gospel music. In *The new Grove dictionary of American music*, edited by H. Wiley Hitchcock and Stanley Sadie, vol. 2, 254–261. London: Macmillan.

Bringing the nations back to God. 1944. Souvenir program for a series of annual gospel concerts, organized by Willie Mae Ford Smith.

Broughton, Viv. 1985. *Black gospel: An illustrated history of the gospel sound.* United Kingdom: Blandford Press.

Dargan, William Thomas. 1983. Traditional gospel songs in a black Apostolic-Pentecostal congregation: A musical and textual analysis. Ph.D. diss., Wesleyan University.

Feintuch, Burt. 1980. A noncommercial black gospel group in context: We live the life we sing about. *Black Music Research Journal* 1:37–50.

Ford Family. 1988. Personal interview with William Dargan, July 12.

Frazier, Doris Fidmont. 1988. Personal interview with William Dargan, July 9.

Gentry, Marabeth. 1988. Personal interview with William Dargan, July 13.

Heilbut, Anthony. 1985. *The gospel sound: Good news and bad times.* New York: Harper and Row.

Holloway, George. 1988. Personal interview with William Dargan, July 11 and 13.

Jackson, Jackie. 1988a. Personal interview with William Dargan, June 21.

———. 1988b. Personal interview with William Dargan, December 28 and 29.

———. 1989. Personal interview with William Dargan, January 4.

Lindsey, Wynetta. 1988. Personal interview with William Dargan, July 13.
———. 1989. Personal interview with William Dargan, January 2.
National Convention of Gospel Choirs and Choruses, Inc. 1950. Souvenir program from annual meeting held in St. Louis.
———. 1962. Souvenir program from annual meeting in St. Louis.
———. 1983. Golden anniversary souvenir program from annual meeting held in Chicago.
Price, Zella Jackson. 1988. Personal interview with William Dargan, July 11.
Randle, Bernadette, 1988. Personal interview with William Dargan, July 9.
Smith, Willie J. 1988. Personal interview with William Dargan, July 10.
Smith, Willie Mae Ford. 1988. Personal interview with William Dargan, July 8, 9, 11, and 14.
Southern, Eileen. 1982. *Biographical dictionary of Afro-American and African Musicians.* Westport, Conn.: Greenwood Press.
Thedford, Dello. 1988. Personal interview with William Dargan, July 13.
White, Katherine Maria. 1982. Analysis of the singing style of gospel singer Mahalia Jackson. Master's thesis, Washington University (St. Louis).
White, Dianne. 1988. Personal interview with William Dargan, June 23.
Wilson, Doris. 1988. Personal interview with William Dargan, June 17.

SELECTIVE DISCOGRAPHY

Cleveland, Rev. James. *Gospel Music Workshop of America: The nineteenth annual G.M.W.A. convention.* Sound of Gospel-King James Records 2D8509, 1987.
Gentry, Marabeth. *From the heart to the heart.* When Singers Meet MG-1, 1985.
Haynes Temple Choir C.O.G.I.C. of East St. Louis, Illinois. *Loving God.* Savoy 14385, 1975.
Ladies and gentlemen of gospel. Produced by Shannon Williams. Nashboro 7157, ca. 1975.
The legends: The O'Neal Twins, Thomas A. Dorsey, the Barrett Sisters, Sallie Martin, Willie Mae Ford Smith. Produced by Milton Biggham. Savoy SL-14742, 1983.
May, Brother Joe. *Search me Lord.* Specialty Records SPS 2132, 1970.
O'Neal Twins. *God's always making a way for me.* Savoy SL14775, 1985.
Russel, Cheryl. *Gifts of the Spirit.* Shekinah Records SR8512-01, 1985.
Salem Inspirational Choir of Omaha, Nebraska. *I don't feel no ways tired.* Savoy DBL-7024, 1978.
Smith, Willie Mae Ford. "Call Him" / "Jesus is the name." Gotham G667, ca. 1950.
———. "Goin' on with the spirit" / "Pilot, take my hand." Sacred 6015, ca. 1950.
———. "Give me wings" / "What manner of man." ca. 1950. (This material has been made available to the authors on cassette tape, but no documentation has been located to date.)
———. "I believe I'll run on." Nashboro 7124, 1973.

———. "Going on with the Spirit." Nashboro 7148, 1975.
Speed, Minister Malcolm. *I give my all to Jesus.* True Foundation Records TF-1002, 1987.
———. *Because He loves us so.* True Foundation Records TF 1001-C, 1985.

APPENDIX A

Give Me Wings

65 Chorus
wings, Lord. Give me wings, Lord. Yes, I want
I IV
69
wings of faith to fly a-way and be at rest. Oh, feel-ing lone-ly. Give me
73
wings, Lord. Give me wings, oh Lord. And I'll
77
fly a-way some-where to be at rest. Oh, give me
81 Chorus
wings, Lord. Give me wings, oh Lord. I want
85
wings of faith to fly a-way and be at rest. Oh, feel-ing
88
lone-ly. Give me wings, Lord. Give me wings, oh
92
Lord. And I'll fly a-way some-where and be at rest.

APPENDIX B

The Lifeboat Is Coming

As performed by Willie Mae Ford Smith

Key
♪ = short pause
⌒ = pause
⊓ = long pause

3

LUCIE E. CAMPBELL WILLIAMS
A CULTURAL BIOGRAPHY

At the tender age of six years, I was introduced to the music director of the National Baptist Sunday School and Baptist Training Union Congress. She was preparing her singers for some kind of pageant. I remember that my sister was given a bit part in the pageant, and as my mother took me toward the stage to meet Lucie Campbell, I could feel the excitement in my mother's being—the kind of excitement that wells up in one when one is in the presence of greatness. My mother proudly introduced me to this great lady, and she shook my hand, which was extended as far as I could reach, because she was on the stage, and I was just in front of the stage. For me, this was an unforgettable moment. There was something about her eyes and her demeanor that captivated me. While I was too young then to appreciate all of the nuances of that moment, years later, reflecting upon it, I've culled out of it some precious impressions. Those eyes were filled with the fire of artistic temperament, and yet there was a veiled peace underneath. She was motherly in her demeanor—stern yet loving; playful, yet serious; a kind of commanding presence that made one a little fearful, and yet at the same time, one could sense a personality of extraordinary warmth, love, and gentleness.

Some years later, as a teenager, I sat in awe as the beautiful music of the Youth Rally Choir rang through the Municipal Auditorium in Shreveport. There was an inspiring pageant entitled "Youth at the Crossroads." This was followed by a consecration period in which youth offered their lives for Christian service both at home and abroad. Underneath all of this pageantry and consecration was the guiding hand of Lucie Campbell. In the annals of the National Baptist history, Lucie Campbell stands out as a dedicated servant of her people and church. There is, perhaps, no area of our denominational work that has not been touched, either directly or indirectly, by the genius of this extraordinary woman.

Her commitment to the gospel mandate of service (Matt. 28:19–20) made her available in many areas of public service, and many of her devoted disciples are still serving today in religion, education, politics, the arts, sports, the legal profession, medicine, and many areas of human service and development. The expanse of her personality made her equally at home with people from all walks of life. She was indeed a grand lady possessed with unusual charm and wit.

Who, indeed, was Lucie Campbell? What were the factors that contributed to the formation of the complex yet transparent personality? What were the roots that produced this spiritual and musical genius? How did she blend those varied talents of hers in the service of her Lord? What is it that makes her music live on in spite of the tremendous evolution of sacred religious music that has taken place in the last several decades?

She burst upon the stage in a very dramatic fashion in the little town of Duck Hill in Mississippi. Perhaps I should say just out of town, because Miss Lucie, as she was called by most of the people who worked closely with her, was born in a caboose when her mother, Isabella Wilkerson Campbell, was returning from a visit with her husband, Burrell Campbell, who was a railroad worker. It was likely that Mr. Campbell worked with the Illinois Central Railroad, since Illinois Central had purchased the Mississippi Central Railroad in 1873. It was this same railroad that was to produce tragedy in Miss Lucie's life even before she could comprehend the magnitude of the tragedy. Her father, filled with excitement as he traveled home to see the newborn Lucie, was killed in a train accident just outside of Duck Hill.

Duck Hill is an interesting little town, located in Carroll County, Mississippi. Carroll County was one of the sixteen counties established by the Mississippi legislature in 1833 out of the area established by the third Choctaw session in the Treaty of Dancing Rabbit in 1830. This was the beginning of the settlement of this territory, even though this area had been claimed for Spain in 1540 by Hernando de Soto. This area was inhabited by the Ibituphos of the Muskogean tribe. According to Norman L. Izell in his *History of Duck Hill,* "The settlement was named for a Choctaw Indian chief (also known as "Doctor Duck" because of his proficiency with medicines made from roots and herbs)" (Izell n.d., 2).

In the year of Miss Lucie's birth, 1885, the town of Duck Hill experienced something of a boom when the big hill was drilled for iron. The Illinois Central Railroad purchased the big hill; lots were sold, and speculators flourished "swapping lots." One of the people who did well during this boom was John A. Binford, the first white man to settle in the Duck Hill area in the 1820s. It was his grandson, Lloyd T. Binford, who owned Miss Lucie's grandmother as a slave. The grandfather, John A. Binford, was treasurer of the Mississippi Central Railroad at its inception. According to Izell:

> Captain Binford owned most of the land that the railroad used in laying tracks from Elliot to Eskridge. When the line was completed, the railroad wanted to name the station "Binford" and had a sign put up so indicating. Captain Binford, being a Quaker, disapproved, and had them remove the sign and call the station Duck Hill. Captain Binford's grandson, Lloyd T., donated the land for the town high school and permitted it to be called Binford High School. In June 1880, the Binfords deeded some land to the local Baptist church for construction of a church building [the local white Baptist church]. Colonel Binford was a very close friend of Jefferson Davis, and when Davis died in New Orleans, Colonel Binford was one of the pallbearers. He accompanied President Davis' remains to Richmond, Virginia, where he was interred. (Izell n.d., 2–3)

It is evident that the Binford family was, indeed, a very prominent family in Duck Hill. I'm sure that old Colonel Binford never dreamed that a genius of such power and international influence as Lucie Campbell would trace her roots to the Binford plantation.

With Burrell Campbell dead and nine children to raise, Mrs. Campbell decided to move to Memphis, seeking a better life for her children. Miss Lucie was not yet two years of age when the family moved to Vance Street in Memphis. Those early years were difficult years for the Campbell family, but Mrs. Campbell was a woman who had great faith in God and extraordinary strength. She took in washing and ironing in order to provide for her children, and she wanted all of her children to have an adequate education. It was also her desire that they be exposed to the fine arts. She could not afford to provide piano lessons for all of her children; so it was decided that the oldest sister, Lora, would be given music lessons.

It appears that Mrs. Campbell took great pride in Lora but not in Lucie. However, in later years, it was Lucie who took care of her mother, and those who knew them testified to their inseparability. When the girls were young, the mother always presented the other girls with pride to the visitors in the home. According to Charles Kennedy, one of Lucie Campbell's students, Mrs. Campbell would call the other girls out for an introduction, and when one would inquire about the other daughter who had not been introduced, Isabella would reply, "Oh, that's old Lucie" (Walker 1986).

Lucie Campbell's discipline and genius helped her to teach herself music. She would listen in the next room while piano lessons were given to Lora and then she would practice the lessons on her own, devising methods of accomplishing the same results as her sister and doing the various assignments. Thus, she in effect taught herself music.

Her elementary and high school education was acquired in Memphis, and she quickly distinguished herself as a bright student. She won the penmanship award in elementary school and in high school, the top prize in the Latin class. She graduated in 1899 from Kortrecht High School, which later became Booker T. Washington High. She had the distinction of being valedictorian of her class. According to Thomas Shelby, formerly Miss Lucie's student, on the day of her graduation, her mother, aware that it was an unusual honor, told her friends, "my daughter is going to get her 'dictory' tonight" (Walker 1982).

Miss Lucie began teaching in public schools in Memphis at the age of fourteen years. It was during the period when one could teach without a college degree or even a high school diploma. She taught at the Carnes Grammar School, and her salary was a grand forty dollars a month. Her high school teaching career began in 1911 at Booker T. Washington High School in Memphis. She presided over the classes of English and American history. She was remembered as a teacher who loved her students and demanded excellence from all of them. Many of the outstanding leaders today were taught by Miss Lucie, and to them she gave a sense of pride, achievement, dedication, and purpose. She did not tolerate inattention to duty. Excuses were not accepted for unfinished assignments, and yet she spent many hours after school tutoring those who had problems with their work.

There were only two "Negro" high schools in Memphis, and as far as Miss Campbell was concerned, Booker T. Washington was *the* high school in Memphis. It was a school of dignity and discipline. She took pride in its traditions and guarded its reputation with all of her energies.

In those days, informal and formal interactions were carefully orchestrated. Politeness, manners, decorum, and deference to elders were emphasized. Students were required to be present for morning devotion at 8:30 A.M. The faculty was required to be present at 8:15 A.M. and fines were levied against faculty members who were tardy, which was rare, indeed. Then, the church influence in the total life structure was more profound, and religion was the dominant influence in the lives of people. In the afternoon at two o'clock, each classroom had its individual devotionals, which were composed of hymns, spirituals, Scripture readings, and prayer.

Social graces were also taught in the school. For example, as part of an alumni program that took place on April 16, 1927, at Booker T. Washington High, addresses were delivered by prominent people from the business and arts community and musical selections were rendered. In the printed program only two preprogrammed items are listed: 7:00–7:30 P.M., Social Intercourse period; and 7:30–8:00 P.M., Discussion of Business Matters. This particular program also began with an invocation by Rev. L. E. Owens (*Booker T. Washington High School: Retrospective* . . . 1927, 29).

The rules for decorum were strict and vigorously enforced by Miss Lucie as well as by other members of the faculty. Each teacher had an assigned floor, and they'd watch everything that happened on their floor, which they ruled with an iron but loving hand. It is said that Miss Lucie kept her door open at all times, so that nothing would happen in the hall that did not immediately claim her attention. It was not unusual for her to call out a name of a student in the midst of her instruction. The student, no doubt on his or her way to some mischief, would be startled to hear his or her name come booming out of Miss Lucie's classroom! She kept close watch over her children. She cared. She prayed for her children. She aided them in every possible way. But she demanded excellence in every area of their lives.

During a time when pregnancy before marriage was considered the most severe mark against the social character of a young woman, Lucie Campbell reportedly had the uncanny ability to tell if a woman had become with child, sometimes before the young lady herself knew it. One of her former students, Thomas Shelby, shared with me an incident that occurred the day before graduation. The students who were to receive their diplomas were naturally excited and filled with anticipation for the next day's graduation exercises. They were in line for the rehearsal of the processional. The student pianist struck the opening chords of the processional, and the processional rehearsal began. Then, from the rear of the hall, the familiar voice of Miss Lucie boomed out, "Just a moment! Come here!" She directed this order to one of the young ladies in the line, who stood there stunned and frightened. "You'll never disgrace this school with two of you in line! Both of you can't march in this line, baby. Sit down. I'll mail you your diploma! Get out of line!" (Walker 1982). This perhaps seems rather harsh and cruel from today's vantage point; however, if one understands the milieu out of which Miss Lucie came and the sacred and spiritual climate that prevailed in that day, her actions were consistent with what was and was not tolerated.

Lucie E. Campbell was a church woman who witnessed the presence and power of Jesus Christ in her life all during the school day, from Monday through Friday. She no doubt would be fired today for being too religious on the job. Her ideas and ideals about Christian womanhood as related to beauty, power, social standing, and behavior represented principles strongly held by Black women involved in educational and church circles during the first half of the twentieth century. These women believed that there was great work to be done in lifting the race and shaping the young.

Campbell's contributions within the Baptist church included her work with women's organizations, which usually got the pulpit only on Women's Day; through her talent as a musician and composer; and through her support of selected male leaders. She was in great demand as a Women's Day speaker and a conference speaker, and the texts of her addresses dramatically document her views on Christian womanhood.

She frequently substituted for Nannie Helen Burroughs, who was president of the Women's Auxiliary of the National Baptist Convention and probably one of the most powerful women in Black Baptist Christendom. Burroughs was a close associate of Mary McCleod Bethune, and there is a school named in her honor in Washington, D.C.

Lucie Campbell's addresses sounded the call to the women of this nation to be proud, devout, and virtuous. In one of her addresses, she said:

> From whatever viewpoint you evaluate a woman, she is the most influential being in the world. She can lead a man to the highest pinnacle of beauty, of purity, nobility and usefulness; or to the lowest depths of shame and infamy. Woman was behind the fall of Adam, the first man; behind the fall of Samson, the strongest man; behind the fall of Solomon, the wisest man. Despite man's boasted strength, courage and intellect, he will follow a woman anywhere. Someone boastfully remarked that man is the head. A quick-witted woman replied, "Then woman is the neck—the head cannot turn without the neck." (Washington 1971, 20)

In another speech, Miss Lucie extolled the virtues of Christian womanhood in this manner:

> Women should feel proud of their esteemed and conspicuous place accorded them in the conception of great Bible writers. When John, the revelator was banished to the Isle of Patmus to be shut off from public society, away from friends and comrades, prohibited from being able to go to the

temple or synagogue for worship, he petitioned Jehovah God to parade before his gaze something or somebody by which the church could be personified. Angels were bubbling over to perform the tasks, but they were not chosen. So they drooped their wings and bowed their heads disappointedly. . . . John still pleads for something or someone by whom or which he can picture the beauty of the Church. The mighty billows of the deep, with the rays of the sun prancing and dancing upon their bosom, resembling the distant beads of pearls, offered themselves. But they were too unreal to personify the Church that must stand the storms and wiles of Satan. . . .

"Who then?" and "Where shall I go?" said John, "to find a fit subject to personify the Church on the Isle of Patmus?" John prayed, supposedly alone, but he was close to heaven—close enough for his vision to behold a new heaven and new earth, no doubt. John had begun to despair—the darkest hour is just before day. John looked again, and said, "And I saw a woman clothed in the sun. A great wonder. A woman who walked on the moon for her silver slippers. At the crown of her head was bedecked with the stars."

. . . Women, we are somebody—clothed in the sun. No need for costume jewelry or real diamonds, rubies or pearls. The sun is enough. You can barely look at the sun with the naked eye. It is too dazzling. A perfectly dressed woman will bear heavily on the eye. (Washington 1971, 27)

Now, this matter of femininity was a serious one for Miss Lucie. She was glorified in her womanhood. She pampered herself. She dressed with modesty. Though a strong woman, she was nevertheless a proud and feminine woman. For example, one of the great experiences at the National Baptist Convention was when Miss Lucie made her grand entrance on the stage. The people would come from miles around to see Miss Lucie strut. She'd throw her shoulders back, and she would strut out on the stage. The people would break out in a frenzy just at her entrance on the stage.

This theme of modesty and femininity was a constant theme in Miss Lucie's speeches. In another speech, Miss Lucie discusses Adam and Eve. She said, "As soon as they began to know right from wrong, they began pinning on leaves. Put on your clothes, women! I know of nothing more beautiful than this array of women in white before me tonight" (Washington 1971, 30).

Miss Lucie was evangelical in her witness, and the evangelism was pronounced and strong. Although she was an intellectual of the first order and an educator of profound depth and power, her heart was in evangelizing. This graduate of Rust College and Tennessee State University, this postgraduate student of Columbia and the University of Chicago, was one who, with great power and persuasion, called many to the Lord Jesus Christ. In a speech entitled "The Call to Arms," Miss Lucie sounds the evangelical call:

The record shows that when Paul and his companions went over to answer the Macedonian call, the first to accept and heed the call was a woman. Women have always been pioneers in the Great Call to Christianity. Lydia was the first convert in Europe. The crying need of the hour is evangelism or "soul-winning." No longer should the Church boast of how much money we raise during the year but how many souls have been saved. Money is a by-product and will surely come if men and women are converted. Lydia didn't have money, but she gave what she had: free room and board. I'm happy to say that the first evangel was a woman—the Samaritan woman at the well. She brought the town to Jesus, and what have you done? He is still calling.

Oh yes, sisters, we were the first at the tomb on the morning of the Resurrection, and the first to see the risen Lord, and greatest of all, the first to hear the call, "Mary." First to get the first command to tell the boys, "The Master is come and calling for thee." Or the words of Martha to her sister, Mary, "Oh, for more Marthas that might introduce Jesus to the world today." (Washington 1971, 16)

Miss Lucie, in all of her pronouncements, in all of her activities, projected a vibrant faith in the Lord Jesus Christ. Hers was a faith that would not shrink. It was as natural as breathing for her. It was the very life force which energized her. You could not long remain in her presence without being gripped by the reality of something momentous.

The mores of the period with the Black Baptist ministry prevented Lucie Campbell from making her speeches from the pulpit. However, one of her students, Charles Kennedy, told me that she could preach better than most preachers. The student said, "Miss Lucie could stand down on the floor and break up a church" (Walker 1986). *Break up a church* means that the depth and power of her speeches would send people into ecstasy. They would shout all over the place, and sinners would come running to be saved.

Not only was Miss Lucie a sought-after Women's Day speaker, but she was also a very dynamic commencement speaker, and her addresses were always filled with pointed words of wisdom. She had a love for young people and was always prodding them to virtue and great achievement. In a commencement address to the Lincoln High School graduation class in East St. Louis, she said, "Society admires its scholars; but society reveres its heroes whose intellect is clothed with goodness. The youth whose loins are girded with virtue is invincible. The inner life dominated by a worthy ideal will have its flower in a beautiful character. Get your values right and begin with yourself. In finding the goalposts, one must follow these three rules: self-reverence, self-knowledge, and self-control" (Washington 1971, 52).

Let not these gems of thought suggest for a moment that Miss Lucie was not very human herself. Let it not be suggested that she, too, was not grappling with the restrictions of her own humanity. Lucie E. Campbell did not reside in the ethereal atmosphere of some Olympian height. She grappled with the same temptation and problems of being human as we all. She was a woman with a fiery temperament and temper. That artistic fire that resided in her soul made itself apparent in her interpersonal relationships. She and her mother had strong and somewhat domineering personalities. She struck fear in many hearts. There was a strength of presence that she had that made you know it had to be done Miss Lucie's way. As long as she had her way, it was all right. It mattered not your station in life; when you met Lucie Campbell, you met a strong, dominant, confident personality.

Miss Lucie and her mother were long-standing members of the great Metropolitan Baptist Church, ministered by the renowned Dr. A. M. Townsend, for whom the Townsend Press is named. Anyway, a good friend of Dr. Townsend reported to me that Mrs. Isabella Campbell was president of the Mother's Board of Metropolitan and that the Townsends and the Campbells were close personal friends. The two families frequently rode to church and other places together, and it is reported that Mrs. Isabella Campbell would not permit Mrs. Townsend to sit in the front seat of the pastor's car because she, Mrs. Campbell, was president of the Mother's Board and must be accorded the honored seat with the pastor (Walker 1986).

It was the Metropolitan Church that nurtured Miss Lucie in the Christian faith. It was this church that encouraged her and aided her in her educational pursuits. The church members took pride in her achievements. She was their "Little Lucie." They watched her grow from childhood into womanhood. She was educated, cultured, intelligent, and creative. There weren't too many people who had achieved as much as Miss Lucie. The love was mutual. Lucie loved Metropolitan and gave her all in its service. Yet she would be deeply wounded at Metropolitan, and out of that trauma would come one of her greatest compositions. It is perhaps that flaw in her personality, a kind of possessiveness of character, that set the stage for what was to be an explosive situation in the Metropolitan Baptist Church.

In 1922, the pastor, Dr A. M. Townsend, resigned to assume the office of corresponding secretary of the Sunday School Publishing Board of the National Baptist Convention, U.S.A., Inc. The church appointed Reverend T. A. Moore as supply pastor. There was some talk of issuing a call to Reverend S. A. Owens, then president of Florida Memorial College. Miss Lucie was against the calling of Dr. Owens and used her influence to block the call.

A call was issued to Reverend J. T. Brown, who was the pastor of the famous Spruce Street Baptist Church in Nashville. After ten months at Metropolitan, Reverend Brown resigned to assume the office of secretary of the Sunday School Publishing Board. When Reverend Brown resigned, the movement to call Dr. Owens surfaced again. This is not surprising, for Dr. Owens was a man of sterling qualities. He was a Morehouse College graduate, a classmate of Mordecai Johnson, and later a member of the Morehouse faculty. In addition to serving as president of Florida Memorial College, he had served as president of Roger Williams College for a period of three years. While pastor of the Bethel Baptist Church in Daytona Beach, Florida, he had licensed the young Howard Thurman as a local preacher and participated in the ordination of Dr. Thurman into the Christian ministry in Roanoke. So he was much sought after. Despite Miss Lucie's objections, the church met and voted to issue a call to Dr. Owens.

Well, Dr. Owens accepted, and the church, by majority vote, elected him its pastor. There was much joy in the congregation as it awaited the arrival of its new pastor. Joy in all quarters except among the followers of Miss Lucie. Unofficial meetings were called at Miss Lucie's home to discuss the strategy to prevent him from assuming the pastorate, and Miss Lucie was the leader of the opposition. The tension and division increased in the congregation. Miss Lucie was a woman of considerable power and influence. She had one of the associate ministers and several deacons in her camp. It appeared as though she would succeed.

The climax came one Sunday morning shortly before Dr. Owens arrived. Reverend T. A. Moore was in charge of the pulpit, but Miss Lucie had decided that a minister of her choosing would preach. The choir was torn with division: the pro-Campbell and anti-Campbell groups. The "pro-Campbellites" took over the choir stand as the time approached for the morning worship. Reverend Moore was brushed aside, and the minister chosen by Miss Lucie began to conduct the service. The members were incensed, but they all remained calm, for no confusion was desired.

Now, Deacon Jeter, a kindly, saintly man who loved Metropolitan with every fiber of his being, stepped into the picture. It was Deacon Jeter who had mortgaged his home in order to purchase pews when Metropolitan moved into its new edifice. It was Deacon Jeter who had shown concern for the widow Isabella Campbell and her nine children. It was Deacon Jeter who had visited the Campbell home to inquire if there was enough food, clothing, and other necessities. He was sort of like a father to Miss Lucie. Deacon Jeter saw that tensions had risen to a dangerous level, and he did not want a disturbance; he did not want the police to be called into his beloved Metropolitan. The wrong man was in the pulpit. Miss Campbell was at the piano. Murmuring could be heard among the congregation, and restlessness and resentment were apparent. Something had to be done!

Members began to speak out in protest. Things were about to get out of hand. Deacon Jeter thought that if Miss Lucie left the piano, the situation would be defused. He went to the piano and gently suggested that she leave the piano. Miss Lucie exchanged words with him. She became infuriated, took her umbrella . . . the congregation exploded! People stood up and crowded the aisles. Fights broke out. It was frightening. One member who was present said, "My girlfriend and I were very frightened. We could not get down any of the aisles to the exits. So we got on the floor on our knees between the pews, and crawled all the way to the side of the church and then out the back door" (Walker 1983). Someone called the police and reported that the worship at Metropolitan was being disturbed. Plainclothes police came. By this time, Miss Campbell's preacher was again in the pulpit. The plainclothes officers merely beckoned to the preacher without uttering a word.

It was reported that the next evening the deacons met and voted to church Miss Lucie and all of her followers. When a member of a congregation is churched, he or she is brought into what is like the trial that precedes what the Catholic church calls *excommunication*. So they voted to church Miss Lucie. This recommendation was brought to the church in a subsequent church meeting, and the vote was placed before the church body. It was passed by a majority vote that the right hand of fellowship be withdrawn from those members involved in this disturbance. Miss Lucie, along with about one hundred of her followers, were put out of the Metropolitan Baptist Church.

One of the deacons who was in this group came back to the church, apologized for his behavior, and was restored. Miss Lucie never came back, never apologized, and began a kind of church "homelessness." She was shocked at the decision of the church. She was embarrassed and hurt. She loved her church. She loved the people there. It was a tragic moment. Naturally, her followers supported her. Their devotion to her bordered on worship. For them, Miss Lucie could do no wrong. Miss Lucie drew that kind of devotion, for she also gave that kind of devotion. If she loved you, you could do no wrong.

On the other hand, many others in the congregation felt that Miss Lucie deserved the treatment that she received. No doubt some were a little less friendly to her. Some, to be sure, were downright hostile towards her. There were ministers who barred her from their churches. There were other ministers who were determined that she would be blackballed throughout the state of Tennessee. All of these factors plagued her. She could not see the inevitable result of her own strength and her own will and her own charisma that drew people to her as avid disciples. She could not understand the dynamics of strong wills colliding within the Baptist structure. Her pain was intense. Her embarrassment was penetrating. Her sorrow was inexpressible. This perhaps would not have been so if she could have shaken the idea that she was misunderstood. However, out of the milieu of that awful experience, Lucie Campbell composed one of her most inspiring gospel hymns, "He Understands; He'll Say, 'Well Done' ":

> If when you give the best of your service
> Telling the world that the Savior is come
> Be not dismayed if men don't believe you
> He understands; He'll say, 'Well done.'
>
> Oh, when I come to the end of my journey
> Wearied of life and the battle is won
> Carrying the staff and the cross of redemption
> He understands; He'll say, "Well done."

Church controversy again brought another classic gospel hymn. This time, the scene was the Central Baptist Church. After the controversy of Metropolitan Baptist Church, Miss Lucie was apparently without a church home for some years. She went to Central Baptist Church after some years and began working with the choir. Her good friend, Reverend Floyd W. Williams, was the pastor. One of the members of Central related to me the beginnings of several controversies that ultimately led to her expulsion from the membership of Central Baptist:

> In 1929, I was a member of the Junior Choir, directed by brother J. D. Cook. It was our responsibility to sing the second and fourth Sundays in each month. Miss Campbell directed the Adult Choir, which sang on the first and third Sundays.
> One fourth Sunday, some important out-of-town guests came, and Miss Campbell wanted the Adult Choir to sing instead of the Junior Choir. The Junior Choir refused to leave the choir stand, and some strong words were exchanged. A church meeting was called to deal with the problem. All the young people of Central came to the meeting ready to express their dissatisfaction. When the meeting was opened and the matter brought to the floor, one young person asked if it was lawful for a nonmember to be present in this meeting. The reason for the question was that Miss Lucie was not a member of Central Baptist Church, even though she directed the choir.
> When the young woman raised the question of membership, Miss Campbell yelled out, "I pay as much money in this church as anybody!"

The young people retorted, "It doesn't matter how much money you give to the church. That does not make you a member!" (Walker 1988).

The church upheld the young people's right to sing on the appointed Sunday, and the meeting was closed without any further action. Pastor Williams and the deacons took Miss Campbell into the church office after the meeting and received her into the membership of the Central Baptist Church. However, a greater conflict was yet to come.

In the winter of 1943, the beginning of the permanent breach with Central began to form. Contrary to popular belief, the conflict was not between the pastor and Miss Lucie but between a Deacon Vesey and Miss Lucie. Reverend Roy T. Morrison was pastor of Central by this time. Deacon Vesey was a strong, outspoken personality, and so was Miss Lucie. A clash was inevitable.

Miss Lucie wrote a letter to the pastor stating that she could not work with such a man as Deacon Vesey. There had apparently been a long-standing feud between the two, and this merely added fuel to the fire. This pastor had a conference with her and asked her to apologize to the deacon. Miss Lucie refused. The pastor then held a meeting with the two protagonists and the Board of Deacons in order to resolve the matter. Miss Lucie remained firm in her rejection of the deacon. A church meeting was called, the facts were presented, and again Miss Lucie was asked to apologize to the deacon. She refused, and the church voted to withdraw the right hand of fellowship.

The very next Sunday, Miss Lucie returned and sat in the audience. After Reverend Morrison preached, he extended the invitation. Miss Lucie came down the aisle and sat in the chair to be received back into the church. Another person came forward also. Reverend Morrison received this person into the membership and left Miss Lucie sitting there. She returned to her pew, got her umbrella . . . a deacon left the sanctuary and called the police. The police came into the church and quietly escorted Miss Lucie and her cook, who had accompanied her to church, out of church.

Many followed Miss Lucie. The membership of the church dropped dramatically. Miss Lucie and her followers filed suit against the pastor and the church. The judge threw the case out of court, saying that he would not adjudicate a church matter (Court Records 1946).

Again, Miss Lucie felt that she was mistreated and embarrassed, and for a moment she thought of leaving church work altogether. She came to realize that what was in store for her had been well worth the pain. She also began to contemplate her contributions to the problem. She came to the point where she lost sight of the earthly purview and became even more fixed on Jesus. Out of this crisis came the composition "Just to Behold His Face," a strong statement of encouragement.

The 1952 song "Even a Child Can Open the Gate" was inspired by her meeting a young man who was to become perhaps the greatest exponent of the gospel hymn, Dr. J. Robert Bradley. This magnificent artist, who serves today as director of music for the Christian Education Department of the Congress of the National Baptist Convention, U. S. A., came to Miss Lucie's attention in 1932. The Convention was meeting in Memphis, and J. Robert Bradley was a little boy on the Mississippi River with his bucket catching crawfish. There on the river he heard the intoxicating sounds of Baptist hymn singing. He left the river, followed the sounds that brought him right on the stage of the National Baptist Convention meeting, and Miss Lucie was leading the singing. One of the choir members saw him and said, "Get that snotty-nosed urchin off the stage! Look at him—every knot standing in a row!" Before he could be removed from the stage, Miss Lucie said, "No, let him stay." He still had the mud from the Mississippi between his toes, the smell of fish still on his hands. But in that little boy dwelled the voice of unusual power and clarity. Miss Lucie took him, took one of her nice lace handkerchiefs, wiped his face, stood him on a chair, and told him to sing. He sang, and the heavens opened. People shouted all over the auditorium, and the Bradley era began. Dr. L. K. Williams, president of the National Baptist Convention, called to Miss Lucie Campbell and said, "Lucie, where'd you get that boy?" She said, "Out the river." He said, "Well, keep him. He's going to be great" (Walker 1984).

This same Dr. Bradley broke tradition when he included Miss Lucie's composition in his London debut in 1955, which took place in Royal Festival Hall. After performing the great arias and recitatives and leider of the great European masters, Dr. Bradley sang "Touch Me, Lord Jesus" and "Something Within." The audience, which included the Queen Mother of England, was strongly moved. Dr. Bradley then turned to the royal box where the royal family sat and announced that the outstanding lady who composed the two gospel hymns and who meant so much to him was present that night in the hall. He presented her to the royal family and the audience. Thunderous applause greeted her. Miss Lucie, graceful as she was, outdid herself in her curtsey to the Queen (Walker 1984).

Miss Lucie's "Something Within" is a famous composition, as is the story behind the composition. The song was dedicated to a blind gospel singer named Connie Rosemond, who inspired it. Mr. Rosemond customarily played his guitar on Beale Street, and people put coins in his little cup and wished him well. Miss Lucie had come to the fish market to purchase some fish. There sat Connie Rosemond, playing hymns and spirituals, as was his custom. It was winter—cold, damp, rainy. Mr. Rosemond's feet were wrapped in burlap bags as he sat and played. Some of the neighborhood men came out of the bar and listened to the musician play and sing. One of them called to Mr. Rosemond after a while and said, "Hey Connie! I'll give you five dollars to play 'Caledonia,' or some other blues," and Mr. Rosemond replied, "Oh no, I, can't do that." The man's partner taunted him.

Connie Rosemond stood his ground and responded again, "I can't do that; all that I know is that there is something within." Campbell, witnessing this scene, was taken with Rosemond's conviction and the image of having "something within." It moved her to write the hymn that brought her to national attention as a gospel hymnodist. In 1919, at the National Baptist Convention, she introduced a promising young contralto named Marian Anderson. She also presented Connie Rosemond, the blind street singer, who performed her composition "Something Within."

Indeed, Miss Lucie had "Something Within." A fire of genius, a fire of spirituality that revealed itself not only in her life but in the gospel hymns that came from her pen.

REFERENCES

Booker T. Washington High School Retrospective Prospective from 1889 to 1927 (G. P. Hamilton Principal, 1892–). 1927. Memphis: Henderson Business College.

Court Records. Chancery Court of Shelby County, TN. 1946. No. 48063, Joe Johnson, A. J. Polk, Marie Sturtyvant vs. Rev. Roy P. Morrison, *et al.* Final Decree of Dismissal issued January 7, 1946.

Izell, Norman L. n.d. *History of Duck Hill* Unpub. MS, Duck Hill Public Library, Duck Hill, MS.

Walker. Rev. Charles. 1982. Interview with Thomas Shelby, Detroit.

———. 1983. Interview with member, Metropolitan Baptist Church, Memphis.

———. n.d. Interview with Deacon Jeter, Metropolitan Baptist Church, Memphis.

———. 1984. Interview with J. Robert Bradley.

———. 1986. Interview with Charles Kennedy, Romeoville, IL, February 6.

———. 1988. Interview with members, Central Baptist Church, Memphis.

Washington, William M., comp. and ed., 1971. *Miss Lucie Speaks: Addresses of Miss Lucie E. Campbell*. Nashville: C. R. Williams (exclusively distributed by the National Baptist Training Union Board).

PART 2

AFRICAN-AMERICAN WOMEN AND CHURCH INSTITUTIONS

4

THADDEUS J. POSEY, O.F.M., CAP.

PRAYING IN THE SHADOWS:
THE OBLATE SISTERS OF PROVIDENCE, A LOOK AT NINETEENTH-CENTURY BLACK CATHOLIC SPIRITUALITY

Traditionally American society has viewed black Christianity as derivative of the European tradition of the Christ event. However, a careful review of early nineteenth-century black Catholic life provides a different portrait of the black religious experience. Far from being a primitive or syncretic Christianity, black American religious belief and practice reveal an eclectic collection of the best of West African beliefs expressed in life-giving Christian terms. As Vincent Harding suggested, "we took the religion of the slave masters and transformed it into an instrument of struggle for truth and freedom."[1]

Black survival in slavery may be understood as related to the "core beliefs" which persisted from their West African belief systems. Henry Mitchell and Nicholas Lewter in *Soul Theology: The Heart of American Black Culture* note that "all cultures have clusters of core convictions about reality, and none can be understood properly apart from the way they traditionally look at the world."[2] These core beliefs became the prism through which blacks of the diaspora (slave or free) addressed the Christianity they encountered. Students of black spirituality acknowledge that the American black spiritual tradition has African as well as European roots.

This article explores the African and European roots of nineteenth-century black Catholic spirituality. By examining the spirituality of the first organized group of black religious in the Catholic tradition, the Oblate Sisters of Providence, it offers some insight into how elements of the cultures of these two continents blended to provide a powerful internal resource for blacks as they faced the hostile environment of bondage. On a broader level, this examination may provide a basis for addressing that ever-present and poignant question: *WHY DO BLACKS IN AMERICA REMAIN CHRISTIAN/CATHOLIC?* Christians initiated slavery in the new world, and Christianity helped maintain it. The spirituality of the free blacks of nineteenth-century Baltimore offers some understanding of a basic value orientation or "core beliefs" which enabled the black community to incorporate and use Christianity to nourish life in a hostile world and to give them the flexibility to survive.

CORE BELIEFS

"Core beliefs," in the life of black America, operate on the fundamental principle that piety must be verified in the life-style of the persons; "do not tell me of your virtue, show me." In this piety "the most treasured and trusted word about our life here on earth is that God is in charge. This faith guarantees that everyone's life is worth living."[3]

In black life experience *"the Providence of God"* is the most essential attribute of God which black core beliefs affirm. In a hostile environment as brutal as slavery, survival was grounded in the unyielding trust in God. It was the salve of sanity in that insane world which helped individuals and communities to keep their balance. "Emotionally balanced persons depend on the Providence of God, holding therefore that life is always worth living. The goodness of God and life will always be disclosed if one will trust enough to wait."[4] Yet Providence is not just common to blacks in the diaspora.

The Providence of God is one of many core beliefs, "common to all or most of the West African religions; but the beliefs were not propagated as such."[5] Africans' societies did not send missionaries to their "heathen neighbors" to preach a "better news." Founders and reformers, scriptures and canons are alien to African religious life. Religion flows from the life of the people. "These very stable peoples simply and quietly assimilate ideas and practices from one another."[6] There was no conversion, however, since religions were coterminous with societies. As the African theologian John Mbiti declared, to convert would "involve propagating the entire life of the people concerned; . . . [thus] to observe a few rituals . . . does not constitute conversion."[7] Clearly the adopting of new ideas as a vehicle for expressing core beliefs (the Midas Touch) was not foreign to the West Africans known in the Americas as slaves.

West African religions hold dear the cycles in life (births, rites of passage and weddings, plantings and harvests, and funerals). "The word celebration is appropriate to all these occasions, and the total community participates. In this sense, everybody is religious and deeply familiar with the tradition."[8] In black spirituality, this is the principle of church without walls; of faith and religion without denomination. Piety is manifest and verified in the halls of human/communal experience and not in church buildings. Mitchell establishes the root of this communal principle when he asserts that for life celebrations:

> All are actively involved, although the tradition does not emphasize meditation and personal mysticism. Again the serving of human needs is strong in the African cultures, but it is assigned to *extended family* and neighborhood ties. The obligation to help persons in need is supported indirectly by religious ideas of community as family but it does not involve conscious religious organizations and practices.[9]

This concept of *extended family* is the foundation of the African and African-American world view. The vocabulary of family (mother, father, brother, sister, aunt, and uncle) is that of life relationships. It is used for Church, for kinship affiliation and for friendship. The African world-view provided the first principle of black spirituality: *Everybody has a place.* We are all family, and the proof of one's piety is in the manner in which one relates to family: *everybody.*

Mbiti has suggested that, "in matters of belief there are clear areas of common ground like God, continuation of life after death, spiritual beings, the works of God, etc. On these both Christianity and traditional religions (African and African-American) overlap to a large extent."[10] On the other hand, in the American (Catholic) experience, theology validated by human experience, piety certified in human interaction, and church seen as a plurality (extended family) in unity, may fall outside the realm of Christianity.

James Cone raises a valid challenge for Christianity when he writes:

> If one's faith is true to life and is thus the defender of life, as the biblical faith most certainly is, then the faith itself forces one to remain open to life as it is lived anywhere.... Indeed it is when we refuse to listen to another story that our own story becomes ideological, that is, a closed system incapable of hearing the truth.[11]

The study of black religion has included numerous notations on black spirituality. However, these notations have rarely provided a framework for exploring black American piety in light of its African roots. And this piety has been given only limited exposure as part of the American Catholic experience. It seems fitting therefore to examine the principles and parameters of a black spirituality soundly rooted in the African/African-American tradition as they have been manifested in the Catholic Church.

As noted in the world-view, Church is a concept rooted in the concept of family, extended family. Thus, for the black Catholic, *Everybody has a place*. The church must be universal—open to all. Recall 'Roots.' A young white man they named "Old George" almost got Tom killed. Yet when he came to the door and asked for food, they fed him. They had no cultural tools for denying food to the hungry. As Mitchell himself reminisced, "when I was pastor of a church, I saw many a 'redneck' who might have spit when he left the building, but who knew that, if he and his family came to my church or any other black church, we simply couldn't send him away without feeding him."[12] It is well known that if, in hard times, you go to the black community, you can at least eat. The issue is extended family; the question is, how can the Church refuse anyone? It is universal!

The human experience for the black community is the Church's lack of respect. In affirming extended family, blacks not only affirm a mutually supportive love, but a deep respect for human personality. To act otherwise would be to affirm only oneself. "This respect is expressed in a kind of awe before each destined-to-be unique personality—a shyness about meddling with or trying to control another."[13] Folks say, "a man has to do what a man has to do." In truth it is a recognition of the right of each person to make his/her own mistakes. When the Church refuses service, the human experience is that "things" (financial, etc.) are more important than people. In black spirituality people are first.

Placing people first is good and correct, but not always reasonable in the European and Catholic mind. For the Pan-African world, as has been noted, Providence is the primary virtue of the community. Nothing is foreign. All belongs to God: people and creation. Do right by people and God will provide. Moreover, the role of the Church is to guide the community in maintaining the balance in life by making the core beliefs a reality. Cheryl Townsend-Gilkes, in her paper "The Black Church as a Therapeutic Community," identifies four historically therapeutic functions that the churches have had in helping black people maintain that balance:

1. the articulation of suffering;
2. the location of persecutors;
3. the provision of asylum for "acting-out";
4. the validation of experience.[14]

But when the Church is the misinterpreter of the core beliefs, or can listen only to its own European heritage, then life experience validates for blacks not only the core beliefs, but that the Church lacks respect as well. It creates the suffering, whereas in black Christianity, the Church should identify the persecutor.

For black Christianity, providence is the virtue; people are first because in God's wisdom everybody has a place; and justice is God's in His time. W. E. B. Dubois notes well that "the long system of repression and degradation of the Negro tended to emphasize the elements in his character which made him a valuable chattel":

Virtues:

PASSIVE CHRISTIANITY: (As Whites taught)	BLACK CHRISTIANITY (Core Beliefs lived)
1. Humility	1. Courtesy
2. Submission	2. Moral strength
3. Long suffering	3. Ability to see the good (beauty beyond the surface)
4. Other world	4. Joy (celebrate life)
5. Patience	5. Avenging spirit (balance & nature)[15]

Dubois' analysis of these value differences in the two types of Christianity helps us to understand the dual interpretations of the virtue of providence by those who have reflected on the black Christian life-style. What has often been valued as passivity on the part of blacks is seen by the wise of the black community in a different light. Simply put, the community calls black Christians to respect all people, but to respect and protect the community first. The lesson learned in a hostile environment grew out of a collective wisdom and provides new directives for keeping the balance necessary for life. Through the centuries, black Americans developed a realistic understanding of how to live as unvalued people. How could blacks continue to proclaim that life is worth living when others counted them as of little worth? A difference in spiritual framework suggests an answer.

Jacques Joubert (1777–1843), a French Sulpician priest charged with the religious education of the children of "free French-speaking people of color" was the co-founder and organizer of the Oblate Sisters of Providence. As their ecclesiastical director, he called four "free women of color" to the sisterhood to give stability to the educational program for "free children of color." Joubert initiated this project among the immigrant black French-speaking Santo Domingans of Baltimore, as two of this community, Elizabeth Lange and Marie Balas, were already running their own school. Joubert describes these beginnings;

> 13 June 1828, Mary Elizabeth Lange, Marie Magdaleine Balas and Rosine Boegue came to live in the house which we had rented from Mr. G. Hoffman at the corner of the street on which the seminary stood, and we began the foundation with eleven boarders and nine externs. They began on this same day to form the community and they began their novitiate by following a few rules given to them. On June 24th Elizabeth Lange was made Superior, and it was agreed by them to change the superior every three years on the feast of St. John the Baptist; but since this first year was to be for all the year of novitiate, Elizabeth Lange's office of Superior would be counted from June 24, 1829.[16]

The development of the *Rule* was no singular project, nor was it accomplished in a single writing. The first few rules developed into several pages. Consultation, reflection and additional ideas were explored to create the final text of the document presented to the archbishop of Baltimore. The *Rule* itself was composed during the first year (1828–29) of the school's operation. Their house was named St. Frances Convent and thus school became St. Frances Academy. While they were novices, Joubert outlined, discussed with the Sisters and consulted as to what would be appropriate.

This "Constitutions des Oblates, Soeurs de la Providence" *(Rule)* makes no reference to any of the basic rules of religious life (Benedictine, Augustinian, Carmelite, Franciscan), so well known in the Church. At the time of its conception Joubert was not certain as to whether the status of religious order would be granted to this society of "free women of color" by authorities. In 1827 Joubert had initiated the Holy Family Society, a lay organization, to support the spiritual growth of Baltimore's free black Catholics. Though the Archbishop had approved the new society, the establishment of an official "religious society of colored women" to educate the young colored girls could have alarmed many in the Church community. Thus, strategically, Joubert penned the Constitution to state clearly that,

they make no vows, but merely a promise of obedience to the Reverend
Director to be appointed by the Most Reverend Archbishop, and to the Superior whom they shall choose from among themselves. Hence their annual engagement, instead of profession, is called *oblation*.[17]

The name, *Oblates, Sisters of Providence*, became their official title.

The first ecclesial approval of the Oblates' rule was actually given by
James Whitfield (1770–1834), the Archbishop of Baltimore, on 5 June
1829. The Rule has eight sections and basically outlines the sisters' life in
the context of basic human and social concerns:

1. Duties of the Superior.
2. Duties of the Sisters.
3. Of Postulants.
4. Of Employment.
5. Order of the Day.
6. Sundays and Festivals.
7. Days of Recreation.
8. General Observations.[18]

On 2 October 1831 the Oblate Sisters of Providence received Papal
recognition. They were religious; they could take vows. As any religious society, the Oblates were founded with a specific service in mind. They "renounce the world to consecrate themselves to God and to the Christian
education of young girls of colour."[19] The *Rule* presents a straightforward
and balanced effort to address what is necessary to maintain an orderly
house and provide for its members' needs and what is appropriate in relating to the public. It speaks of equality, respect, and sanctification. The superior, elected for three years, was the mother of the household. With
sincere charity, she would receive, listen to, advise, and when it fostered the
good order of the house, yield to the sisters' requests!

It will be her duty to see that the Sisters be not burdened with occupations,
that they take sufficient repose when necessary; that in health or in sickness
they never be left destitute of those little comforts which may be necessary;
in a word, she will conceive for them all the tenderness of a mother.[20]

The first of these tender mothers, who nurtured this unusual group in
the shadows of the Church of Baltimore, was Sister Mary Elizabeth Lange.

If Joubert created an acceptable *Rule* for the Oblate, Sisters of Providence, then Sister Mary Elizabeth Clovis Lange gave that rule life. She was the spirit of the *Rule*. Not only was Sister Mary the superior general for three terms within the Oblates' first thirty years; she also was the mistress of novices for three terms, assistant general for one term and one of the first three sisters to work outside of the confines of St. Frances Convent. More than anyone else she saw clearly the possibilities for the black community of Baltimore and the role St. Frances could play in moving possibilities to reality. The spirit of the Oblates is a heritage brought to life by the one they affectionately called "Mother Lange."

Mother Lange was the epitome of Catholic presence among those women who became the pillars of antebellum black American life. While she did not write novels and poems or give lectures as her fellow Baltimorean,[21] Frances Ellen Watkins Harper (1825–1911); nor did she publish as Mary Ann Shadd Cary (1823–1893) who had, at one point, fled to Canada; nor did she give a performance at Buckingham Palace for Queen Victoria as Elizabeth Taylor-Greenfield (1809–1876); nor was her courage exemplified by a great escape as was Ellen Craft's (c.1826–1897) or by anti-slavery lecturing as was Sojourner Truth's (1797–1883), Mother Mary Lange was an educator with a vision of the black community as to what could be realized and an inspiration from God as to how it might be accomplished. She exemplified how to walk that tightrope among the forces of prejudice and hatred, often inclined to violence, and an unenlightened Christianity. Mother Lange's heroic contribution is reflected in her steady, persevering commitment not only to educate those who were considered unteachable, but to nurture in them the self-confidence essential for them to become productive citizens. White Protestants and Catholics alike; in principle, proclaimed a place for everyone; their mind-set did not permit their actions to reflect that proclamation. Catholics, according to Maria Caravaglios, sought to address their own inconsistent perception of human categories:

> The pastoral letters of the years preceding the Civil War, both those from the bishops and those from diocesan or provincial synods, give evidence of the southern hierarchy's efforts to keep the Church safe from any suspicion or change of abolitionism, at the same time that they strove to remind their slave-owning parishioners of their responsibilities as Catholics.[22]

Free blacks created an even greater confusion for Catholics. Baltimore was caught between the traditional English-speaking American approach to

race relations and the immigrant French-speaking tradition. It had successful and contributing citizens of color. It also had a community of "free
women of color" who had institutionalized themselves as women of God.
Their French roots curbed the aggressiveness of many, while the disdain for
their black roots made them a point of ambivalent curiosity. Catholics, outside of Baltimore, made assertions on both sides of the argument as to
whether a viable, functional and contributing black community was an actual possibility. The pluralism of the American Catholic Church had not
grown enough to grant blacks an identity or assure them a secure place in
the Church. Thus, the fate of the sisters was at this point uncertain. Bishops
were left to make prudent and expedient decisions.

John England (1786–1842), bishop of Charleston and a spokesman for
the Catholic position supporting slavery, visited St. Frances in November
1829. The Oblates' Annals record:

> He approved very much of the institution, that it would produce much
> good and he proposed to establish one similar in his diocese as it had a
> large number of colored people: it was fitting that Archbishop Whitfield
> had set them an example.[23]

Yet England, particularly, was at a loss to give "the Church's" reflection
on the status of "free people of color." Perhaps this was due to the fact that
the Northern Europeans lacked that experience. Only the Catholic countries with colonies (France, Portugal and Spain) could offer any such insight. Thus the immigrant French procedure for relating to free people of
color, indeed a curiosity for the old English-speaking American Catholics,
proved to be the influential Catholic element.

This French influence was reflected in the Oblates' spiritual life. Their
rule states a twofold purpose: "The Oblates renounced the world to consecrate themselves to God, and to the Christian education of young girls
of colour."[24] They were founded to do a job: to educate "girls of colour" at
a time when the education of people of colour met with great opposition.
They were asked to do so in the Catholic tradition of convent schools,
which had an agenda not completely suited to life in the black community
of 1828.

Convent schools were French in origin, though started by an English-
woman, Mary Ward (1585–1645), in St. Omer in the early seventeenth century. Mary Ward and her community tried to establish, as historian Eileen
Brewer discovered,

the female equivalent of a Jesuit schooling, and incorporate religion, Latin, reading, writing, the native tongue, arithmetic, French and Italian, into her curriculum. The girls also learned needlework, nursing and basic medicine.[25]

Over the years this approach to education became the Catholic model for preparing young ladies for family life. Given the French background of Joubert, Sister Mary Lange, and the founding sisters, the principles of the convent school were the point of reference for some aspects in the development of St. Frances Academy. But the Baltimore of the 1820s was not France. And the black community, as was the case with other American communities, adapted the curriculum to suit its needs.

The Oblates, in the French tradition, recognized the need for an education that would train the young women for their actual duties in life. They, too, saw the importance of a strong spiritual foundation and of the manners and demeanor essential to black survival in nineteenth-century Baltimore. But of greater historical value is the fact that the Oblates brought into being a new balance, the convent school setting and the vision and educational interest of the black community of the United States. As a standard account of Maryland Catholic education concludes:

> The establishment of this unique enterprise was to eventuate in setting up a stable organized school and a body of teachers to perpetuate that institution. It marks the beginning of an organized effort in behalf of Negro education among Catholics.[26]

Joubert wanted to teach youngsters to read so that they might recite the catechism. His initial concern had a singular purpose. The black community's vision, however, has always looked at education as the panacea for overcoming the ills that the American experience provided. Again "core values" and Christian intent merge to enhance the black community. Nowhere do we see this merger more evident than in the spiritual vision and life of the sisters.

VISION IN THE SPIRIT
Yahweh, who has the right to enter your tent
or to live on your holy mountain?
The one whose way of life is blameless
who always does what is right

who speaks the truth from his heart
whose tongue is not used for slander
who does no wrong to his fellow
casts no discredit on his neighbour.
(Ps. 15:1–4)

The *Annals* tell us about the aspirations of Elizabeth Lange and her close friend, Marie Balas. "For more than ten years, they wished to consecrate themselves to God for this good work, waiting patiently that, in His own infinite goodness, He would show them a way of giving themselves to Him."[27] "Grace builds on nature!" The period in which they taught in their own private school proved to be a valuable preparation for their future. Their service in the school is symbolic of Elizabeth's and Marie's sacrifice for the sake of God's call to serve the needs of the community. Joubert elicited a greater commitment, as he describes in the *Annals:*

> They promised to do everything that I should think of to further this work, and they put themselves and all they had, entirely at my disposal, which necessitated their discontinuing a small free school which they had been having for a number of years at their home. Assured of the good will. I felt myself bound to prepare the way.[28]

William Andrews, in looking at the spirituality of nineteenth-century black women, reminds us that once someone had experienced the "call," the question became, "how radically to break with the world? More specifically, how much could one deny the world's traditional expectations of a Christian woman?"[29]

In the confusion and ambivalence of Catholic Baltimore there were few if any expectations made of Christian black women. Mother Lange and the Oblates not only established the standard for what it meant to be black religious women in the Catholic Church in the United States, but they also created a new standard for young black women in general. The Oblates also instilled the values of Christian living and "productive citizenship" in this segment of American society that the white community ignored. More importantly, the values were not merely stated; they were lived. St. Frances Convent and Chapel became the center of black Catholic spiritual life in Baltimore. By 1853 the Catholic Almanac listed the Chapel as the church for "the colored people." The Oblates' preaching was by example; they shared their own spirit and life with their students and the entire community.

Much has been written recently about Mother Lange because of the promotion of her cause for canonization. Many articles refer to the basic sources, others reference earlier articles, thus preserving the "oral tradition." What then do we know of Sister Mary Elizabeth Lange? The most common response concerning her was that she, "was very good but a very strict observer of the Rule and made no allowances for small omissions."[30] Indeed, stories are related in which her vigilance shifted to show with clarity the consistency of her love and care. Perhaps the best story is that of Sister Mary's trickster, Eugenia:

> This night after the ringing of the bell she went to one of the girls who was mortally afraid of Sr. Mary. She tickled this child and caused her to scream with fright. Everyone was silent. Sr. Mary called the child to her to ascertain what was the matter. She tried to tell Sr. Mary what the mean girl (Eugenia) had done, but not being able to say the word [tickle] in French, she tickled Sr. Mary in order to show her what she meant. The Sisters could not refrain from smiling; but one of the Sisters who had seen Eugenia's trick, explained to Sr. Mary and the latter comforted the child, but gave a severe reprimand to Eugenia.[31]

Sister Mary always maintained a balance in life. "She was a model of piety and extreme mortification and self-abnegation."[32] "Sr. Mary was a good kind Mother and when anyone was sick or in pain, she would do the last [sic] thing to give them ease and comfort."[33] She was a great teacher and really loved little children."[34] As most people remember teachers who were task masters with love and respect, so was Mother Lange remembered. She was the sister who had a heart; a woman of great love. She was the sister who, on 12 July 1830, became godmother for Marie Helen Thomas (future Sister Gertrude Thomas, fifth superior general);[35] she was the sister who, on 23 February 1840, honored the request of a dying mother to take in her children, five-year-old Sarah (the future Sister Theresa Catherine Willigman, sixth Superior General) and three-year-old Charity Willigman.[36] Sister Theresa Catherine recalled that

> Sister Mary never spared herself; work had no terrors for her; very seldom did she rest, and as it was one of Fr. Joubert's expressed advises [sic] that the Sisters should never be idle, even in the hours of recreation, they

would always have their hands busy with work; even the children were taught knitting to prevent idleness.[37]

Her zeal for the children and her tireless efforts for the community set an example for all the sisters. The amended Rule of the Oblates (1833) was the result of three factors: the desire of Sister Mary and her companions to be religious, the guidance offered by Joubert and their lived experience. Joubert's original thought was not specific; "I thought of founding a kind of religious society."[38] The sisters' lived experience, characteristic of Oblates life under the initial rules, brought about both the Rule and the revisions (1833, 1839 and 1868).

Oblate life is contemplative but not cloistered; strict in following the Rule, but not rigid. "The Oblate Spirit" evolved with two ever-present existential factors being considered: the desire of the sisters "to consecrate themselves to God, and to the Christian education of young girls of color"[39] and a hostile environment that did not want "religious women of color." Theirs was an unwanted commitment. Thus they *prayed in the shadows!* For some, the very notion of "religious women of color" was a contradiction in terms. These factors created a duality of perspective as well as life.

These dualities made the Oblates "bi-cultural." On the one hand, they had to relate to a Church and Catholic community whose roots were primarily European. On the other hand, they were black women, dedicated to the service of the Black community. This "bi-cultural" dynamic was equally reflected in their spirituality. Theirs was a bi-cultural life that reflected a classical French asceticism expressed in an African mode. The asceticism called them to perfection in an imitation of Christ (an Incarnational approach), and the African belief system called them to a genuine life in service of the community. Perhaps no devotion brings this to light more clearly than their membership in the Association of Holy Slavery of the Mother of God.

While cursory view of Oblate history provides an appreciation of their devotion to the Eucharist, the ascetical practices of the Association of Holy Slavery appear strange, if not repulsive. A devotion initiated by St. Louis De Montfort (1673–1716) adherents see Our Lady as, "a means of acquiring Wisdom; that is, of being united to her Divine Son. Devotion to her is only a means, but it is the most perfect means, and according to St. Louis-Marie the only means we have of being constantly united to Christ."[40] Therefore, to freely give oneself to a slavery that would secure a constant union with Christ was in complete harmony with the Oblate Rule. This slavery gave new meaning to life. The sisters, in their early history, were fully aware of what slavery required (Sister Angelica was bought out of slavery by Joubert, and Sister Louise Gabriel was freed by Richard Caton).[41] In their burning desire to serve God, their willingness to join the Association of Holy Slavery to the Mother of God speaks volumes of their commitment to God and the children of black community whom they served. These freed women took the classic model of the abused of the black community and turned it into a mode of service and a model of grace. This was a definitive expression of the old core values in a French ascetical framework. Joubert incorporated in the Oblates' *Rule* the importance of the external manifestation of this internal disposition. Concerning the duties of the Sisters he wrote:

> The Sisters will strive to the utmost of their power to observe the rule of the house; in this each one will endeavour to give an example of the most perfect obedience. Their sanctification depends on their fidelity with which they observe the rules. Their great object shall be to entertain amongst themselves a perfect union and for this end they will act with unanimity, with simplicity and openness of heart.[42]

Following the rule and giving good example were key elements of the Sulpician spiritual heritage passed on to the Oblates. The Sulpicians, who had helped lay the spiritual foundations for the Oblates, did not stress physical mortification. They believed "there was a tendency toward pride in such behavior."[43] In Sulpician life, as well as in Oblate life, asceticism was expressed in the highly structured regimen of the community schedule. Joubert actually published it in the Rule. The Oblates inherited an asceticism of the French school that emphasized the manifestation of the divine life within as opposed to the "Rigorism" of those influenced by the Jansenists. The principle of inner discipline was not new to the black religious experience.

Christianity, as sifted through the centuries in the Caribbean and the United States, was distinctly manifested in the twofold spiritual heritage of the Oblates. Theologian Jamie Phelps, O.P., describes this heritage:

> The spiritual traditions of the Catholic church, for example, were transmitted to the sons and daughters of Africa without any consciousness of the cultural-specific ways—Spanish, Irish, German, English, French, or Italian—in which they were being transmitted. In addition, these ministers of God's good news sometimes maintained a disdain for the natural religious expression of blacks. For them, blacks needed to be elevated and rescued from their immorality by their participation in what was perceived to be a

universal spirituality that was, in fact, a particular cultural-ecclesial spirituality and way of life. White missionaries assumed that blacks had no culture worth preserving, and that their religiosity was a natural disposition
based primarily on fear and ignorance. Christianity would provide them
both with culture and the true faith.[44]

Black American spirituality must always be seen in light of the American
ecclesial and political dilemma: the ongoing conflict centered around race,
religion, ethnicity and morality. Thus, in the black style, the Oblates, while
maintaining their identity, their belief in the "crucified Christ" and accepting all of His precepts, created "ways of finding meaning, worth, hope and
purpose in different and decidedly difficult contexts."[45] Paramount in the
development of their life-style was the critical balance between ecclesiastical demands and an authentic response to the Spirit. "For Blacks, authenticity rests always with truthful *practice* of biblical religion, especially in the
pursuit of love and justice."[46] It is a part of that personal integrity fundamental to black spirituality—what the Sulpicians considered to be the manifestation of the internal divine life. Therefore two elements became
"spiritual imperatives" for the young community of "free Black women religious": discernment and example.

Discernment has always been a "sine qua non" for balance. It is the pre-
lude to wisdom. Oblate life was established on the age-old precepts of getting to the issue through charity, patience, meekness, humility and a belief
in the common good. The sisters placed a special emphasis on harmony in
their environment. The convent permitted both the discernment of self and
the sharing of self for the common good. For example, the superior was forbidden to correct faults in the presence of others, "unless the fault was such
that for the edification of those who should have seen it happen, it requires
a prompt correction, which in this case she will make in such a fashion that
blaming the fault, she will relieve the one at fault."[47] Life had taught the
Oblates enough lessons of embarrassment. Their esteem and respect for
each other balanced the disdain and rejections they received elsewhere.
Thus, for the sisters the example set was extremely important.

Working with Joubert, they were able to capture in the Rule the vital importance of example. The sisters were quite aware, in these situations, that
negative responses to their actions could easily be taken out on someone
else—those blacks who had little possibility of eliciting an ecclesial concern.
As black religious that example was of the utmost importance, for it preserved the common good of the convent and called forth the good of the
black community.

The absolute criterion of authentic Black Spirituality is its impact on the quality of the believer's life. It assumes that the true nature of our faith is reflected in the way in which we relate to other human beings, and the created order, and that our concern for others will naturally generate witness and actions directed toward the realization of freedom for all human beings to live a liberated and joyful life, energized by the power of the spirit.[48]

This multifaceted black life-style, recognized as religious life by the Catholic Church, was probably one of the few places a black person could truly practice the faith to its fullest. The Oblates had the rare opportunity to live an authentic Catholic/Christian life and, in so doing, model authentic bi-cultural Christianity for the entire black community. A notable practice of the sisters was that of granting residence to senior women. Sometimes this was accomplished by following the patterns of the Church at large in order to express Christ's universal love. The *Annals* on 10 December 1837 record "the reservation that was made of the six benches in the back of the chapel for the White people who came to the service."[49] At other times the bi-cultural dimension of French religious life and African-American core values required a firm and clear challenge to the Church and its officials in order to call forth the love and respect for all individuals, black or white. Such was the tone of Sister Mary's letter to the Sulpician Superior, Louis Deluol, on the occasion of his request for the sisters to manage the housekeeping at the Sulpician seminary.

Sister Mary began her letter to Deluol with a reminder of the unique aspects of Oblate life, the freedom of discussion and the open consultation and prayer concerning the issues of their life. Indeed this principle of equality found in the Rule was maintained throughout the Oblate's first sixty years.[50] The letter, with a traditional black spirit, recognized both the personal call of each member of the community and the discernment necessary to truly "respond to the Spirit." But mother's letter included more significant points which expressed not only the graciousness of the community but their understanding of themselves as black religious women and their dedication to their state of life.

Mother Lange thanked Deluol because he had provided an opportunity for them to repay some of the kindness they had received from the Sulpicians over the years. She called to the attention of the superior of the seminary formation program their twofold reality, that she and her sisters were both "persons of color and religious at the same time." But more significantly she proclaimed and exemplified the balance that black spirituality demanded by presenting the dangers of speaking from such a position—"in such a manner as not to appear too arrogant on the one hand and on the other, not to miss the respect which is due to the state we have embraced and the holy habit which we have the honor to wear."[51] In so doing, Mother Mary not only identified the problem—damned if you do and damned if you don't—in the classic black ecclesial sense, but she also modeled the humility and honesty appropriate for a Catholic religious. In this framework she then provided Deluol with the conditions for any contractual employment of Oblate Sisters of Providence in the Seminary community.

The Oblates' spiritual journey was a religious life that encompassed a bi-cultural reality. Within the framework of traditional Catholic religious life, the Oblates forged a life of service in a milieu of confrontation and abandonment. As Jamie Phelps noted,

> White missionaries assumed that Blacks had no culture worth preserving, and that their religiosity was a natural disposition based primarily on fear and ignorance. Christianity would provide them both with culture and the true faith.[52]

Though Catholic, Mother Lange and the early Oblates could see American Catholicism from a point of view formed of a blend of French and African-American experience. As Mother Lange so often manifested in her life, God granted them a spirituality whereby they could look at the members of their own Catholic religion as well as other citizens of Baltimore and still find Christ in the faces that surrounded them. The Oblates developed spirituality that was flexible enough to address the religious diversity within the same ecclesial communion.

Although the ambivalence of the American Catholic community brought pain and insecurity into the sisters' lives, they willingly responded when called upon. Their strong self-identity allowed them to willingly serve with zeal and an honest spirit. They were called to exemplify God's love shining through "people of color." To this truth each Oblate Sister of Providence surrendered herself, surrendered herself as a slave to the Mother of God. But this surrender was one that demanded life—celebrating life for the honor and glory of God—not death. The Oblates, it would seem, did not just go along with the program put before them by churchmen. It can be said that they set an example for the entire black community on how to live this dual life of black and Catholic.

In a society where significant truths and values are racially determined, issues of identity, a proper relationship with God and other human creatures, and worthiness to be included in the peculiar concern God reserves for those created in God's own image can be clouded and frequently compromised. But the Black Church perceived itself as an expression of the divine intent that, however nefarious may be the strategies of others, the faith cannot be robbed of its power and the righteousness of God will not be left without a witness.[53]

The Oblate Sisters were the center, the heart of the black Catholic Church of Baltimore. The sisters shared their vision with the community, walked the pilgrim way and helped establish the proud roots of black Catholicism in America's first archdiocese. If the criteria of authentic black Spirituality is the impact it has on the quality of life of the believers, then the Oblates have fulfilled their *Rule*. They were a clarion example for all Catholics in nineteenth-century America. For in black Spirituality,

the central focus is the preservation and the strengthening of the life-force and power that dwells within each individual and the community. This life-force is the Spirit of God.[54]

The Incarnational spiritual posture of the Oblates leads them to respond to the needs of all in the community in "Imitation of Christ." The primary need they addressed was the education of the community. True to their black spiritual roots, the Oblate Sisters of Providence lived this Incarnational spirit in an "extended family" context. In their responses to epidemics, to visitors, to residents, and to the seminary community, the sisters' commitment to personalist service is evident, while at the same time they maintained that "schedule of asceticism" which gave each sister the time and space to rekindle the strength and the zeal necessary to "respond to the Spirit." This contemplative dynamic gave them the freedom to receive God's presence in the lives of those they served.

They were living examples to the entire black community of Baltimore as to how to be freely bi-cultural on the margins of society.

NOTES

1. Vincent Harding, "The Acts of God and the Children of Africa." *Roads to Faith: Black Perspectives in Church Education.* (Atlanta: United Church Press, 1973), p. 6. Harding calls it 'the Black Midas Touch.'

2. Henry H. Mitchell and Nicholas C. Lewter, *Soul Theology: The Heart of American Black Culture*, (San Francisco: Harper & Row, 1986), p. ix.

3. *Ibid.*, p. 14.

4. *Ibid.*, p. 155.

5. Henry J. Mitchell, *Black Belief: Folk Beliefs of Blacks in America and West Africa*, (New York: Harper & Row, 1975), p. 61. Henceforth: *Black Belief.*

6. *Ibid.*

7. John Mbiti, "Christianity and Traditional Religions in Africa," *International Review of Mission LIX*, 236 (October 1970): 435.

8. Mitchell, p. 62.

9. *Ibid.*

10. Mbiti, p. 435.

11. James Cone. *God of the Oppressed*, (New York: Seabury Press, 1975), p. 104.

12. Henry H. Mitchell. "The Continuity of African Culture," *This Far by Faith: American Black Worship and Its African Roots*, (Washington: National Office for Black Catholics and the Liturgical Conference, 1977), p. 11.

13. Mitchell, *Black Belief*, p. 90.

14. Cheryl Townsend-Gilkes. "The Black Church as a Therapeutic Community" (unpublished paper: Northeastern University, 1978), p. 1.

15. W.E.B. Dubois, *The Souls of Black Folk*, (Greenwich: Fawcett Publications, 1961), p. 146–147.

16. *Annals of the Oblate. Sisters of Providence.* Vol. I:2. Henceforth: *Annals.* They are an incomplete chronological ledger of the events in Oblate life from 1827–1874.

17. *Original Rule of the Oblate. Sisters of Providence.* (OA. Box 41), p. 1. Henceforth: *Rule*.

18. *Rule,* p. 1–3, 5–6.

19. *Ibid.*

20. *Ibid.*

21. The Abolitionist had a number of women active in the freedom movement during Mother Lange's lifetime, but the activities of free black women were not limited to speaking engagements: Frances Ellen Watkins Harper, who delivered her first anti-slavery lecture and published her first book in 1854. She became respected for her dedication to her people. Mary Ann Shadd Cary, the first black American woman to edit a newspaper (*Provincial Freeman*), encouraged blacks to take refuge in Canada after the passage of the Fugitive Slave Act (1850). Elizabeth Taylor-Greenfield, the opera singer known as the "Black Swan," whose performance at Buckingham Palace received the praise of the London press in 1851. Ellen Craft, known as a "master of disguise," who was able to pass as a White gentleman with her husband as "his" slave and escape to Philadelphia from Clinton, Georgia. Sojourner Truth, the pilgrim of freedom, who spent forty years traveling back and forth freeing slaves.

22. Maria G. Caravaglios. "A Roman Critique of the Pro-Slavery Views of Bishop Martin of Natchitoches, Louisiana," *Records of the American Catholic Historical Society of Philadelphia.* 83 (1972): 67–81. See also: Bishop Ignatius Reynolds, "Pastoral of April 8, 1844," *U.S. Catholic Miscellany:* "Pastoral of the

Provincial Council of St. Louis." *Catholic Mirror,* November 3, 1855; "Pastoral of the Bishops of the Province of Baltimore," *Catholic Guardian,* June 5, 1858; "Pastoral of the Second Provincial Council of St. Louis," *Freeman's Journal,* October 2, 1858.

23. *Annals,* I:7.

24. *Rule,* p. 1.

25. Eileen Mary Brewer, *Nuns and the Education of American Catholic Women: 1860–1920,* (Chicago: Loyola University Press, 1987), p. 5.

26. Michael F. Rouse, *A Study of the Development of Negro Education Under Catholic Auspices in Maryland and the District of Columbia.* (Baltimore: Johns Hopkins University, 1935), p. 39.

27. *Annals.* I:1.

28. *Ibid.* Joubert's comments are critical, since Duffy, Lannon and others give the impression that Mother Lange and later the Sisters are continually saved from their economic failures. Their later failures have more to do with ecclesial racism than economic ineptness.

29. William L. Andrews, ed. *Sisters of the Spirit: Three Black Women's Autobiographies of the Nineteenth Century.* (Bloomington, IN: Indiana University Press, 1986) p. 12.

30. Sr. Theresa Willigman, *First Foundress of the Oblates,* OA Box 40:10, p.9. Henceforth: First.

31. *Ibid.,* p. 10.

32. "Fifteen Facts about the Foundress of the Oblate Sisters of Providence: Mother Mary Elizabeth Lange," (Mother Lange File) OA. ML. I:3.

33. Sr. Theresa Willigman, *First,* p. 9.

34. OA. ML. I:3.

35. *Annals.* I:9.

36. *Annals.* I:74–75.

37. Sr. Theresa Willigman, *First,* p. 10.

38. *Annals.* I:1.

39. *Rule,* p. 1.

40. Wilfred Jukka. S.M.M., "The Spirituality of St. Louis-Marie de Montfort." *St. Louis-Marie de Montfort (1673–1716),* ed. Ronald Lloyd, S.M.M. (Liverpool: Rockliff Brothers), p. 45.

41. OA. Box. 79:15. (Manumission papers).

42. *Rule,* p. 2.

43. Christopher J. Kauffman, *Tradition and Transformation in Catholic Culture,* (New York: Macmillan Press, 1988), p. 17.

44. Jamie Phelps, O.P., "Black Spirituality," *Spiritual Traditions for the Contemporary Church,* (Nashville: Abingdon Press, 1990), p. 346.

45. William B. McClain, "American Black Worship: A Mirror of Tragedy and a Vision of Hope," *Spiritual Traditions for the Contemporary Church,* (Nashville: Abingdon Press, 1990), p. 352.

46. *Ibid.,* p. 355. Bold print is not in the original text.

47. *The Original Rule of the Oblate, Sisters of Providence: Revision of 1833,* (OA. Box 41), p. 3.

48. Jamie Phelps, p. 344.

49. *Annals,* I:52. It would seem that the Sisters followed the tradition of the time; space was provided for those different from the majority.
50. "15 September 35 the director assembled the Sisters today to make known to them the proposition which was made so him by the Superior of the Seminary, to have two of the Sisters of Providence manage that house. He said that this unexpected request worried and troubled him and that he wished to remain neutral in the affair, which concerned all at one time. . . . He said that they should by the following Sunday make known, by writing, their intention to the Superior of the Seminary. He also said that the Sisters should have no fear of making the conditions which they judged agreeable." *Annals,* I:38, 96. The *Annals* contains too many examples to cite.
51. *Annals,* I:38–39.
52. Phelps, p. 346.
53. McClain, p. 358.
54. Phelps, p. 344.

5

STEPHEN WARD ANGELL

THE CONTROVERSY OVER WOMEN'S MINISTRY IN THE AFRICAN METHODIST EPISCOPAL CHURCH DURING THE 1880s:
THE CASE OF SARAH ANN HUGHES[1]

Sarah Ann Hughes, a member of the African Methodist Episcopal Church in North Carolina in the 1880s, very much wanted to be a full-fledged minister in her denomination. Other A.M.E. women shared her aspiration during that same decade, especially Margaret Wilson of New Jersey. Both women were accepted for several years as pastors in their own right, and Hughes achieved ordination as a deacon. But the all-male club they so boldly sought to join seemed determined to exclude them.[2] It is not divulging too much of the plot to state at the outset that their male opponents eventually prevailed. Possibly this story would have ended differently if these women, like Jarena Lee, Zilpha Elaw, Amanda Berry Smith, and the women of Mr. Wesley's Methodism[3] had not felt impelled by the Holy Spirit to seek placement in a pastorate or formal ordination, but had remained free-lance evangelists. As long as preaching women stayed outside of the male power structure, nineteenth-century male preachers were less likely to see them as a threat. Hughes, however, sought the benefits and recognition that status equality with her ministerial brethren could bring. She did not welcome the prospect of confrontation with her church, as had Rebecca Jackson in leaving the A.M.E. Church to begin a Shaker community in Philadelphia, or as had Anne Hutchinson, who fearlessly challenged the male authorities in the seventeenth-century Massachusetts Bay Colony.[4] Hughes attempted to mark out a quieter, less obtrusive course of action, but unwanted controversy still dogged her steps.

Church records disclose little about Hughes' life before she undertook her ministerial work. She was born in 1849.[5] Her birth place is not known. She was married by the time that her name first appeared in A.M.E. records, but no information about her husband, not even his name, is given. We know a little more about the early life of another A.M.E. woman preacher, Margaret Wilson, who was ten years older than Hughes. Wilson was born to parents who belonged to the A.M.E. Church in Baltimore, Maryland, and attended Sunday School there.[6] Hughes' early background was probably dissimilar to that of Wilson. It is unlikely that Hughes had been in a participant in the A.M.E. Church during her childhood, particularly if she was a North Carolina native, since that denomination was not organized in North Carolina until the arrival of the Union Armies during the Civil War.

At the age of 32, Hughes began her labors in the North Carolina A.M.E. Annual Conference as a free-lance evangelist living in Raleigh. At the Annual Conference Session in November 1881, an evening was devoted to "religious exercises conducted by Sister Sarah Hughes, the Evangelist of the North Carolina Conference." Her audience responded warmly to her eloquence as she preached on the subject of repentance. Her listing under appointments for 1881–1882 as the "evangelist of the North Carolina Conference" seemed non-controversial.[7] Margaret Wilson at this time occupied a similar position in the New Jersey Annual Conference. In April 1881, New Jersey A.M.E. ministers approved the following resolution:

> Whereas, Sister Margaret Wilson, a member of the A.M.E. Church in Cape
> May, and an Evangelist, desires to be recognized by this conference,
>   Be it resolved that this Conference recommend her to each of the Pas-
> tors of our Church in this State.[8]

The unsalaried title "evangelist of the conference" clearly implied that Hughes and Wilson would travel throughout the area of the annual conference, conducting regular or special worship on a one-time-only or limited-time basis. Thus, they would conform to the pattern set by Amanda Berry Smith, who was then witnessing to people on four continents.[9] Most of their ministerial brethren eagerly supported women engaging in this kind of ministry, as the New Jersey resolution attested.

By the time the North Carolina Annual Conference met in November 1882, Hughes had apparently become dissatisfied with such a makeshift ministry and sought to obtain a pastorate. No overt obstacles were placed in her way. Her formidable skills as an evangelist probably facilitated her initial entry into the pastorate. As Benjamin F. Lee later noted, "it has been said that her ministry has been attended by great power."[10] Undoubtedly her eloquence outstripped that of many male A.M.E. preachers. Hughes was listed as a licensed preacher on the pastor's roll that year and began the process of becoming a member of the North Carolina Annual Conference, and thus a candidate for a pastorate. She was appointed to the Committees on Missions and Sunday Schools and paid her one-dollar dues to the Conference's Historical and Literary Association and to its Mission Society. She and nine other candidates for membership in the Conference were called before the altar by Bishop Daniel A. Payne. Each of the ten were given another year to study the rules of the church before they were examined for membership. Finally, Hughes was given her first appointment, an important one. She was assigned to Fayetteville Station, a sure sign of the high regard in which her preaching and evangelistic skills were held.[11]

Six months later, when the New Jersey Annual Conference met, Margaret Wilson asked for and received an appointment to a pastorate also. She was given a smaller charge, the Haleyville Mission.[12] Almost simultaneously, Wilson and Hughes had begun to expand the boundaries of women's ministry in the A.M.E. Church. They were beginning the process of seeking compensation and titles equivalent to those of their ministerial brethren. They wanted to share both the benefits and the work.

The following year would not be an easy one for Sarah Hughes. She stayed for only a short time at Fayetteville Station. According to Presiding Elder J. G. Fry, he "relieved Rev. S. A. Hughes from the charge at Fayetteville by her own request." The reason for her action, however, was fairly clear. The congregation at Fayetteville was extremely restive during her tenure there, presumably because they were unhappy about having a woman pastor. Her male successor was able to quiet the tumult. Fry stated that "with Rev. E. D. Roberts in charge, peace and quietude prevail there. . . . Our work is not at a par value, but there is a premium on it. That charge needs an able pastor to serve it in every sense of the word."[13]

Hughes accepted an assignment to Roberts' old pastorate at Wilson's Mills, North Carolina, and was allowed to minister there the remainder of the year. Perhaps her major accomplishment during that year was to oversee the erection of a frame for a new church building, with dimensions of 47 feet by 28 feet. She also assisted in laying the cornerstone of St. Stephen's Chapel, part of the Erie Mills Mission.[14] Hughes' 131-member church at Wilson's Mills provided her with plenty of opportunities for ministry; twelve marriages, two funerals, and five infant baptisms took place during the year.[15] Although the conference records are not explicit at this point, presumably she presided at most or all of these occasions, aided by the only local preacher in her congregation. Her presiding elder claimed that Hughes made "thirteen additions . . . to that work," but the statistical records list just five converts. She therefore performed all of the activities expected of A.M.E. pastors, including the construction of churches and the conversion of the unchurched. Meanwhile, Margaret Wilson had been acquiring church property as well. She bought a lot and a building separately, and intended to move the building onto the lot. She had paid for both the land and the building.[16]

Neither Hughes nor Wilson were given equal pay for equal work. In 1883, Hughes received an annual salary of $45, fifth lowest among the 64 paid A.M.E. ministers in North Carolina. The highest salary received by a North Carolina minister was $908.21; the lowest, $10; the median, $128. Unlike the four lowest-ranked churches, Wilson's Mills was not a terribly impoverished church, and its members could have afforded to pay their pastor a larger salary. Thus, for example, it contributed $31 toward the Presiding Elder's salary of $674.71.[17] Others who received more than Hughes complained that they did not get a living salary. The Mission Committee of the North Carolina Annual Conference regretted that its home missionaries were paid only $88 per year:

> Now, consider the fact that the majority of them have families depending on them for support; what must naturally be the result? Want, suffering, discouragement, and perhaps death . . . Brethren, let us double our diligence in doing for our home missionaries, by urging our people to contribute to their support.[18]

In the New Jersey Annual Conference, the pay disparity between Wilson and her male colleagues was even greater. She was the lowest-paid pastor in the conference for three consecutive years. Her salary was $64 in 1883; $28 in 1884; and $42 in 1885. The lowest-paid male pastor in New Jersey received $195 in 1883; $74.50 in 1884; and $55.50 in 1885. The median salary for all New Jersey A.M.E. pastors in 1883 was $428.[19] The first blow received by A.M.E. women pastors in the 1880s, and in many ways the most grievous, was salary discrimination.

When Hughes attended the North Carolina Annual Conference in November 1883, suspicion and covert hostility replaced the friendliness with which she had been greeted in previous years. Although she had been appointed a member of the conference's Sunday School Committee, the men on that committee had met without notifying her and conducted the committee's business. They prepared a report for the Annual Conference and merely asked her to sign it. With some misgivings, she complied. Hughes was angry enough about this occurrence to raise it on the floor of the Annual Conference, although, with understandable caution, she couched her complaint in indirect terms. She merely asked Bishop Payne "to state the meaning and duty of a committee," admitting that she had "felt a little grieved" that the other Committee members had failed to invite her to their meetings. Payne responded to her query in a superficial manner and instructed conference members on committee procedures. He apparently did not grasp the opportunity to chastise the men on the committee for their unwarranted exclusion of a woman colleague from their labors.[20]

Hughes also signed the conference's 1883 report from the Committee on Home and Foreign Missions, along with R. H. W. Leak, George D. Jimmerson, George Hunter, and Scipio Sauls. Leak, who was fairly supportive of Hughes, apparently did invite her to committee meetings.[21] Missions were an issue of great concern to her. She spoke before the Annual Conference that year about Christian missionaries and their work, and she was again listed as having paid her missionary dues. The committee report recommended vigorous action on behalf of both home and foreign missions. It urged that ministers form missionary societies in every church where there was not one already. Both church attenders and Sunday School students should contribute one cent per month toward missions. It is doubtful whether Hughes wrote any part of this report. That was probably a responsibility that Leak himself had undertaken, as the first-named committee member; Hughes' name is third on the list of five.

Annual Conference usually provided an opportunity for its newer members to show off their literary attainments, and the 1883 session in North Carolina was no exception. Four young men read essays during the conference. Hughes had been expected to read an essay also, but she had been unable to prepare one. Payne invited her to make some extempore remarks, but she asked to be excused from that oratorical exercise.[22] It would be natural to inquire why she had neglected to prepare an essay and refused to speak extemporaneously, but no obvious answers present themselves. Reading between the lines, one could say that she probably experienced a growing fright on account of her isolated position as the only woman in an otherwise all-male annual conference. In regard to essay preparation, perhaps family and ministerial responsibilities consumed so much of her time and energy that she had little left over for writing a polished literary composition. It is also possible that she found writing to be a great struggle (as opposed to extempore speaking, at which she excelled.) She apparently possessed at least a rudimentary level of literacy, but her education may not have adequately equipped her for writing polished essays.

Puzzlement, more than overt hostility, was evidenced by the many titles that male ministers utilized to address her. There was a lack of agreement on what to call her. Her presiding elder, J. G. Fry, called her "Reverend S. A. Hughes" or even "Reverend Sister S. A. Hughes."[23] The editor of the *Christian Recorder*, B. F. Lee, referred to her as the "Reverend Mrs. Hughes;" another correspondent for the same paper called her "Mrs. Sallie Ann Hughes."[24] In the proceedings of the North Carolina Annual Conference, she was sometimes listed as "Sister S. A. Hughes" or "Mrs. S. A. Hughes." She was listed on the Conference Roll in 1883 as "S. A. Hughes" and in 1884 as "Sarah A. Hughes." When she signed the offending report of the Sunday School Committee which had excluded her from their meetings, her name appeared in Annual Conference Records as "Sallie Ann Hughes." She seems not to have been given the title of "Mother," by which such women as A.M.E. Church leader Rachel Moman of Mississippi were known at this time.[25] Male ministers were called either "Reverend" or "Brother," with "Reverend" probably used more frequently. It would appear that Hughes was given the title "Reverend" somewhat less often than men were. In any event, men never settled in their minds the relative importance of titles signifying her ministerial vocation, her marital status, and her equality with other men and women in the community, but they merely used those titles in whatever combination came to their minds at the moment.

It may be recalled that the North Carolina Conference in 1882 had accepted Hughes and nine men as provisional members. At the 1883 Annual Conference, she was one of thirteen persons whom Payne called before the altar to accept into full membership in the connection. It was a momentous occasion, signifying that the bishop (and at least some of her ministerial brethren) recognized her permanent usefulness in the ministry. Full members of the A.M.E. connection were entitled to receive an appointment as pastor every year, with few exceptions. She was the only one in the group not yet ordained, as each of the twelve men had already been ordained a deacon or elder.[26] She received an appointment to Charlotte Mission. This mission consisted of two points, Matthew's Station and Monroe, but it possessed no property. It was a small charge, but undoubtedly it was one that looked promising. Very likely Hughes began to look for property for her mission church almost at once. The Annual Conference appropriated thirty-five dollars to assist her in her work.[27] From later reports, it seems that the lay members of the Charlotte mission church were fond of their new pastor.

Hughes travelled north to Baltimore six months after receiving her appointment to Charlotte in order to attend the quadrennial A.M.E. General Conference.[28] Two hundred and eleven delegates, the vast majority of them men, converged for this important gathering of the supreme governing body of the A.M.E. Church. Numerous issues occupied their attention, including the need to lobby for a bill in Congress to reverse the 1883 decision of the Supreme Court voiding the federal Civil Rights Act of 1875. Such eminent visitors as the elderly Frederick Douglass addressed the Conference.[29] Other female ministers also were present at this General Conference. Hughes met Margaret Wilson of New Jersey there, probably for the first time. At least five other A.M.E. preaching women attended, namely, "Mrs. Williams of South Carolina, Mrs. Cooper of Baltimore, Mrs. Palmer, Mrs. Hall, [and] Mrs. Askins."[30] The home states of the last three women ware not specified. The subject that most interested them, the possibility that the A.M.E. Church would formally endorse the preaching of women, was not broached until the thirteenth day of the conference. Toward the end of his lengthy Quadrennial Address on Wednesday, May 17, Bishop William F. Dickerson praised the work of the woman preacher. It was time, he said, for the General Conference "to fix her status in the church:"

> You will please address yourselves to the answer of this question: "May they be regularly licensed to preach?" Should an affirmative answer be given to this interrogative, a proper adjustment of the pronouns [in the A.M.E. Book of Discipline] may serve to give notice to all that we have risen to that height where sex is no barrier to the enjoyment of some of the privileges of the Gospel Ministry.[31]

If, as a result of this mild endorsement of female preaching, a few female pronouns had been scattered through the *Book of Discipline,* it would hardly have constituted wholehearted acceptance of women's ministry. Nevertheless, the issue had been posed in such a way that the General Conference could not ignore it.

On the following day, Butler Derrick introduced a resolution stating that women "shall be eligible to any of the offices that are now filled by the male members of our churches, providing it does not come into conflict with the laws of the States in which they live." Many persons spoke in favor of Derrick's resolution, so much so that the scribe for the *Christian Recorder* believed that most of the gathering supported it. Outspoken opponents, however, forced the resolution to be recommitted to committee. When the matter was brought again to the conference floor by George Sampson a few days later, the scope of the resolution had been severely restricted. Instead of authorizing women to fill any office of the A.M.E. Church, the new resolution only permitted the licensing of women preachers—something that Hughes and Wilson in effect had already received. Sampson proposed to grant women licenses in order to control their ministries. They would become "amenable to the Quarterly Conference of the church of which they were members." The General Conference approved this much narrower resolution.[32]

Some of the North Carolina delegates wanted to roll back the status of female ministers so that they would no longer have to face competition from women like Sarah Hughes for jobs. A resolution which seemed to affirm the status quo consequently dissatisfied them. W. D. Cook, a North Carolina elder, offered a resolution on May 22 which would forbid the assignment of women to a separate charge. If Cook had his way, women could only minister as free-lance evangelists. Less than half of the delegates were present and voting when Cook introduced his resolution, but most of this small group sympathized with his position. Baltimore A.M.E. minister James H. A. Johnson opposed women preaching from the pulpits: "There is no advantage to be gained from it. God has circumscribed her sphere, and whenever she goes out of it, injury is done to society. The Bible said she should keep silence in the church." A more vulgar note was sounded by G. W. Bryant, who expressed himself "in favor of their staying home and taking care of the babies." Sixty-five men voted in favor of Cook's resolution forbidding women to pastor churches, while only eleven opposed it, and hence it passed.[33]

There is no record of the immediate reaction of Hughes and other A.M.E. women to this disastrous train of events, but their responses can easily be imagined. It seems that they were extremely dispirited by the sorry spectacle that they had witnessed. Hughes immediately came under pressure to surrender everything that the North Carolina Annual Conference had given her. Male preachers complained that the thirty-five dollars provided by the 1883 Annual Conference to Hughes for her missionary labors had been illegally appropriated. She paid thirty dollars directly to Elder George D. Jimmerson, money which he then applied to his own ministry. The remaining five dollars she gave to R. H. W. Leak, who redeposited the sum in the conference treasury.[34] When the North Carolina Annual

Conference convened in November 1884, Hughes was absent for the first time in four years.[35]

From the conference records it is unclear exactly when she relinquished her pastorate, but it probably happened soon after the close of the 1884 Annual Conference, possibly in the first quarter of 1885. Not only she but also her congregation were quite disspirited. "Charlotte Mission lost all when Sister Hughes left it," her presiding elder reported. "Since then they have lost heart—nearly every other member has joined other churches." She had not succeeded in acquiring property before disaster had struck; the conference's rescission of its earlier appropriation for her ministry undoubtedly hindered her efforts in this area. The presiding elder could not find a new preacher to take charge of the now non-existent work, nor was any appointment made for that mission at the Annual Conference in 1885. The Charlotte mission simply disappeared from the A.M.E. connection.[36]

Since it is highly doubtful that she ever pastored again, it is safe to say that Hughes' career as a pastor had ended. So, perhaps, should this story come to a conclusion, except for an unexpected circumstance. Bishop Dickerson, who had been assigned to the episcopal district which included North Carolina, died suddenly and prematurely.[37] His interim replacement was Bishop Henry McNeal Turner, famed proponent of African emigrationism and an outspoken supporter of female preachers. As a U.S. Army chaplain in 1865, Turner had helped to establish the North Carolina Annual Conference of the A.M.E. Church, but he was less successful in his mission work in North Carolina than he would later be on his home turf in Georgia.[38] Turner was quite supportive of women assuming a wide variety of leadership roles in the A.M.E. Church. When confronted by assertions of female preachers that God had called them to become ministers, Turner responded that their claims might well be valid. He believed that women were often better ministers than men and was distinctly unimpressed by the preaching and pastoral skills of many men then in the A.M.E. itinerancy:

> When a man cannot succeed at anything, can't draw the people, can't sing, can't preach, can't pray decently, can't build, can't raise any money, can't get up a revival, can't read respectably, can't write legibly, can't increase the Sabbath school, etc., of what use is he? Is he of any more use than a horse?[39]

In particular, he stridently condemned North Carolina male ministers for the extremely small size of the A.M.E. Church in their state, believing that their insufficient missionary zeal had been responsible for the denomination's poor showing there.[40]

Turner presided at the 1885 session of the North Carolina Annual Conference, which convened at Company Shops (present-day Burlington) on November 25. Sarah Hughes was present at this session. On the morning of November 29, the service for the ordination of deacons was scheduled. Turner invited ten men and Hughes to come up to the altar, and he ordained all eleven as deacons. He then made a boast which would later serve him ill. Following the "usual, solemn ceremonies, . . . the Bishop said that he had done something that had not been done in 1,500 years—that was the ordination of a woman to the office of a deaconess in the church, but he trusted that it would rebound to the honor and glory of God."[41] A prudent explanation of the precedents for his action, especially those drawn from early Christian history with which he was somewhat familiar,[42] would have helped him to justify the proceedings to the rest of the A.M.E. Church. It was the supposed uniqueness of Hughes' ordination that provided an especially effective argument to the A.M.E. opponents of women's ordination.

Male A.M.E. ministers in North Carolina seem at first to have viewed the ordination of Hughes to the office of deacon as a consolation prize. In any event, no one protested against this action at the 1885 Annual Conference. Turner did not give her a pastorate, thus honoring the letter of Cook's resolution at the 1884 General Conference. Her brethren seem to have received her quite amicably, as they had not done since 1882. She was invited to deliver a guest sermon at a local Baptist Church, and in the final session of the Annual Conference, she was asked to lead the gathering in prayer. W. D. Cook, sponsor of the resolution which had deprived Hughes of her pastorate, thanked the local pastor and congregation at Company Shops for their hospitality. Then the North Carolina Annual Conference adjourned.[43]

The aura of glory surrounding her ordination, if such ever existed, seems to have dissipated quickly. The editor of the *Christian Recorder,* B. F. Lee, was present when she was ordained, and reported on the event for his newspaper. While he conceded that ordination was a logical accompaniment to her 1883 reception to full membership in the A.M.E. connection, he expressed profound misgivings about the idea of permitting women to pastor churches at all:

Mrs. Sallie Ann Hughes has been a member of the North Carolina Annual Conference four years and has had regular charge of a church part of that time. . . . If it was right and legal to receive her on probation and into full membership, it is right and legal to ordain her, provided she answers all the requisites for ordination. It is a serious question, however, whether this innovation upon the customs of all varieties of the Episcopal Church, made in the North Carolina Conference and threatened in the New Jersey Conference, is warranted by any development in Christian work. Where is the demand for such change? Our last session of General Conference seemed to declare against lady pastors altogether. We have not run out of men for pastors. Women have always been great helpers; they have enough work of this kind.[44]

The communication of Hughes' ordination to the whole denomination fanned the flames of controversy which were still raging following the General Conference eighteen months previously. An urgent question was whether ordinations of women would occur elsewhere. Lee feared that Bishop John M. Brown might ordain Wilson as a deacon in New Jersey. Alice S. Felts wrote a letter to the *Christian Recorder*, challenging its editor's assertions that there were no scriptural or church historical precedents for this event. She based her argument partly on the inconsistency with which most men applied the apostle Paul's teachings. Ecclesiastical law in the A.M.E. Church

infers, or seems to believe, [women] have a place in making arrangements for its Sunday school or the growing church, wherein it provides for female superintendents and teachers, overlooking Paul's injunction . . . when he says that he does not suffer a woman to teach in public.[45]

No one attempted to answer her query as to why Paul's words should be understood to apply to female preachers but not to female Sunday School teachers. Felts' defense of Hughes' ordination was only one of the contributions to the debate. Oberlin-educated Bishop Brown sent a lucid defense of women's ordination to the fledgling *A.M.E. Church Review*. It was published in the April 1886, issue, along with Bishop Jabez Campbell's attack on women's ordination.[46]

Opponents to women's ordination proved to have the power to work their will. Wilson was not ordained, and she did not receive a pastoral charge after 1885. Turner ran into problems with the faction-ridden North Carolina Annual Conference, although it is unclear what part the women's ordination issue played in the conflict. R. H. W. Leak, a supporter of Hughes, started a publication called *The Forerunner* to complain about certain of the bishop's actions; he apparently was unhappy about the appointments that had been given to some ministers. At Turner's request, the task of presiding over the 1887 session of the North Carolina Annual Conference was assumed by Bishop Campbell, a vocal oppponent of women's ordination. Hughes was absent from this conference. On the morning of the second day of the conference, the list of deacons was read, and included within the list was Hughes' name. Campbell ruled that "her ordination was contrary to all law, therefore she is not a deacon and her name must be stricken from the list of deacons." Leak appealed this decision to the 1888 A.M.E. General Conference in Indianapolis,[47] but to no avail. That body ratified Hughes' de-ordination (without naming her) by taking Turner severely to task for ordaining her in the first place. According to the resolution endorsed by the conference, the most damning aspect of Turner's ordination of Hughes was its supposedly unique character.[48] His boastfulness had come back to haunt him. Thus, Hughes' ordination had been irrevocably stripped from her, just as she had been deprived four years previously of the opportunity to pastor an A.M.E. Church. The delegates to the 1888 General Conference may not have known it, but the relationship of their action to the recent precedent of at least one Wesleyan group was entirely too close for comfort. The General Conference of the Methodist Protestant Church in 1884 had de-ordained Anna Howard Shaw, only four years after she had been ordained by the New York Conference of the Methodist Protestant Church.[49]

That Hughes was able to accomplish as much as she did over a five-year period is eloquent testimony to her energy and her talent as a public speaker. When she sought to fulfill her aspiration to become a pastor, not just an evangelist, however, she found that she had few supporters either inside or outside her Annual Conference, and she did have many vocal opponents. Thus, after an apparent opening, Hughes was cast out of the North Carolina A.M.E. connection not once but twice, the first time as a pastor, the second time as an ordained member of the clergy. She had experienced passive discrimination for reasons of gender (for example, a committee of which she had been a member met without her), active discrimination short of a severance in her relationship (pay discrimination, congregational rebellion against her assignment to their church, revocation of a conference appropriation already disbursed to her), as well as the double severance resulting from being stripped of her ordination and her membership in the North Carolina connection. Hughes' name does not appear in any of the A.M.E. records after 1887 that I have seen. Understandably, given the tremendous opposition that she confronted, she seems to have dropped out of church work.

It is probable that the controversy surrounding Hughes and other women pastors in the 1880s strengthened two trends within the A.M.E. Church:

1. A.M.E. women in the 1890s seemed to have learned from Hughes that a woman could not challenge male authority structures and hope to prevail when largely in isolation from sisters with similar dreams and aspirations. Thus, they became extremely conscious of the importance of mutual support of each other in their religious vocations. Where there had not been women's missionary societies organized prior to the mid-1880s, especially in the South, new branches of such societies were formed. Areas with existing mission societies experienced a re-invigoration of their work. Other church work of interest to women, especially Sunday School committees, also made headway. Supporters of the women's ordination movement were well-represented in the ranks of the African missions movement of the 1890s. Bishop Turner had been instrumental in both, and his second wife, Martha Turner, and his secretary and future fourth wife, Laura Lemon, also were indefatigable workers in the mission movement. The women's missionary societies showed that no A.M.E. woman who aspired to a ministerial or church-related vocation needed to suffer the loneliness and vulnerability which Hughes had experienced.[50]

2. A.M.E. women in the 1890s were no less confident that there was moral and scriptural justification for their involvement in such traditionally male ministerial tasks as preaching and church building, but they had become more cautious in the way they asserted much claims. Furthermore, they were far less likely to seek validation of their ministerial claims from men. The A.M.E. male ministers in the 1900 General Conference established a separate order of deaconnesses, and they were quite definite in stating that the office of deaconness was not subject to ordination. Consider, however, the case of Millie Wolfe, a deaconess in Waycross, Georgia, in the 1890s and early 1900s. Women who took part in the missionary societies, such as Sarah Duncan, referred to Millie Wolfe as "Reverend" heedless of male strictures. Wolfe assumed some traditionally male ministerial roles, preaching and causing at least one church to be built, but she never asked the male ecclesiastical structure to ordain her. Bishop Turner enthusiastically endorsed Wolfe's work, but he did not offer to provide her with ordination. After A.M.E. men overruled Hughes' ordination in the late 1880s, it seems that women and men in that denomination tacitly agreed to disagree on the issue of women's ordination. Neither side conceded the argument to the other, but renewed confrontation was avoided.[51]

NOTES

1. Most of the research on which this article is based was conducted in the archives of Wilberforce University in Wilberforce, Ohio, and was supported by a dissertation research grant from Vanderbilt University's Graduate School of Arts and Science. Sincere thanks are extended to both. Thanks also to Lewis Baldwin, Dale Johnson, and Emily Cheney, who read and commented upon various versions of this article; and to Jualynne Dodson and others who gave me the benefit of their comments at the meeting of the American Academy of Religion in Boston, Massachusetts during December, 1987.

2. The broader picture of women's ministry in the A.M.E. Church has been ably sketched by Jualynne Dodson, "Nineteenth-Century A.M.E. Preaching Women: Cutting Edge of Women's Inclusion in Church Polity" in *Women in New Worlds,* ed. by Hiliah F. Thomas and Rosemary S. Keller (Nashville: Abingdon, 1981), pp. 276–289. For the attitude of A.M.E. men toward the preaching of women, see David W. Wills, "Womanhood and Domesticity in the A.M.E. Tradition: The Influence of Daniel Alexander Payne," in *Black Apostles at Home and Abroad: Afro-Americans and the Christian Mission from the Revolution to Reconstruction,* ed. by Richard Newman and David Wills (Boston: G. K. Hall, 1982), pp. 133–146; and my chapter on "Henry McNeal Turner's Advocacy of Women's Leadership within the Black Church" in Stephen W. Angell, "Bishop Henry McNeal Turner and Black Religion in the South, 1865–1900" (Ph.D. Diss., Vanderbilt University, forthcoming).

3. William R. Andrews, *Three Black Women's Autobiographies of the Nineteenth Century* (Bloomington, IN: Indiana University Press, 1986); Rosemary R. Ruether and Rosemary S. Keller, *Women in American Religion: Volume One: The Nineteenth Century* (San Francisco: Harper and Row, 1981); Earl K. Brown, *Women of Mr. Wesley's Methodism* (New York: Edwin Mellen Press, 1983).

4. Jean M. Humez, *Gifts of Power: The Writings of Rebecca Jackson, Black Visionary, Shaker Eldress* (Amherst, MA: University of Massachusetts Press, 1981); Richard E. Williams, *Called and Chosen: The Story of Rebecca Jackson and the Shakers* (Metuchen, NJ: Scarecrow Press, 1981); Francis J. Bremer, *Anne Hutchinson: Troubler of the Puritan Zion* (Huntington, New York: Robert E. Krieger Publishing Company, 1981).

5. *Minutes of the North Carolina A.M.E. Annual Conference* (hereafter abbreviated NCM), 1885, p. 21.

6. Joseph H. Morgan, *Morgan's History of the New Jersey Conference* (Camden, NJ, 1887), p. 51.

7. NCM, 1881, pp. 22, 34.

8. *Minutes of the New Jersey A.M.E. Annual Conference,* 1881, p. 17.

9. Smith had loose ties with the A.M.E. Church, but she also maintained connections with Quakers and other varieties of Methodists. See her *Autobiography: The Story of the Lord's Dealings with Mrs. Amanda Smith, the Colored Evangelist* (Chicago, IL: Christian Witness Company, 1921), pp. 198–204, passim.

10. *Christian Recorder,* December 10, 1885.

11. NCM, pp. 13, 16, 19–20, appointment list.

12. Morgan, *History of the New Jersey Conference,* p. 51.
13. NCM, 1883, pp. 40, 41.
14. NCM, 1883, pp. 44.
15. NCM, 1883, statistical tables.
16. Morgan, *History of the New Jersey Conference,* pp. 45–46, 51.
17. NCM, 1883, Statistical tables.
18. NCM, 1883, p. 55.
19. Morgan, *History of the New Jersey Conference,* Statistical tables.
20. NCM, 1883, pp. 18, 56–57.
21. NCM, 1883, pp. 54–56.
22. NCM, 1883, p. 15.
23. NCM, 1883, pp. 40, 44.
24. *Christian Recorder,* June 5, 1884; December 10, 1885.
25. Rachel Moman joined the A.M.E. Church in Jackson, Mississippi, in 1869. After Bishop Henry M. Turner designated her "Mother of the Mississippi Conferences," probably in the early 1880s, she attended several Annual Conference sessions in her home state. She also was active as a stewardess, deaconess, officer in the women's missionary society, and president of her WCTU chapter. Revels A. Adams, *Cyclopedia of African Methodism in Mississippi* (Natchez, Mississippi, 1902), pp. 139–140.
26. Local preachers, and licensed preachers who were not members of the A.M.E. connection, were sometimes accepted as pastors on a temporary or trial basis. Full membership in the connection showed that the recipient was recognized as a minister of great and long-lasting usefulness. Connectional members generally received appointments as pastors every year, unless they were declared supernumerary. Ordinarily, only ordained ministers were given such recognition. NCM, 1883, p. 30; on A.M.E. polity, see any edition of the A.M.E. book of discipline, as well as Henry M. Turner's *Genius and Theory of Methodist Polity* (Philadelphia, 1885).
27. NCM, 1883, p. 34, statistical tables; 1884, pp. 38, 91–92.
28. *Christian Recorder,* June 5, 1884.
29. *Ibid.,* May 15; May 22; May 29, 1884; C. S. Smith, *A History of the African Methodist Episcopal Church* (Philadelphia, 1922), pp. 139–145.
30. *Christian Recorder,* June 5, 1884.
31. *Minutes of the 1884 A.M.E. General Conference,* p. 133.
32. *Christian Recorder,* May 29, 1884; *Minutes of the 1884 A.M.E. General Conference,* p. 253.
33. *Christian Recorder,* June 5, 1884; see also J. H. A. Johnson, "Female Preachers," *A.M.E. Church Review* 1 (October, 1884): 102–105.
34. NCM, 1884, pp. 91–92.
35. She remembered, however, to contribute her dollar to the Missionary Society of the North Carolina Conference, in spite of all the troubles which afflicted her. NCM, 1884, p. 51; 1885, pp. 70–71.
36. See NCM, 1885, pp. 32–33, 43.
37. Dennis C. Dickerson, "William Fisher Dickerson: Northern Preacher/Southern Prelate," *Methodist History* 23 (April, 1985): 151.

38. Edwin S. Redkey, "Henry McNeal Turner: Black Chaplain in the Union Army," Unpublished paper presented at the AAR Annual Meeting, Atlanta, Georgia, November 24, 1986; Stephen W. Angell, "Bishop Henry McNeal Turner and Black Religion in the South, 1865–1900" (Ph.D. Diss., Vanderbilt University, forthcoming).

39. *Christian Recorder,* August 14, 1884; March 25, 1880. See also his unsigned editorial in the *Voice of Missions,* May, 1897.

40. *Ibid.,* December 6, 1877; August 1, 1878.

41. NCM, 1885, pp. 20–21; *Christian Recorder,* December 10, 1885. His *Methodist Polity* explores in some detail the early Christian precedents for ordaining women to ministerial offices.

42. In his *Genius and Theory of Methodist Polity* (1885), p. 60, Turner mentioned the prophetesses of ancient Israel and the deaconesses of the apostolic period as establishing a precedent for women's ordination in modern times.

43. NCM, 1885, pp. 30–33, 75.

44. *Christian Recorder,* December 10, 1885.

45. *Christian Recorder,* February 18; March 18, 1886.

46. Both bishops' articles were given the title "The Ordination of Women: What the Authority for It?" and appeared consecutively in the *A.M.E. Church Review* 2 (April, 1886): 351–361.

47. NCM, 1887, p. 8; Edward W. Lampton, *Digest of Rulings of the Bishops of the African Methodist Episcopal Church* (Washington, DC, 1907), p. 189.

48. Smith, *History,* p. 159.

49. William T. Noll, "Laity Rights and Leadership: Winning Them for Women in the Methodist Protestant Church, 1860–1900," in *Women in New Worlds,* ed. by Hiliah Thomas and Rosemary Keller (Nashville: Abingdon, 1981), I, 227. My attention was first called to this incident by Edie Rice-Sauer, in an 1984 seminar presentation on Anna Howard Shaw in a class on women's religious history at Vanderbilt University.

50. On the roles of women in the A.M.E. Church of the 1890s, see David W. Wills, "Aspects of Social Thought in the A.M.E. Church," (Ph.D. Diss., Harvard University, 1975), pp. 166–189.

51. On Wolfe, see the *Voice of Missions,* October, 1896; Sarah J. Duncan, *Progressive Missions in the South* (Atlanta, 1906), pp. 213–214. On the attitudes of A.M.E. men toward the deaconess movement at the turn of the century, see Dodson, "Nineteenth Century A.M.E. Preaching Women," pp. 288–289, and Wills, "Aspects of Social Thought," pp. 187–189.

6

RICHARD NEWMAN

"WARRIOR MOTHER OF AFRICA'S WARRIORS OF THE MOST HIGH GOD":
LAURA ADORKOR KOFEY AND THE AFRICAN UNIVERSAL CHURCH[1]

At 9 P.M. on Thursday, March 8, 1928, Laura Adorkor Kofey[2] was shot and killed by an unknown assassin as she addressed a large crowd in Liberty Hall, Miami, Florida. According to her followers she was, as she had claimed, an African princess; a prophetess of black pride, self-help, and African repatriation; and the divinely appointed "Warrior Mother of Africa's Warriors of the Most High God." According to her critics she was merely a fraud: an American Negro named Laura Champion from Athens, Georgia, who betrayed the black community either by luring people from the established churches, or by subverting the nationalist goals of Marcus Garvey's Universal Negro Improvement Association (UNIA) with the divisive nature of her leadership, her unauthorized collection of funds, and the religious character of her message.

Laura Kofey first appeared in the South in 1927, the last year Garvey served in Atlanta Penitentiary before his release and deportation. According to local residents, she "came up out of nowhere,"[3] although, in fact, she seems to have entered the United States from Canada and became active in the Detroit branch of the UNIA. Amy Jacques-Garvey remembers her as a particularly effective organizer.[4] Appealing to the Miami branch of the UNIA, which was vulnerable because of the imprisonment of the President-General,[5] she claimed to be a friend of Garvey's and said she had his approval for carrying on his work. She later announced that she had been sent to the United States by her father, King Knesipi of the Gold Coast, to organize Negroes and take them back to Africa.

An eloquent orator whose appeals to racial pride, the African heritage, and community self-reliance both reflected and spoke to the black nationalism of the period, Laura Kofey soon gathered dedicated disciples. Her mission, however, began to cause serious divisions within the black community. In Miami, her popular Sunday evening addresses emptied the black churches, thereby alienating the powerful Ministerial Alliance. The UNIA at first opened their doors to her, but became doubtful of her alleged alliance with Garvey. On August 1, 1927, she visited Garvey in federal prison in Atlanta in the company of several Miami UNIA members who had recommended the Princess to Garvey as "worthwhile." In the following months, however, there were complaints of her money-raising to buy a sawmill and ships for an African exodus. Garvey pointed out that he had given her no authority to collect funds; he assumed she was involved in a scheme using his name to extract money from a "dense" public, and he advised that she be reported to the police. In October, Garvey revoked the charter of Division 286 which was entertaining her and inserted a warning notice in the *Negro World*.[6]

In their investigations, Garveyites claimed to discover Laura Kofey to be, in reality, a native of Athens, Georgia, who had worked for the American Red Cross, travelled to New York, England, and Africa, and who had taught school in New Orleans before her advent in Florida.[7] Garvey's followers were further alienated when she claimed to be responsible for the commutation of Garvey's sentence late in 1927. The denunciation by the UNIA led to Laura Kofey's establishing a rival organization, the African Universal Church, under whose auspices she then began to organize and speak.[8] Details of the founding of the church are not clear, although it seems to have been legally established in Jacksonville in 1928 by Clarence C. Addison and others. One tradition has it that Laura Kofey first began a church in 1924 in Asofa, ten miles from Accra, where she lived with her husband.[9]

Pressured both by the UNIA and the Ministerial Alliance, Laura Kofey withdrew for a time to Jacksonville, but returned to Miami early in 1928. She spoke at a series of evening meetings, drawing large and enthusiastic audiences, but there were disturbances caused by Garveyite hecklers. In one struggle between friends and enemies of the Princess over the use of a hall, both sides asked for police protection, and the authorities finally padlocked the building.[10] On a subsequent evening, March 8, while preaching in Liberty Hall at N.W. 15th Street and Fifth Avenue, someone fired a pistol through a crack in the door direction of the pulpit, a distance of about fifty feet. Two shots struck Laura Kofey in the head. She died instantly.

Pandemonium broke loose among the two hundred people in the hall. The Princess's enraged followers seized Maxwell Cook, a Jamaican who was a captain in the uniformed branch of the local UNIA, and beat him to death on the spot. A squad of detectives, motorcycle policemen, and deputy sheriffs armed with sawed-off shotguns halted the riot.[11] The police gathered thirteen suspects, but arrested only Claude Green, president of the Miami UNIA, and James Nimmo, the Colonel of Legions (military head of the branch).[12] Nimmo recalls that only the fact that he was in custody and handcuffed to the steering wheel of a police car kept him from being attacked by the crowd. Both Green and Nimmo were charged with murder in the first degree, a charge sustained by the indictment returned by the grand jury on June 28. Green was alleged to have shot and killed Laura Kofey, "alias Princess Laura Kofey," and Nimmo was held to be "then and there aiding and abetting," and therefore an accessory before the fact.[13]

At the trial, witnesses testified that Cook had signalled to Nimmo and that Nimmo was seen firing the shots. Evidence was also introduced, however, indicating that Green, a diabetic, was at home ill. In Nimmo's defense, friends stated that they had feared trouble since Nimmo had been a prominent heckler at the Princess's talk the previous evening, and therefore were in the process of escorting him away from the hall at the very moment the murder took place. On July 10, the jury found both defendants "not guilty." To protect Green and Nimmo from Laura Kofey's supporters, the judge ordered them to spend several days with Albert Stokes, a Negro who was both a member of the UNIA and on friendly terms with the white community. Nimmo subsequently returned to the Bahamas, his birthplace, and Green eventually immigrated to Canada.

Following the assassination, funeral rites for the thirty-five-year-old Laura Kofey were conducted in Miami. The body was then moved to Palm Beach where another service was held. It was said that seven thousand people followed the funeral procession between the two cities. The body was moved again, this time to Jacksonville where a fee of twenty-five cents was charged to view the corpse. The crowds were so large that they caused traffic congestion at the undertaker's parlors. Her followers first claimed that the remains were to be shipped back to the Gold Coast,[14] but final rites, which allegedly drew more than ten thousand people, were held at Duval Cemetery in Jacksonville on August 17. Laura Kofey's body was draped in silk and linen and laid to rest in a mausoleum especially constructed by her disciples. There was some indication that her father, King Knesipi, had engaged American attorneys and planned to come to the United States to investigate the murder, but apparently his visit did not take place.[15]

Laura Kofey's preaching was essentially a blend of Garveyism and religion. She criticized the UNIA for holding dances to raise funds, and advocated prayer meetings in their place. She opposed the uniform department's drilling on Sunday. She was against the donation of funds to the Garvey movement, but allegedly collected $19,000 herself in a few months of speaking through the South. The *Negro World* claimed not only that she took money for emigration, but also that some people actually disposed of their property to await the ships she claimed would be sent by African kings to Miami and Jacksonville to transport them back to Africa.[16] Despite her criticisms of the UNIA, it is clear that the main motifs of her message were borrowed from Garveyite ideology. What she added was a rather traditional religious dimension, but one that she and her followers transformed into a religious sanction for the black nationalist themes of racial pride, African identification, and community building.

As recalled by her followers,[17] the essence of her proclamation was: "Negroes you have lost your name, you have lost your language, you have lost your heritage. My God showed me, it come [sic] a time you will wish you were as black as the ace of spades. Negroes be proud of your woolly hair and the color of your skin. Go back to yourselves, that's back to Africa and that is back to God." The message was directed against those who believed that "Negroes must think white, not black. We ain't lost nothing in Africa."

A note of authority was added by Laura Kofey's account of her own background and experience:

I am a representative from the Gold Coast of West Africa, seeking the welfare of Africa's children everywhere. God called me out of Africa to come over here and tell you, His people, what He would have you to do. I travelled from place to place in Africa trying to keep from answering the Call. I could not get away from that All-Seeing Eye. He prevailed with me wherever I went. He finally afflicted me with a fearful sickness unto death three times until I said Here Am I Lord sent me. . . . I have come to bring you a message of good news and glad tidings . . . . Your kings and leaders of Africa who are your fathers and your native people who are your brothers and sisters have also given me a MESSAGE to ask you: They say you have been a long time away from home, why have you not made PREPARATIONS to come home? They say, if you want to come let we [sic] know, and if you don't want to come let we know. In the Gold Coast of West Africa there is a DOOR (to all Africa) OPEN to you and a hearty welcome waiting you there.

Racial self-affirmation combined with the idea of the African diaspora led Laura Kofey to advocate both repatriation and, like the spokesmen of other black nationalist movements, economic self-sufficiency. She is reported to have said:

> Negroes, learn to help yourselves, create your own jobs, build your own enterprises. Clean up your lives—love one another, patronize one another. If you don't learn to help yourselves and build industries and commerce with your Motherland Africa you are doomed and done for. Don't send preachers to Africa who don't know nothing else to do but preach. Send dedicated and God-fearing men and women skilled in the trades and qualified in the professions.

The Africa she described was "the kind of Africa the people had not been told about," one with cities and towns with modern conveniences, black mayors and legislative houses, industrial and commercial activity. In the words of her followers, "She was emphasizing that Africa is so big that the surface has not yet been scratched. She was, indeed, opening the eyes of the people urging them to participate in the economic development of their motherland Africa for the benefit of all concerned." Taking from Garvey the notion of a commercial shipping line that would also serve as a carrier for African return, the Princess reportedly collected funds to charter Japanese ships that would sail from New Orleans to West Africa.

Laura Kofey's nationalism was built on a religious foundation intertwined with her own prophetic and charismatic personality. "Children," she stated, "my hand's in Jesus' Hand and Jesus' Hand in God's Hand and my other hand in my children's hand." Her addresses were all based upon the reading of Scripture; she would interpret the Bible in the light of contemporary racial conditions and then announce how "my Old Man God" would have people respond. At the conclusion of her preaching services she would extend her right hand and say, "Enroll your names with your Mother, children. If you don't have but one drop of black blood in you, and know you cannot pass for white, enroll your name with your Mother."

With this "Gospel of Love and Race Redemption," Laura Kofey preached throughout the South for eighteen months. Despite the large number of followers she attracted, Miami was not the only place where she met with opposition. She was arrested in St. Petersburg at the instigation of "enemy race leaders to whom she first came 'but they received her not,'" leading the Princess to comment, "Some of my children good, some of my children bad, but your Mother loves every one of you." Arrested in Jacksonville, she was stripped while in prison to discover if she had, as her enemies claimed, "voodoo roots" on her body to account for her power.[18]

Faced with arrests, harassment, and deportation attempts, Laura Kofey is said to have stated:

> Children, now your Mother knows how St. Paul felt and how all the Apostles felt when they were put in jail for His Name's Sake. My God told me if I go back to Africa it is death and if I stay here it is death, but if I die in His Program over here, then I can be in HIS SPIRIT and be able to take care of my Africa's children everywhere. If God deem me worthy to suffer and die in His Program for His people, then I tell Him "thankee." No man taketh my life, I give up my life that I might take it up again. All I've asked my Old Man God is to take me in the presence of my children that they may be witnesses I went down for them.

Following her death, Laura Kofey's adherents continued the African Universal Church, but now with the added purpose of perpetuating her memory as well as to carry out her ideology and program. The title "Universal" was chosen to signify the nondenominational character of the church. The church's motto is Garvey's "One God, One Aim, One Destiny." In the early period there were local churches in Miami, Jacksonville, St. Petersburg, and Tampa, Florida; Mobile and Belforest-Daphne City, Alabama; Atlanta, Georgia; and New York City, but these have now decreased in number. The first leadership was African—not men who had known or been associated with Laura Kofey, but African students in the United States who were attracted to the church because of its African interests. DeWitt Martin-Dow of Gambia was the Church's first Supreme EIder. E.B. Nyombolo from Central Africa was the first Managing Director, followed by a Reverend Ajaye from Sierra Leone. A Nigerian named Idowu was also an early leader.[19]

With the denomination's decline and the elimination of a central administration, the local churches are now essentially autonomous although there is some voluntary cooperation. One governmental characteristic is that each congregation has both a pastor (often ordained in another denomination) and a lay chairman who is in effect overseer of the church. Services are in the free church tradition. Infant baptism and Holy Communion are celebrated as sacraments. Perhaps the most unique feature is that March 8, the anniversary of Laura Kofey's death, is kept as a memorial to her and every fourth Sunday is celebrated as Mother's Day. The church in Liberia, a black section of Dania, Florida, is called St. Adorkor's African Universal Church. The church in Carver Ranches, a black neighborhood of West Hollywood, Florida, has a large framed portrait of the Princess over the chancel and a banner on the central pulpit which reads "In Memory of Princess Mother Laura Adorkor Koffey of Gold Coast West Africa, Assassinated in Miami, Florida, March 8, 1928, May She Rest in Peace."

The church's hymnal consists of gospel songs and Negro spirituals, but also of some African group songs in the Xhosa language as well as American black nationalist lyrics by Rabbi Arnold J. Ford and others. A number of hymns are original or adaptations that have been rewritten to incorporate references to Africa and Laura Kofey. Two examples:

> How bright our mighty hosts of Light
> With blest Adorkor by Thy Grace,
> Our Mother whose body united
> Africa's remnants in Thy Name.[20]

> O Africa my zion!
> My paradise serene
> Land of my Leader Jesus,
> Home of my hopes and dreams;

> I know now, yes, I know now,
> Since Mother set me free;
> That thou art God's anointed
> And shelter for oppressed.[21]

An adaptation of "Were You There?":

> Were you there
> When Adorkor brought the Light?
> When she preached in Jesus' Name?
> When my Mother shed Her tears?
> When they stripped Her in the Jail?
> On that day She prayed all day?
> On that night She paid the price?
> When the bullet pierced Her Head?
> When She fell in Jesus' Name?
> When this righteous blood was shed?[22]

The African Universal Church's creed summarizes its articles of belief:

I believe in God, the Father Almighty, Maker of heaven and earth, Father of all races of mankind; and in His holy Word as set down by His Prophets and Apostles, in the Old and New Testaments.

I believe in the fulfillment of God's Word and the destiny of my race, that the scattered sons and daughters of Africa shall again be redeemed in the name of Jesus of Nazareth who glorified the Cross a sacrifice for the salvation of the hearts of men.

I believe in St. Adorkor the saintly Messenger of God who so nobly emulated the life and teachings of our Blessed Lord and Savior Jesus Christ and suffered martyrdom for the Cause of her race of people.

I believe in God's Words, that before the end of time, the second coming of Christ, we shall have worked our way back to the homeland.

I believe in the Christ way of life and life more abundantly here on earth, and in the brotherhood of all men.

I believe in the Universal Church for African people at home and abroad with Jesus Christ as the Chief Corner Stone and Laura Adorker as the Sainted Mother of the race at home and abroad.

I believe in the forgiveness of sins, eternal salvation, the power of the Holy Ghost, and life everlasting. Amen.[23]

This is a remarkable document, synthesizing as it does conventional Christian teachings, an underlying belief in brotherhood, a race with a destiny to fulfill, a homeland to which believers must "work our way back," and a sainted martyr who is "Mother of the race at home and abroad."

The African Universal Church thus obviously constitutes a cult of Laura Kofey, who became "Mother Kofi," the "Patron Saint for African-American Relations," and whose motto was "I'll Take Care of Mine." She is also referred to as "Remnants Gatherer—Soul of Africa By Precept, Example, and Martyrdom" and "Warrior Mother of Africa's Warriors of the Most High God." The church distributed free copies of "Mother's Sacred Album" which contained her picture, a picture of the mausoleum, and "The Holy Fan on which Her Blood was spilled." In addition, it advertised "7 Days' Free Closet Prayer Treatment" in the form of "Mother's Closet Prayer Book" which promised "No Matter How Bad Your Condition, Divine Help in Your Affairs." These objects elicited testimonials such as the following from Oklahoma City, Oklahoma:

I was having such a hard time, it seemed like everything was working against me. I sure appreciate Mother's Sacred Album and the Closet Prayer Treatments you sent me. I have also been very sick but much better.

The church emphasized, however, the nationalist themes Laura Kofey
had articulated. It announced, "A people who are a people, are people who
pride themselves in their own." The church encouraged the use of African
language by distributing free lessons in Xhosa-Zulu. E.B. Nyombolo wrote
a "Sentence Maker" as well as primer and vocabulary books for "conversation and Scripture passages." "Miracle blessings" were claimed by "growing
numbers of her [the Princess's] children in Alabama, Florida and elsewhere" who prayed in Banta, which was advanced as "among [the] best
known of original African languages." Tshaka, or the Reverence Eugene
Preston McCarroll, the A.U.C.'s Territorial Director, wrote a *Biblical Key*
"chock full of Biblical research tracing our Lord Jesus to both Houses of
Shem and Ham." The Church also offered free copies of *How to Read and
Understand Drawings of the Land of Ham.*

In 1931 the African Universal Church sent six missionaries to Africa,
three to the Gold Coast and three to Nigeria. There was insufficient financial support from the directors in the United States, however, and the project failed. The three missionaries in Nigeria returned home and two of the
missionaries in the Gold Coast secured employment in Accra from a West
Indian baker named Shackelford. The one missionary who remained, Carey
Harold Jones, was a Floridian who had been active in the Garvey movement and was ordained in the A.U.C. in Jacksonville by Martin-Dow. He
began a mission in Apam where he cooperated with Ebenezer Bresi-Ando,
a Ghanaian who was, at the time, Bishop of The Primitive Church.[24] Jones
split from Bresi-Ando, tried unsuccessfully to carry on the A.U.C. mission
alone, and finally in 1945 returned to the United States to make contact
with the African Orthodox Church, the religious body most closely identified with the Garvey movement.[25] He and the people of six mission stations
were received under its jurisdiction in 1955, and he was later made Archbishop of the African Orthodox Church Province of West Africa.[26]

The African Universal Church has also sought to combine the nationalist characteristics of African identification and economic self-help. Laura
Kofey herself reportedly gathered goods to be shipped to Africa for sale.
Ernest Sears, chairman of the church in Carver Ranches, joined the A.U.C.
because "the black man is looked down upon" and needs a "bread and but-
ter program" of racially organized industries for self-esteem and financial
betterment. It is part of the church's ideology to construct a commercial
program of international investment that would both contribute to African
development and benefit the black community in the United States. Sears
himself has visited Ghana twice, in 1968 and 1971, looking toward the establishment of business, as well as a church and school, in that country. The

holder of an import-export license, he was favorably received by members of Laura Kofey's family and officials of the Ga tribe.[27]

In addition to its hopes for commercial ties to Africa, the church did develop a rather extensive domestic program of economic self-reliance. The national denomination encouraged "field workers" to "establish your own work" through an industrial club as well as through racially conscious clubs, such as Africa study or Negro history, and more conventional religious organizations, such as prayer bands and Bible study. The church in Belforest-Daphne City, Alabama, advertised a "Thriving Community Pioneered by Mother's Children," consisting of a church edifice, educational building, Samaritan Home, guest dormitory, dining hall, and community enterprises. The most extensive program seems to have been in Jacksonville, where Adorkaville, "A Self-Help, Non-Profit Church Community," was established in the early 1940s. Off U.S. Highway No. 1, on Dabula Drive, the church built and offered "homes within the means of her [Laura Kofey's] children" in a "year-round, quiet, cheerful Christian community." The church advertised Adorkaville as a "symbol of God's miraculous victories for the welfare of his people."

Under the leadership of E.B. Nyombolo, it was decided in July 1944 to establish a community. The reasons were the war-time housing shortage, the desire to improve living conditions, and a commitment to group cooperation and protection, the latter reason being particularly consistent with Laura Kofey's teachings. As a result, eleven acres on the edge of Jacksonville were purchased in August, 75 percent of the funds being provided by Nyombolo, who was employed at the time at the Walker Business College. The land was cleared communally, and it was decided to construct houses and to erect a church building. There is one deed and title to the property, in the name of the African Universal Church, but the houses are owned by the dozen or so families who moved there. The selection of families to occupy the community was made by the group itself, with places going to those who were felt to be most qualified and deserving.

The aims of Adorkaville were to create (1) a law-abiding Christian community, (2) a memorial to Laura Kofey, (3) a vehicle for cooperation, (4) an opportunity to educate the group's children, (5) a means for cooperation with the political state, and (6) a way to live an African-American existence. A school was established that taught African history, languages, geography, and culture. Plans were drawn for an African International Center where there would be vocational and cultural training, all for the purpose of greater cooperation between Africa and the United States, including a dormitory for visiting Africans. In fact, no buildings besides houses were ever constructed except a temporary wooden church and the foundation for a larger cinder-block church.[28]

The commitment to repatriation continued within the group. When Senator Theodore Bilbo of Mississippi sponsored a bill to use war debts owed to the United States to finance sending American Negroes to Liberia, he received the following telegram dated April 23, 1939, from the Missionary African Universal Church, Inc., of Jacksonville:

> Your law-abiding citizens, followers of the martyred African Princess Laura Adorkor Koffey, assassinated Miami, Fla., March 8, 1928, in hearty accord with your views as published under your name in Chicago Defender of April 22, 1939. Prayerful wishes for your continued interest and courageous efforts in this cause so thoroughly misrepresented by an element of our visionless misleaders![29]

Archbishop Addison kept up his own campaign against civil rights, calling integration "sinful"[30] and arguing for an economic self-sufficiency, a position which was allied with the Louisiana Sovereignty Commission, the Congress of Christian States of America, and other conservative white groups.

Since he met people who claimed to be her relatives, Ernest Sears's trips to Ghana have settled the question of the authenticity of Laura Kofey's African origin. Also, Sears holds a letter dated April 24, 1969, from the Ga Mantse, Paramount Chief of the Ga (Accra) State, which says, "The late Adorkor Cofie hailed from Sempe Division of the Ga (Accra) Traditional area."[31] Sears's visit also disclosed that before her coming to the United States, Laura Kofey was pastor of a church in the village of Asofa and that she had a mission in Kumasi. Her original scheme appears to have been to travel to America and then return to spread her nationalist-religious-commercial program throughout Africa. It is well known that, through the role of medium, women may have an extremely significant place in traditional Ga religion and society.[32] Given this cultural background combined with her Christianity, her exposure to Garveyism, and her own personal charismatic gifts, reasons exist to explain how Laura Kofey was prepared to assume her position of leadership.

Is the phenomenon of Laura Kofey unique? On the surface, it certainly seems unusual that an African woman of royal blood in the 1920s left a religious career in her own country, absorbed the philosophy of Marcus Garvey,[33] emigrated to America, led a black nationalist movement, and had a church established in her memory. On the other hand, the richness of black history—African, West Indian, and American—has yet to be explored, and until that is more fully done there can be no adequate criteria to determine either norms or uniqueness. This is probably particularly true of that most continuous, influential, and neglected of institutions, the black church. In the meantime, it can be said that Laura Kofey expressed the heart of the black religious nationalist tradition with her exhortation, "Go back to yourselves, that's back to Africa and that is back to God." It is because of her articulation of that sentiment—with all its connotations for the black experience—that Laura Kofey's followers could say, "It was revealed and made manifest to her children that their Blessed Mother is the Daughter of the Most High God—that she is a living spirit in Christ Jesus for the Welfare of her children and whosoever will, everywhere."

NOTES

Portions of this essay in an earlier form were read at the American Academy of Religion, National Meeting, Chicago, Ill., November 10, 1973; American Academy of Religion, National Meeting, St. Louis, Missouri, October 29, 1976; Department of American Studies, Florida State University, February 16, 1977; Department of Special Studies, College of the Holy Cross, October 27, 1978; and the African Studies Center, UCLA, May 17, 1982

1. I am indebted to a number of people for their assistance in the preparation of this paper, particularly Robert A. Hill, Alma Marcus, Garth Reeves, and those cited in the notes who granted interviews.
2. Kofey, in any of its variant spellings—Kofi, Coffie, etc.—is a common Ghanaian surname. See H. Dwight Beers, "African Names and Naming Practices." *LC Information Bulletin* (March 25, 1977), 206. For consistency I have used Kofey unless it is spelled differently in a direct quotation.

    It is the custom on the Akan Coast to name children after the day of the week on which they were born. Kofi is the name for Friday. Plantation blacks in the New World followed the same custom. Coffee is mentioned among names of slaves of the Royal African Company in 1680. Before the nineteenth century, Cuffee, Cof, and its variants were the most common given names of African origin among male slaves in the South, among free Southern blacks, and among free Northern blacks in the Revolutionary War. In the nineteenth century, the use of African names declined significantly. See Murray Heller, ed., *Black Names in America: Origins and Usage* (Boston, 1974), passim.

    Prof. Marion Kilson informed me that Adorkor is a common given name among the Ga people.
3. Interview, the Rev. Leon Brown, West Hollywood, Florida, July 24, 1973.
4. Letter to the writer, January 31, 1972.
5. Interview, Jacob Dean, Miami, Florida, July 26, 1973.

6. I am indebted to Robert A. Hill for copies of the exchange of telegrams between Garvey and his followers which document this.

7. Interview, James Nimmo, Miami, Florida, July 28, 1973.

8. *Chicago Defender* (March 31, 1928).

9. *The Church; Why Mother Established the Church and What It Stands For* (N.p. [Jacksonville, Fla.?], n.d.), p. ii. The history of the church itself, both in the United States and Africa, needs very much to be explored.

10. *Miami Daily News* (March 9, 1928), 6. This report also carries an account of Laura Kofey's assassination which seems to have been the basis for the story in the Kingston, Jamaica *Daily Gleaner* of April 3, 1928.

11. *Miami Herald* (March 9, 1928), 6.

12. Consisting of some seventy men, the uniformed rank was a paramilitary department of the Miami UNIA. It drilled in a park with wooden rifles and was prepared to confront racial enemies, particularly the Ku Klux Klan. Major Nimmo refers to the department as "a counter-revolutionary force."

13. Files no. 14 and 19, Criminal Court records, Dade County Courthouse, Miami, Florida.

14. *Miami Herald* (March 12, 1928), 2.

15. *The New York Times* (March 21, 1928), 13. For additional coverage, see the *Negro World* for July 14, 1928; July 21, 1928; and July 28, 1928.

16. April 7, 1928.

17. The following quotations are taken from *Mission Crusader* unless they are otherwise identified.

18. "Voodoo roots" probably means plant roots used as charms or fetishes worn next to the skin to allow for the most efficient transference of their power, letter to the writer from Michael E. Bell, April 6, 1978. An interesting parallel occurred in 1656 when the first two Quakers to arrive in Boston, Ann Austin and Mary Fisher, were also imprisoned, stripped, and searched for "tokens" of witchcraft on their bodies; see Charles A. Selleck, *Quakers in Boston, 1656—1964; Three Centuries of Friends in Boston and Cambridge* (Cambridge, 1976), p. 1.

19. Interview, the Rev. John Dean, Dania, Florida, July 28, 1973.

20. *African Universal Hymnal* (Jacksonville, 1961), p. 6.

21. Ibid., p. 30.

22. Ibid., p. 28.

23. Ibid., pp. 64–65.

24. After a disagreement with Jones, Bresi-Ando (who was also known as Ebenezer Johnson Anderson) was on his way to the United States to meet the A.U.C. hierarchy when he became involved with *episcopi vagantes* in London; he emerged as His Beatitude Mar Kwamin I, Prince-Patriarch of Apam. See Peter F. Anson, *Bishops at Large* (London, 1964), pp. 278–279.

25. See Richard Newman, "Archbishop Daniel William Alexander and the African Orthodox Church," *International Journal of African Historical Studies*, 16 (1983), 615–630: see also "The Origins of the African Orthodox Church," introductory essay. *The Negro Churchman: The Official Organ of the African Orthodox Church* (Millwood, N.Y.: Kraus Reprint Co., 1977), pp. iii–xxii [and see above].

26. Interview, the Most Rev. Carey Harold Jones, Accra, Ghana, July 1, 1971.

27. Interview, Ernest Sears, Miami, Florida, July 25, 1973.
28. Interview, Robert E. Keyes, Jacksonville, Florida, December 2, 1975.
29. F. David Cronon, ed., *Marcus Garvey* (Englewood Cliffs, N.J.: Prentice-Hall, 1973). The Bilbo bill was also supported by the UNIA as well as by Garvey personally (see Robert A. Hill, ed., *The Black Man* [Millwood, N.Y.: Kraus-Thomson, 1975]. Introduction, pp. 26–28, and Ethel Wolfskill, "Earnest Cox and Colonization: A White Racist's Response to Black Repatriation, 1923–1966," unpublished Ph.D. dissertation, Duke University, 1974, Ch. IV).
30. *New Orleans Times Picayune* (August 28, 1956), 16.
31. This is confirmed by a letter to the writer from Henry Adjei of Accra dated September 16, 1973. Laura Kofey's nearest living relative is Mr. Buitiful Ouaye, Chief Linguist of the Sempe Division and a personal friend of Mr. Adjei's.
32. See Marion Kilson, "Ambivalence and Power: Mediums in Ga Traditional Religion." *The Journal of Religion in Africa,* IV, 3: 171–177. For a more complete account of Ga religion, see Marion Kilson, *Kpele Lala: Ga Religious Songs and Symbols* (Cambridge, Mass., 1971), which also contains a full bibliography on the Ga people. For the role of women in the African independent church movement, see David Barrett, *Schism and Renewal in Africa: An Analysis of 6,000 Contemporary Religious Movements* (Nairobi, 1968), pp. 146–150.
33. According to Archbishop Jones, Laura Kofey read Garvey's newspaper *Negro World* while still in Africa and was converted to his ideas and thus inspired to travel to the United States and identify herself with the Garvey movement.

7

CLARENCE G. NEWSOME

MARY MCLEOD BETHUNE AND THE METHODIST EPISCOPAL CHURCH NORTH:
IN BUT OUT

The fifteenth of seventeen children, Mary McLeod Bethune was born in the tiny farming hamlet of Mayesville, South Carolina, on July 10, 1875. She died at her home in Daytona Beach, Florida, nearly eighty years later on May 18, 1955. Born two years before the Rutherford B. Hayes–Samuel J. Tilden compromise sounded the death knell of Reconstruction in 1877, she was raised in the shadow of the plantation. Both her parents were freed slaves who depended upon employment from their former owners to make ends meet. Like countless thousands of other freedmen, the McLeods felt the full weight of racial discrimination, political disfranchisement, and economic deprivation that characterized the plight and predicament of black men and women during the post-Reconstruction period. But despite all the disadvantages one could imagine, including that of female gender, Mary Bethune emerged as one of the nation's foremost leaders barring race and gender, during the first half of the twentieth century.

She scored, as it were, a number of firsts. The product of a meager formal education herself, she was the first black woman to establish a four-year institution of higher learning in the world, Bethune-Cookman College; the first African-American woman to found a national organization to lobby the federal government primarily on behalf of black women and children, the National Council of Negro Women; and, as director of the Negro Division of the National Youth Administration (NYA) during the Franklin D. Roosevelt presidency, she was the first African-American woman—in fact, the first African-American person—to hold such a high-level federal appointment. Over the course of her career she was an advisor to three presidents (Herbert Hoover, Franklin D. Roosevelt, and Harry S. Truman) and the recipient of many of the nation's most coveted awards, including the NAACP's prestigious Spingarn Medal.

Between 1933 and 1945, Mary McLeod Bethune was arguably the most powerful African-American person in America. By her own account, this was due largely to the exercise of her religious faith. Hers was a faith born within the environment of a devout Christian home and nurtured during its early stages within the fellowship of an all-African-American Methodist Church. Interestingly, she would not officially affiliate with Methodism until she was nearly fifty years old. For the better part of her life she practiced her faith under the banner of Presbyterianism. Within the context of discussing her involvement with organized religion up to the time she withdrew from the Presbyterian Church, in this article I would like to provide insight into the sequence of events that led her to join the Methodist Episcopal Church; the nature of her formal involvement with the Methodist Episcopal Church; and the sense in which her relationship with the Methodist Episcopal communion, for reasons of race, gender, and perception of the church in American society, can be described as one in which she was "in but out."

EARLY CHURCH INVOLVEMENT

Mary McLeod Bethune was the offspring of parents who converted to Christianity during the period of their enslavement. Both her father and her mother, Samuel McLeod and Patsy McIntosh (their surnames derived from their respective owners), belonged to men who were regarded throughout the community as being God-fearing, Christian, church-going gentlemen. Perhaps as a result of their initiative, and certainly with their permission and maybe even blessing, Samuel and Patsy were introduced to the tenets of the Judeo-Christian faith.

Both Samuel and Patsy were people who, despite the constraints of servitude, took seriously their commitment to the Faith. This is evident, in part, by their insistence that they be permitted to have a Christian wedding. The couple met at a harvest party sometime during their mid- to late-teens. Shortly afterwards they requested permission to marry and made known their predilection for a Christian ceremony. Atypical of the times, they were allowed to employ the services of a local prayer-meeting leader. To have such a person preside was sufficient for them to believe that their marriage had the endorsement of the church and that it was consequently legal in the eyes of God.

During their enslavement Mary Bethune's parents were often forced to attend church with their owners. We may safely speculate that when it was possible to do so, they stole away with other bondsmen and bondswomen to worship by means of the celebrated "invisible institution." At any rate, at the conclusion of the Civil War, one of the first things the couple did was join, and perhaps even help organize, an all-African-American Methodist congregation in the Mayesville area. If they were not founding members, they were clearly leaders in the life of the congregation by the time Mary Jane was born ten years later.

Mary Jane McLeod attended this church during the first eight years of her life, but never joined, curiously enough, because of an answer to prayer. It was around the time of her eighth birthday that Mary Bethune experienced, as she put it, the first real wound to her body and soul. She spoke of it in this way:

> I think that possibly the first real wound that I could feel in my soul and my mind was the realization of the dense darkness and ignorance that I found in myself—when I did find myself—with the seeming absence of a remedy. What I mean by that was the recognition of the lack of opportunity. I could see little white boys and girls going to school every day, learning to read and write; living in comfortable homes with all types of opportunities for growth and service and to be surrounded as I was with no opportunity for school life, no chance to grow—I found myself very often yearning all along for the things that were being provided for the white children with whom I had to chop cotton every day, or pick corn, or whatever my task happened to be.[1]

Seeking a way out of her predicament, she prayed earnestly day and night. The answer came one day in the person of Miss Emma Wilson, an African-American Presbyterian missionary who had been assigned by the Board of Missions for Freedom of the Trinity Presbyterian Church to organize a school for colored children in Mayesville.

Of the children still living at home, Mary Bethune was the one chosen by her parents to enroll. The school began operating in October 1884 in Trinity Presbyterian Church, an all-African-American congregation affiliated with the Presbyterian Church, U.S.A. By its second year of operation, the school, Mayesville Institute, occupied its own facility, a two-room yellow-brick building constructed adjacent to the church edifice. Through her enrollment in the school, Mary became involved with Trinity Presbyterian Church, choosing to attend there on Sunday rather than the church of her parents. The record shows that more than worshiping there she got quite involved in the life of the fellowship, participating in Sunday school and numerous church programs and projects. Her choice of church seems never to have become an issue with her parents. Upon graduating from Mayesville Institute, Mary Jane McLeod, like all the other candidates, was required to present herself "before the elders of the church to be questioned as to her religious tenets—her belief in God and in eternal salvation. Her Catechism and Confession of Faith being duly accepted, she was (at age twelve), received as a member of Trinity."[2]

Her affiliation with the Presbyterian Church continued when she received a scholarship in 1887 to attend Scotia Seminary for Negro Girls in Concord, North Carolina. Scotia was founded by a Yankee Presbyterian and, like Mayesville Institute, was supported by the Presbyterian Church, U.S.A. Upon graduating from Scotia in 1894, Mary Bethune enrolled in the Moody Bible Institute, the first African American to do so. A year before completing her studies at Mayesville Institute, she had a revelation that she would become a Presbyterian missionary in Africa. She saw Moody Bible Institute as the final stage in her formal preparation for such an assignment.

While a student in Chicago she received, via the intercession of the venerable Dwight L. Moody himself, a "mighty baptism of the Holy Spirit."[3] This experience, she confessed years later, made her effective in all that she thought, said, or did thereafter. Consistent with D. L. Moody's own tendency to assign secondary, if not tertiary, importance to denominational identification, it was an experience that, in tandem with her parents' liberal stance on denominationalism, doubtless raised her consciousness beyond any inclinations to equate denominational loyalty with Christian witness.

Spiritual baptism was for her a liberating experience. No longer would she feel unduly constrained or circumscribed by protocol or convention. This is not to suggest that she became cavalier in her attitude toward organized religion. Quite the contrary, she continued to see the church at both the local and general levels as vital communities in which the converted and the faithful should conscientiously locate themselves for their spiritual well-being and edification. She continued to believe this even after the Presbyterian Church, U.S.A., dealt her the harshest blow in her life. Upon graduating from Moody Bible Institute in 1895, she applied to the Board of Foreign Missions for a position in Africa. She was told that there were no openings at that time for African Americans. The pain of their decision perhaps forced her to consider leaving the Presbyterian fold, but she chose not to do so for another thirty years.

The Board's decision left her in a quandary as to her future. Reasoning that she had misinterpreted the revelation of her childhood, she concluded that it was intended for her to become a missionary in the South among her own people. Consequently, she accepted an appointment by the Presbyterian Board of Education to a teaching position at Haines Institute in Augusta, Georgia. Haines was founded in the late 1800s by an outstanding African-American Presbyterian woman, Lucy Craft Laney, a former slave. Working side by side with Lucy Laney confirmed Mary Bethune in her belief that she was to spend her life serving her people in her native southland, although the precise nature of her work would not be clear for almost another decade. In the following year, 1896, Mary McLeod moved to Sumter, South Carolina, to take a position at another Presbyterian-supported school and to be near her aging parents. She became involved in a local Presbyterian church where, as a member of the choir, she met Albertus Bethune and they were subsequently married.

Four years later, after a few years in Savannah where their only child, a son, was born, the couple took up residence in Palatka, Florida. Mary Bethune was invited there by an African American Presbyterian cleric who, having learned of her interest in organizing a school, asked her to establish one in conjunction with the church he was pastoring. She did and with considerable success, but not without some difficulty. The record is silent as to the nature of the difficulty. But it is probable that on the one hand she did not enjoy the freedom she hoped for in running the school and on the other she had to contend with her husband's abiding concern that she was willing to work for too little in return; she was willing to sacrifice too much. In either case, she characterized her three years in Palatka as a time of "rough sledding."

In pursuit of her destiny, she, with her son in tow, moved to Daytona Beach in late summer of 1904. It was here, she concluded after reconnoitering the area, that she was to do the special work she was born to do: organize a school for African-American girls in the Deep South where living conditions for the African-American masses had not advanced appreciably beyond those during slavery. Despite her husband's initial objections and reluctance to join her, despite vociferous and hard-core opposition in both the black and white communities, and with virtually no money, she succeeded in opening the doors to her school in October 1904. Situated in a little shanty, with only five little girls and her son enrolled, upturned crates for desks, and crushed elderberry juice for ink, it was nothing worthy of a boast.

But in her eyes it clearly represented the power of faith in action, with or without the support of others, with or without denominational endorsement. In fact, she did not seek denominational backing. "I had no sponsorship when I went to Daytona," she wrote years later. "I knew no employer but God."[4]

Devising and employing any number of tactics to raise money for her school, from selling pies on Daytona Beach street corners to canvassing door to door in New England neighborhoods, Mary Bethune managed to develop the Daytona Normal and Industrial Institute for Negro Girls into a junior college by 1924. However, by this time the burden of raising enough money to keep pace with the financial demands of the school was more than she could carry alone. She decided that it would be best to seek denominational support and wrote to the Presbyterian Board of Education. Reminiscent of the Board of Foreign Mission's response years before, the board turned her down, citing financial hardship. In turn she petitioned the African Methodist Episcopal Church, the African Methodist Episcopal Zion Church, the Colored Methodist Episcopal Church, the Episcopal Church, and the Methodist Episcopal Church North. It is highly likely that she would have accepted an offer from the Episcopal Church. It so happened that the offer from the Methodist Church reached her desk first, even while emissaries from the Episcopal Church were en route. With the offer from the Methodist Church in hand, her church involvement turned in another direction.

METHODIST EPISCOPAL CHURCH INVOLVEMENT

As practical and pragmatic as she was principled, Mary Bethune strategically withdrew from the Presbyterian Church and joined the Methodist Episcopal (M. E.) Church in 1924. There is no indication that the decision to do so was a difficult one. After all, she had suffered major disappointments in the Presbyterian camp. Moreover, she was far too ecumenical in outlook to feel obligated or bound to the Presbyterian ecclesiastical persuasion. As her reputation as an outstanding educator grew between 1904 and 1924, numerous Presbyterian organizations throughout the nation, particularly women's organizations, called upon her to speak to regional and national groups and to serve on any number of different regional and national committees, primarily those concerned with issues of education and race. But locally her identification with the Presbyterian Church was minimal. In fact, prior to joining the M. E. Church, she frequently attended an African

Methodist Episcopal (A. M. E.) church on a corner adjacent to her school. Her involvement with this congregation likely made her transition to the M. E. Church smoother.

Mary Bethune entered the M. E. Church fold by seeking and gaining membership in an all-black fellowship that worshiped near her school, Stewart Memorial. She maintained her membership there until her death in 1955. According to her pastor for the last fifteen or so years of her life, Rogers P. Fair, she participated in the life of the church just like any other congregant. She made no attempt to dominate the church's program. She participated in the activities of the church in ways that significantly under-spoke her reputation from the 1930s on as one of the most powerful persons in America. If anyone in Daytona Beach and its environs doubted this reputation, an overnight visit to her house by Eleanor Roosevelt in 1940 made the point. According to Reverend Fair, when asked to prepare a dish for a fund-raising event or special program, she did so like any other church member. Except for the fact that frequently on Sundays she sat alone in the front pew, she would have been indistinguishable amid the congregation. According to Reverend Fair, she sat quietly, often looking straight ahead. When he preached, he recalled, it seemed as though she looked clear through him. On the whole, he concluded, her involvement in the life of Stewart Memorial was rather low key.

It was a different story, however, on the jurisdictional level. In contrast to her posture in the local church, here her approach was more high powered. Within five years of her Methodist membership she was elected a full delegate to the General Conference, a remarkable achievement for a newcomer. Between 1928 and 1952 she served either as a reserve or full delegate to each consecutive meeting of the General Conference and as a full delegate to each Annual and Jurisdictional Conference from 1924 until the year she died. During this time she also served on a number of important committees that addressed such issues as education, federation, books, episcopacy, foreign missions, hospitals and homes, itinerancy, pensions and relief, state of the church, temperance, prohibition, public morals, and temporal economy.

Mary Bethune's membership on numerous committees attests to her range of concerns and activity in the Methodist Church. It also attests to her desire to keep in touch with the church leadership where she could bring the full force of her influence and prestige to bear as one of the nation's most powerful leaders. By the early 1930s, for example, few people had as much direct or indirect access to the president of the United States as did she. One church leader with whom she regularly corresponded was Dr. D.

S. Davage, Secretary of the General Education Board. Frequently she would say to Davage, as she would say to other church leaders, "Remember, what strength and influence I have is at the disposal of the Church to help do the things that will help carry us on to greater service."[5] Such influence she often used in the politics surrounding the election of bishops. For this reason, men aspiring to the bishopric, black and white, frequently sought her support. Seldom did the candidates she endorsed lose.

IN BUT OUT

The fact that Mary Bethune could help to "make" bishops suggests the extent to which she was able to infiltrate the Methodist structure. There is a sense in which she was clearly "in" the Methodist Church. She was, beyond doubt, "into," let us say, the work and the workings of the Methodist Church. She was also "in" in the sense that she enjoyed the respect and esteem of the Church leadership, if not uniformly among the general membership.

But it is also the case that she was never wholly "in" the Church in the sense that the general Church was willing to embrace her without reservation or she likewise embrace the general Church. Many in the Church felt that her standing in Church circles derived not so much from her commitment and actual contribution to the life and work of the Church as it did from her achievements and power base external to the Church. There were many people, African American and white, who did not like her, to put it bluntly. In the opinion of some, she "sought to exert too much influence."[6] It was said (in view of her size, perhaps lightheartedly) that she often tried "to throw her weight around."[7] Many believed she ought to use the Church, that is, her contacts in the Church, to further her own interests as they related to the financial needs of her school and the sociopolitical agenda she promoted through the National Council of Negro Women and her duties as director of the Negro Division of the NYA. For many, her soul and her passion remained forever outside the Church.

From Mary McLeod Bethune's vantage point, this was probably an accurate assessment. In no way did she take her membership lightly, but nothing had claims upon her soul above the intimate and personal relationship she believed herself privileged to have with God, and nothing claimed her passion more than her school, which she believed she and God, as allies (or in a holy alliance), had raised literally from a trash heap. But beyond this, there were other factors that contributed to her sense of being outside the spiritual mainstream of the Methodist Episcopal Church. They include racism, chauvinism, and the failure of the Church, like organized religion in general, to be true to its gospel mandate.

Nothing suggested more to Mary Bethune that the Methodist Episcopal Church was overcome with racism than the move to organize the Central Jurisdiction in 1936. When she joined the church in 1923 she was aware of the movement to reunite the northern and southern branches of Methodism, along with the Methodist Protestant Church. She herself strongly favored the idea of Methodist union. Unity was one of her cardinal principles. She fervently believed in it and preached it in season and out. But it appeared hypocritical and racist to her that union should come at the expense of the African-American membership or for that matter at the expense of systemically segregating any group. The thought of organizing all African-American members of the M. E. Church North, via their annual conferences, into a single jurisdiction predicated upon race rather than geography was the highest and most blatant form of institutional racism.

As the discussions concerning the Plan of Union became more intense, she became more and more vocal in her opposition to it. Like the author of an article that appeared in an issue of the *Christian Advocate* in 1936, she regarded the Plan as "unChristian, unsocial, and unjust because it tended to perpetuate the vicious practice of race discrimination and segregation."[8]

On the day that the Plan of Union came up for vote on the floor of the 1936 General Conference in Columbus, Ohio, she rose to her feet in noticeable anger to speak her piece. "I have not been able to make my mind see it clearly enough," she said in a measured, stern tone of voice, "to be willing to have the history of this General Conference written, and the Negro youths of fifty or a hundred years from today read and find that Mary McLeod Bethune acquiesced to anything that looked like segregation to black people."[9] Indeed, racial integration was at the top of her sociopolitical agenda. As the foremost leader of her race, she could not afford to endorse any policy anywhere at any time that appeared to aid the flight of Jim Crow. Nonetheless, despite her protest and that of the overwhelming majority of the African American membership, the Plan passed. With passage doubtless came her resolve, or a reaffirmation of the same, to keep the Methodist Church from ever binding her soul, from ever having to serve God and the cause of Christ in servility.

It was her sense that some in the Church desired to put her in a subservient position in the operation and management of her school that made chauvinism a factor. Although she was grateful for Methodist sponsorship, in truth she actually wanted her school subsidized by the Protestant Episcopal Church. From the time that she first entered into discussion with representatives of the Episcopal Church she felt that she might have more freedom in directing the course of her school. It seemed to her that they would likely adopt a hands-off policy. She was anxious about Methodist involvement because she suspected that the Methodist Church would be inclined to exercise greater control, particularly in view of the fact that she was a woman, and African American besides.

In negotiating with Methodist officials she anticipated that one of their conditions would be that she relinquish control altogether. Their decision not to require this partly accounts for her readiness to accept two other conditions: (1) merger with Cookman Institute, a Methodist black school in Jacksonville, Florida, that was in financial straits; and (2) change from an all-girls school to a coeducational institution. To her pleasant surprise, they not only refrained from asking her to relinquish control, but asked her to serve the new school, Bethune-Cookman Institute, as president.

In that position, Mary Bethune endeavored to exercise the same level of authority as she had previously, but the requisite Methodist representation on the Board of Trustees mitigated against this. She was not long in realizing that she had not underestimated the desire on the part of the Church to be directly involved in the operation and management of the school. It seemed that the Methodist membership of the Board wanted to tie her hands. She often found their comments condescending and patronizing. It sometimes seemed that they did not trust her judgment. Occasionally she confided in those closest to her that they were set on ruining her school. At one point she called privately upon an African-American member of the Board, a man who would later become a bishop, and pleaded with him to help her save her school.

Part of the problem, it seems, had to do with the sense in which she continued to regard the school as hers. "She failed to see," a church official once said, "that no individual is larger than an institution. . . . Her failure to see this," he continued, "prevented the Church from ever rallying behind the school to the degree that she and others would have liked."[10]

From Mary Bethune's side of the issue, the Church, as represented by the Board, failed to comprehend the special work she felt called to do on behalf of African American girls and her unique qualifications to address their particular needs. It was her belief that a race could rise only as high as its womanhood and that without special attention to the moral component of the educational process, African-American women would forever remain the most abused, dispossessed, disfranchised, deprived group in American society. They would forever remain at the bottom of the social order. In a speech entitled "A Philosophy of Education for Negro Girls," she asserted that

> if there is to be any distinctive difference between the education of the Negro girl and the Negro boy, it should be that of consideration for the responsibility of this girl in the world today. The challenge to the Negro home is one which dares the Negro to develop initiative to solve his own problems, to work out his own problems, to work out his difficulties in superior fashion. . . . This is the moral responsibility of the education of the Negro girl. It must become a part of her thinking: her activities must lead her into such endeavors early in her educational life; this training must be inculcated into the school curricula so that the result may be a natural expression born into her children. Such is the natural endowment which her education must make it possible for her to bequeath to the future of the Negro race.[11]

On one, if not two, occasions. Mary Bethune orchestrated a move to return her institution to an all-girls school, but to no avail. There is reason to believe that for some of the male members of the Board her objective reflected the sentimentality of an aging woman whose rationale was unconvincing and fiscally unsound.

Whether these attempts were made prior to 1930 is uncertain. What is clear is that by that time she decided to direct more and more of her attention and energy to the task of creating another organization, one over which she would most certainly have and maintain control: the National Council of Negro Women (NCNW). It had become evident that a male-dominated hierarchical institution like the Methodist Episcopal Church was too formidable a foe for her to have her way with the school as much as she would have liked. Consequently, she began to lobby black women's organizations all over the country, trying to convince them of the value of a confederation that would provide black women a forceful voice on the national level. The numerous organizations working separately and alone on issues of common concern were much like an open hand that delivers a slap to the face, she argued. A council of organizations, like a balled up fist, would be capable of delivering a mighty blow in shaping national policy to the needs of black women and children. It took five years of constant negotiation, but in 1935 the National Council of Negro Women came into existence and with it a power base for her from which to operate outside the school and, by extension, outside the Methodist Episcopal Church.

Beginning in 1935 Mary Bethune looked to Washington, D.C., as the primary seat of operation for her many activities. Her appointment to the

NYA position that year provided her a justifiable reason to be away from the school for extended periods of time. In 1943, eight years after NYA was voted in by an act of Congress, it was voted out in the interest of federal spending reforms. But a year earlier, in 1942, Mary Bethune had succeeded in establishing a national headquarters for the NCNW in Washington. This enabled her to continue on in Washington with a commitment to develop the NCNW into one of the most powerful organizations in the country.

In order to provide the level of leadership the NCNW needed at that juncture in its history, Mary Bethune reasoned that she needed to resign her post as president of the school. She did so and was subsequently granted the title president emeritus. In 1942, Dr. James Colston was appointed to succeed her. But always the matriarch who sought to dictate her will whether near or far, she continued to exercise as much influence in the life of the school as she could. Her efforts to do so soon compelled Colston to resign. "I refused," he later confided to an associate, "to be subject to petticoat rule."[12]

In 1944 Mary Bethune felt that she had no other choice than to return to the presidency of Bethune-Cookman. Despite all of her national commitments, she stayed on for another three years. By 1947, however, the responsibility, in view of her age, had become too onerous for her to continue. She was able to handpick her successor, Richard V. Moore, thinking that she could essentially continue to run the school through him. But, knowledgeable of Colston's experience, Moore strategically cultivated and nurtured alliances within the Methodist structure, alliances that made it possible for him to minimize, and in some cases neutralize, her influence. Feeling somewhat betrayed and abandoned, Bethune's direct participation in the daily life of the school diminished with each passing year. There is ample evidence to suggest that she had long harbored the hope that her son would someday succeed her. With him as president she could be a factor in the shape and character of the school right up until the end. But for many reasons this hope did not materialize. In the final analysis, she had to yield control to another man, whose interests, she believed, were largely not her own.

In 1949 Mary Bethune resigned her position as president of the NCNW and returned to her home on the campus of Bethune-Cookman College. Somewhat pathetically, she lived as if she were in exile. To curb her influence on the life of the school, some instructors whom she had hired and who admired the ground upon which she walked were expressly forbidden by the school's administration to visit her during the normal operation of the school.

In retirement she continued to be active in Methodist Church circles, but by this time her participation was so low-key that many in the church, even African Americans, did not know she was a Methodist. During the final two years of her life, Mary Bethune chose to identify publicly more with the Moral Rearmament Movement than the Methodist Church. The Moral Rearmament was, according to Sydney Ahlstrom, a religious movement with ostensibly no interest other than "changed lives." It was founded by Frank Buchman (1878–1961), a charismatic Lutheran pastor of pietistic background. Buchman, wrote Ahlstrom, was a "Lecturer in Personal Evangelism at Hartford Seminary en route to the world Disarmament Conference in Washington, D.C., when he received from God a commission to convert the world—through a program of Moral Rearmament."[13]

In Mary Bethune's way of thinking Moral Rearmament was more representative of the Gospel mandate than the Methodist denomination or any other denomination, for that matter. For Bethune the Methodist Church, like all church bodies, had largely failed in its mission. The mission of the church, its Gospel mandate, was the welfare and total well-being of each individual. Throughout her career she believed that the church fell short of its calling because it tended not to promulgate "a religion that had meaning for this world and the present age."[14] African American churches, in particular, she sometimes argued, needed to rethink the kind of religion they were promoting. According to Bethune,

> there are many false ideas about the spiritual glow which is supposed to characterize the Negro soul. The truth is the Negro long lived a revivalistic emotion and was taught to think of heaven as a land of luxury to which he would pass after a life of burden in this world. The Negro needs an equality of religion. He needs a religion in which his religious feeling has matured into social passion.[15]

For Mary Bethune "the full teaching of Jesus concerning the abundant life" could be actualized in history only if churches carried out the "full implications" of religion.[16] Throughout the ages the church, she stressed in several of her speeches, had been a courageous voice in denouncing wickedness. But it needed to do much more than censure evil; it needed to offer in its place a constructive program of human relations.[17]

The Moral Rearmament Movement was, for the most part, theologically and socially conservative. Theologically speaking, it focused largely on spiritual rebirth; socially speaking, it was status quo oriented and avowedly controversially anti-communist. Buchman, for example, once commended Hitler in a roundabout way for stemming the tide of communism in Europe. Nonetheless, Mary Bethune was drawn to Moral Rearmament because of the program of human relations it preached. Concentrating on people with prestige, influence, and power, "houseparties" would be organized in different parts of the world. People of different nationalities and races were introduced informally to the "Five C's," (confidence, conviction, confession, conversion, continuance), and to a "God-guided" life under the "Four Absolutes" (honesty, purity, unselfishness, and love).[18]

Aside from the Movement's platform, it is possible to understand the attraction Moral Rearmament held for Mary Bethune in that she readily identified theologically with the language of spiritual rebirth. In her mind, the strategy and the platform of Moral Rearmament represented what all churches and denominations should have been aggressively pushing and practicing. "There is evidence," she once indicated in a speech entitled "Girding for Peace," "that the church is beginning to acquire new courage in the application to life of the great moral truths. . . . If nothing else, the pressures of the times are stimulating effort toward the *practice* of religious principles. But too often," she contended, "these principles are merely preached in beautiful language when there is the pressing need to set them forth in the specific language of deed."[19]

As Mary Bethune sized up the situation, the institutional church too often failed in its obligation to impart spiritual values through the practical application of the same. "What do the churches mean to . . . folks. . . , black and white?" she once asked. "They admonish us to, 'Be ye doers of the Word, and not hearers only.' " But "what sort of values are they providing [concretely]. . . ?"[20] Her response to these queries was then and is now prophetic:

> The church has been and must continue to be the great gateway to these spiritual influences which lead us to the realization of the Fatherhood of God and the brotherhood of Man. But this influence can be willed only by a living, breathing church that puts this concept into practice, whatever its denomination or the power of its affiliation.[21]

"We must look to the church," she added, "for the leadership that recognizes the 'pigment of the divine' in all the Children of God, whether they are natives of the Kentucky hills, or the plains of India, or the backwoods of Mississippi."[22] But its voice has not been heard, clearly. A strong, unequivocal acceptance of the truth that there is no second-class citizenship in God's world has been lacking. The church has trailed social advance. Many times the words of the great old hymns have been sung off key.[23]

On the evening that Mary Bethune died at her home, the Retreat, as she called it, students gathered around the house and sang her two favorite songs: "Let Me Call You Sweetheart" and "What a Fellowship, What a Joy Divine, Leaning on the Everlasting Arm." Throughout her life she had leaned on the "everlasting arm," albeit not so much within the context of institutional church as outside it. Her participation in the institutional church in general and the Methodist Episcopal Church in particular proved problematic along the lines of race and gender. On the whole the institutional church proved to fall too short of its mandate for her wholly to commit her soul to its care. Consequently, she participated in the life of the church, the Methodist Episcopal Church especially, but, in order to witness to the Faith in a way she felt comported with the Gospel mandate and the gift of the Holy Spirit, she elected to operate largely outside it.

NOTES

1. Transcript of interview by Dan Williams with Mary McLeod Bethune, Mary McLeod Bethune Foundation Papers, Daytona Beach, Florida, n.d., 6.
2. Rackham Holt, *Mary McLeod Bethune* (Garden City, N.Y.: Doubleday, 1964), 29.
3. Mary McLeod Bethune, untitled autobiographical statement, Mary McLeod Bethune Foundation Papers, Daytona Beach, Florida, n.d., 4–5.
4. Mary McLeod Bethune, "What My Faith Means to Me—An Education," *The Church Women* (The General Department of United Church Women, National Council of the Churches of Christ in the U.S.A.) 20 (December 1954):15.
5. Mary M. Bethune to Dr. M. S. Davage, June 12, 1943, Mary McLeod Bethune Foundation Papers, Daytona Beach, Florida, 2.
6. Interview with Rogers P. Fair, Daytona Beach, Florida, May 4, 1978.
7. Ibid.
8. Timothy B. Echols, "Unification? Yes! But What Kind," *The Christian Advocate,* 58 (April 30, 1936): 277.
9. Henry Nathaniel Oakes, Jr., "The Struggle for Racial Equality in the Methodist Episcopal Church: The Career of Robert E. Jones, 1904–1944," (Ph.D. diss., The University of Iowa, 1973), 432.
10. Interview with Bishop James Thomas, Duke University, Durham, N.C., October 1978.
11. Mary McLeod Bethune, "A Philosophy of Education for Negro Girls," Mary McLeod Bethune Foundation Papers, Daytona Beach, Florida, n.d., 8.

12. Interview with L. S. Cozart, Charlotte, N.C., June 1980. Cozart was president of Barber Scotia College for more than a decade.

13. Sydney Ahlstrom, *A Religious History of the American People* (New Haven, Conn.: Yale University Press, 1972), 926.

14. Earl Martin, "Mary McLeod Bethune: A Prototype of the Rising Social Consciousness of the American Negro" M. A. thesis, Northwestern University, 1958), 73.

15. Ibid., 73.

16. Ibid.

17. Ibid.

18. Ahlstrom, *A Religious History of the American People*, 926.

19. Mary M. Bethune, "Girding for Peace," Mary McLeod Bethune Foundation Papers, Daytona Beach, Florida, n.d., 6.

20. Ibid.

21. Ibid.

22. Ibid., 7.

23. Ibid., 6.

8

EVELYN BROOKS HIGGINBOTHAM

RELIGION, POLITICS, AND GENDER: THE LEADERSHIP OF NANNIE HELEN BURROUGHS

For the past two decades, scholars in a variety of disciplines have examined the relationship between the black church and the socio-political struggle of black Americans. The prominent role of the clergy in the Civil Rights Movement, as well as the flourishing of black pride and consciousness in the late sixties, influenced scholars to reexamine the church—the single most important institution in the black community—and to reveal its historic role in the preservation and progress of that community. Eugene Genovese and Albert Raboteau portray the church of the slaves as a vehicle for the assertion of human dignity amidst the brutal and dehumanizing environment of the slave system. James Cone, Cornel West, Peter Paris, and Deotis Roberts address the nexus of religion and politics from both a historical and contemporary perspective, and they present black religion as a liberating force in the struggle for racial equality.[1]

The great value of this research notwithstanding, there still remains a conspicuous absence of the feminine in the black religious tradition. While all of the aforementioned scholars, and there are many others, have greatly enhanced our knowledge of the church as an integral and dynamic component of the black experience, these works do not give any serious attention to women, and thus we are left with very little toward an understanding of the feminine presence.[2] The omission of women from the literature makes a statement not only about research methods and the selective use of sources, but also about the working definitions and assumptions that scholars bring to their investigations.

First of all, the androcentric bias found in these works can be seen in their exclusive focus on the ideas, pronouncements, and activities of the male clergy. The ideas and actions of the female clergy, evangelists, and missionaries are rendered invisible because scholarship has defined religious leadership as singularly male in character and composition. Women leaders are, at best, subsumed under the generic category "clergy" or "clergyperson," if you will, and, at worst, dismissed and disregarded on the premise that they have no historical presence, theological insight, or noteworthy influence. Secondly, some researchers rely upon the archives, records, minutes, and speeches of the male-dominated religious bodies, since these bodies represent the officially sanctioned voice of both men and women in the various denominations. Unfortunately, in their pursuit of truth, these scholars make no effort to examine the records of the auxiliary women's organizations which, unlike the male-run bodies, do not purport to speak for anyone other than women. In the final analysis, this research can provide only partial truth. Thirdly, scholars have failed to incorporate any type of feminist discourse into their analysis of theology. The present literature on black theology and the black Christian tradition fails to capture the dialectic of being separately and together black and female, and thus the theology of the oppressed is not portrayed in terms that capture the meaning of the black woman's dual oppression. Since women have historically constituted the majority of church members—they make up the greater portion of the body of Christ—we do ourselves an intellectual if not an ethical disservice to continue to study the church as if it were solely the terrain of men—to construe it as if it were devoid of the presence and influence of women.

Like the church, the study of politics, too, has been narrowly defined as male, and thus any discussion of the relationship between religion and politics has served to reinforce the invisibility of women. A critique of studies in political science reveals that an important part of the problem lies in the distinction between the private and public spheres of life and the placement of women within the private. Women's attitudes and activities are conventionally identified within the private sphere—within the realm of self, family, and other personalized connections. Moreover, women's political attitudes are depicted as mere reflections of men's attitudes—of husbands, fathers, brothers, and other male leaders to whom women seemingly "defer" in the representation of their interests in the public realm. The public sphere and public activities, on the other hand, extend beyond the personal and impact upon the larger society. Equating the private/public dichotomy with the nonpolitical/political, while making gender a function of this equation, has served to depoliticize women's activities and remove them from political study.[3]

In an effort to address the issue of religion, politics, and gender, this paper focuses on the black Baptist women's movement in the early decades of the twentieth century, and especially on the leadership of Nannie Helen Burroughs.[4] The minutes and recorded speeches of the organized black Baptist women reveal the feminine presence as both a spiritual and political force within the black community. Burroughs, the most articulate and dynamic voice of this movement, served as an important political mentor to the female religious community, and it might be added that she had many followers among the male clergy.

In 1900 in Richmond, Virginia, Nannie Burroughs launched her long and illustrious career as a nationally acclaimed religious leader when she delivered the speech "How the Sisters Are Hindered from Helping" at the annual meeting of the National Baptist Convention (NBC). Expressing the discontent of black women and proclaiming their "burning zeal" to be coworkers with Baptist men in the Christian evangelization of the world, Burroughs's appeal met with a favorable response and resulted in the NBC's approval of the establishment of the Woman's Convention (WC), Auxiliary to the NBC. By the close of the meeting, the women had elected the following officers: S. Willie Layten of Philadelphia, president; Sylvia C. J. Bryant of Atlanta, vice-president-at-large; Nannie H. Burroughs of Washington, D.C., corresponding secretary; Virginia Broughton of Nashville, recording secretary; and Susie C. Foster of Montgomery, Alabama, treasurer. The minutes for 1900 listed twenty-six state vice-presidents, including one each from Indian Territory, Oklahoma Territory, and Washington, D.C. The women described their mission as coming to the rescue of the world, and they adopted the motto: "The world for Christ. Woman arise. He calleth for thee."[5]

In her first open letter to the Baptist women of America, S. Willie Layten urged all existing societies to affiliate with the WC, to work closely with the state vice-presidents, and to welcome the formation of new societies where none existed at the state and local level.[6] Layten had a long familiarity with the organized work of black Baptists. Her father, William H. Phillips, has been described as a pioneer among the trained ministry during the early years of black freedom and as an organizer and participant in the formation of the NBC. Layten's youth was spent in Memphis, where she acquired her early education and probably her first knowledge of women's missionary activities. As a young bride in the late 1880s, she resided in California and served as the first president of the Woman's Auxiliary to the Western Baptist

Association of California. Theodore S. Boone, historian of black Baptists, has observed that Layten was well acquainted with the history of women's efforts to form a separate convention and in fact was a "student" of the movement in 1890 to organize a woman's foreign mission convention.[7]

Officers of the Foreign Mission Board of the NBC aided the fledgling WC. The board furnished the women with office space at its headquarters in Louisville and allotted Virginia Broughton, recording secretary of the WC, a page in its newspaper, the *Mission Herald*. Nannie Burroughs, already employed as a secretary in the office of the Foreign Mission Board, used the Louisville headquarters for the new women's convention. Burroughs, an eloquent speaker and organizational genius, was the dynamic force behind the convention. Born in Culpepper, Virginia, in 1878, Burroughs moved to Washington, D.C., at the age of five with her mother and remained there until after her graduation from the city's colored high school. In 1896 she wrote to Booker T. Washington in hope of finding employment as a typist and stenographer at his school. Although she failed to secure a job at Tuskegee, she became the bookkeeper and editorial secretary for L. G. Jordan, corresponding secretary of the NBC's Foreign Mission Board. She continued to work for Jordan when he relocated the board's headquarters in Louisville. Until her return to Washington, D.C., in 1909, Burroughs participated in the Baptist women's societies in Louisville and established an industrial club with classes in bookkeeping, shorthand, typing, sewing, cooking, child care, and handicrafts.[8]

In her first annual report to the WC, Nannie Burroughs related the eagerness with which existing missionary societies affiliated with the national body. She found willing supporters in hundreds of churches. She sent the local women's societies tracts, envelopes, cards, report blanks, and coin mailers to aid their work. During her first year in office, she labored 365 days, traveled 22,125 miles, delivered 215 speeches, organized a dozen societies, wrote 9,235 letters, and received 4,820.[9]

Only twenty-two years old when elected corresponding secretary of the WC, Burroughs did not spawn the feminine consciousness that gave birth to a national Baptist womanhood. Beginning in the 1880s black Baptist women had organized into separate conventions at the state level and in the 1890s expressed their dream for a national organization. Leaders such as Virginia Broughton of Nashville and Mary [Cook] Parrish of Louisville had preceded Burroughs and, in fact, influenced her by citing scriptural justification for women's rights within the church and the larger, secular society.[10] Broughton and Parrish would also join in the founding of the WC in 1900 and serve among its earliest officers.

In 1901 Elias Camp Morris, president of the NBC, hailed the work of the woman's auxiliary, particularly that of its corresponding secretary, Nannie Burroughs. Despite his praise of the convention, he expressed his reservations as to the feasibility of a separate woman's convention and suggested that the women operate as a board of the NBC. A Woman's Home and Foreign Mission Board, Morris posited, should be established according to the same criteria as the other boards of the NBC; it should, like the other boards, have a distinct headquarters; and should, also like the other boards, report annually to the male-controlled convention.[11] S. Willie Layten, having acquiesced to Morris's suggestion, recommended in her second annual address that the "name of our organization be changed from Convention to Board, in order that we become perfectly harmonious to the policy of the National Baptist Convention." The women, led by Burroughs, countered her recommendation by passing resolutions to retain both the title "Convention" and the existing format of the constitution.[12]

In 1903 Richard H. Boyd, the powerful corresponding secretary of the Home Mission Board of the NBC as well as head of its publishing board, observed the reluctance of the women to relinquish their autonomy and admitted himself willing to yield to their stubbornness. Between 1902 and 1904, Robert Mitchell, auditor of the NBC, also defended the women's separate status. His report for 1902 called for the NBC's "unqualified support and endorsement" of the WC and particularly applauded the efficiency of its corresponding secretary. Mitchell further stated that the NBC should allow the women to work unfettered by specific requests and dictates.[13]

Throughout the first decade of the twentieth century, the WC extended its influence among black Baptist women in America. In 1903 the corresponding secretary, Nannie Burroughs, reported that the WC represented nearly a million black Baptist women. In 1904 she reported further growth in women's organizational work as a result of the WC. During the past year, 408 new local societies and 102 children's bands had been organized. Each year, Burroughs filled hundreds of orders for guides, pictures, buttons, and leaflets, and she received thousands of letters and postcards.[14]

Burrough's charisma and leadership abilities epitomized the essence of the black Baptist women's movement, and indeed she led it from 1900 until her death in 1961.[15] This movement afforded black women the opportunity to share knowledge of their state and local activities and, more important, to begin to carve out their own national arena for leadership and action. At the foundation of their movement rested a religious tradition that combined the eschatological vision of that "Great Gettin' Up Morning" with the dream of human equality and human dignity in the America of their own time. Peter Paris describes the principle of human freedom and equality under God as the prophetic principle of the black Christian tradition:

> It was out of the crucible of racial oppression, then, that the black Christian tradition emerged as a nonracist appropriation of the Christian faith. As such it represented the capacity of the human spirit to transcend the conditions of racism in both thought and practice. In addition, this tradition has been represented as a fundamental principle of criticism justifying and motivating all endeavors by blacks for survival and transformation.[16]

For the WC and its leadership, this prophetic principle of human equality and the goal of survival and transformation as a race contained both spiritual and political implications and demanded struggle on two fronts—struggle against the forces of oppression within the race as well as on the outside. Their discussion of the struggle within fostered an idealistic, even conservative analysis. Indeed, if our research stopped at this point, we would draw an otherworldly, passive, and compensatory image of black women and the church relative to the sociopolitical context of black life in the Jim Crow America of the early twentieth century. The WC's outspoken emphasis on cleanliness, thrift, temperance, personal hygiene, sexual morality, and proper public conduct often blamed blacks for their victimization. The women's missionary work and later social service programs that emerged in urban centers after 1910 reflected a behavioral approach to racial progress. The behavior of each black person, they reasoned, had the power to confirm or refute racist stereotypes and racism in general. This emphasis on individual struggle at the level of personal values and conduct linked institutional racism and social relations to individual intentions and behavior and thereby privatized racial discrimination and rendered it less subject to government regulation, to the authority of the public realm. In 1904 S. Willie Layten, president of the WC, idealized home and motherhood within this conservative schema:

> Mothers be stern, be firm, and yet you can be kind and sympathetic. As a race we cannot afford to contribute ONE single life to the bad, though the individuals force it upon us. We are impoverished; unfortunately the minority or bad Negroes have given the race a questionable reputation; these

degenerates are responsible for every discrimination we suffer. The misfortune not to be judged as other people, behooves us to become more careful until we have gained a controlling influence to contradict the verdict already gone forth.[17]

In 1913 Burroughs reflected a similar conservativsm in her analysis of alley dwellings in Washington, D.C. Although she did not overlook the role of slum landlords in perpetuating poor housing, she placed greater responsibility on her own people:

In Washington City there is much talk about getting the seventeen thousand Negroes out of the alleys. To the student of euthenics, who believes that the shortest cut to health is by creating a clean environment in which to live, this plan is most feasible, but to do a work that will abide we must first "get the alley" out of the seventeen thousand Negroes, and it will be an easy task to get them out of the alley.[18]

The Baptist women's moralistic emphasis and concern for "respectable" behavior translated into a belief in the primacy of spiritual over material progress, and yet their emphasis offered each striving soul an attempt to gain personal dignity and worth in this world despite its racism and poverty. Although focusing on Christian tradition within slave culture, Eugene Genovese has captured its essential applicability for blacks in the early twentieth century:

If it [Christianity] calls for political submission to the powers that be, it also calls for militant defense of the freedom of the spirit and the autonomy of the personality.[19]

Nowhere is this more clearly visible than in the writings and speeches of Nannie Burroughs. She rejected all theories that bound blacks to a culture of poverty. To her, personal achievement was ultimately a question of individual will and effort, although she acknowledged the damaging effects of institutional racism. In 1905 Burroughs decried the abridgement of her people's civil and political rights but exalted the resultant rise of black-owned businesses and other expressions of racial self-help. Submission to the Jim Crow laws, she asserted, denied blacks civil equality, but never human dignity:

Men and women are not made on trains and on streetcars. If in our homes there is implanted in the hearts of our children, of our young men and of our young women the thought they are what they are, not by environment, but of themselves, this effort to teach a lesson of inferiority will be futile.[20]

The records of the WC reveal equally a concerted commitment to struggle against the structural and systemic underpinnings of racial inequality—the external agents of black oppression. In this regard, Burroughs led her convention in an outward attack on institutionalized racism and the laws that sanctioned it. Strategies to overcome the structural problems of inequality took the form of petitions, verbal protests, calls to action, and the advocacy of alliances with other groups. The annual meetings of the WC functioned as an important arena through which black women learned about and addressed the political questions of their day. The meetings, held always in conjunction with those of the NBC, climaxed each year's work. At the annual gatherings of the WC, reports and speeches were delivered not only by the national leaders, but also by delegates and invited speakers. Outstanding speakers brought varied and informative messages to the Baptist women. Burroughs's leadership played the most important individual role in the political socialization of black Baptist women, who represented all walks of life and hailed from all parts of the nation. Burroughs transmitted her ideas and values to the thousands who gathered to hear her highly acclaimed annual reports. Her report and the address of the president S. Willie Layten were the high points of the annual meetings.

The political philosophy of the convention can be seen in the 1913 minutes, which recorded their seven-point manifesto, "What We Want and What We Must Have." The women clearly outlined what they perceived to be the pressing needs of black Americans:

1. Well-built, sanitary dwellings . . . and streets that are paved and kept just as clean as others in the town are kept.
2. Equal accommodation on common carriers.
3. Franchise for every Negro—North, South, East, and West—who is an intelligent and industrious citizen.
4. Equal treatment in the courts.
5. Equal division of school funds.
6. Lynching stopped.
7. Convict lease system broken up and better prisons and humane treatment of Negro prisoners.[21]

Jim Crow segregation, especially the segregated railroad lines, provided a perennial target for the black Baptist women's protest. In 1904 the report of the executive board and corresponding secretary called attention to the separate car policies of railroad companies. Their early protest, however, focused on the unequal conditions of the separate cars and not on the principle of segregation. The report called for united protest against the unsanitary toilet facilities for blacks. Another concern was the absence of step boxes for alightment. Identifying by name the particularly racist railroad companies, corresponding secretary Burroughs promised to continue to "annoy" the railroads until facilities were upgraded. She alerted her sisters to the positive response of the few lines that installed the step boxes, but she demanded continued insistence on equal accommodations. The women present at the conference in 1910 signed a petition that demanded separate toilets for black men and women, and separate washbasins.[22]

In 1914 the minutes of the Woman's Convention reveal that the women aligned with the National Association for the Advancement of Colored People (NAACP) in a campaign against the caricaturing and stereotyping of blacks in literature, film, newspapers, and on the stage. The minutes advocated boycotts and written protests to editors and others who practiced this type of racial slurring. The women also called for the elimination of school textbooks that ridiculed blacks. The leaders and members of the WC greatly respected the NAACP and in 1914 passed a resolution that pledged to cooperate with it. In 1919 the annual conference of the WC greeted the speech of John R. Shillady, secretary of the NAACP, with loud and enthusiastic applause.[23]

Lynching proved another target for the concerted action of the women and the NAACP. The Baptist women's pleas to halt lynching pointed out what was often overlooked—that black women were among the fatalities of lynch law. In 1919 a study undertaken by the NAACP revealed that between 1889 and 1918 a total of 2,472 black men and fifty black women met their deaths at the hands of mobs.[24] In 1918, the report of the executive board of the WC recommended support for the ill-fated Dyer anti-lynching bill. In 1919 the report of the executive board of the WC again demanded anti-lynching legislation and enjoined every black American to stand behind the NAACP in its fight against lynch law:

> Let 15,000,000 Negroes line up with the National Association for the Advancement of Colored People. Any man who is not a member of that organization stands with the mob. There is no middle ground.[25]

The report in 1919 also called for greater sophistication in the exercise of the franchise. It encouraged blacks to study the record of political candidates and cast their ballots for those who sought to suppress mob violence. Immediately after World War I, S. Willie Layten advocated that blacks turn their Great Migration to the northern cities into a political advantage for the race. Without racist voting restrictions, northern states afforded many of these southern migrants an opportunity to wield the ballot for the first time. Layten challenged her sisters, although disfranchised because of sex, to educate the migrants as to the political gains to be won. The church, Layten reasoned, remained the most logical institution to promote a voter education program.[26]

World War I evoked a mixture of patriotism and protest from the WC. In 1918 the women heard the defense reports of outstanding blacks in the government—Emmett J. Scott, assistant to the Secretary of War, and George Haynes, specialist in black affairs for the Department of Labor. Filled with patriotic fervor, the annual speech of S. Willie Layten in September 1918 served as the rallying cry for women to help win the war. Layten advised her sisters to conserve food and fuel, purchase Liberty Bonds and war stamps, and to raise liberty gardens. Layten did not exhibit a blind, unquestioning love for her country, for she admitted that even patriots on the front line become "restless and discontent when their rights are abridged at home." In the same year Burroughs, ever the protesting patriot, reminded the convention that their fight against race prejudice in America figured no less than their fight against autocracy abroad. Her report called for the passage of anti-lynching legislation and for the repeal of the separate coach law. Having assumed the control of the railroads as a war expediency, the federal government, according to Burroughs, could suspend the Jim Crow laws as another war expediency. Nor did she bite her tongue when she referred to President Woodrow Wilson and his war slogan, "Make the world safe for democracy":

> He likes to write—he likes to say things. He has used up all the adverbs and adjectives trying to make clear what he means by democracy. He realizes and the country realizes that unless he begins to apply the doctrine, representatives of our nation would be hissed out of court when the world gets ready to make up the case against Germany and to try her for her sins.[27]

Protest ran throughout the annual conference in 1919. As Woodrow Wilson cried loudly to the American people for a League of Nations, Burroughs pointed to his silence on lynching and segregation. The WC voted to send Burrough's report for 1919 to Wilson, the United States Congress, and to the governors of the states. At the conclusion of the speech by the representative from the NAACP, the convention choir sang "We've Fought Every Race's Battles but Our Own." Meeting on September fifteenth, 1919, the executive board of the WC recommended that Baptist churches and Sunday schools throughout the nation dedicate the Sunday before Thanksgiving to fasting and prayer in order to protest the "undemocratic and un-Christian spirit of the United States as shown by its discriminating and barbarous treatment of its colored people." The NAACP and the National Association of Colored Women joined the black Baptist women in advertising the day of protest. The December 1919 issue of the NAACP's magazine *Crisis* reported the commemoration of the day on November Thirtieth with a noontime prayer hour having been observed for the denunciation of lynching and racial injustice.[28]

The principle of human equality and dignity under God related not only to racial concerns. It also spoke to gender concerns. This is the great contribution of women of the black Christian tradition. They infused into that tradition the belief in the capacity of the human spirit to transcend not only the conditions of racism but also sexism. The feminist theology of the black Baptist Church has been discussed elsewhere.[29] This theology did not constitute a break from orthodoxy, but it did entail the restatement of orthodoxy in progressive, even liberating language for women. This is best expressed in the biblical verse: "Neither bond nor free, neither male nor female in Christ Jesus." By expounding biblical precedents, black Baptist women presented the intellectual and theological justification for woman's rights.

During World War I, the WC spoke out for greater employment opportunities for black women. In 1918 delegate Mamie Steward of Kentucky delivered the speech, "What the Colored Woman Can Do with Her New Industrial Opportunities." In the same year Burroughs applauded the opening up of industrial work previously closed to black women, and reserved special praise for women who worked in such male jobs as section hands on railroads. She recommended petitioning industrial management to promote black women to supervisory positions in sections with high concentrations of black female workers. However, her optimism waned by the time of the annual meeting just one year later. By 1919 the aftermath of war swiftly taught black Americans the meaning of being "last hired and first fired." Reminding her sisters in 1919 of her forewarning of black layoffs, Burroughs condemned the firing of black workers and urged her audience to patronize only businesses that re-tained black workers.[30]

Woman's suffrage was also championed by the WC. In fact the WC was joined by the leaders of the NBC in its advocacy of the right of suffrage for both blacks and women. In 1914 E. C. Morris, president of the NBC, sup-ported woman's suffrage on the principle of justice and representative gov-ernment. Morris reprimanded the United States Congress for its failure to represent the millions of black Americans and linked the disfranchisement of women and blacks to the principle of "taxation without representation."[31]

Although black Baptist women argued from the principle of justice, the proceedings of their annual meetings contain a greater number of feminist references to the expediency of the ballot for women. Layten and Bur-roughs often spoke of the black woman's vote as redeeming the race from man's misuse of the ballot, and repeatedly noted that the black woman's vote would enhance the black struggle for freedom. In the *Crisis* in 1915, Nannie Burroughs argued the expediency position when she observed the importance of the vote in protecting black women from male dominance and abuse. At the same time that Booker T. Washington's influential voice did not dare to oppose openly black disfranchisement, the WC called for a united leadership that would "neither compromise nor sell out." In 1912 the minutes of the WC recorded: "If women cannot vote, they should make it very uncomfortable for the men who have the ballot but do not know its value." Three years earlier, the Baptist women had specified that woman's political input in state legislatures and the federal government would en-sure an improvement in the status of black women.[32]

In 1912 the WC committee on the state of the country asserted women's full capabilities in assisting men in social reform and affirmed that reform would occur only when women were included in the electoral process. In 1912 the same committee also officially endorsed the presidential candi-dacy of Theodore Roosevelt and The Progressive Party platform, which in-cluded woman's suffrage, prohibition, and child labor legislation. In 1914 the temperance committee of the WC linked the passage of a woman's suf-frage amendment to that for prohibition and argued that each worked to eliminate the liquor traffic.[33]

When the WC met in St. Louis, Missouri, in 1918, Mrs. Hannah Red-dick addressed her sisters on the subject "What Women Will Do with the Ballot" and employed the "home protection" argument for woman's suf-frage. She contended that the vote would make divorces more difficult for men to obtain and marriages less easy to enter into. At the St. Louis con-ference a white representative from the Equal Suffrage League of St. Louis spoke on woman's right to vote and invited all WC members from Missouri to join her organization. In 1919 Mrs. Gertrude Rush, a prominent black lawyer and delegate from a Baptist church in Des Moines, Iowa, posited that the vote would enable women to fight for better working conditions, higher wages, and greater opportunities in business. Through the suffrage, Rush maintained, women could better regulate moral and sanitary conditions, end discrimination and lynch law, obtain better educational opportunities, and secure greater legal justice.[34]

In its annual gathering in 1920, the WC hailed the passage of the Nineteenth Amendment. President Layten urged black women to exercise their newly won right and to enter politics. Corresponding secretary Burroughs commended by name such white suffragists as Susan B. Anthony, Anna Howard Shaw, Alice Paul, and Carrie Chapman Catt. At the same time, she pointed to the racism of white suffragists as a cause for the limited participation of black women in the organized suffragist movement.[35] By perceiving the vote as a weapon in the struggle for both race and sex advancement, leaders of the WC recognized that woman's suffrage, when coupled with black northward migration, would enlarge the black electorate in northern cities and provide important political advantages. In 1919 Layten assigned to the church the responsibility of supervising and directing black political gains as a result of migration. In 1920 she again urged the churches to assist in the political modernization of the rural migrants, so that they might understand the advantages and political leverage open to them.[36]

In 1920 Burroughs argued that the ballot would aid women in fighting for labor laws designed to protect women and children: "For industrial and economic reasons, the ballot will be a sure defense for women in industries who should demand equal pay for equal service." Like Layten, Burroughs advocated that the church politicize its members to exercise their right to vote. Burroughs exhorted her sisters to organize suffrage clubs in their churches. Predicting a wave of protest by those who would separate religious from political issues, she continued to assure her sisters that practical Christianity included the exercise of the ballot.[37] Throughout the 1920s Burroughs involved herself directly in electoral politics by mobilizing the women's vote throughout the nation. Her leadership served as a linchpin that united the political work of the National Association of Colored Women, the National League of Republican Colored Women, and the larger religious community.[38] During election time, Burroughs, along with the black and white candidates whom she supported, could be found addressing church congregations and soliciting support for the upcoming election. Harold Gosnell's classic study of political activities among black Chicagoans observes the common occurrence of candidates speaking to congregations during the regular worship service:

> The congregations do not ordinarily resent their presence. Many of their listeners are hard-working people who do not have the time or energy to attend the evening political meetings during the week.[39]

Finally, in promoting the principle of human dignity, the WC, and especially Nannie Burroughs, kept before the eye of the public the need to respect black womanhood. At times this meant publicly attacking the hypocrisy of white women reformers who advocated social purity for white women but ignored the sexual exploitation of black women by white men. At other times, calling attention to the dignity of black women meant castigating the sexism of black men. Burroughs found the black press to be a great outlet for the expression of her feminist consciousness. She wrote a column for the *Pittsburgh Courier* throughout the 1920s and 1930s. Black newspapers around the nation regularly covered her speeches and activities. On one occasion she editorialized in the *Courier:*

> The Negro woman "totes" more water; grows more corn; picks more cotton; washes more clothes; cooks more meals; nurses more babies; mammies more Nordics; supports more churches; does more race uplifting; serves as mudsills for more climbers; takes more punishment; does more forgiving; gets less protection and appreciation than do the women in any other civilized group in the world. She has been the economic and social slave of mankind.[40]

In 1933 the *Louisiana Weekly* covered her speech to an overflowing audience of young people at the Bethel A.M.E. Church. Burroughs spoke on the topic "What Must the Negro Do to Be Saved." Her speech relayed three messages—the combination of which underscores the prophetic principle of the feminine in the black religious tradition. The first was a spiritual one—to glorify the things of the spirit and to get a correct sense of values through a God-centered life. There was no substitute for the spiritual—not in the form of philanthropy or any man-made institution. For Burroughs, there could be no compromise or shortcuts to heaven. The second was a race-focused message. She told her young listeners that blacks must serve

154 notice to the world that they are willing to die for their rights. She admonished them not to wait for a deliverer and uttered the mandate:

> I like the quotation, "Moses my servant is dead. Therefore, arise and go over Jordan." There are no deliverers. They're all dead. We must arise and go over Jordan. We can take the promised land.

Her third message insisted upon a new perspective on black womanhood.

> We must have a glorified womanhood that can look any man in the face—white, red, yellow, brown, or black, and tell of the nobility of character within black womanhood. Stop making slaves and servants of our women. We've got to stop singing—"Nobody works but father." The Negro mother is doing it all. The women are carrying the burden.[41]

This is the legacy of Nannie Helen Burroughs. She influenced several generations of progressive race leaders both male and female by asserting the crucial relationship between religion, politics, and gender. No scholar of the black church can overlook or disregard her presence and influence. She stands among the finest representatives of the black Christian tradition. Nannie Burroughs is the feminine in our religious tradition.

NOTES

1. Eugene D. Genovese, *Roll Jordan Roll: The World the Slaves Made* (New York: Random House, 1974), 161–284; Albert J. Raboteau, *Slave Religion: "The Invisible Institution" in the Antebellum South* (New York: Oxford University Press, 1978); James H. Cone, *God of the Oppressed* (New York: Seabury Press, 1975); Cornel West, *Prophesy Deliverance!: An Afro-American Revolutionary Christianity* (Philadelphia: Westminster Press, 1982): Peter J. Paris, *The Social Teaching of the Black Churches* (Philadelphia: Fortress Press, 1985); and J. Deotis Roberts, *Roots of a Black Future: Family and Church* (Philadelphia: Westminster Press, 1980).

2. See, for example, C. Eric Lincoln, ed. *The Black Experience in Religion* (New York: Anchor Books, 1974); Olin P. Moyd, *Redemption in Black Theology* (Valley Forge, Pa.: Judson Press, 1979); Gayraud S. Wilmore, *Black Religion and Black Radicalism* (New York: Anchor Books, 1973). An exception to the trend of omitting women is James H. Cone and Gayraud S. Wilmore, eds., *Black Theology: A Documentary History, 1966–1979* (Maryknoll, N.Y.: Orbis Books, 1979), 363–442.

3. Joseph Bensman and Robert Lilienfield, *Between Public and Private: The Lost Boundaries of the Self* (New York: The Free Press, 1979), 171–185; Susan C.

Bourque and Jean Grossholtz, "Politics as an Unnatural Practice: Political Science Looks at Female Participation," *Politics and Society* 4 (Winter 1974): 225, 228, 258, 261.

4. Much of the following information appears in expanded form in Evelyn Brooks, "The Women's Movement in the Black Baptist Church, 1880–1920" (Ph.D. diss., University of Rochester, 1984), ch. 4.

5. See National Baptist Convention, *Journal of the Twentieth Annual Session of the National Baptist Convention, Held in Richmond, Virginia, September 12–17, 1900* (Nashville: National Baptist Publishing Board, 1900), 10, 64, 68, 195–196.

6. Ibid., 197–198.

7. Theodore S. Boone, *Negro Baptist Chief Executives in National Places* (Detroit: A.P. Publishing Company, 1948), 29–30; Thomas O. Fuller, *History of the Negro Baptists of Tennessee* (Nashville: National Baptist Publication Board, n.d.), 201.

8. NBC, *Journal of the Twenty-first Annual Session of the National Baptist Convention and the Second Annual Session of the Woman's Convention, Held in Cincinnati, Ohio, September 11–16, 1901* (Nashville: National Baptist Publishing Board, 1901), 20–21; Nannie H. Burroughs to Booker T. Washington, 18 February 1896, Booker T. Washington Papers, Library of Congress; Earl H. Harrison, *The Dream and the Dreamer* (Washington, D.C.: Nannie H. Burroughs Literature Foundation, 1956), 9–12.

9. NBC, *Twenty-first Annual Session, 1901,* 19–21.

10. See Evelyn Brooks, "The Feminist Theology of the Black Baptist Church, 1880–1900," in Amy Swerdlow and Hanna Lessinger, eds., *Class, Race, and Sex: The Dynamics of Control* (Boston: G. K. Hall, 1983), 31–59.

11. NBC, *Twenty-first Annual Session, 1901,* 29, 59.

12. NBC, *Journal of the Third Annual Session of the Woman's Convention, Held in Birmingham, Alabama, September 17–22, 1902* (Nashville: National Baptist Publishing Board, 1901), 20, 38.

13. NBC, *Journal of the Twenty-second Annual Session of the National Baptist Convention, Held in Birmingham, Alabama, September 17–23, 1902* (Nashville: National Baptist Publishing Board, 1902), 107; NBC, *Journal of the Twenty-third Annual Session of the National Baptist Convention and the Fourth Annual Session of the Woman's Convention, Held in Philadelphia, Pennsylvania, September 16–20, 1903* (Nashville: National Baptist Publishing Board, 1904), 82, 157.

14. NBC, *Third Annual Session of the Woman's Convention. 1902,* 24; NBC, *Fourth Annual Session of the Woman's Convention, 1903,* 229.

15. See Evelyn Brooks Barnett, "Nannie Helen Burroughs," in Rayford W. Logan and Michael R. Winston, *The Dictionary of American Negro Biography* (New York: W. W. Norton, 1983).

16. Paris, *Social Teaching,* 11.

17. NBC, *Journal of the Twenty-fourth Annual Session of the National Baptist Convention and the Fifth Annual Session of the Woman's Convention, Held in Austin, Texas, September 14–19, 1904* (Nashville: National Baptist Publishing Board, 1904), 324.

18. NBC, *Thirteenth Annual Report of the Executive Board and Corresponding Secretary of the Woman's Convention, Auxiliary to the National Baptist Convention, Made at Nashville, Tennessee, September 17–21, 1913*, 15.

19. Genovese, *Roll Jordan Roll*, 165.

20. NBC, *Journal of the Twenty-fifth Annual session of the National Baptist Convention and the Sixth Annual Session of the Woman's Convention, Held in Chicago, Ill., October 25–30, 1905* (Nashville: National Baptist Publishing Board, 1905), 270.

21. NBC, *Thirteenth Annual Report, 1913*, 33.

22. NBC, *Fifth Annual Session of the Woman's Convention, 1904*, 346; NBC, *Seventh Annual Report of the Executive Board and Corresponding Secretary of the Woman's Convention, Auxiliary to the National Baptist Convention, Made at Washington, D.C., September 1907*, 9–10; NBC, *Journal of the Tenth Annual Session of the Woman's Convention, Held in New Orleans, Louisiana, September 14–19, 1910* (Nashville: National Baptist Publishing Board, 1910, 37–38.

23. NBC, *Journal of the Thirty-fourth Annual Session of the National Baptist Convention and the Fourteenth Annual Assembly of the Woman's Convention, Held in Philadelphia, Pennsylvania, September 9–15, 1914* (Nashville: National Baptist Publishing Board, 1914), 173, 178; NBC, *Journal of the Thirty-ninth Annual Session of the National Baptist Convention and the Nineteenth Annual Session of the Woman's Convention, Held in Newark, New Jersey, September 10–15, 1919* (Nashville: National Baptist Publishing Board, 1920, 243–244.

24. See Table No. 2 and Table No. 4 in NAACP, *Thirty Years of Lynching in the United States, 1889–1918* (New York: National Association for the Advancement of Colored People, 1919), 33, 39.

25. NBC, *Sixth Annual Session of the Woman's Convention, 1905*, 269; NBC, *Journal of the Eighteenth Annual Session of the Woman's Convention, Auxiliary to the National Baptist Convention, Held in St. Louis, Missouri, September 4–9, 1918* (Nashville; National Baptist Publishing Board, 1919), 168; NBC, *Nineteenth Annual Session of the Woman's Convention, 1919*, 233.

26. NBC, *Nineteenth Annual Session of the Woman's Convention, 1919*, 203, 209, 211.

27. NBC, *Eighteenth Annual Session of the Woman's Convention, 1918*, 140, 142, 160–161, 168–169, 191.

28. NBC, *Nineteenth Annual Session of the Woman's Convention, 1919*, 232, 261; "Meetings," *Crisis* 19 (December 1919): 85.

29. Brooks, "Feminist Theology," 31–59.

30. NBC, *Eighteenth Annual Session of the Woman's Convention, 1918*, 163, 166, 194; NBC, *Nineteenth Annual Session of the Woman's Convention, 1919*, 166, 219–220, 250.

31. NBC, *Thirty-fourth Annual Session of the National Baptist Convention, 1914*, 36; NBC, *Thirty-eighth Annual Session of the National Baptist Convention, 1918*, 30.

32. Burroughs, "Black Women and Reform," *Crisis* 10 (August 1915): 187; NBC, *Journal of the Twelfth Annual Session of the Woman's Convention, Held in Houston, Texas, September 11–15, 1912* (Nashville: National Baptist Publishing Board, 1913), 39; NBC, *Journal of the Twenty-ninth Annual Session of the Na-*

tional Baptist Convention and the Ninth Annual Session of the Woman's Convention, Held in Columbus, Ohio, September 15–20, 1909 (Nashville: National Baptist Publishing Board, 1909), 256–257.

33. NBC, *Twelfth Annual Session of the Woman's Convention, 1912,* 93; NBC, *Fourteenth Annual Assembly of the Woman's Convention, 1914,* 151, 229.

34. NBC, *Eighteenth Annual Session of the Woman's Convention, 1918,* 197, 100; NBC, *Nineteenth Annual Session of the Woman's Convention, 1919,* 250.

35. NBC, *Journal of the Fortieth Annual Session of the National Baptist Convention and the Twentieth Annual Session of the Woman's Convention, Held in Indianapolis, Indiana, September 8–13, 1920* (Nashville: National Baptist Publishing Board, 1920), 305, 338–339.

36. NBC, *Nineteenth Annual Session of the Woman's Convention, 1919,* 203, 209, 211; NBC, *Twentieth Annual Session of the Woman's Convention, 1920,* 305, 316.

37. NBC, *Twentieth Annual Session of the Woman's Convention, 1920,* 338–340, 383.

38. See discussion of Burroughs's leadership in the mobilization of black Republican women during the 1920s in Evelyn Brooks, "In Politics to Stay," in Louise Tilly and Patricia Gurin, eds., *Women in Twentieth-Century American Politics* (New York: Russell Sage Foundation, forthcoming).

39. Harold F. Gosnell, *Negro Politicians: The Rise of Negro Politics in Chicago* (Chicago: University of Chicago Press, 1935), 46, 94–96; St. Claire Drake and Horace R. Cayton. *Black Metropolis* (New York: Harcourt Brace, 1945), 413.

40. Quoted in Jacquelyn Dowd Hall, *Revolt Against Chivalry: Jessie Daniel Ames and the Women's Campaign Against Lynching* (New York: Columbia University Press, 1979), 78.

41. Burroughs, "Unload Your Uncle Toms," in Gerda Lerner, ed., *Black Women in White America: A Documentary History* (New York: Vintage Books, 1973), 550–553. Reprinted with changes from the dissertation, *Women's Movement in the Black Baptist Church, 1880–1920.* Chapter 4. Copyright 1984.

9

ROGER D. LAUNIUS

A BLACK WOMAN IN A WHITE MAN'S CHURCH: AMY E. ROBBINS AND THE REORGANIZATION

Like all institutions, the Reorganized Church of Jesus Christ of Latter Day Saints has struggled throughout its existence to deal with tensions between races in the house of faith. The example of one black woman's family in the first half of the twentieth century illustrates the difficulties inherent in the effort for both Church authorities and individuals in this painful process of mutual accommodation. Amy E. Robbins (1884–1956) left a remarkable personal memoir about her experiences as a black woman in a church run by white males. It presents a truly remarkable story of faith and perseverance, her love of God, her concern for her family, and her commitment to the gospel. It also describes in a moving way her lifelong labor against bigotry and injustice in the context of the Reorganization. Through the lens of Amy Robbins's life, new perspectives on these subjects can be illuminated, reinforced, or perhaps altered.

The Reorganization never imposed official restrictions on black members, as did the Latter-day Saints under Brigham Young. Yet Reorganization leaders and members have generally accepted American middle-class racial concepts of black subservience and this tacit decision has affected its operations among black Americans.[1]

Furthermore, the institutional Church has allowed the pursuit of two race policies, one ideal and the other practical. The ideal has remained unchanged since the Church's organizational meeting: the gospel of Jesus

Christ is for all humanity. Christian salvation is universal, without regard to race, color, or condition. The atonement of Christ is available for all.[2] The Reorganized Church adopted an official policy accepting this basic scriptural position as early as 1865, near the conclusion of the Civil War, and it has remained in effect ever since.[3]

This official position, however, tells only part of the story, for there has been a wide divergence between the ideal and its implementation. The Reorganized Church has been, since its inception in the 1850s, and continues to be, a white, Midwestern-based religious movement with strong ties to the larger society. Its leaders and members have usually been firmly incorporated into the American values system and have been, or aspired to be, middle class. They have usually followed the American mainstream in its social practices, including whatever restrictions on racial equality might exist in the United States.[4]

Because of this internal discrepancy between the Church's belief and its practices, Amy Robbins shouldered the burden of racial prejudice throughout her life in the Reorganization. The fact that she was a woman added a second burden, that of gender discrimination, which ironically was almost invisible but no less crushing. Darlene Clark Hine argues that black women had fundamentally different experiences from white women because many gender prejudices were masked by the overarching problem of racial bigotry. As a result, black women were unaware of much gender discrimination and tended to see race as the explanation of the pattern of prejudice they encountered. Amy Robbins also fits this pattern. She developed a sensitivity to racial discrimination over the course of her lifetime but apparently remained unaware of the extent to which gender discrimination was also a burden.[5]

Amy Elizabeth Thomas Burke Robbins was born on 30 March 1884 at Minden, Haliburton County, Ontario Province, Canada. The daughter of Charles Edward Thomas and Eliza Jane Pearl Thomas, Amy grew up with heroic stories of her family's struggles against oppression. Her paternal grandfather, John Dorsey, escaped slavery in the American South through the famous "underground railway" and made his way to Canada where he married Catherine Ann Thomas, a freed woman, and took her name to mask his identity as an escaped slave. Catherine Thomas, an octoroon, had been sexually abused by her master to whom she bore a child. In a fit of remorse he had freed her but periodically tried to locate her and either persuade or force her to come back to the South with him. John Dorsey Thomas had then fought in a black regiment in the Union Army during the Civil War and liked to tell how he helped rid the United States of slavery.

Amy's maternal grandparents, Henry Pearl and Mary Patterson Pearl, had mixed ancestry: German, Irish, Cherokee, and black. From Greene County, Pennsylvania, they had never been enslaved but regarded the institution with loathing.[6] Because of this heritage, Amy, a relatively light-skinned black, spent most of her early life around whites and could not remember experiencing racial prejudice growing up in Canada.

When she left home as a teenager to work as a domestic in Lindsey, Canada, Amy met and later married Jack Burke, the son of an Irish immigrant. They were married only a little more than a year when he was drowned in a river while on a trip. She says little about him in her memoirs except that this mixed marriage taught her that all people needed to be accepted "regardless of their color or station in life. It is a glorious feeling to have no prejudice rankling in my heart and love in my heart for everyone." She was pregnant at his death and lived with an aunt in Detroit until her son was born.[7]

Amy's aunt, a member of the Reorganized Church, began to take Amy to worship services. Amy remembered:

> One evening we went to a missionary service downstairs. The people there belonged to the same Church. The young priest, William Smith, preached about the restoration of the gospel in these latter days and the coming forth of the Book of Mormon. It all sounded wonderful and I believed all he said without question. It had such a ring of truth that I could doubt nothing. After the service was over he asked if there were any questions. A minister from another Church asked many and offered objections to some of Mr. Smith's claims, especially about the Book of Mormon. I listened feverishly, for I did not see how he could answer some of the inquiries. My tension was relieved when every question and inquiry was answered from the Bible. I thought I had read the Bible through, but nothing I had read in the Bible sounded like what he read, and I thought it just could not be the same kind of Bible. I was thrilled beyond words with what I heard.

The local Reorganization members began meeting regularly with Amy, and she soon asked for baptism.[8]

Amy was baptized at sunrise in the Detroit River on 9 July 1905 by Elder George Shippy, a service she described as "the highest mountain peak of my life." Attended by only four people, Amy related that this baptismal service was laced by an irony that she relished, despite her unmistakable sincerity. She described the "Motley group" assembled: "there was a Mr. Black, who was white and my aunt, Mrs. White, was black, and . . . I was brown and the Elder was white. These different colors were one in Jesus Christ." That same morning she was confirmed a member at the Evergreen Branch of the Church at the corner of Fourth and Holden in Detroit. She recalled that in the prayer the elder confirming commanded that the Holy Spirit rest on her: "I felt the spirit envelope me in a wonderful power that cannot be described in words, only that I was baptized by the Holy Ghost. At that time I received a definite knowledge of the truthfulness of the restored gospel of Christ. This was a turning point in my life and I experienced peace, joy and happiness in my endeavor to serve God."[9] This deeply significant experience sustained Amy throughout her life as she dealt with difficulties of all forms.

Amy stayed in Detroit, working in a variety of settings and participating in the life of the Saints. "I was happy during those years," she wrote, "with just enough heartache to balance my joy and make me appreciate my blessings." While there, she met Herbert M. Robbins, a black farmer living near North Buxton who had been a widower for five years, and married him on 15 March 1909 in a ceremony presided over by a Reorganization priesthood member, even though Bert was a strong Baptist. She thought it an idyllic marriage. Before they went to bed on their wedding night, Bert suggested that they kneel in prayer. "I was moved to tears as I listened to the beautiful, all inclusive prayer he offered," she wrote. "I knew God would bless our lives together. Every morning and evening from then on it was an established rule to have family worship."[10]

They returned to Robbins's farm after the wedding, and Amy enjoyed country living. To her son from her previous marriage and Bert's daughter from his, they added eight more children, the last one born eight months after Bert's untimely death. Although they were too far from town to attend church, the first three years were peaceful and outside pressures were few. Bert owned the farm; and while the work was hard, the rewards were theirs. Then he mortgaged his land in an effort to forestall a foreclosure on his parents' home but could not maintain payment. In 1912, after they lost the farm, they moved to Battle Creek, Michigan, where Bert began work on a railroad.[11]

Amy Robbins was disappointed that there was not a Reorganized Church congregation in Battle Creek; but about 1915, a young priest came into the area and began holding meetings. When Amy saw a notice for a Reorganization worship service in a Saturday newspaper, she "was so happy for I had hoped and prayed for the Church." Joyfully, she told Bert her news and was very pleased when "he said he would go with me."[12] She did not realize that close contact with the Church would present her with special challenges.

The Robbins family reached the meeting location on Sunday at the appointed time and were received "very cordially," but the minister in charge immediately changed his sermon topic. Amy described the scene:

> [The minister] introduce[d] us to about ten people by telling them that we were their cousins because we were one of their brothers, but our father was cursed with a black skin and though we still carried that curse we were still cousins ect. ect. [sic]. My husband was unusually quiet and had no comments at all and when I asked him to go to Church with me Sunday he said he did not care to go to Church to hear of his cursings he heard enough of that every day. When he went to Church it was to hear of God's goodness and blessings and he never again went to our Church. But he was a wonderful husband and lived [as] an upright Christian in every sense he knew. I always found in the life of Roy M. Young [the minister in charge of that service] a very ad[m]irable follower of the Christ.[13]

This incident expresses, with brutal honesty, the painful division between belief and behavior that has marked race relations in the history of the Reorganization. It demonstrates that many Reorganized Church members, while honestly believing that the gospel was for all, tacitly accepted an inferior position for blacks beneath whites. In part that was the result of the common religious conception incorporated into Mormonism at leàst by the 1840s that God cursed Cain with a dark skin for murdering Abel. As offspring of a "cursed" lineage, blacks therefore had less stature than whites.[14] Clearly the minister in Battle Creek accepted this position and offered the theory of the curse of Cain as a fact. And certainly Roy Young's explanation would have seemed acceptable to white members who accepted the social values of the larger American society.

Although Amy does not comment on the aspects of gender discrimination this incident shows, they were no less important.[15] Amy Robbins was a Church member but, as a woman, was not eligible for priesthood. She was, consequently, automatically placed into an unequal position in relation to the minister who made his position plain. A member of the priesthood had the right to speak in the worship service; she did not. He answered to a hierarchy which she could never be a part of, and that hierarchy did not then envision his racist introduction of her and her husband as problematic or contradictory of larger gospel values.[16] It is interesting that she accepted the minister's remarks about her and her race without complaint, even while she recorded her husband's quiet but staunch rejection of the racial stereotype. Unfortunately, she does not explain why she accepted this labeling. I conjecture that she did so partly from cultural influences, partly because of the Reorganized Church's traditional deference to the authority of priesthood, and partly because her hunger for the church to which she was so thoroughly and deeply converted made her willing to forgive Young, seeing beneath his racism to his more "admirable" qualities.

What of Bert's reaction? As a Baptist, he did not attach the same significance to priesthood authority as Amy. His response—first courteous endurance, then dignified withdrawal—is a reaction of his stronger self-esteem, that must have been partly gender related. It says much about his respect for Amy, however, that he made no public protest during the meeting. Amy accepted her second-class status and continued to participate in the Battle Creek congregation.

In spite of persistent racism, Amy found worshipping with the Battle Creek Saints tremendously rewarding. Her home life was also pleasant. Children were born every couple of years. Bert's steady work made it possible for them to buy a house with some acreage on the outskirts of town where they had a barn and some livestock. Amy had the unusual luxury, for a black wife, of being a full-time mother and homemaker.[17] She participated in a local women's service group, and was part of a sewing circle that made quilts and other items. Her friends were mostly black, but neither they nor she thought much about race. Her light complexion let her move without challenge in white society. Her awareness of both her race and her gender lay dormant.[18]

This idyll ended abruptly on 17 February 1919 when Bert died after a three-day illness, thrusting Amy into a totally different world. The crisis of losing a spouse has long been recognized as a major turning point in an individual's life, both emotionally and practically. For a woman economically dependent on her husband, the crisis is exacerbated.[19] Amy was newly pregnant with her eighth child by Bert, born eight months after the father's death, while her oldest child, Bert's daughter from his earlier marriage, would soon graduate from high school. The happiness and reliance developed in her decade-long partnership with Bert created emotional ties that her first widowhood could not match. As another crushing blow, her eleven-month-old son, Eugene Wentworth Robbins, died in his sleep on the very night of Bert's funeral. Amy had him buried in Bert's grave.[20]

Doubly bereaved, Amy Robbins received advice from friends, but little help. Virtually all of them agreed that she should put the children up for adoption. "They were so sure I could never provide for them," she remarked, "but they didn't reckon with a mother's love for her fatherless brood, or with God's love for his children." She did not want to work outside the home, leaving her children to take care of themselves. Instead she got a primitive washing machine and took in laundry. It was a practical solution for the time. It allowed her to stay home with her children, as she believed was important. Even if entrepreneuring a small business had been a practical possibility, she had few resources except her own labor and few skills except housekeeping. Being a laundress, on the other hand, did not violate any cultural expectations about appropriate behavior for a woman, particularly a black woman. She had thus selected a profession that would draw no uncharitable commentary.[21]

Frugally Amy remade old clothing into clothes for herself and her children. When three of her daughters were about the same size she liked to dress them alike. She even had a little fun with it, calling them "Robbins Brown Breasts"—Twitter, Chirp, and Peep.[22]

Five months after Bert's death when Amy was six months pregnant, Amy's brother, Charles W. Thomas, came to visit in July 1919 and realized her dire condition. Without a wife or family, Thomas decided to stay, found work, and was soon contributing to the family's upkeep. He was a stabilizing influence in the Robbins's lives for the next two years. Thomas also helped Amy get a "Mother's Pension" through the County Poor Commission, a small allowance to help with the upkeep of children below the ages of fourteen.[23] Almost immediately, Amy Robbins introduced Thomas to the Church and he was baptized in late July or early August. Bringing a convert's zeal to his membership, Thomas ensured that Amy's family was active in the local branch while he was there. He even took them to district reunion a few weeks later, an annual week-long family camp held at Indian Lake, during late August of 1919. She recalled, "We enjoyed the association of the Saints." She also remarked that living in tents at the reunion was trying when a hard storm blew down their tent, "soaking all our clothes and bedding and running in pools on the tent floors." But that was outweighed by the good experiences: "It didn't dampen our spirits as we sang praises, prayed, and gave thanks."[24]

At this camp, an unfortunate incident occurred, underscoring the racial discrimination Amy had to face. Some nonmembers objected to blacks using the same beach at the lake as the white Reorganization members, and the Battle Creek pastor asked her to use a different part of the lake front. Amy wrote:

> "There was a place farther down the lake shore good enough for us," he said, and the Elder took us there where there was a couple of old planks extending out among long weeds and a mud bottom, with mud and weeds also along the shore.
>   The shame and humiliation were very depressing to us, for, during the hours that were set aside for swimming and recreation, we stayed away from the beach and wandered around the ground feeling very much like packing up and returning home. We felt that if the saints had stood together and demanded their rights for the whole group to their leased property, there would have not been too much opposition, however, my brother being from that part of Canada where discrimination was not known, was crushed and disappointed in the attitude of the saints.[25]

Although this incident cut Amy deeply, she was able to forgive the white Saints for this slight; but it hurt her children even more. Her adolescent son, Russell Robbins, left the Church for a time as a young man; but although he later returned, he was still bitter about the Indian Lake incident more than thirty years later.[26]

During the same month (though it is not known whether it was before or after the reunion), an experience at an RLDS worship service in Battle Creek provided a deeply affirming and consoling experience for Amy. Lilly Barmore, a woman in the congregation, "spoke through the gift [of] the Spirit to the congregation." When she finished, she turned to Amy and told her in prophecy that God acknowledged her as His servant. "I was told," Amy recalled, "that my prayers had been heard and recorded and I was admonished to 'worry not because of your children, for mine arms are around them and I will care for and protect them.'" The message was a significant confirmation of Amy's sense of self-worth, a mark of God's love for her and her family.[27]

In short, the months immediately following Bert's death were a time of shattering blows and growth that made Amy understand herself in new ways, both positively and negatively. Amy gained a greater sense about her own strengths but also learned more about the handicap of being a black woman in a white man's church. In time she came to believe that the great trial of Bert's death had brought blessings of forcing the family to pull together. Amy's grandmother had taught her to memorize poems and give concerts. She worked with her children, who were quite talented musically, to put together a program of dramatic readings, dialogues, and music. They raised seventy-five dollars at one performance at the Second Baptist Church in Battle Creek. Other performances followed, less lucrative but still financially helpful.[28]

Amy remained deeply and passionately committed to the Reorganized Church and to her congregation in Battle Creek. Most of the time, the family attended church without apparent difficulties. This positive record should receive its full value in Amy's spiritual life; but racism remained a persistent problem, even though it surfaced only occasionally over Amy Robbins's next forty years in the Church. She remained a strong advocate of the Restoration until her death; but her faith in the justice and mercy of God gave her the moral authority and energy to label prejudiced behavior for what it was, to protest it (though usually without satisfactory results), and to put her perceptions on the record. It was not always an easy task. It is in this context that we should understand the instances of abuse and neglect that occurred in her largely white Battle Creek congregation. From our current perspective, her faith, energy, and diligence would have made her a valuable member—and almost certainly a priesthood leader—in any congregation; instead in a hundred small ways she and her family were made to feel unwelcome.

Amy's children were musically talented (two became professional musicians) and willingly contributed their gifts to the congregational choir. However, some members refused to allow them to be seen in the choir loft during the service and insisted on seating them behind a curtain at the back of the loft. It was an exceptionally belittling episode. Most white members would not have accepted such a plan if they had been its targets. Hurt and humiliated, Amy, too, considered staying away; that she forebearingly accepted the arrangement says much about her commitment to the Church. However, she was anguished about the effect of such experiences on her children, for she desperately wanted them to feel an attachment to the Church: "I realized that the salvation of my children was at stake when they mingled with the world and were denied the privalege [sic] of hearing and association with the gospel."[29]

On another occasion, some of the local Saints told the pastor they were ashamed to bring friends to Church because there were black members in the congregation. Amy's recollection of this experience is heartrending:

> Only the Master could know the humiliation I underwent, because I was a
> Negro wholly dependent upon my white brethren for the spiritual food for
> which I was starving and for the teaching of the truths of the gospel for my
> children and my own encouragement. There was a motion made . . . that
> I stay away from Church, for a while at least, that they have a chance to
> bring their friends; there was much discussion and finally the motion was
> lost, however I offered to remain away from the Church for a period of six
> months or longer and though some were much opposed to it, I did stay
> away. I did stay away which was about the hardest thing I have ever done.
> What they did not know was that I did, as it were, "lick up the crumbs that
> fell from the Master's table," when I would stand under the window and
> get what instruction that might sift through, and, in my heart sing the
> songs of Zion with them. I would feel like a sneak because I was reaping
> good that was not intended for me.[30]

When she finally got up the courage to go back inside the meeting house one Wednesday night for prayer meeting, most of the members exclaimed how pleased they were to see her and expressed surprise that she had not been attending. It was as if they were not even aware of the problem.

Nor were the prejudices expressed only at a local level. In the early 1930s, an old priesthood member named Philemon Pement moved to Battle Creek. He was a dynamic and well-read minister who, according to Robbins, helped to revitalize the local branch. He was elected branch president by the members, but the ex-pastor and a few supporters opposed his efforts at every turn. They could find no acceptable means of getting rid of Pement until he "preached a sermon on love and brotherhood and how God made of one blood all nations, and we were all descendants of Noah, and how Moses married an Ethiopian woman and how his sister was stricken with leprosy when she rebuked him for it, etc., etc." The opponents of Pement asked the district president to remove him as branch president on the grounds that he had stirred up racial tensions in the congregation. The district president relieved Pement of his responsibilities and asked him to leave Battle Creek. The real issue, Robbins thought, was that the district president and many others in the area opposed Pement's defense of the rights of black members of the congregation. The affair greatly upset Amy, but she was powerless to effect any change, both as a voiceless woman and as an obviously unpopular ethnic minority. Once again, she considered withdrawing from the congregation but felt that she could not deprive herself of needed spiritual sustenance.[31]

The problems of prejudice extended even to the highest levels of the Church, and this also deeply troubled Amy Robbins. In 1920 she attended another reunion at Indian Lake, where the guest minister was Reorganization president Frederick M. Smith, a grandson of the founding prophet. "I was very anxious to meet the prophet of God," she wrote, "as it had always been my wont to place saints upon a pedestal, and the president was on the highest of them all, and I felt greatly honored to have this opportunity of meeting him." She commented that when she finally met him the Spirit of God confirmed his prophetic ministry and "As he stood to speak that morning, he was, in my eyes, a little lower than an angel; a chosen representative of Christ; a man of God who was to lead us, the people of God, to Zion." Then Smith began his remarks by talking about a "nigger" who worked for him. Amy wrote poignantly:

> I did not remember anything more that was said in that talk. I don't think in all my life I ever had such a hurt, such a bitter disappointment, my angel, or saint, or prophet had fallen from the pedestal on which I had placed him. Many eyes were turned on me and my aunt, the only colored people on the grounds. My eyes were filled with tears, my face burned with shame and humiliation and I at once felt like an outsider, an outcast with no part in the Zionic scheme because I was what the Prophet would call a "nigger." As soon as the benediction was pronounced I fled to my tent where I gave way to my bitter tears; my weekend was spoiled and I wanted to go home.[32]

In fact, she left the reunion as soon as she could get a ride, disappointed and chagrined that the prophet could be just a "man" subject to all the prejudices of any other.

Amy Robbins's powerlessness in the face of these discriminatory actions was very real. She perceived clearly that as a black woman she had no access to the normal channels of administration. But even with all internal mechanisms for justice shut in her face, she was unwilling to leave the Church. Why? Although any social dynamic has multiple sources, certainly Robbins's strongest motivation was her firm commitment to the ideals of the Reorganization even in the face of internal prejudices. Her writings were laced with statements of belief and commitment. Perhaps the most telling evidence of this was her poetry, primitive but emotional and powerful. One poem, "The Restoration," captured the angles of Amy Robbins's life and belief.

The Church was brought out of the wilderness,
    The gospel gifts have all been restored.
Showing forth God's love and great tenderness,
    To all those who put all their trust in the Lord.

If man will have faith and truly repent,
    Be baptized and his sins washed away,
The gifts from above will surely be sent
    As promised in this latter day.

True to form the prophet in this latter day
    Gave his life as a martyr for Truth.
He searched in the scriptures to find the true way
    And God called him while yet in his youth.

And so God has in these latter days,
    Made available to man a new birth,
Faith, repentance, baptism, just as in old ways
    When Jesus was here on the earth.

Let us spread glad tidings of the restoration
    And work while it is yet called today
Until we have reached out into every nation
    And spread the gospel of truth all the way.[33]

Her son Russell urged her to "leave those ungodly, sinning, scornful Church members alone," and a few of her children were driven away or sustained some periods of inactivity.[34] However, she remained a committed member, and she searched for ways to better the situation.

This search became more active as time passed. Perhaps she became less timid, perhaps maturity brought greater appreciation of what was at stake, perhaps the changes in the larger American society made it easier to speak out on these issues, and perhaps she eventually decided that the issue was significant enough for her to risk injuring others' feelings. Certainly, she went a long way in her efforts toward overcoming the Church's conservative strictures on her race. For example, during the 1930s, she proposed an alternative branch in Battle Creek that would meet in her house. While she explained this should not have been necessary, it was better than suffering abuse from the local Saints, especially the propensity they had to alienate her children. She wrote: "Since God has accepted us as members of the body of Christ and has acknowledged us as His children, I am unable to understand why the rest of His children would assume the attitude that they were better than their father."[35] She obtained this permission, but the mission was never successful at attracting enough attendees to satisfy the local Church leadership and was eventually discontinued. It was revived in the early 1940s under the direction of her son Arnold, a priest, but it was again discontinued after several months of futile effort.[36]

About 1946 some members of the Battle Creek branch made it very uncomfortable for the Robbins family to attend services. By then, the family included some of Amy's married children and their children, so they decided to begin meeting in her home again. She did not ask official sanction but independently began a new mission. This time, instead of concentrating on adults, she invited local children who did not attend any services into her home on Sunday mornings for music, fellowship, and religious instruction. These family meetings quickly attracted thirty-five children, and more might have come but for want of space. This mission was successful, and Amy remarked in February 1949:

> In the two and one half years that we have been meeting by ourselves we have had two sermons preached by the District Missionary. My son [Arnold] has conducted quite a few Communion Services and has taught us in class the Restoration by E. A. Smith, the Membership Manual, and now we are studying The Call at Evening. We are trying to prepare ourselves by study that we might better be able to defend and teach the gospel we know is true.[37]

Meetings in the Robbins home continued through most of the rest of Amy's life. While it was not a fully satisfactory arrangement, it served its purpose, and Amy Robbins and others were willing to support it.

Perhaps heartened by her success, Amy also raised the issue in a public way with a letter to the editor of the *Saints' Herald* in 1948, responding to an article on the rise of the Church among other cultures and races appearing in an earlier issue. She suggested that the Reorganized Church did not treat all equally because of race. She commented:

> As Latter Day Saints, we were given the custody of the Restored Gospel to share equally with every nation, kindred, tongue, and people, and we should be able to say to other races and colors, "Do Not Move—We Are All Equal Here." Instead, many say, "You move out—We are not equal here or anywhere else because your skin is dark." . . .

Why is the gospel of the kingdom preached to the colored people, and why are they baptized into the body of Christ, and why are they confirmed and receive the gift of the Holy Ghost if they are not equal with every other person who obeys the same ordinances?

She concluded with a question about whether the "people of God" would be able to overcome these societal prejudices and carry out the great commission. If not, she believed the Church would ultimately fail.[38]

Partly because of these developments, in the late 1940s Wilford G. Winholtz, a young and idealistic elder in Chicago, sought contact with Amy and her family. He was making a concerted effort to get the Church to acknowledge the inequalities of how it dealt with race and to develop a set of resolutions and a plan of action to reform the institution. Amy willingly supplied information and ideas. Winholtz unsuccessfully sponsored resolutions on racial equality at the General Conferences. In 1950 he also assembled the research he had gathered with help from Amy and others into a report to the First Presidency and Joint Council of the Reorganized Church. In it he asked that the Church's leadership acknowledge an institutional problem with racial equality and then take the initiative to rectify it.[39]

Amy Robbins's partnership with Winholtz gave her a long-desired hearing for her situation in Battle Creek. Unable to overcome the prejudices of others alone, she allied herself with a white male who did not have to deal directly with bigotry. It was apparently satisfying, even though the results were not fully satisfactory. It would be the 1960s, in the midst of the civil rights crusade, before the Church officially acknowledged the prejudices that Robbins, Winholtz, and others recognized.[40]

Meanwhile, Amy Robbins was winning many small victories. For example, even when the church mission was operating in her home, she would periodically return to the Battle Creek congregation and be welcomed by all. On one occasion, 14 November 1954, she proudly attended the ordination of her youngest son, LaVern Robbins, to the office of deacon in Lansing, Michigan.[41] "At the age of 35," she recalled, "he consecrated his life to the service of the Master who had spared and protected his life thus far. I am sure if his father was living he would be very proud." Then she added, "LaVern's desire to follow after righteousness has been a great comfort to me, and my prayer is that he and Arnold together in the priesthood will do a great work in building the Church and kingdom of God, and in spreading the light of the restored gospel among the nations."[42]

172

Less than two years later, Amy Robbins died in Battle Creek on 24 April 1956 at the age of seventy-two. She penned a fitting epitaph for herself seven years earlier. She testified that "God's work shall roll on no matter what vain attempts man may make, . . . we believe in the precious truths of the gospel, which . . . will, in time, go out indiscriminately to *all races* and *colors*. We believe that the work of the Lord will be accomplished and Zion will be built up as a place for the Saints of God, without segregation and discrimination."[43]

How can one assess the life of Amy Robbins? Frozen out of the mainstream of Church life, she clung to her beliefs and worked within the circumscribed avenues available to her toward ridding the Reorganized Church of bigotry. She did not live to see these problems overcome; indeed, they are still very much present. A black woman who joined the Reorganized Church in 1905, the granddaughter of slaves, she spent the next fifty years worshipping with the Saints, rejoicing in the Restoration concept, and trying to overcome racial prejudice. Robbins never held priesthood office nor any branch office more significant than Sunday School secretary. She never occupied a pulpit. A happily domestic woman, she reacted to the world on a personal level. No ideological reformer operating from intellectual premises, she defended herself and her children, as best she could, from the wrenching effects of racial prejudice in a Christian church.

Much earlier, the Apostle Paul spoke to another minority group of Christians disdained by a majority group when he wrote to the Galatians: "There is neither Jew nor Greek, there is neither bond nor free, there is neither male nor female: for ye are all one in Christ Jesus" (Gal. 3:28). Amy Robbins, by her practice and, perhaps even more, by her unflinching presence, wounded though she sometimes was, held that ideal before her family, her congregation, and the Reorganized Church.

NOTES

1. For histories of blacks in the Reorganization see William D. Russell, "A Priestly Role for a Prophetic Church: The RLDS Church and Black Americans," *Dialogue: A Journal of Mormon Thought* 12 (Summer 1979): 37–49; Arlyn R. Love, "The First Presidency's Response to the Civil Rights Movement," *John Whitmer Historical Association Journal* 4 (1984): 41–50; and Roger D. Launius, *Invisible Saints: A History of Black Americans in the Reorganized Church* (Independence: Herald Publishing House, 1988).

2. See *Book of Mormon* (Independence: Herald Publishing House, 1966 ed.), II Nephi 11:113–15; *Book of Doctrine and Covenants* (Independence: Herald Publishing House, 1970 ed.), Section 1:1b.

3. The General Conference adopted race-related resolutions in 1875, 1948, 1950, 1956, and two in 1968; see *Rules and Resolutions* (Independence: Herald Publishing House, 1980 ed.). Each of these resolutions espoused the ideal of Christ's salvation through repentance, regardless of race or condition.

4. No demographic studies of Church population have been done for the nineteenth century, but see discussions of Church growth and development in Roger D. Launius, *Joseph Smith III: Pragmatic Prophet* (Urbana: University of Illinois Press, 1988), chap. 13; Roger D. Launius, "Quest for Zion: Joseph Smith III and Community-Building in the Reorganization, 1860–1900," in *Restoration Studies III,* edited by Maurice L. Draper and Debra Combs (Independence: Herald Publishing House, 1986), 314–32; and Norma Derry Hiles, "Lamoni: Crucible for Pluralism in the Reorganization Church," ibid., 139–44. For the perceptions that white nineteenth-century Americans held of blacks, see William Stanton, *The Leopard's Spots: Scientific Attitudes Toward Race in America, 1815–1859* (Chicago: University of Chicago Press, 1960), and George M. Frederickson, *The Black Image in the White Mind* (New York: Harper and Row, 1971).

5. Darlene Clark Hine, "Rape and the Inner Lives of Black Women in the Middle West: Preliminary Thoughts on the Culture of Dissemblance," in *Unequal Sisters: A Multi-Cultural Reader in U.S. Women's History,* edited by Ellen Carol DuBois and Vicki L. Ruiz (New York: Routledge, 1990), 292–97. For an essay that approaches gender discrimination in the RLDS Church, see Patricia Struble, "Mite to Bishop: RLDS Women's Financial Relationship to the church," *John Whitmer Historical Association Journal* 6 (1986): 23–32.

6. Amy E. Robbins, "Just Amy: Autobiography," n.d., mimeographed booklet in my possession. On sexual abuse and its effect on women, see Hine, "Rape and the Inner Lives of Black Women"; Rennie Simpson, "The Afro-American Female: The Historical Construction of Sexual Identity," in *The Power of Desire: The Politics of Sexuality,* edited by Ann Snitow, Sharon Thompson, and Christine Stansell (New York: Monthly Review Press, 1983), 229–35; Darlene Clark Hine, "Lifting the Veil, Shattering the Silence: Black Women's History in Slavery and Freedom," in *The State of Afro-American History: Past, Present, and Future,* edited by Darlene Clark Hine (Baton Rouge: Louisiana State University Press, 1986), 223–49.

7. Robbins, "Just Amy," 21–22, 24.

8. Ibid., 22.

9. Ibid., 23.

10. Ibid., 24.

11. Ibid., 24–34; Amy E. Robbins to Wilford G. Winholtz, 17 February 1949, copy in my possession.

12. Amy E. Robbins, "My Experience as a Negro in the Battle Creek Branch of the Reorganized Church of Jesus Christ of Latter Day Saints," p. 1, n.d., copy in my possession.

13. "Bert's Last Sermon," in Notes from Materials from the Library of Amy E. Robbins, typescript by Richard Hawks, 14 June 1979, copy in my possession.

14. The religious dimension to black inferiority arguments have been analyzed in V. Jaques Voegeli, *Free But Not Equal: The Midwest and the Negro During the*

174

Civil War (Chicago: University of Chicago Press, 1967); Winthrop D. Jordan, *White Over Black: American Attitudes Toward the Negro, 1550–1812* (Chapel Hill: University of North Carolina Press, 1968); Anne C. Loveland, *Southern Evangelicals and the Social Order, 1820–1860* (Baton Rouge: Louisiana State University Press, 1980); and Donald G. Mathews, *Religion in the Old South* (Chicago: University of Chicago Press, 1977). On the issue within Mormonism, see Newell G. Bringhurst, *Saints, Slaves, and Blacks: The Changing Place of Black People Within Mormonism* (Westport, Conn.: Greenwood Press, 1981); Lester E. Bush, Jr., and Armand L. Mauss, eds., *Neither White Nor Black: Mormon Scholars Confront the Race Issue in a Universal Church* (Midvale, Utah: Signature Books, 1984).

15. How women's subordination has closed them off from power and authority in American society has been traced in several recent penetrating works: Carl N. Degler, *At Odds: Women and the Family in America from the Revolution to the Present* (New York: Oxford University Press, 1980); Jacqueline Jones, *Labor of Love, Labor of Sorrow: Black Women, Work, and the Family from Slavery to the Present* (New York: Basic Books, 1985); Gerda Lerner, *The Majority Finds Its Past: Placing Women in History* (New York: Oxford University press, 1979); Nancy F. Cott, *The Bonds of Womanhood* (New Haven, Conn.: Yale University Press, 1977).

16. The priesthood structure of the Reorganized Church is a hierarchical system in which authority to act and perform certain functions is granted to its members according to the position occupied in the system. Priesthood members hold all important offices in the church at every level from the local congregation to the Joint Council. It is an enormously significant institution and has defined the overall direction of the Reorganization. A good deal of deference to priesthood holders by the membership has been a part of the Reorganization from its earliest years, with quiet acceptance of their decisions in most instances. When dissent in the church has arisen, it has generally been the result of perceived abuses of authority by priesthood members. On the Reorganized Church's priesthood structure see Alfred Yale, *The Priesthood Manual* (Independence: Herald Publishing House, 1972 ed.).

17. It was unusual in black marriages for the husband's earnings to constitute a living wage. See Elsa Barkley Brown, "Womanist Consciousness: Maggie Lena Walker and the Independent Order of Saint Luke," in *Unequal Sisters*, edited by DuBois and Ruiz, 208–23.

18. Robbins, "Just Amy," 23–44.

19. General discussions of this subject can be found in Lisa Wilson, *A Death in the Family: Widows in Pennsylvania, 1750–1850* (Philadelphia: Temple University Press, 1992); Thomas Bender, *Community and Social Change in America* (Baltimore: Johns Hopkins University Press, 1986); Peggy Pascoe, *Relations of Rescue: The Search for Female Moral Authority in the American West, 1874–1939* (New York: Oxford University Press, 1990); Kathleen Underwood, "The Pace of Their Own Lives: Teaching Training and the Life Course of Western Women," *Pacific Historical Review* 55 (November 1986): 513–30; and David J. Russo, *Families and Communities: A New View of American History* (Nashville: American Association for State and Local History, 1974). For a socio-psychological

perspective on Reorganized Church members, see Marjorie Troeh, "Role Changes of Widows and Widowers in Relation to Voluntary Organizations" (M.A. thesis, University of Missouri at Kansas City, 1982).

20. Robbins, "Just Amy," 34.

21. Robbins, "Just Amy," 34. On the stereotypical roles of widows see, John Harriss, ed., *The Family: A Social History of the Twentieth Century* (New York: Oxford University Press, 1991).

22. Robbins, "Just Amy," 48.

23. Ibid., 50.

24. Ibid., 49–50.

25. Robbins, "My Experience as a Negro," 3.

26. V. Russell Robbins, Letter to Amy E. Robbins, 21 February 1950, copy in my possession. After recalling the Indian Lake incident, he reported, smarting, that he had been called "boy" at church one day in Detroit, Michigan. "I am 34 years old, the father of two children, a husband, a citizen, a body-repairman, a union member, a voter, a good risk to my credit references," he wrote, "*BUT* to a good brother of the church, I am a boy."

27. Robbins, "Just Amy," 50.

28. Ibid., 36–37.

29. Amy E. Robbins, et al., to Elder A. C. Barmore, President of Battle Creek Branch, [ca. 1930], 5, in Notes from Materials from Library of Amy E. Robbins, n.d., typescript by Richard W. Hawks, 14 June 1979. On her children's musical success see Frances Ashby, "Music Is Her Life," *Saints' Herald* 109 (1 March 1962): 164–66; [no author], "They Sang for Mattie," *Saints' Herald* 111 (15 June 1964): 416–17.

30. Robbins to Winholtz, 17 February 1949.

31. Amy E. Robbins to Wilford E. Winholtz, 18 March 1949, copy in my possession.

32. Robbins, "My Experience as a Negro," 4.

33. Excerpt from Amy E. Robbins, "The Restoration," in "Amy's Pomes," part 3, pp. 13–15, photomechanical publication of typescript, n.d., copy in possession of author.

34. V. Russell Robbins to Amy E. Robbins, 21 February 1950.

35. Robbins, "My Experience as a Negro," 3–4.

36. Robbins to Winholtz, 17 February 1949.

37. Robbins to Winholtz, 17 February 1949. Elbert A. Smith was the son of David H. Smith, the youngest son of Joseph Smith, Jr. His book, *The Restoration: A Study in Prophecy* (Independence: Herald Publishing House, 1946) was a fundamental religious instruction book for the Church for more than a generation. Jessie Ward, *The Call at Evening* (Independence: Herald Publishing House, 1920), was a missionary tool masquerading as a novel about conversion and faith.

38. Amy E. Robbins, "Racial Equality," *Saints' Herald* 95 (13 November 1948): 1104.

39. Wilford G. Winholtz to First Presidency and Members of the Joint Council, 15 March 1950, with a lengthy report and attachments enclosed, copy in my possession. For more information on Winholtz, see Launius, *Invisible Saints*, 212–15.

40. See Launius, *Invisible Saints*, 219–54; Russell, "A Priestly Role for a Prophetic Church," 45–49; and Love, "The First Presidency's Response to the Civil Rights

Movement," 41–50. Consistent with its earlier history, the Reorganized Church again mirrored the larger American society by breaking down racial barriers that it had earlier maintained.

41. In spite of the periodic emergence of racial prejudices, and certainly because of Amy Robbins's perseverance, with the exception of Russell Robbins all of her children remained active in the Reorganization after her death. Members of this family are leaders of the Reorganization to the present. One of her grand-children, Richard W. Hawks, is one of the Seven Presidents of Seventy.

42. Robbins, "Just Amy," 57–58.

43. Robbins to Winholtz, 17 February 1949.

10

BETTYE COLLIER-THOMAS

MINISTER AND FEMINIST REFORMER: THE LIFE OF FLORENCE SPEARING RANDOLPH

The Reverend Florence Spearing Randolph's[1] achievements as an evangelist, minister, missionary, suffragist, lecturer, organizer, and temperance worker rank well with those of the most celebrated Americans in our history. Yet, as important as her contributions were and as well-known as she was, less than a decade after her death she became an obscure figure. Unfortunately, this has been the plight of many African-Americans, particularly females, whose papers remain uncollected and whose lives rarely are celebrated on the pages of our history books.

Florence Spearing Randolph was born in Charleston, South Carolina on August 9, 1866, the seventh child of John and Anna Smith Spearing. She was born into a family of privilege and culture, whose free black lineage stretched back almost two generations before the Civil War. As the daughter of a prosperous cabinet maker and a member of the black elite, it was expected that she would become educated and would pursue a career in one of several professions available to women of color. Because of her race and gender, her choices were limited primarily to teaching and dressmaking. She chose dressmaking.

Florence attended local public schools and was a graduate of Avery Normal Institute in Charleston. Since most Southern public schools for African-Americans were limited in their offerings and usually covered grades one through three, normal schools were established for students who desired additional training and who wished to teach. For many years a certificate from a normal school was acceptable for teaching in most Southern black public schools, particularly in the rural South. The majority of African-Americans, recently freed from slavery, were poor and uneducated and had few options beyond working in the fields, or at the most in menial and servile jobs. Large numbers of black girls of this class worked in domestic service, or in the fields. Following her graduation from the Avery Institute, Florence became a dressmaker and an instructor in a dressmaking school.

In 1885, at the age of nineteen, she moved to New Jersey, taking up residence with an older sister in Jersey City. In Jersey City she could earn as much as a dollar fifty a day as a dressmaker, as compared to fifty cents a day in Charleston, and she could move and work in a freer environment. It was here that she met and married Hugh Randolph of Richmond, Virginia, who worked on the railroad as a cook in the dining car service of the Pullman Company. The marriage was very successful, lasting until the death of her husband in 1913. The Randolphs had one child, a daughter, Leah Viola, who was born in February of 1887. Leah Viola married J. Francis Johnson, a successful physician in Washington, D.C.

In 1886, Florence Spearing Randolph became a member of the Monmouth Street African Methodist Episcopal Zion Church, where she was appointed Sunday school teacher and class leader for the young people. As a child in Charleston, she had frequently accompanied her blind grandmother, who made house visits to pray with the sick and to explain the scriptures. This experience left a deep impression on the young Florence, who was later determined to pursue a career in the ministry. In the late 1880s, under the tutelage of George Biddle, an A.M.E. Zion minister and Yale graduate known as a Greek and Hebrew scholar, she began studying the Bible. In 1925 she completed a "synthetic Bible course" from the Moody Bible Institute of Chicago, Illinois, known for its training of missionaries. In 1926, following her appointment as minister to Wallace Chapel in Summit, New Jersey, she enrolled in an advanced course at Madison and Drew Seminary, later known as Drew University. Although she was an auditor in the Seminary School and did not pursue a degree, she was frequently referred to as a distinguished graduate of Drew Theological Seminary.

Throughout the late 1880s and early 1890s, Florence Randolph operated a flourishing dressmaking business from her home, located in downtown Jersey City. It was in this period that she began to exhort and do very active temperance and church work. In biographical notes, Randolph speaks of her early experiences, which drew her to the ministry. Reflecting on her early work, she stated that:

For several years I conducted a very successful dressmaking business, with seven in my workroom beside myself. Two dressmakers and 5 apprentice girls. Then one day while setting by my window trying to design a pattern this happened: . . . A crowd gathered in front of a saloon just across from my house (for one had saloons those days on almost every corner). With the curiosity of a woman, I walked across to discover the trouble. It was there that I saw quite a young man whom I suppose was not accustomed to saloon drinking and perhaps gambling, become intoxicated and noisy. The Saloon Keeper disregarding his youth soon called the police and a patrol wagon had come to take him away, hence the crowd— Speaking aloud to myself, I said, if I had my way I would close every saloon before night. A white woman standing near, a president of the WCTU, told me "if you feel that way come and join the WCTU and help us bring about prohibition." Finding the lady lived on the very next block to me, I became a member of No. 1 WCTU of Jersey City, soon became one of the local members, which marked the beginning of 14 years of real missionary work among those who suffer from strong drink and from poverty. Thus as a WCTU, Christian Endeavor, Kings Daughter and Sunday School Teacher I soon developed into a Bible student, discovering that one can do a real telling work for God and humanity.

During the unexpected illness of Reverend R.R. Baldwin, the pastor of the Jersey City A.M.E. Zion church, she was granted permission to start a meeting which turned out to be one of the greatest revivals in the history of the church. Her youth and gender attracted large crowds, which helped to increase the membership of her church and others in the vicinity. Local press coverage and word-of-mouth revelations increased her visibility and popularity. Invitations to speak and conduct revivals came from small churches and missions, white and black. Because of her success she was made a class leader and an exhorter, and was finally granted a local preacher's license. Randolph states that it was at this time that "the ball of criticism, fault finding and persecution began rolling. In 1897 I was granted head preacher. Not that I wanted honors, nor sought them but pressure was brought to bear by the pastor."

In 1898 Randolph was admitted to the New Jersey Conference and became Conference Evangelist. Her acceptance followed a lengthy and somewhat bitter debate. Opposition by the presiding Bishop set the tone for disaffection among fellow ministers who were opposed to elevating women to positions of authority in the church. This was just the beginning of her many years of struggle to be accepted and treated as an equal in the A.M.E. Zion ministry.

At the May 1900 A.M.E. Zion Church Conference meeting in Atlantic City she was ordained a deacon, and in August of that year she was a delegate to the Ecumenical Conference meeting in London. During this trip she also traveled to Scotland, France, and Belgium, speaking and lecturing.

Between 1897 and 1901, Randolph pastored several churches in New York City; Newark, New Jersey; and Poughkeepsie, New York. During her career, she pastored five churches in New Jersey, working without salary for the first twelve years. The churches to which she was assigned were small, poor, and struggling, with few members. Once the churches became solvent she would be replaced by a "nice young man" and reassigned to another "problem." Her last "problem" in her ministerial career was Wallace Chapel in Summit, New Jersey, where she served for twenty-one years. Serving as pastor of this church from 1925 to her retirement in 1946, she continued as Pastor Emeritus until her death in 1951.

Randolph's work with the Women's Christian Temperance Union (WCTU), as an organizer and lecturer against the liquor traffic, influenced her ministerial thought and style. Working in this capacity until after the repeal of the Eighteenth Amendment in 1933, she reflected the fiery zeal of the WCTU reformers. As a young minister, she was described as "a militant herald of temperance and righteousness. She adopted the technique of the period and fought fiercely and furiously." Her lectures and speeches were frequently direct in their attack on racism, colonialism, and sexism. Even though her public posture was strong and direct, and she spoke and worked on behalf of woman suffrage, she was accepted and supported by a number of men because of her feminine demeanor. In 1905, a reporter for T. Thomas Fortune's paper, the *New York Age* stated that: "Her sermons, lectures and public addresses are all the more attractive and impressive because of the modest womanly manner in which they are delivered. In the pulpit, or on the platform she is always a woman, and when she speaks [she] has something to say." This public posture served her well throughout her career.

Very early in her career, Randolph became identified with educational and religious movements in Africa's interest. In 1921 and 1922 she traveled in Africa, spending many months as a missionary in Liberia and more than a year on the Gold Coast, lecturing, preaching, and studying conditions on the African continent. She made seven trips into the interior, traveling by truck, oxcart, canoe, and native carriers. She became well known in Africa for her work on behalf of the Quittah A.M.E. Zion Mission Sunday School and Varick Christian Endeavor Society. Randolph served as a preacher and teacher in Africa for thirteen months without salary, paying her own traveling expenses. Returning to the United States, she conducted a series of lectures designed to educate Americans about the conditions in Africa. She educated three African children, a native boy and two girls.

In 1912 Randolph's concern about the cause of foreign missions led to an appointment as the A.M.E. Zion Secretary of the Bureau. In 1916 she was elected President of the Women's Home and Foreign Missionary Society of the A.M.E. Zion Church, a post she held for twenty-five years. In addition to missionary work in the United States, her work included the fields of Demerara in South America and Africa. Most of the fund-raising for missionary work was conducted by women. Randolph always led in the raising of missionary money.

Florence Randolph's work in the A.M.E. Zion Church was singular and distinguished. In many ways she was a pioneer, expanding opportunities for women in the church through her achievements. Licensed as a local preacher in 1897, and ordained as a deacon in 1900, she was among the first black women to be ordained. She was the first woman to be made an elder in the New Jersey Conference and one of the first in the church. In 1933, Livingstone College bestowed upon her the honorary degree of Doctor of Divinity. She was the first woman of the A.M.E. Zion denomination to receive this honor from the college.

We have spoken at length about Randolph's work as a minister, missionary, and temperance worker. What about her work as an organizer? The New Jersey Federation of Colored Women's Clubs was organized by Randolph in 1915. Like most of her endeavors, the founding of the federation was influenced by her temperance work. Specifically, the federation was an outgrowth of a conference of women of color representing thirty societies of the WCTU of New Jersey, who met in October 1915 to develop plans for arousing greater interest in the temperance union movement among African Americans in the state. Randolph served for a number of years as the state president of the Temperance Union League, whose members included white and black women.

The National Association of Colored Women (NACW), founded in 1896, represented a coalition of women's clubs. To systematize and organize its work more efficiently, by 1915 the NACW had established state federations comprised of clubs within a state. Initially the New Jersey Federation was composed of temperance societies; later the ranks were increased by missionary societies and, by 1917, included any women's clubs "doing work for human betterment, church, civic, literary, business or political." In 1917, eighty-five clubs were enrolled with a combined membership of 2,616, and the objectives of the federation were expanded to meet the needs of its diverse membership. By 1924, the federation had fifty-six active clubs with a total membership of 3,500. It is significant to note that, of the thirty-six delegates represented at its eighth annual session convened in Atlantic City in October 1923, among the wives of lawyers, physicians, college professors, teachers, and businesswomen, a large number of the club representatives were domestics, and some were day workers.

During the early years, the work of the New Jersey Federation of Colored Women's Clubs was influenced by the philosophy of Randolph. While she served as founder and first President from 1915 to 1927, from 1927, and later as President Emeritus and a member of the board of trustees, she continued to influence organizational structure and policies. Moreover, her position as the national chaplain of the NACW and her extensive contacts and visibility provided her with leverage for a continued leadership role. Commenting on Randolph's leadership ability, a reporter for the *Southern Workman* covering the federation's convention in 1923 observed that: "She possesses unusual ability, tact, and cleverness, with a keen sense of humor. The effects of eight years of convention manipulation and education of delegates were plainly evident as one sat through the three days' proceedings."

What were the tenets of Randolph's leadership which influenced the development of the New Jersey Federation? First and foremost, she was an integrationist and a feminist. Having grown up in the stultifying racial climate of post-Civil War Charleston, South Carolina, she had witnessed segregation and discrimination during the years when Southern whites were attempting to define the new relationship between former slave and former master. Even though her family's class and status shielded her from some of the worst elements of racism, in her daily life she saw the evidence of abuse, neglect, and the omnipresent oppression of her people. One of the key themes of her life was the need to work for the elevation of the race and to stamp out racism. The lynching of a close family friend, Postmaster Crum, in Charleston during the late nineteenth century had convinced her that an all-out assault on lynching was necessary. Thus the federation was an ardent supporter of the antilynching campaign.

Randolph was very skillful in the use of politics to effect change. The New Jersey Federation established contacts and made known its concerns to elected state and national officials. Through its Legislative Department, it conducted studies of legislation pertinent to race and gender issues. Members were encouraged to seek appointments to key boards and commissions where they could influence policy making. Letters and appeals articulating the federation's concerns were sent to key political figures, and the press was skillfully utilized to publicize their activities and concerns.

Understanding the power of interracial coalitions, the federation frequently invited white women to work with them on public issues.

In 1919, the New Jersey Federation joined with an unspecified group of white women to present an appeal to President Woodrow Wilson to "personally interest himself in the adjustment of race differences in this country." The group told the President that "You have spent many months in France [negotiating the Treaty of Versailles] in an earnest effort for interracial harmony. We beg that you will give a like skillful attention to interracial harmony here." The appeal addressed specific concerns related to the riots occurring in cities throughout the nation. A number of riots occurred following charges of black men assaulting and raping white women. In the appeal the federation stated:

> We ask that the present system of quelling riots by the sending of white troops only to crush colored men into submission be abandoned and that a system of control of lawlessness more worthy of the undoubted patriotism and loyalty of colored soldiers be employed. Excuse for lynching colored men and for rioting against them is everywhere made on the ground that colored men assault white women's honor. As a student of American history you know that the story of assaults white men have made on colored women's honor is written on the faces of our race.

In support of black women, the white women told President Wilson:

> The excuse always presented for lynchings and maltreating colored men is the charge that white women are not safe where they are. We know, Mr. President, that colored women have not been safe in this country where white men are. As white women—representing the so-called victims of the racial situation—we call upon you for justice for black men and women.

The Reverend Florence Randolph's feminist leadership included work as a suffragist for the passage of the Nineteenth Amendment, and diverse efforts to elevate the status of women, particularly African-American women. For years she served as a member of the executive board of the New Jersey State Suffrage Association. Randolph was a key factor in securing ratification of the suffrage amendment, speaking before the state legislature in its behalf. Shortly after the passage of the Nineteenth Amendment, in 1920, she was invited by former governor Edward C.

Stokes, then chairman of the New Jersey Republican Party, to assist Mrs. Lillian Feichert, head of the Republican women's division, in organizing and leading the women of New Jersey in the Warren G. Harding presidential campaign. In the 1930s she became a candidate for nomination for assemblywoman on the Republican ticket.

An ardent believer in black history, Randolph joined the Negro History Movement engendered by Carter G. Woodson, and the founding of the Association for the Study of Negro Life and History in 1916. The federation was among the first of the New Jersey organizations to argue for African-American history and to sponsor programs during Negro History Week. In 1924 the federation, under the auspices of its Race History Department, held a statewide meeting to organize state activities for the celebration of Negro History Week.

Other issues addressed by the New Jersey Federation during Reverend Randolph's tenure included fund-raising for an educational fund for scholarships for students who excelled at the New Jersey Manual Training and Industrial School for Colored Youth at Bordentown; development of health programs; establishment of homes for underprivileged girls; demands that the state and national press exercise more responsibility in reporting news about African-Americans; appeals to Congress to enforce the Fourteenth and Fifteenth Amendments; and requests to the Attorney General and Department of Justice to abolish peonage.

Although the full dimensions of Randolph's work in the A.M.E. Zion Church and the New Jersey State Federation are yet to be known, she influenced the life of blacks and Americans through her ministry and her work, particularly in temperance and suffrage.

NOTES

An expanded biography of the Reverend Florence Spearing Randolph, along with her sermons, will appear in a forthcoming book by Bettye Collier-Thomas.

REFERENCES

Dickerson, Gloria H. and Hicks, J. Maurice, "Florence Spearing Randolph, 1866–1951," in *Past and Promise: Lives of New Jersey Women*, 1990. Metuchen, NJ: Scarecrow Press, 1990.

"Dr. Florence Randolph." *Star of Zion*, October 10, 1935.

Nichols, James L. *The New Progress of a Race*. Naperville, Illinois: J.L. Nichols & Company, 1929.

"Not to be Ministered Unto, But to Minister." Chicago *Defender*, December 11, 1937.

Richardson, Clement. *The National Cyclopedia of the Colored Race*. Vol. 1. Montgomery, Alabama: National Publishing Company, 1919.

"Rev. Florence Randolph Given Honorary Degree." New York *Age*, July 8, 1933.

"Useful Life of the Reverend Mrs. Florence Randolph." Baltimore *Afro-American*, September 28, 1912.

Who's Who in Colored America, 3rd ed. Brooklyn, NY: Who's Who in Colored America, 1932.

"Woman Missionary Honored by Zion." New York *Age*, June 1, 1916.

COLLECTIONS

The Reverend Florence Spearing Randolph's papers, sermons, and memorabilia are in the possession of Bettye Collier-Thomas.

PART 3

AFRICAN-AMERICAN WOMEN AND CHRISTIAN MISSIONS

11

RANDALL K. BURKETT

ELIZABETH MARS JOHNSON THOMSON (1807–1864): A RESEARCH NOTE

I am prompted by Mary S. Donovan's recent article, "Women and Mission: Towards a More Inclusive Historiography," (*Historical Magazine*, December 1984), to set aside for a moment my current research project and offer a sketch of a fascinating woman on whom much more research needs to be done. While compiling information on the first twenty-five men of African descent who were ordained in the Episcopal Church between 1795 and 1865, I have come upon a number of "and his wife" references which have been dutifully squirreled away for future investigation. Of particular interest were two women whose husbands enrolled in the African Mission School, formed in 1828 at Washington College (now Trinity College), Hartford.[1]

The African Mission School was a short-lived effort on behalf of Connecticut Episcopalians to develop a black leadership for the church in Liberia. In their Second Annual Report, directors of the school reported on the progress of the three formally enrolled students, Edward Jones, Gustavus V. Caesar and William Johnson. It also noted the following:

> The Board have also the satisfaction of announcing that much valuable assistance to the mission is anticipated from the labours of two females connected with it. One of them, the wife of Mr. Caesar, has for a year past received the benefit of the school; while the other is now engaged in one of the infant schools in Hartford, with the intention of making herself thoroughly acquainted with the system of instruction pursued in that institu-

tion. The value of having two female assistants, of highly respectable attainments and exemplary piety, to aid in conducting the primary schools, cannot be too highly appreciated; and the Board view with great satisfaction this addition to the effective strength of the Mission.[2]

I have had little luck in locating information on "the wife of Mr. Caesar,"[3] but a letter from Lydia H. Sigourney, published in the *African Repository* in July 1830, provides the key to identification of "the other" female. Mrs. Sigourney, one of the most widely read authors of the first half of the nineteenth century, was secretary of the Hartford Female African Society, which had been organized just one year after the African Mission School Society. Both associations supported the American Colonization Society, and Mrs. Sigourney reported the Hartford women had decided that the year's contributions should be expended to help pay the passage of freedwomen desirous of emigrating to Liberia. She also remarked that the annual meeting had been attended by a group of black women who were members of "The Charitable Society in the African Sunday School" at Hartford. These women, based in the Talcott Street (Presbyterian) Church, formed an auxiliary to Mrs. Sigourney's group and were also committed to the Colony of Liberia. Mrs. Sigourney wrote:

> The young woman who holds the offices of Treasurer, and third manager in this [Charitable] Society, is to go on to Liberia, the approaching Autumn, at the same time with three young men from the African School in this City, two of whom will officiate as Missionaries, and one as a Teacher. Betsy Mars, will I think, be a valuable inhabitant and assistant in the New Colony, being a capable and intelligent woman, and having been for some time engaged in the instruction of children of her own colour.[4]

Elizabeth Mars was born in Connecticut in November 1807. Her brother, James Mars, was born a slave in Canaan, Connecticut, in March 1790. From his short autobiography, *Life of James Mars, a Slave Born and Sold in Connecticut,* we learn that their father, Jupiter Mars, was a native of Columbia County, New York, and that he had at least five different owners, the last of whom was a clergyman named Thompson, pastor of a church in North Canaan, Connecticut. Their mother (name not mentioned) was born in Loudin County, Virginia, and was brought north with the other possessions of Thompson's wife. Elizabeth and James' parents were apparently of sturdy stock, as James writes,

My father was a man of considerable muscular strength, and was not easily frightened into obedience. I have heard my mother say she has often
seen her mother tied up and whipped until the blood ran across the floor
in the room where she was tied and whipped.[5]

Elizabeth was raised in the home of Thomas H. Gallaudet, the prominent
Hartford Congregationalist who founded the Asylum for the Deaf and Dumb
in that city in 1817.[6] She "became pious" at the age of sixteen and was educated by friends in Philadelphia. While in Philadelphia, she met the Quaker
philanthropist and ardent advocate of colonization, Elliott Cresson. A letter of
introduction for Cresson, written by two secretaries of the Domestic and Foreign Missionary Society (Jackson Kemper and Peter van Pelt, Jr.) in 1831,
stated that Cresson "has exhibited great kindness to some coloured members
of our communion who are about to embark for Africa; and has lately been instrumental in forming an association among a few ladies of the Society of
Friends for the purpose of sending out and supporting two excellent coloured
females, Episcopalians, as teachers of schools at Liberia."[7] These were, of
course, Mrs. [Elizabeth] Caesar and Elizabeth Mars.

Some time in 1830, Elizabeth Mars married William Johnson, the young
man who was studying at the African Mission School to be a teacher in
Liberia. In August 1830, the board of directors pronounced Gustavus Caesar and William Johnson fit for service in Liberia, respectively as minister
and as teacher. The Domestic and Foreign Missionary Society Board in
New York at first unanimously accepted the recommendations from their
Connecticut brethren and voted to send both couples, along with the
Amherst College graduate Edward Jones,[8] to Liberia. Problems soon developed, however, when Caesar and Johnson met with members of the foreign committee in New York. Serious questions were raised about their
academic qualifications; after the interview the committee expressed its
"heartfelt regret—that Mr. Caesar does not appear sufficiently well prepared for the profitable exercise of his ministry; and that Mr. Johnson is utterly destitute of those qualifications, which a teacher in the humblest
elementary department ought to possess."[9] They proposed that the appointment be suspended for three months and private tutoring be provided
for the two men; meanwhile, an appointment was arranged for Elizabeth
Johnson as assistant teacher at the Gaskill Street Coloured Infant School in
New York, where, according to minutes of the foreign committee, "She will
be expected to attend from 8 o'clock in the morning until the children have
left the School in the afternoon—to divide the exercises with the present
Teacher—to aid in cleansing the room and yard & keeping all things in per-

fect order—and to commence her duties on the 18th inst."[10] For this work she was to be paid at a rate of $100 per year.

However, problems continued to mount. One week after appointing her as teacher at the Gaskill Street School, committee members raised questions about a possible "want of attachment on the part of Mrs. Johnson to the mode of worship in the Protestant Episcopal Church," and the foreign committee decided to interview her on the matter. Two days later, at seven o'clock on a Friday night the interview took place.

> In reply to certain questions proposed to Mrs. Johnson, she informed the committee that for the last six years she had been a Communicant in the Presbyterian Church and still considering herself a member of that body of professing Christians—that she was more attached to the mode of worship in the Presbyterian Church than to that of any other—and had never conversed with any one but the Rev. Mr. Cesar (*sic*) in relation to the peculiarities of the Episcopal Church or read anything on the subject.[11]

The committee resolved to give several books to Mrs. Johnson, which she was to read carefully before reporting back to them. When still further complications arose, over the loyalty of Edward Jones to the cause of Liberia and to the Colonization Society with which the mission school was so intimately associated, the whole enterprise collapsed. The committee finally decided to revoke its connection with Jones, the Caesars, and the Johnsons.

In spite of the fact they no longer had the imprimatur of the Domestic and Foreign Missionary Society, the Johnsons and the Caesars resolved to go to Liberia. Gustavus Caesar had been ordained, along with Edward Jones, as deacon on 6 August and as priest on 6 September 1830 by Bishop Thomas C. Brownell of Connecticut. Only five Afro-Americans had been ordained in the Episcopal Church before them. The *African Repository* reported that the Caesars sailed for Liberia on the Brig *Criterion* on 2 August 1831, arriving in Monrovia three months later on 30 October, and the Johnsons left the following year.[12] Their arrival in Liberia denoted a significant black Episcopal presence in the tiny colony, in spite of the fact they were not formally recognized by the Episcopal Church as missionaries. Caesar did retain his connection with the diocese of Connecticut, appearing on the clergy list for the diocese in November 1834 (just prior to his death) as serving in Caldwell, Africa.[13]

William Johnson died within two weeks of his arrival in Liberia of the "acclimating fever," along with his infant son, William Johnson, Jr., and Elizabeth soon married another Episcopalian, James Madison Thomson, who had emigrated to Liberia in 1832. Thomson was born in Demerara (British Guyana) around 1806, was educated in England, and lived for a time in New York City, where he was a member of St. Philip's Church. Peter Williams, Jr., rector of St. Philip's, noted that he had given Thomson letters of recommendation and provided him with sufficient books so as "to enable him to introduce the Episcopal service" in Monrovia.[14] Thomson served as lay reader to the small group of Episcopalians in Monrovia, who formed themselves into a religious society under the title of St. James Church. They wrote to Episcopal authorities in the United States, requesting help in building a church, but insufficient funds were raised to make that possible.[15]

A long letter from Elizabeth Thomson to John Dillingham, Esq., dated 18 February 1834, provides a glimpse of her activities during her first three years in Liberia.

Honored Sir:

Three years have elapsed since I first promised to you faithfully, that I would write to you of my health and situation. You have doubtless heard of all my afflictions and misfortunes that I have met with, and I will mention none of them. My health is quite good now. I am troubled with nothing but the agues and fevers, now and then, which are common to this country. I have never regretted one moment coming to this place; although it is the astonishing mercy of God that my life is spared, when so many have fell on my right and left, and that God has made me, though unworthy to bear the name, an instrument in his hands of doing good. I have quite a flourishing school of about seventy children—about forty-five of them I teach on the infant school system. I find some of them quite apt and others who are quite dull. I have some native girls that learn very fast. All of them are spelling—three of them are writing—and one of them is quite fond of composing letters. Some of them, I think, are more intelligent than the Americans. I sometimes wish that my school consisted entirely of them—but you cannot get them from the country unless you pay something for them, and then their parents will often come and take them away. I had two little girls living with me, who I took much pride in, but as soon as they began to learn to talk English and sew, they took them away. I also had two Vie or Cape Mount boys. They are much more given to learning than any other tribe. The youngest is very smart. He has a taste for the book, and printing the alphabet and words of three or four letters. His father has sent for him, but I am loth to part with him.

The climate is very pleasant—not so warm as we imagine in America. The sun is very powerful in the middle of the day, but we always have a plenty of air, and sometimes it appears almost cold enough for a frost. There are but few people here from the north, but what are here appear to enjoy very good health. The expedition that came last from Charlestown, numbers of them died, but it was owing greatly to their imprudence, as well as the want of medical aid. The first attack was gentle, but the second, third and fourth relapses carried them off.

We have not had a very flourishing Sunday School since I have been here, but I have tried to keep my scholars together on the Sabbath. I have quite an interesting Bible Class, which I take much delight in. I never can regret the time that I spent in the Sabbath School in America. The knowledge I there received, I think I can now impart to others. We much want such a person as yourself, and then our Sabbath Schools would flourish. The other Schools continue, but I do not think they are making much progress, excepting the one taught by Mrs. Caesar, at Caldwell. There are one or two more settlements about to take place on the coast. Mr. T. my present husband has now gone to Cape Palmas to see the place. The Missionaries that lately arrived here are all sick, but not dangerous. We have lost one—the wife of Mr. Wright. Time will not allow me to say more. I hope I shall soon hear from you and the family, as I often think of the little girls. I beg an interest in your prayers; that I may continue faithful unto the end, and what I do do all to the glory of God, is the desire of Your most obedient servant.[16]

The same week that Elizabeth wrote to her friend in Pittsfield, her husband wrote a long letter to Bishop Thomas Brownell of Connecticut, requesting that he be considered a candidate for orders in that diocese. He reported that he had just moved with Dr. James Hall, agent of the Maryland State Colonization Society, to Cape Palmas, where he would serve as Hall's secretary. He also stated that he and his wife would welcome employment by the Episcopal Church as teachers of a school they were planning to establish in Cape Palmas. Accompanying Thomson's letter were testimonials signed by John B. Pinney, Gustavus V. Caesar, James Hall, John B. Russwurm, and other prominent residents of Monrovia.[17]

In both 1834 and 1835, James Thomson appeared as a candidate for orders in the diocese of Connecticut. In June 1835, the Executive Committee of the Domestic and Foreign Missionary Society appointed the Thomsons as teachers of a mission school in Cape Palmas.[18] Mount Vaughan School was begun in March 1836 and in late December, the medical missionary, Dr. Thomas S. Savage, was sent to join them. A sanguine report on the mission, and especially on the work of the Thomsons, was published in the 1837 proceedings of the Board of Missions:

At St. James' Hill, Mr. Thomson has been occupied since March 1836, in clearing and planting the land, three acres being already in provisions, in erecting a Mission house and building for the scholars, and in superintending the school. His family, in the mean time, continued at Harper, whither he has returned weekly, to spend Sunday, and where also, with his school, his family and a few others (says Dr. Savage,) "he pours out on the altar, which he has here consecrated to God, the sweet incense of prayer and thanksgiving." The Committee have no hesitation in approving the wisdom, good sense and persevering zeal, evinced in Mr. Thomson's preparatory measures, and notice his sacrifices in often denying himself and family, that the work might go on. In speaking of Mr. and Mrs. Thomson's early labors in the Mission, Dr. Savage remarks: "God has signally blessed our Mission in raising up such devoted servants. In their self-denying labors, he sends over a voice to the Church at home, for the prayer of faith—for persevering effort—for greater self-denial, and greater consecration of money, body, and soul, to the great work of Africa's redemption."[19]

Alas, these happy prospects were not fulfilled, for the very next year the foreign committee reported that "Circumstances affecting Mr. Thomson's standing as a religious teacher led to his removal from the Mission early the past year . . . on the facts being laid before them by Dr. Savage."[20] Mrs. Thomson promptly resigned her position as well.

James Thomson died in Liberia in December 1838. A deathbed reconciliation with the church may have paved the way for Elizabeth Thomson's return to service of the mission, as she was again listed among the mission staff at Cape Palmas by 1842. Her relationship to the Foreign Mission Society continued to be strained to the breaking point, however, as is evident from correspondence in the Mission Board Archives. In July 1845, Mrs. Thomson returned with her son, James Madison Thomson, Jr., to the United States, where she stayed for a number of months with her brother, James Mars, in Hartford. In a letter dated 29 July 1845, she requested financial assistance from funds being held for her by the Mission Board, stating that her brother's family was in straightened circumstances due to illness.[21] Receipt of these funds was acknowledged in a letter written twelve days later, and there is no further correspondence until 24 March 1846, when Mrs. Thomson wrote requesting the balance of funds in her account in the treasury of the Mission Board. To that short letter she appended the following note:

Your letter of last fall, and one of the present month, addressed to the Rev. George Burges (*sic*) of this City, have been presented to me by him, the information which they bore, of the Committee being decided not to send me out to the Mission again, was so unexpected, that it has thrown me into deep anxiety and regret. Having been engaged, and deeply interested in the Mission since early in the year of 1836. taught the first native *school*, witnessing its first risings with great interest. being a partaker of its joys and sorrows and ever being ready to lend a helping hand, while others have been sinking around me. My children being acquainted with the language and being consecrated to the Mission by their father. . . . Under these circumstances, I have not felt that I could conscientiously engage *anywhere else, especially* until (*sic*) I heard from the Missionaries in Africa, but as the Committee are *decided*, I shall be obliged to do so, as I do not wish to remain in this Country if a good opportunity offers me of returning.[22]

Subsequently Mrs. Thomson reluctantly accepted an offer from her husband's old friend, Dr. James Hall, and made arrangements to return to Cape Palmas under the auspices of Maryland in Africa.[23] Precisely what motivated the board to dismiss her we have been unable to determine, though a thorough search of the Foreign Mission minute books should reveal the basis for their actions. In any case, by September 1849, the board reversed its position and returned her to the missions staff, an affiliation she would retain until the end of her life. A tribute to both James and Elizabeth Thomson by Anna M. Scott, in her book *Day Dawn in Africa*, suggests the esteem with which the two were held by those "on the ground" in Liberia:

The Mount Vaughan buildings are beautifully located on a high hill, three miles back of Cape Palmas, commanding an extensive sea and land view. This mount was the first home of our missionaries in Western Africa. When Dr. T. S. Savage . . . arrived, on the 25th of December, 1836, he found here Mr. and Mrs. Thomson, actively and profitably engaged in teaching a school. . . . Mr. Thomson was instructed . . . to select such a spot as he should deem suitable for the establishment of a mission-school. After consulting with Dr. James Hall, then Governor of Liberia, and others, Mr. Thomson decided to locate the school at what is now called Mount Vaughan. This was the beginning of our missionary work at Cape Palmas. Few missionaries, white or colored, have labored more faithfully in the cause than Mr. and Mrs. Thomson. He has long since passed away to his reward, but she still remains, a blessing to the Mission.[24]

On 9 February 1854 the Thomson's only daughter, Mary Agnes, married Garretson W. Gibson, who had been among the first men ordained in

Liberia by its new bishop, John Payne.[25] Illness forced Mrs. Thomson to re-
tire from her work in Mount Vaughan that year, and in November 1855, her
daughter died of the epidemic that was afflicting the whole colony. The following year, Mrs. Thomson was able to return to work at Mount Vaughan,
but in December 1856, disaster struck when war broke out between
colonists and natives. "The natives retaliated by burning several unpro-
tected houses in the colony, and among them the Mission buildings at
Mount Vaughan. This occurred on Christmas evening. The principal suf-
ferers were Mrs. E. M. Thompson (*sic*) and the Rev. G. W. Gibson. The former lost everything except her clothes; the latter nearly all his personal
effects, including his library."[26]

In 1861, Elizabeth Thomson returned as a teacher at Mount Vaughan.
Illness forced her to resign this position the following year, and in 1863 she
was placed in charge of St. Mark's Hospital. She died there the following
year on 26 April 1864. The unusually detailed account of her death and her
funeral, as reported in the *Spirit of Missions* in August 1864, attests to the
extraordinary respect with which she was held throughout the community.
In part it read,

> During an unusually protracted life in Africa, Mrs. Thomson's course has
> been that of a consistent Christian, a faithful Christian teacher, and con-
> stant friend, so far as her ability extended, to all friendless persons. It
> was particularly toward orphans and little children that her lively sympa-
> thies seemed most to flow out to the extent of, and even beyond her
> means.
>
> She evidently sought not this word's goods but only how she could be
> useful. Her pastor, in his funeral address, well said she had been a mother
> in Israel, and a succorer of many, adding the fit apostolical words, "of my-
> self also." Only this last phrase should include every member of the mis-
> sion, who, during Mrs. Thomson's long connection with it, ever came in
> contact with her. The writer, during a missionary life, almost commensu-
> rate with hers, gratefully adds this testimony. More than this she needs
> not, would not desire to have said. Her own modest estimate of her ser-
> vices and of her faith, so perfectly corresponding with the unaffected
> tenor of her whole life, was well expressed in a few words to her pastor a
> few hours before her death. "I am conscious of many shortcomings and
> failures, but all my hope is in Jesus."[27]

Elizabeth Mars Johnson Thomson was a major figure in early Liberian
educational history, a figure in her own right, and not simply by virtue of

marriage. Indeed, her decision to go to Liberia appears to have preceded her decision to marry her first husband, William Johnson, and the deaths of her two husbands in no way deterred her life-long commitment to her educational work in the infant colony of Liberia. This is a point worth emphasizing, I think, since it builds upon and perhaps takes one step further Mary Donovan's call for the investigation of "the husband and wife as a missionary team."[28] She argues that the women were as crucial as the men in shaping the particular missions where they worked and that the women deserve equal attention if we are accurately to understand the process of mission. In the case at hand, it is clear that the woman was far more important and effective, over many years, than were the husbands with whom she served. A confidential letter written by Jackson Kemper, secretary of the Domestic and Foreign Missionary Society in March 1831, anticipated this very fact. Writing about the circumstances under which Gustavus Caesar and William Johnson would get to Liberia with their wives, even though not under the formal auspices of the Episcopal Church, Kemper wrote, "Both men are dull but worthy. They will make good settlers. Their wives I expect will prove to be by far the best teachers in the colony."[29] One cannot always count on such prescience among ecclesiastical bureaucrats (especially if they are male), and one can rarely hope to find it in writing. It is such tidbits, however, that make the researcher's heart leap for joy.

NOTES

1. Research for this article was made possible in part by a "Travel to Collections" grant from the National Endowment for the Humanities, awarded in 1984. Research was undertaken in the National Archives of the Episcopal Church, Austin, Texas. The author is grateful for the generous assistance provided by the Archives staff. I am also grateful to the College of the Holy Cross, which awarded a fellowship leave making possible the completion of this article. In addition to a collective biography of antebellum Black Episcopal clergy, I am currently preparing an article on the African Mission School.

2. *Report of the Board of Directors of the African Mission School Society* (Hartford: G. F. Olmsted, 1830), pp. 4–5. The African Mission School is discussed briefly in Vincent P. Franklin, "Education for Colonization: Attempts to Educate Free Blacks in the United States for Emigration to Africa, 1823–1833," *Journal of Negro Education* 43 (1974), 91–103.

3. Her first name was Elizabeth. On 24 June 1835, shortly after the death of her first husband, she married A. W. Anderson of Millsburg, a small village up the St. Paul River above Monrovia. *African Repository* 11 (1835), p. 343.

4. "Female African Society," *The African Repository, and Colonial Journal* 6 (1830), 150–154. I have been unable to locate in Hartford any records of the Female African Society, though two of its officers, Mrs. Mary Grew (President)

and Mrs. Ann E. Morton (Treasurer) were also officers of the Female Beneficent Society of Hartford, and a number of the women involved (including Mrs. Grew and Sarah and Ann Terry listed as Managers) had attended the Hartford Female Seminary, directed at this time by Catharine Beecher. Betsy Mars maintained her connection to and friendship with Lydia Sigourney throughout her life. In 1864 her son, when informing the Foreign Mission Board of his mother's death, requested that one person in the United States (Mrs. L. H. Sigourney) be apprised of his mother's passing. A.L.S. J. M. Thomson to Rev. S. D. Dennison, 16 May 1864, in Papers of the National Council (Domestic and Foreign Missionary Society), Liberia Records, RG 72—19, Episcopal Church Archives, Austin, Texas.

5. James Mars' *Life*, originally published in Hartford, 1864, is reprinted in Arna Bontemps, Introduction, *Five Black Lives* (Middletown, CT: Wesleyan University Press, 1971), pp. 35–58. See especially, pp. 38, 39 and 45. James Mars states that he "took a very prominent part in the organization of the Talcott Street Church" (p. 56), in which the Charitable Society was formed. David O. White states that "Probably the hardest working and most fervant Christian [J.W.C.] Pennington had in his church was James Mars . . . a deacon of the Talcott Street Church." In "The Fugitive Blacksmith of Hartford: James W. C. Pennington," *The Connecticut Historical Society Bulletin* 49 (1984), p. 12.

6. *Journal of the Proceedings of the Bishops, Clergy, and Laity, of the Protestant Episcopal Church . . . In a General Convention* (New York, 1835), p. 10.

7. A.L.S. Jackson Kemper and Peter van Pelt, Jr., to Dandeson Coates, Secretary of the Church Missionary Society, 19 July 1831, in Church Missionary Society Archives, London. In a letter from Jackson Kemper to New York clergyman Jonathan Wainwright, dated 16 April 1831, Kemper states, "Mr. Cresson has kindly interested himself in the welfare of Mrs. C. & Mrs. J. He has induced a few quaker ladies to appoint them teachers in Liberia at a salary of 200 to each." Copy in Jackson Kemper Papers, 11 G 109, State Historical Library, Madison, Wisconsin.

8. On Edward Jones (1808?–1865), see Hugh Hawkins' essay, "Edward Jones, Marginal Man," in David W. Wills and Richard Newman, eds., *Black Apostles at Home and Abroad; Afro-Americans and the Christian Mission from the Revolution to Reconstruction* (Boston: G. K. Hall & Co., 1982), pp. 243–253.

9. Foreign Committee Book of Records 1830–1835, entry for 27 September 1830, in Papers of the Domestic and Foreign Missionary Society, RG 41-28, Episcopal Church Archives, Austin, Texas.

10. *Ibid.*, entry for 10 November 1830.

11. Foreign Committee Book of Records 1830–1835, entries for 17 November and 19 November 1830.

12. *The African Repository, and Colonial Journal* 7 (1831), p. 217. The Johnson family arrived in Monrovia with a small contingent of emigrants on the schooner *Margaret Mercer* in 1833. See, U.S. Congress, Senate, Doc. 150, *Emigrants that Have Been Sent to the Colony of Liberia, Western Africa, by the American Colonization Society and its Auxiliaries, 10 September 1843, & c.* Public Document No. 9, 28th Cong, 2d Sess., 1845, p. 251. I am grateful to Tom L. Shick for bringing this valuable document to my attention.

13. George D. Browne was both right and wrong in concluding, with respect to the Caesars and the Johnsons, that "One thing is sure—after this time [1830] their names do not appear in the history of the Liberian Church." He was, of course, unaware of the connections provided through the life of Elizabeth Mars Johnson Thomson. See his "History of the Protestant Episcopal Mission in Liberia to 1838," *Historical Magazine of the Protestant Episcopal Church* 39 (1970), p. 20.

14. Thomson's name is frequently misspelled Thompson. Peter Williams, Jr., (1786–1840), the second Afro-American ordained in the Episcopal Church, describes his efforts on behalf of Thomson in *The African Repository, and Colonial Journal* 10 (1834), p. 187.

15. *Proceedings of the Domestic and Foreign Missionary Society of the Protestant Episcopal Church* (Philadelphia, 1835), pp. 41–42, which also contains biographical information on James Thomson.

16. *The African Repository, and Colonial Journal* 10 (1834), 188–189. John Dillingham (b.1797) was from Pittsfield, Massachusetts, the town to which James Mars moved from Hartford. I have been unable to locate further information on John Dillingham, but his brother Charles (1799–1834) graduated from Williams College in 1819 and helped Thomas Gallaudet to found the Asylum for the Deaf and Dumb in Hartford. Calvin Durfee, *Williams Biographical Annals* (Boston: Lee and Shepard, 1871), pp. 388–389.

The rate of mortality in Liberia among the early settlers was devastating. Tom W. Shick, in his excellent study *Behold the Promised Land; A History of Afro-American Settler Society in Nineteenth-Century Liberia* (Baltimore: The Johns Hopkins University Press, 1979, 1980), reports that although 4,571 Afro-Americans emigrated to Liberia between 1821 and 1843, only 2,388 persons survived in 1843 (including those born in the country). See esp. pp. 27, 28. An appalling average 22% of all emigrants died within their first year of arrival. Shick describes the system, alluded to in Mrs. Thomson's letter, whereby children of Africans were "pawned" to Afro-Americans, in order that they could be educated. "The ward system that evolved from this practice," Shick writes, "became an important channel of contact and communication between the settlers and their African neighbors." p. 31.

17. Both letters are found in Standing Committee Papers, Diocese of Connecticut, Hartford.

18. The Committee voted salaries of $500 to James Thomson and $200 to Elizabeth Thomson. Foreign Committee Book of Records, 1830–35, entry dated 9 July 1835 in RG 41-28, Episcopal Church Archives, Austin, Texas.

19. *Proceedings of the Board of Missions of the Protestant Episcopal Church* (New York, 1837), p. 101. See also E. F. Hening, *History of the African Mission of the Protestant Episcopal Church, with Memoirs of Deceased Missionaries, and Notices of Native Customs* (New York: Stanford and Swords, 1850), pp. 22–24.

20. *Proceedings of the Board of Missions of the Protestant Epicopal Church* (New York, 1838), p. 78. Penelope Campbell, in her book *Maryland in Africa; the Maryland State Colonization Society 1831–1857* (Urbana: U. of Illinois Press, 1971), reports that James Thomson was accused, though never convicted, of having seduced colonial and African girls (p. 169).

21. A.L.S. E. M. Thomson to P. P. Irving, 29 July 1845, in Liberia Records, RG 72-19, Episcopal Church Archives, Austin, Texas.

22. A.L.S. E. M. Thomson to P. P. Irving, 24 March 1846, Liberia Records, RG-19, Episcopal Church Archives, Austin, Texas. George Burgess, at this time rector of Christ Church, Hartford, was consecrated as the first bishop of the Diocese of Maine in 1847, a position he held until his death in 1866.

23. A.L.S. Elizabeth M. Thomson to P. P. irving, 30 March 1846, in Liberia Records, RG 72-19, Episcopal Church Archives, Austin, Texas. I have been unable to consult American Colonization Society or Maryland in Africa archives for correspondence with Mrs. Thomson.

24. Anna M. Scott, *Day Dawn in Africa; or, Progress of the Prot. Epis. Mission at Cape Palmas, West Africa* (New York, 1858), p. 156.

25. Garretson Walter Gibson (1832–1910) served as president of Liberia College in the early 1890s and became President of the Republic of Liberia in 1901. Born in Maryland, he emigrated with his family to Liberia in 1835 and returned to the United States in 1850, where he was tutored for the priesthood by the Rev. Dr. H.V.D. Johns, rector of Christ Church, Baltimore. See *Liberia* Bulletin No. 17 (November 1900), pp. 1–3.

26. *An Historical Sketch of the African Mission of the Protestant Episcopal Church in the U.S.A.* (New York, 1884), p. 25.

27. *The Spirit of Missions* (August 1864), pp. 214–215. Her physical stamina, probably inherited from her hardy slave parents, permitted her thirty-three long years of arduous service, a tenure approximated by only one other early 19th-century Episcopal missionary in Liberia, John Payne, the likely author of this obituary notice. Her tenure in West Africa was precisely matched by that of Edward Jones, who served in Sierra Leone, under the auspices of the Church Missionary Society, from 1831 until 1864. Jones left Sierra Leone that year, due to ill health, and travelled to England where he died the following year.

28. Mary S. Donovan, "Women and Mission: Towards a More Inclusive Historiography," *Historical Magazine of the Protestant Episcopal Church* 53 (1984), pp. 298–300.

29. Copy of a letter from Jackson Kemper to Rev. Dr. Ducachet, March 1831 in Jackson Kemper Papers, II G 98, State Historical Library, Madison, Wisconsin. There is much to be learned about this extraordinary woman, about her education in Philadelphia, her early work in Hartford and the type and format of schooling which she originated in Monrovia and elsewhere in Liberia. Most of the sources on her life and character are white and male in origin; there are a few of her letters in the Domestic Foreign Missionary Society Papers, but none that I have been able to locate addressed to her family, to other Afro-Americans, or to Americo-Liberians. Some records may survive in Liberia; additional information would be found in a careful search of American Colonization Society and Maryland State Colonization Society Papers. Certainly, a thorough survey of the minutes of the Foreign Mission Board and other records in the Liberian Papers in the Episcopal Archives at Austin will yield further insight into her life and work.

After this article was completed, I came upon an extraordinarily interesting dissertation by Debra Lynn Newman which sheds substantial light on Elizabeth

Mars Thomson and the context within which she worked in Liberia. "The Emergence of Liberian Women in the Nineteenth Century" (Ph.D. Dissertation, Howard University, October 1984) provides access to a significant array of sources for understanding her life and work which it has not been possible to incorporate in the present essay. Newman's excellent study confirms, however, that Elizabeth Thomson was one of a handful of leading Liberian educators during the 19th century.

12

JUDITH WEISENFELD

"WHO IS SUFFICIENT FOR THESE THINGS?" SARA G. STANLEY AND THE AMERICAN MISSIONARY ASSOCIATION, 1864–1868

The literature dealing with those women and men who dedicated themselves to teaching the newly freed slaves in the South during Reconstruction has grown considerably in recent years. From W. E. B. DuBois's *Black Reconstruction in America* in 1935, with its positive depiction of the role of these teachers through Henry Lee Swint's 1941 work, *The Northern Teacher in the South,* with its negative stereotype, to more recent works, we now have a body of literature which has begun to examine this group in a more thorough and complex manner.[1] The general stereotype which often appears in the literature is of the missionary teacher as a white woman from New England, fresh from the abolitionist movement. While it is true that many teachers fit into this category, there were also many African-American teachers and missionaries, both women and men.[2] A good deal of the literature has dealt, at least briefly, with the ways in which African-American men functioned in the context of such organizations as the American Missionary Association (AMA). However, the experience of these men was different from that of African-American women, in part because these men were more likely to be given administrative positions in the organizations, either as principals, field agents, or supported missionaries. Most of the women, then, were more likely to remain "in the trenches" as teachers during their tenure with the missionary society.[3]

African-American women who worked in the field through the American Missionary Association during Reconstruction have not received the attention due them, in part because of the widely accepted stereotype of the Yankee schoolmarm. In addition, because they were not usually the administrators in these schools, their reports and letters to the home office were sent intermittently. Those African-American women whose teaching work through various religious organizations is more widely known, like Charlotte Forten, Mary Still, Mary Peake and Sara Jane Woodson Early, left extensive journals or monographs with which scholars can easily work. At first glance, it seems impossible to glean anything substantial from the few documents which other teachers left. However, the existence of this material calls out for attention. Using the letters to the American Missionary Association from one teacher, Sara G. Stanley, and her few other remaining documents, it is possible to present a sketch of her work with the AMA. Stanley was a thoughtful and complex individual and her career allows us a unique window on this missionary work. She leads us to ask questions concerning the dialectical nature of the relationship of these African-American women and their sponsoring missionary society. Stanley gained a great deal from her opportunity to work with the freedpeople under the auspices of this organization which had high religious ideals. She always remained in dialogue and in tension with the association, however, in ways in which white teachers and even African-American men, whose status in the work was higher, might not have felt necessary. Consideration of her perspective points the way to possibilities for further research to bring out the many voices of women like Sara Stanley.

In March of 1864 Sara Stanley, then twenty-eight, responded to the American Missionary Association's call for workers to aid the newly freed slaves in the South. In her application she wrote of her gratitude for the ability and privilege which God had given her and of how toil among the freedpeople would bring her nearer to God. She added, "My reasons for seeking to engage in the work of instructing the Freed people of the South are few and simple. I am myself a colored woman, bound to that ignorant, degraded, long enslaved race, by the ties of love and consanguinity, they are socially and politically, 'my people'." Stanley felt herself truly called by God to brave any "suffering and privation" and even death "to devote every power with which he has endowed me to the work of ameliorating [the former slaves'] condition." Her commitment to the freed slaves was obviously strong, as was her belief that the teachers, with God's help, could accomplish great things. "I feel assured, that an inscrutable providence has appointed a destiny far greater and more glorious [for the freedpeople] than any political charlatan or statesman has yet conceived of, such a testimony as Christian men and women rejoice to contemplate—of intellectual power and spiritual greatness." She expressed no particular concern for salary or location and wished to commit herself for as long as she was found "worthy and efficient."[4] Stanley was enthusiastically recommended by a number of people who certified that she was a church goer, intelligent, and a hard worker. Mr. Thomas Tucker, for example, wrote from Oberlin to George Whipple, the corresponding secretary of the AMA, that, "Ladies of color of high intellectual culture and personal accomplishment as she, can both serve the Freedmen as teachers and at the same time be a strong vindication before the Southern secessionists of the equality of the races."[5]

Stanley was sent to the mission in Norfolk, Virginia which was overseen, at the time, by Superintendent Professor Woodbury and William Coan. The AMA's involvement in education in Norfolk had begun in September of 1861 when the school run by Mary Peake, a free black woman, was brought under AMA auspices. As the work became more taxing, Peake became ill and finally died in February 1862. She was considered by AMA workers to be the first martyr for the cause, and replacements were sent in to build on her work.[6]

Only one of Stanley's letters from Norfolk to the central AMA office in New York describes her teaching activity in the mission school. It is possible, however, through letters written by some of her colleagues, to formulate a general sketch of what life was like at the Norfolk mission. Stanley herself wrote that, although the work was strenuous, both physically and emotionally, it was tremendously rewarding. She had expected to find the children to be more difficult to manage but wrote that they were instead "far more docile and tractable than I supposed possible for such illiterate and undisciplined children. . . . Through their affectionate nature, I find that they are very easily governed." Strong disciplinary measures were unnecessary because the children were committed to their studies and eager to learn. In this first report to the home office, Stanley outlined and emphasized her view of the role of the AMA and its teachers. Their mission, ordained by God, was to set these young people on the "paths of righteousness," to mold their minds for their future, both in this world and the next. As humans acting with human capacities alone, the work could not be accomplished, according to Stanley's vision. Only by relying completely on God would the workers be "sufficient for these things."[7]

Conditions during the war made missionary work difficult in Norfolk. This is clearly indicated in a letter of April 1864 from a white missionary teacher, Mary Burdick, who wrote of the negative influence of "the gay military." "I have been earnest in doing my part that the prayer-meetings should be sustained. *There* Sir I feel is our only safety," she wrote. In addition, the war caused the missionaries and the freed people to be moved from place to place, causing discontinuity in numbers at the meetings.[8] Another indication of conditions in Norfolk is given in a letter of June 1864 in which William Coan, one of the supervisors of the mission, wrote to the home office. "I write to you in haste—not wishing to frighten you or anyone, but simply to say that there is more than ordinary sickness here and I feel it due to you and every interest to advise that no more teachers be sent here before this Autumn."[9] The combination of the hard work and the southern climate caused many teachers not accustomed to either to take ill and some to die. Overcrowding was another feature of these schools, both day schools and Sunday religious instruction. In the postcript of William Coan's June 1864 letter, he noted that there were eight hundred in his Sabbath school that week. The April 1864 report from the school in which Sara Stanley taught, under the direction of Ms. M. E. Bassette, states that they had 250 different pupils in a building designed for 130, with average attendance at 195.[10]

In many of the letters from the Norfolk mission house, the teachers referred to themselves as being part of "the family." Ultimately, however, the Norfolk mission experienced many conflicts of personality and a significant clash of ideals. The year 1864 saw a clash between Prof. Woodbury and William Coan, the supervisors of the mission, which led them to discontinue contact with each other for a period of time. They eventually resolved the argument and began to work together again, but the incident created a tense environment for all the workers at the mission.[11] Such conflicts were not at all unusual given the close living quarters and difficult working conditions.

In the summer of 1864 an incident occurred in which Sara Stanley would become very involved. A white teacher from one of the other Virginia missions was on her way home and stopped en route in Norfolk. Edmonia Highgate, a black teacher at the mission, offered to share her room with the visitor, an acquaintance of hers. Samuel Walker, a white teacher, wrote to the home office that William Coan, one of the supervisors of the mission, was highly offended by this arrangement. Walker also noted that another white teacher, Mary Reed, was vocal in her support of Coan's position. Of the whole incident, Samuel Walker wrote, "I wish there was some way of testing the Anti-Slavery views of our teachers before coming here so they might practice what they preach."[12] For her part, Mary Reed wrote candidly to George Whipple in the home office, emphasizing her honesty in this matter, saying, "I remember saying that I came from home expecting to make sacrifices and great ones too for these people but that I did not anticipate living with them as we do here. . . . Recently, they with their friends have sometimes outnumbered us at the table and assumed so much that I have *almost thought* that persons who said, 'Give them the opportunity and they will take advantage of your very kindness' were right."[13]

The response by William Coan and Mary Reed to this "incident" enraged Sara Stanley and Edmonia Highgate. Stanley wrote to Prof. Woodbury, who was in New York at the time, that Coan, with his "peculiar secession, pro-Slavery and Christian negro-hating principles" was seriously damaging the work of the mission. Her protest was framed in terms of Coan's faithlessness to the gospel message. Quoting a comment which John Brown once made about a southern clergyman, she said, "He needs to learn the A.B.C. of Christianity."[14] She insisted that the underlying "motive to action" for missionaries must be "God is man, Christ clothed in the habiliments of flesh, the Son of God in the person of a negro." Arguing that, under other circumstances, individuals should be free to choose their acquaintances, Stanley emphasized the extraordinary nature of their situation at the time. "He has no right to pursue any course that will militate in the slightest degree against the Cause he professes to serve. For the success of our efforts there should be a Christian unity and sociality among the laborers."[15] Coan was ultimately transferred to another mission station as a result of the incident, but not dismissed as American Missionary Association ideals and rules actually required.[16] This, too, Stanley protested, but Coan was allowed to continue his work.

Some months later, Stanley wrote to George Whipple in New York of a Miss Gleason and her racist tendencies. Gleason had demanded that all of the African-American teachers be moved from the mission house because she did not desire to live with them. Stanley was particularly shocked because, having often been mistaken for white, she had been completely unaware that her presence was considered "obnoxious" to anyone. If Gleason had not been told that Stanley was black, she could never have known to be offended by her presence, Stanley commented. "Oh the profound wisdom of this prejudice against color!" she exclaimed, "When one half shade difference is to determine whether an individual is to be respected or despised." Again, she was shocked that so-called Christians, claiming to labor in the name of Christ, could display such attitudes. Stanley wrote that she would have liked to excuse Gleason on the basis of the influence of the woman's past surroundings and lack of "intellectual training." She argued that this would be destructive to the cause, however, because society as a whole cannot express right principles if individuals do not. "Oh! . . . if we could have in this work only earnest, humble, true hearted Christians—regarding all mankind as brothers, God's children, Christ's redeemed, feeling not that the great desire of all hearts should be to near a Saxon complexion."[17] Edmonia Highgate added a postcript to this letter, stating her agreement with all that Stanley had expressed and underlining that their protest was not to any attack on themselves, but to an attack on their divinely ordained mission. Sara Stanley posed a strong challenge to the well-intentioned northern white missionaries with whom she worked. In challenging these particular workers in Norfolk to "practice what they preach," she was ultimately disappointed by their inability to rise to that challenge. Stanley's experience of the racism of co-workers was, by no means, an uncommon occurrence for black teachers in the South.

Blanche Harris, another Oberlin graduate, who had been principal of an AMA experimental school run by African-American teachers in Norfolk in 1863, was forced to resign in April of 1864 for health reasons. When she recovered, she requested to return to Norfolk but was sent, along with her sister, to Natchez, Mississippi instead. She wrote to the home office that the black teachers in Natchez were left to their own devices and the aid of the black community to find lodging and pay their board. They did not even receive assistance in finding a school room or supplies. "The distinction between the two classes of teachers [white and colored]," she wrote, "is so marked that it is the topic of conversation among the better class of colored people."[18]

Two months later Harris wrote that she had been ill for a week when Superintendent Wright from the mission house in Natchez (where the white teachers lived) insisted that her board was too expensive for the association to pay while she was ill and that she must move into the mission house. There were strict conditions attached to this, however. "I would be obliged to room with two of the domestics, and . . . I must not expect to eat at the first table [when the white teachers ate], and might come into the sitting room sometimes. My room was to be my home."[19] Superintendent Wright also asserted that the black teachers "could not compare with the white ladies" and, thus, did not deserve to have a school of their own. Only with the help of the local black community was Harris able to avoid the degradation of being secluded in a room at the mission house or being transferred to a much more dangerous back woods location. She formally requested to be transferred back to the Atlantic coast a number of times. One year later Harris, frustrated and discouraged, resigned from the AMA and went to North Carolina as a teacher for the Society of Friends.[20]

Sallie Daffin, one of the staff members in Harris's Norfolk school, later had a similar experience in North Carolina where she was made to board with a black family because it was felt that her presence would create tension in the mission house.[21] It was also sometimes charged that the AMA purposely did not send black teachers to urban east coast areas but sent them instead to places like Natchez, Mississippi and Mobile, Alabama, situations which were certainly more difficult and extremely dangerous for African-American women alone. Edmonia Highgate, whose health forced her to take a leave of absence from her work in Virginia in 1864, requested to return there early in 1865. The AMA sent her instead to Darlington, Maryland to teach in a school with thirty-four students. She complained, saying that it was not her "duty to stay here in the woods" for such a small school when many schools had few teachers and hundreds of pupils. "Colored teachers when *imbued* with the right *spirit and properly qualified* [should be] *in the front ranks of this work.*"[22] Highgate was ultimately successful in obtaining a transfer and became principal of a school in New Orleans. Many black teachers who were not as forceful remained "in the woods." Highgate continued to encounter difficulties with white AMA workers, as did Stanley. In 1869 and 1870 Highgate worked as a lecturer and fundraiser for the AMA. In a speech in 1870 she discussed the consequences of this racism for the school children. "Even in the instruction given to the ignorant there lacks some of the main essentials of right instruction. The teachers sent out by the evangelical organizations do very little to remove caste-prejudice, the twin sister of slavery. We need *Anti-Slavery* teachers who will show that it is safe to do right."[23]

Many of the African-American teachers in the American Missionary Association related their experiences of racism to the home office but few did so as strongly as Sara Stanley. Perhaps her perceived "haugtiness" and outspoken nature caused her downfall at Norfolk, for Miss Gleason and Clara Duncan, another black teacher and Oberlin graduate, soon turned against her.[24] Clara Duncan "found" a letter in Stanley's trunk and wrote to George Whipple in the home office about it. He, in turn, wrote to Gleason concerning the disturbing contents of that letter. Gleason then went into Stanley's trunk and mailed the letters she found to Whipple. While the details of this incident are not clear and the contents of the letter unknown, it seems that Stanley was involved with Samuel Walker, a married white teacher. He had also been a vocal defender of the rights of the black teachers at the mission. Walker stated that "his efforts had been solely to protect her [Stanley] from the animosity of others." Walker resigned his post at this time over this incident and also stated that other teachers had charged that he had been squandering AMA money on travel.[25] Stanley was removed from the situation but not deemed unfit for future AMA service.[26] Two months later she was sent to St. Louis, Missouri.

This assignment was very different from Norfolk, primarily because Stanley now taught in a free school paid for by the local Colored Board of Education. The Board did not have access to great funds and, thus, the school was situated in a dingy church basement which lacked many of the necessary supplies. Stanley was greatly impressed, however, by the warmth and gratitude of the members of the Board and the black community in general, as well as by their determination to establish a sound school system under their own control.[27] The Colored Board in St. Louis had been working in conjunction with the AMA since 1863. A white AMA agent supervised the city schools and paid out the Board's money in salaries to the AMA teachers. This agent, George Candee, desired to place "superior" white teachers in the schools but the Board refused to allow this. Candee concluded from this that, "The colored people are exceedingly jealous of the whites; they hate them."[28]

The Board put full confidence in Stanley and her abilities as a teacher. She described her students in St. Louis as "scrupulously clean," some as well dressed as northerners. Many of the children were from families which had been free before the war. Others were poor orphans and the majority were of mixed parentage. Stanley noted, "the great preponderance of the mulattoes over the blacks immediately arrests the attention of the spectator. Of the whole number (one hundred) there are not I think twenty blacks. The caucasian element is largely ascendant, many of the children have blond and red hair and the peculiarly white transparent complexion which is their usual accompaniment. A woeful commentary on the hideous iniquity of Slavery."[29]

The poverty of the school prevented Stanley from creating the kind of atmosphere she would have liked to provide for her students. "An airy, cheerful, attractive schoolroom I have always considered essential to the success of a school, and to the proper moral and intellectual culture, as well as the physical well being of the pupils. Its importance cannot be overrated."[30] She was eventually able to obtain a blackboard and some maps. Working without supplies posed a challenge to her imagination which she grappled with constantly. All of her students soon were able to read using McGuffy's readers and she also taught geography, grammar, and mental arithmetic. The rapid progress of the students she humbly attributed to their own efforts.

Stanley also ran a Sabbath school in St. Louis with a large number of devoted children. "I am much encouraged by the interest manifested by my scholars in their book, and their industrious application and by the earnest endeavor of many to talk humbly to God. I have enjoyed precious hours of prayer with my little ones, and the Spirit of God has been with us."[31] Stanley felt a great sense of accomplishment in both the spiritual and academic progress of her students and was proud to convey this to other AMA workers. She wrote for the *American Missionary,* the AMA's monthly magazine, of one boy, bitter from his experience as a slave and "a hardened sinner." He was converted and set himself to train "to preach the gospel to his people." He soon found that he could not pay for school and felt that the Savior had abandoned him. Fortunately, "kind Christian friends" provided the money for him to continue.[32]

In May of 1865, two months after Stanley first began to teach in St. Louis, the free schools run by the Colored Board of Education closed and she was asked to oversee a school for which tuition was charged. She accepted the position but in July the state legislature made provisions for free schools beginning the following fall. Stanley wrote to the AMA that she could not be part of this new school system "as teachers will be provided in the fall by the Board of Directors (white) of Public School, whose preference, it is presumed, will be for indigent females of their own state, whom the rebellion impoverished."[33] Stanley left this post in debt, in part because the AMA had been negligent in sending the salary and travel expenses owed her. She had also refused to accept tuition from indigent parents when "their utmost endeavors were necessary to provide for their daily wants."[34]

Stanley's next position was in Louisville, Kentucky. The school there was also under the direction of a Colored Board of Education, but was not free. She noted that, unfortunately, this meant that only those families with money beyond what was needed for basics could afford to send their children to school. Her description of Louisville shows the limitation of the work of benevolent associations in comparison with the great need. "Hundreds of filthy, squalid untaught children are to be seen about on the streets, apparently indifferent to their wretched condition, because hopeless of any effort being made for its mitigation, or the hand of Christian charity being extended for their relief. . . . The brutalizing influence of slavery remains stamped upon mind and soul in its pristine horror."[35] The neglect of this city by benevolent associations made Stanley's work much more difficult, but her reports show great progress. She had charge of eighty students who required a great deal of attention and effort which Stanley reported she was happy to give. Her efforts were rewarded and in May of 1866 she was appointed principal of her school. Held in the basement of the Colored Methodist Church, the school had grown in a few months from eighty to one hundred and ninety. Her pride in this achievement was evident when she wrote that even whites who were "originally 'secesh' " [secessionists] were pleased with the "order, decorum and general proficiency of the pupils."[36]

The progress in Louisville was primarily in the area of academic endeavor, and Stanley wrote to the AMA that in terms of religious education, she had made little progress. Her assessment of the situation was that the students would only convert at "exciting revivals." Gradual instruction and exposure to the Bible did not effect conversions in her experience. She wrote that "the idea seemed to be inherent with them, that the duty of Christians consists primarily in boisterous prayers and weird singing and shouting, which characterizes the worship of their elders. Many of the freed people in this portion of Kentucky have but little conception of practical religion; with them religion is theoretical or emotional and manifests itself in noisy and demonstrative praise, rather than in pure and upright living."[37] Unfortunately, again, Stanley did not have the opportunity to be with these students over an extended period to convert them to her religious perspective. The school was taken over by a public school system, run by the Freedmen's Bureau and paid for by taxes on the property of black residents.[38]

After a gap of two years, Stanley again took a position with the AMA, this time in Mobile, Alabama.[39] A great conflict developed here when Stanley made plans to marry Charles Woodward, a white war veteran. She had initially intended to postpone the marriage until after the school year was completed, but her health had made it impossible for her to continue teaching. Mr. Putnam, a white AMA worker in Mobile, threatened to resign if the marriage took place. A great deal of his objection had to do with the performance of the wedding ceremony in the Mission House for fear it would "create a talk." He also claimed that the black community would object to the marriage. Stanley vehemently denied that the black community viewed this marriage in the same way that Mr. Putnam did and wrote that prominent members of the community would have made public Putnam's attitudes had Mr. Woodward not asked them to refrain. The Mission House was her home and she refused "to be required to skulk away as if I were committing a crime."[40] Stanley and Woodward were not married in the Mission House, but in a friend's home in Mobile. With this, Stanley ended her career as a fieldworker for the AMA.[41] The marriage did not cause a stir in Mobile and the Woodwards remained there for some years while they worked as cashier and assistant cashier for the Freedman's Bank.[42]

In many ways Sara Stanley's short career as a teacher for the American Missionary Association is typical when compared to the careers of white teachers during the same period. She was a young, unmarried evangelical Christian, educated at Oberlin College, the training ground for many of the AMA's teachers and administrators. She adhered to a view which saw the role of the teacher as "uplifting" the freedpeople to a level which would qualify them to become full citizens and with this came a measure of paternalism on her part. However similar her experience may appear to be to those of white teachers, Sara Stanley was an African-American woman from the South with a unique family background which provides us with a special window on Reconstruction missionary work.

Sara G. Stanley was born in New Bern, North Carolina in 1836 to a prominent free, "brown" family. Her grandfather, John Carruthers Stanley, was born a slave in 1722 in North Carolina, the son of an Ibo slave woman and a wealthy white man, John Wright Stanley. John Wright Stanley was a planter, a shipper, a lawyer, and one of the founding fathers of New Bern.[43] Interestingly, it was not the typical master-slave relationship which resulted in the birth. John Carruthers Stanley's mother was not owned by his father, but by Mrs. Lydia Carruthers Stewart who eventually manumitted the child in 1798 for faithful service. John Wright Stanley did acknowledge his son, however, leaving him an inheritance which was divided with other "illegitimate" heirs as well as with the "legitimate" heirs.[44]

A local historian wrote that, after this, John Carruthers Stanley, "By his industry and speculations . . . acquired a large property, consisting of two or three plantations, about sixty slaves, and some houses in New Bern."[45] He also ran a barber shop in town. By 1816, he had freed twenty slaves, including his wife, their two children and his wife's brother.[46] Most of the slaves which Stanley held worked on one of his plantations or were mortgaged out to other plantation owners. By 1830 Stanley was the largest slave owner in the county and extraordinarily wealthy when compared with other free people of color in the South at the time and many whites as well.[47]

Members of the Stanley family were also leaders in the religious community of New Bern. Sara's grandmother, Kitty, was listed as one of "The Thirteen," those present at the first meeting of the Presbyterian church in New Bern. When a permanent structure was built, the Stanley family purchased two pews (in the rear of the church) for 150 dollars each, placing them among the founding members and the few who could afford a family pew.[48] Sara's parents, John Stewart Stanley and Frances Griffith Stanley, had six children and operated a school for free blacks in New Bern, as well as a store.[49] The family continued to acquire and own slaves in New Bern and the vicinity and John Stewart Stanley managed one of his father's plantations. The Stanley families, white and black, were well respected members of the New Bern community and John Carruthers Stanley maintained a good relationship with prominent white citizens. John Carruthers Stanley was even designated the executor and trustee of the estates of white neighbors. He was also called upon at one point to rescue his white half-brother, John Stanley, from financial difficulties.[50] The Stanleys were also connected to a network of African-American families of New Bern which would achieve some status after the war.[51]

After preparing at her parents' school, Sara Stanley went on, at the age of sixteen, to study at Oberlin College. While she was there her family also moved to Ohio, first to a town called Delaware and later to Cleveland.[52] She remained at Oberlin for three years as a student in the college level "Ladies' Course." Stanley received her teacher's certificate in 1857 and then taught for a number of years in the public schools of Ohio before applying to teach in an American Missionary Association school.[53] A devout Presbyterian, Stanley's tenure at Oberlin prepared her, both academically and spiritually, for her position as an AMA worker. Stanley's religious convictions seem to be typical of northern evangelicals and abolitionists who committed themselves to work in the south after the Civil War. She articulated a strong criticism of America placed firmly in the context of the ideals of Christianity. In an address before an anti-slavery society in 1856, Stanley pressed the theme that America was failing in its claim to be a "Christian Democratic Confederacy." While its flag declared "Liberty and Independence—Free Government—Church and State," the "clank of chains on human limbs" indicated that "American religion [teaches] adoration to the demon Slavery, whom it denominates God." For Stanley, failure to act on behalf of the slaves could not be tolerated in light of this infidelity to the claim of Christian Democracy.[54] Stanley's answer to the AMA's call for teachers was one of the ways in which many people chose to act.

The reality of the work in the South for African-American women added another dimension to Stanley's view, however, which set her apart from white teachers. Almost from the outset, Stanley's interactions with white teachers forced her to realize that there was not always a connection between anti-slavery views and a willingness to view African Americans as truly human and as Christian brothers and sisters. Stanley never failed to make her position clear in situations in which white workers attempted to de-humanize African-American workers or the community in which they worked. For Stanley, the freed people often provided a much better example of true Christianity than the teachers sent by the missionary societies.

Stanley's emphasis on equality is clearly grounded in her Christian perspective, but it also grows out of her particular experience as a black Southerner. Although she was from a slave-holding family, she was unquestionably influenced by the brutality of slavery for both slave and owner and committed to abolition. In the midst of this paradox, her background in a family network of African-American and white members provided her with a unique experience of the real possibilities of a different kind of relationship between whites and African Americans, both in the South and the nation as a whole. Her perception of Reconstruction was one which saw it as a time of great promise in which her vision could be applied to create a new South, one in which all were accorded the rights of the true democratic America. Her role and her duty towards that end were to educate African Americans to assume their rightful position and she committed herself fully. Ultimately, Sara Stanley became disillusioned with the American Missionary Association as a means to carry out her vision. She respected the goals of the Association, but was continually forced to challenge the instruments used to achieve these goals: racist, paternalistic, "Christian negro-hating" white teachers.

Stanley always attributed the difficulties she encountered with the Association to racism and never to other factors such as anti-feminism, as other African-American women sometimes did.[55] From her activities as teacher in the south, it is clear that Stanley accepted an activist role for women in the work ahead. She decisively chose this work, this mission, over employment in a northern public school system. Stanley, however, does not seem to have been involved in the struggles of African-American women on the question of the "emancipation of the sex." Active in such organizations as the Ladies' Anti-Slavery Society of Delaware, Ohio, Stanley was certain that African-American women could find avenues to play a role in the work. Her abilities as a teacher were clear and she knew that she could advance the cause of obtaining equal rights of citizenship for her people. When she felt thwarted in this, it was because of racism.

One of the ways in which Stanley attempted to challenge the racism of many of the teachers was by providing stories of her experiences for the AMA's magazine, *American Missionary*, which presented the freed people in all of their complexity. She was a talented writer and saw the political uses of this talent.[56] One of these stories was used in the 1866 Annual Report of the Association. Stanley wrote of a white Northerner visiting her school:

> "Now, children," said he, "you don't think white people are any better than you because they have straight hair and white faces?" "No, sir," cried

> the children, with intuitive comprehension of the great truth uttered by Paul on Mars' hill. "No, they are no better, but they are different; they possess great power; they formed this great government; they control this vast country; they invent telegraphs and steamboats; they construct railroads and war steamers. Now, what makes them different from you?" The answer, "Education," seemed inevitable; but, instead, a chorus of little voices instantly responded, "*MONEY.*" "Yes," said the speaker, "but what enabled them to obtain it? *How* did they get that money?" A simultaneous shout burst forth, "Got it off us; stole it off we all."

Stanley concluded, "A different answer might have been returned, but hardly a truer one as applied to the people of the South." The AMA, in printing the story, diffused its power and attempted to force Stanley into its paternalistic framework by prefacing it as follows: "Miss Stanley furnishes a pleasant little sketch of negro logic and shrewdness."[57]

A close reading of Sara Stanley's few documents from her tenure as an AMA teacher, placed in the context of her family background, as well as the context of the Reconstruction South, reveals a woman in constant dialogue with the world around her. She returned to the South filled with the same ideals as northern white abolitionists. As Stanley became increasingly aware of the inability of many of these white workers to put their ideals into practice, she was forced to expand the scope of her mission. Not only was she required to provide the freed people with an education, but she also felt her duty to hold the American Missionary Association and its workers to their stated Christian ideals. This very real tension added to the difficulties Stanley faced in her work, as it must have for many other black teachers. Similar examinations of less well known African-American teachers, both male and female, would greatly add to the scholarship on the period and contribute to a more complex understanding of educational and missionary work among the freed people.

NOTES

I would like to thank Albert J. Raboteau, John F. Wilson, Martha Hodes, Dennis Dickerson, and Glenda Gilmore for their comments on earlier versions of this essay, which was presented at the December 1989 meeting of the American Society of Church History.

1. Among the works in this growing field are Clara DeBoer, "The Role of Afro-Americans in the Work of the American Missionary Association," (Ph.D. diss., Rutgers University, 1973); Robert C. Morris, *Reading, 'Riting and Recon-*

struction: the Education of Freedmen in the South, 1861–1970 (Chicago, 1976); Jacquelin Jones, *Soldiers of Light and Love: Northern Teachers and Georgia Blacks, 1865–1873* (Chapel Hill, 1980); Joe Richardson, *Christian Reconstruction: The American Missionary Association and Southern Blacks, 1861–1890* (Athens. Ga., 1986) and James D. Anderson, *The Education of Blacks in the South, 1860–1935* (Chapel Hill, 1988). Ellen NicKenzie Lawson's excellent collection, *The Three Sarahs: Documents of Antebellum Black College Women* (New York, 1984), introduced me to Sara Stanley's writings.

2. Clara DeBoer in "The Role of Afro-Americans in the Work of the American Missionary Association," states that of 467 black workers identified, 174 were women. The number of male workers is not necessarily the same as the number of male teachers. Some of those men included in her number were local or imported ministers whose church work was supported by the American Missionary Association. These ministers did not engage in teaching. DeBoer, p. 492.

3. See Morris, *Reading*, ch. 3, "The Black Teacher," in which he primarily deals with African-American men, many of whom were school principals, AMA field agents, or AMA-supported ministers.

4. Sara Stanley to American Missionary Association, 4 March 1864. American Missionary Association Archives, Amistad Research Center, Tulane University, New Orleans, La.

5. Thomas Tucker to George Whipple, 22 February 1864, AMA Archives.

6. Lewis C. Lockwood, *Mary S. Peake: The Colored Teacher at Fortress Monroe* (Boston, 1863).

7. Sara Stanley to George Whipple, 28 April 1864, AMA Archives.

8. Mary Burdick to George Whipple, 23 April 1864, AMA Archives.

9. William Coan to George Whipple, 12 June 1864, AMA Archives.

10. Monthly report of the Bute Street School, April 1864, AMA Archives.

11. This information comes from Mary Burdick's letters to George Whipple during 1864. AMA Archives.

12. Samuel Walker to Prof. Woodbury, 9 July 1864, AMA Archives. Apparently, Woodbury was visiting the home office in New York at the time and had left the mission to Coan.

13. Mary Reed to George Whipple, 18 July 1864, AMA Archives.

14. Sara Stanley to Prof. Woodbury, 21 July 1864, AMA Archives.

15. Sara Stanley to Prof. Woodbury, 29 August 1864, AMA Archives.

16. The list of qualifications to become an AMA teacher were: "A Missionary Spirit, Good Health, Energy, Culture and Common Sense, Good Personal Habits, Experience, Conquering of Prejudice." This last one was for the white teachers. The rules required that they do this or be dismissed. DeBoer, pp. 227–228.

17. Sara Stanley to George Whipple, 6 October 1864, AMA Archives.

18. Blanche Harris to the AMA, 23 January 1866, AMA Archives.

19. Blanche Harris to the AMA, 10 March 1866, AMA Archives.

20. Dorothy Sterling, ed. *We Are Your Sisters: Black Women in the Nineteenth Century* (New York, 1984), p. 277.

21. Richardson, *Christian Reconstruction,* p.206.

22. Edmonia G. Highgate to George Whipple, 13 April 1865, quoted in Richardson. *Christian Reconstruction,* p. 196.

23. Address of Edmonia G. Highgate to the Massachusetts Anti-Slavery Society, February 1870, quoted in Sterling, *We are Your Sisters,* p. 301.

24. George Whipple, who obviously admired and respected Stanley, and who she respected tremendously, considered her too "haughty" from the start. Sara Stanley to George Whipple, 25 March 1865, AMA Archives.

25. Captain Brown to George Whipple, 8 January 1865. Brown was from the Quartermaster's Office for Negro Affairs in Norfolk.

26. Miss Gleason to George Whipple, 6 January 1865; Captain Brown to George Whipple, 6 January, 1865; Captain Brown to George Whipple, 8 January 1865. AMA Archives.

27. Sara Stanley to George Whipple, 25 March 1865, AMA Archives.

28. George Candee to S. S. Jocelyn, 26 April 1864.

29. Sara Stanley, Formal Report from St. Louis, May 1865. AMA Archives.

30. Ibid.

31. Sara Stanley to the AMA, 9 June 1865. AMA Archives.

32. Sara Stanley, *American Missionary,* March 1867.

33. Sara Stanley to the AMA, 27 June 1865, 19 July 1865. AMA Archives.

34. Sara Stanley to the AMA, 10 July 1865; 1 August 1865. AMA Archives.

35. Sara Stanley, Formal Report from Louisville, Ky., March 1866. AMA Archives.

36. Ibid.; 7 June 1866. AMA Archives.

37. Sara Stanley, Formal Report from Louisville, Ky., 18 July 1866. AMA Archives.

38. Sara Stanley to the AMA, 7 June 1866. AMA Archives.

39. Stanley's health had begun to deteriorate during her work in St. Louis and continued to be taxed in Louisville. She might have been recovering and visiting her family during this period. Sara Stanley to the AMA, 19 July 1865; Formal Report, March 1866. AMA Archives.

40. Sara Stanley to the AMA, 6 April 1868; 2 May 1868. Jacob Shiperd to Mr. Putnam, 7 May 1868. AMA Archives.

41. Lawson, pp. 63–64. It appears that she taught in an AMA training school for black teachers for a short time.

42. Carl R. Osthaus, *Freedmen, Philanthropy and Fraud: A History of the Freedman's Savings Bank* (Chicago, 1976), p. 49.

43. Rev. L. C. Vass, *History of the Presbyterian Church in New Bern North Carolina,* (Richmond, VA, 1886), p. 73.

44. Another of John Wright Stanley's sons by a black woman, John P. Greene, became the first black legislator in Ohio. Lawson, p. 321.

45. Vass, *History,* p. 135.

46. John Hope Franklin, *The Free Negro in North Carolina, 1790–1860,* (Chapel Hill, 1943), pp. 31–32.

47. Loren Schweniger, "John Carruthers Stanly and the Anomaly of Black Slaveholding," *The North Carolina Historical Review* 67 (April, 1990): 177, 182. The family name was originally spelled Stanly.

48. Vass, *History,* p. 183 and chart following p. 126.

49. Lawson, p. 48.

50. The 1830 census shows the family as owning 163 slaves. Schweninger, pp. 177, 187; 184–186.

51. For an account of the path of one family which had been owned by John C. Stanly, see Glenda Elizabeth Gilmore, "Gender and Jim Crow: Sarah Dudley Pettey's North Carolina, 1876–1900," *North Carolina Historical Review*, forthcoming. Also see Lawson for information on the Hazle family of New Bern, pp. 46, 49, 309.

52. Lawson, pp. 49–51.

53. AMA archives, Brown Co., Ohio, 14 November 1857; Sara Stanley to the AMA, 19 January 1864. AMA Archives.

54. Sara G. Stanley, "Address of the Ladies' AntiSlavery Society of Delaware, Ohio," 1856 in Lawson, pp. 65–70.

55. See, for example, Lucy Stanton Day to the AMA, 21 May 1864. AMA Archives.

56. In addition to the "Address of the Ladies' Anti-Slavery Society," there is also extant an essay which Stanley wrote for the the *Weekly Anglo-African* in April of 1862 on the poetry of John G. Whittier. In this issue of the paper, she, along with Frances Ellen Watkins Harper and Mary Shadd Carry, was made an honorary member of a literary society of African-American men. See Lawson, p. 53, 70–79.

57. *American Missionary Association Twentieth Annual Report*, 1866, p. 40.

13

SANDY D. MARTIN

SPELMAN'S EMMA B. DELANEY AND THE AFRICAN MISSION

This essay seeks to examine, on a limited basis, the role of black women in the African mission movement, specifically as that role pertained to the use of black educational institutions as vehicles for such a movement. This study shall concentrate on Emma B. DeLaney, in relation to Spelman College, her alma mater, and her work as a missionary. DeLaney spent a total of eleven years in the African mission field (1902–1905, 1912–1920). Spelman College, founded in 1881 in Atlanta, enjoyed early the strong support of the American Baptist Home Missionary Society, a predominantly white, northern group, and the black Baptists of Georgia. Established as a school for black women, Spelman presents itself as an ideal case study for examining the role of Baptist women in the African mission field.

Such a story is significant from many standpoints. First, within the last decade, a number of secular historians have rediscovered the importance of studying the African mission movement as a key to a better understanding of African and Afro-American history. Second, students of American and, more specifically, Afro-American religion can profit from a more critical study of African missions, a long-neglected aspect of these two disciplines. For the African mission movement helps to explain both the self-concept of the black church in the United States, and the black church's concept of African religious systems. The evangelistic and educational dimensions of the African mission movement represent the most systematic and consistent connection between grassroots black America and Africa.

Third, this study is but another contribution that demonstrates the active participation of black women in Afro-American history. In this regard, increased attention must be devoted to the role of black women in promoting and supporting African missions, their service in the mission fields as comissionaries with their husbands, and, given the example of Emma B. DeLaney, their function as independent missionaries. Although not ordained ministers, many served the mission cause in the spheres of education. This was often the best means of securing converts. Finally, this paper will disclose the impact of black educational institutions in the promotion and support of African missions.

This study proceeds in two stages: (1) as a background on the development of the African mission movement among black Baptists in the nineteenth and early twentieth centuries; and (2) as a case study of the role of Emma B. DeLaney in African missions.

HISTORICAL DEVELOPMENT OF AFRICAN MISSIONS AMONG BLACK BAPTISTS[1]

Sustained African mission work by black American Baptists had its origins in the founding of the Richmond African Baptist Missionary Society in 1815. Throughout the antebellum period, black Baptists in Virginia spearheaded efforts to Christianize Africa by utilizing black American missionary-colonists settling in Liberia. They channeled these activities through the General Convention of the Baptist Denomination, or Triennial Convention founded in 1814 and, after it divided into northern and southern segments, the Southern Baptist Convention.

SPELMAN COLLEGE: EDUCATION AND AFRICAN MISSIONS

Various religious organizations and churches established a host of schools, institutes, and colleges for blacks during the 1865–1900 period. Some folded, but others have remained viable educational institutions. The American Missionary Association (AMA), mainly a Congregational group, founded colleges such as Fisk (Tennessee) and Tougaloo (Mississippi), in the 1860s. In 1867, the Episcopalians established St. Augustine's in North Carolina. The Northern Methodists founded Rust College (Mississippi), Morgan State (Maryland), and Clark College (Georgia), all by 1870. In the 1860s and 1880s,

Northern Baptists led the way in establishing schools such as Shaw University (North Carolina), Benedict College (South Carolina), and Morehouse and Spelman Colleges (Georgia).[2] Blacks, particularly ministers, played key roles in helping to collect funds for constructing and maintaining these schools.[3]

These educational institutions promoted African missions in a number of crucial ways. First, the schools themselves were missionary in character, founded for the purpose of educating and evangelizing blacks, often with the expressed desire of encouraging both domestic and African missionary sentiment. They also cultivated these interests in their students. Second, they trained future missionaries and mission supporters for work in Africa. Third, they served as a link between the Africans and Afro-Americans by educating many of the former and returning some of them to their home continent. Finally, many of these schools formed missionary support groups or societies which collected and dispensed funds for African missions in general and/or designated African missionaries.

Spelman College[4] is a prime example of the link between Baptist schools and African missions. Established as a place of learning for black girls and women, Spelman began with the tireless, committed efforts of two white, Northern Baptist women, Sophia B. Packard and Harriet E. Giles, and the black pastor of Friendship Baptist Church in Atlanta, the Reverend Frank Quarles. The school established a nurses' training department in 1886, a missionary's training department in 1891, a teachers' training department in 1892, and, in collaboration with the future Morehouse College, in 1897 began a liberal arts college curriculum. Beginning in very humble surroundings with two teachers and eleven students in the early 1880s, Spelman had grown to a teaching staff of forty-two and 700 students, with buildings having a total value of $350,000, by 1902.

In 1902, a writer for the college newspaper, the *Spelman Messenger*, articulated the purpose of the College:

> This is no ordinary educational enterprise. It exists primarily and pre-emi-
> nently for the formation of intelligent Christian character, and for the appli-
> cation of Christian principles, through its students, to all affairs of life, and
> in intercourse with all people. Its objective aims are to make better
> women, better wives, better mothers, better homes, better society, bet-
> ter schools, better churches, better citizens. . . .[5]

Mrs. M. C. Reynolds, the white corresponding secretary of the Woman's American Baptist Home Mission Society, wrote, "The loving Father by his tender providence has given you opportunities for service through education and culture."[6] It was clear to all that education at Spelman was always to be saturated with Christian ideals in the pursuit of Christian objectives. Put succinctly by Reynolds, "Education separated from Christ and his word is a curse. . . ."[7]

Graduates of Spelman have, over the years, voiced similar concerns. Mrs. Isabel Kelly Glenn, a 1917 Spelman graduate, agreed that one should be prepared, "both intellectually and morally," for one's profession. In her essay, "The Value of Education," Glenn envisioned education as vital to bridging the economic gulf between whites and blacks. She wrote, "Education, the basis upon which revolves the whole of progress, is not only the basic principle of civilization, but also the intermediary through which we place ourselves on a par with our supposed superiors."[8] Another Spelman graduate, Georgia M. Gilliard, who completed her high school work in 1917, also spoke of the connection between education and black progress. As had so many before her, Gilliard condemned slavery but saw it as "a necessary evil" in that it introduced blacks to, and prepared them for, participation in "the most advanced civilization of the world."[9] The astounding success of blacks in education, she felt, demonstrated their capacity to compete with whites and proved that they deserved emancipation. Although blacks owed a great debt to white pioneers in the education of Afro-Americans, Gilliard expressed pride in the progress blacks made in taking increasing responsibility for educating their own people.

It was quite easy for supporters of education for blacks to connect such a concern with that of African missions. Again, Reynolds of the Home Mission Society addressed the students on the connection between foreign and domestic work. "With the masses of colored people here or amid the dense darkness of Africa's millions you are called to labor. . . ."[10]

Lillie Belle Wilson, 1919 graduate of Spelman, exemplified this concern for African missions in an article, "Africa in the New Day," published in the October 1919 issue of the *Spelman Messenger*. Wilson, often recounting the sacrifices made during World War I, challenged her fellow Spelmanites to an even nobler goal than freedom—the redemption of the black motherland. Pressing needs of the age, she contended, were African Christianization and education "to hasten a new day for Africa."[11] Alluding to the sacrifices made by Spelman graduates on the African mission field, she asserted that women had a major responsibility in helping to bring these things to pass. She wrote:

> In order to bring about this new day, we, the women of today, must take the leading part. We, like our forerunners, must go as torch-bearers to the

dark shores of Africa and let our ministrations redeem her by leading her people to a higher plane of thought and action; by teaching them clearer views of life and duty; and by inspiring their souls with loftier aims.[12]

During this period, both liberal arts and industrial education were promoted by black Baptists. It is interesting, however, to observe the great emphasis placed upon industrial education in connection with African evangelism. In an essay, "The Relation of the Missionary Enterprise to Industrial Missions," Lucy Houghton Upton, a white woman who had served in various capacities at Spelman for twenty-two years, asserted that industrial education in particular suited the needs of Africa. Already in various parts of Africa, she contended, this type of training had produced amazing results, such as the banishment of famine among the "Kaffirs."[13] Backward people, she said, especially needed the type of education which

. . . teaches the dignity of labor . . . is a resource in times of persecution, is a help to self-respect and self-support, develops confidence and strength, and trains in diligence, honesty, and steadfastness of character: . . . it is indispensable in dealing with all backward races, for it lays the basis, for a better social order.[14]

Spelmanites, as well as other missionaries journeying to Africa, would attempt to transplant industrial education. For example, Emma B. DeLaney traveled to the interior of Liberia in 1912 and established the Seuhn Industrial Mission.[15]

A number of Spelman graduates became African missionaries between the 1880s and 1920s. Though some traveled to the Continent as co-missionaries with their husbands, others set sail as independent pioneers. By 1920, four black American women graduates of Spelman had served or were serving in the African mission field. In 1889, Nora A. Gordon began the missionary tradition at Spelman. After her death, the Reverend R. C. Gordon, her husband, married the former Ada Jackson. The second Mrs. Gordon died in service on the field in 1910. Miss Clara A. Howard, in 1891, traveled to Africa as an independent missionary. Two years later she had to leave the station at Lukungu, Congo, where she served with Nora Gordon, because of illness. But Clara Howard devoted much time at Spelman College, promoting and collecting funds for African missions. In 1902, Emma B. DeLaney continued the Spelman tradition, but unlike others who served in the Congo, she embarked for southern Africa.[16]

Not only did Spelmanites sail to Africa, Africans traveled to Spelman. By 1900, five African women had matriculated at Spelman. Two remained in the United States after completing their work. The others returned as missionaries to Africa. For example, Margaret Rattray and Lena Clark came to Spelman with the help of Clara Howard. Both returned to Africa. Lena Clark Whitman, after marrying a missionary, traveled to the Sudan. Rattray returned to the Congo and appeared to have been instrumental in directing Flora Zeto to the United States.[17] Emma B. DeLaney brought Daniel Malekebu from southern Africa to the United States. He and Zeto, who graduated from the high school department in 1915, married and returned as missionaries to southern Africa in the 1920s. Thus, they both fulfilled earlier plans to return to the motherland.[18] A writer in the January 1919 issue of the *Spelman Messenger* made an observation that was applicable not only to the Congo but also to southern and western Africa.

> This coming and going of Spelman girls to the Congo has brought the land very near to us, and the interest thus aroused is strengthened by the work of the Congo Mission Circle [at Spelman] under the direction of [former missionary] Miss Howard.[19]

EMMA B. DELANEY: A SPELMANITE IN AFRICA, 1901–1920

The missionary career of Miss Emma B. DeLaney vividly demonstrates the connection of the African mission movement, black Baptist educational institutions, and black women's role in the mission movement. DeLaney, originally of Fernandina Beach, Florida, attended Spelman College, graduated from the high school department in 1894 and the missionary training department in 1896. She completed nurse training in 1900. In 1902, the Florida native sailed to southern Africa under appointment of the Foreign Mission Board of the National Baptist Convention (NBC). She remained in the Chiradzulu area for three years. After returning to the United States in 1905, she expended considerable time and energy collecting funds for mission work in the African Republic of Liberia. In 1912, she once again journeyed to Africa, into the hinterlands of Liberia. There she founded the Seuhn Industrial Mission. In 1920, after eight years in Liberia, she left Africa for the last time. She died two years later.[20]

In the February 1902 issue of the *Spelman Messenger,* DeLaney set forth a few details about her personal life and her reasons for applying as a missionary to Africa. She said that, early in her life, her interest had been aroused by a returned missionary's accounts of his labors.[21] Could this returned missionary have been the Reverend E. B. Topp of Mississippi, who, in the early 1880s, served in West Africa? In February 1888, Topp came to Florida and spoke to the black Baptist General Convention about the significance of "sending the Gospel to the heathen in Africa." Whatever the identity of the missionary, DeLaney was touched by the event and, like the Baptists in Florida, could rhetorically ponder:

> Did not our hearts melt within us as he depicted the horrors of darkness that hang over our brethern in our Fatherland, and set forth the many reasons why we who have the light should send it to those who have it not?[22]

Her desire for personal service in Africa was enhanced after her conversion. During her twelve-year stay at Spelman, her desire intensified and her plans crystallized. After spending over three years in home mission work, she presented herself as an African mission candidate. DeLaney spoke in clear and strong terms on the influence that Spelman had upon the shaping of her final decision.

> After entering Spelman Seminary and spending twelve years there, where our duty to God and humanity, both at home and abroad, is daily set forth, the mere desire for the work was changed to duty and a longing for the work that nothing else would satisfy. . . ."[23]

Spelman, like many other black educational institutions, had indeed become a focal point for producing and encouraging both home and foreign mission activities.

DeLaney's statements indicate that she had wrestled intensely with her decision. Perhaps in reply to critics who charged that she was venturing far from home to do work much needed in this country, the future missionary stated that she did not consider work to be done at home less important, but she also knew that nine out of ten young women trained in missionary work would remain in the United States. She approached African missions realistically, seeking neither personal "gain" nor a "pleasure trip." Many of those dear to her advised her not to go. Probably the strongest objection came from her father. She knew that she was opposing "the bitterest protest of a father whose wishes have always been sacred."[24]

To sever ties with community, culture, and homeland requires a major, personal commitment and an abundance of courage. Most parents would undoubtedly find it difficult to encourage or consent to their children embarking upon a journey which would take them into parts unknown, especially to a place that was frequently regarded as barbaric, heathen, uncivilized, and godless. Such fears were often grounded on a well-known fact that many such persons died of sickness or other dangers in the field or returned in broken health. One could very well imagine the strength it took for DeLaney to elect such a course and the opposition she, as a woman, must have received, particularly at that point in history.[25]

The courage and strength required to make such a firm, unshakable commitment developed at least in part from her strong belief that "I go because I am commanded to go." DeLaney, like many others, was convinced that the church must do more for missions to save the "heathens" from their pitiful state. She was prepared to risk all, including her life and the disapprobation of a beloved father, to help redeem the lost.[26]

DeLaney's application was approved. With a strong commitment and faith in the necessity of her task, she set sail for Chiradzulu, then British Central Africa. Getting to her post was certainly not a simple task. She missed a steamship connection and had to remain in Capetown, South Africa, from February 18 until March 6. If she held any illusions that residing in Africa would shield her from the kind of racism and discrimination that blacks experienced in the United States, they soon disappeared. In dealing with the ticket office, she encountered adumbrations of the treatment that she, as many other black Americans, would face in southern, British-controlled Africa. She wrote of her experience:

> The agent gave me an order to three different places. I tried them and received the same answer from each. "We are crowded out." I soon saw this was a polite way of turning a Negro away. Let me say that there is as much prejudice in some places in Africa as in America. . . .[27]

Of course, during the next few years DeLaney would have ample opportunity to witness the pervasiveness and depth of white racism in British-ruled southern Africa. Indeed, other black missionaries noted the fear that the English government had regarding them. The government viewed them suspiciously as agents sent to ferment violent revolution against it. Indigenous ministers often had to place themselves under the supervision of white missionaries in order to secure adequate freedom of operation.[28] The white ministers themselves were often culprits in stifling black Baptist organizations in Africa. In the early 1900s, the National Baptist Convention (NBC) attempted to organize a South African Baptist Association working through indigenous Africans who had previously visited the United States. There were many white preachers who refused to support this mood of black independency within their denominations. Rather, they convinced the colonial government that these moves were part of the Ethiopian movement, which they envisioned as an attempt by the Africans to claim equality with whites and overthrow the white government.

> In many ways and many cases the government is now helping these white ministers to hold the black members within said denominations against a desire for their own. Those religious teachers have succeeded in scaring the masses of white people and put the government in position to guard with suspicion the coming of any American man of color.[29]

Miss DeLaney also attested to the environment of suspicion and harassment. Soon after her arrival, she noted "the inhuman treatment of the natives from the chief employees of steamer companies."[30] DeLaney also wrote from the field describing the ordeal of the Branch family, black American missionaries of the Adventist Church. The Branches had to persist in their efforts to be admitted into the area. They had to persuade the authorities that they were not part of a grand conspiracy to ferment revolution. Branch apparently convinced them that war and the Bible were not partners. Yet, DeLaney was not surprised at such anxiety on the part of the authorities. "[T]hey do treat the natives like beasts and they are afraid someone will come to oppose their way of doing. . . ."[31]

But, as noted earlier, the problems between the colonial government and the black missionaries did not dissipate with the latter's admission into the region. For a year, DeLaney called attention to a situation in which the government apparently sought to deprive the National Baptist Convention of mission land. Although her missionary colleague and senior, the Reverend L. N. Cheek, had been attempting to settle these matters, he, up to that time, had been unsuccessful.[32]

Beyond the problems with the government and white missionaries, black missionaries faced other fearsome challenges affecting mission work, personal safety, and health. Soon after her arrival, DeLaney felt herself succumbing to fever. At one point she mentioned in her letters that she contracted fever more than once every month. In 1903, John Chilembwe, an African missionary trained in the United States, shot a leopard near her quarters and advised her to close her windows for safety. For a while she also suffered from the lack of female companionship, since there was no "civilized" woman in the area.[33]

Despite such personal and social obstacles, DeLaney launched into her missionary tasks. One of her first goals was to learn the Nyanja language. She noted with sorrow the spiritual, medical, and social conditions of the Africans, especially the women. A letter in the January 1904 issue of the *Spelman Messenger* contains this quote from the missionary: "According to heathen customs the worst of everything must be put on women."[34] Her missionary zeal and her nurse training provided a good combination for her work. She lamented, in a letter dated December 11, 1902, the lack of means to accomplish the things she wanted to do. How can one talk about the love of Christ, she wondered, and not be able to demonstrate that concern because of the many medicinal services needed?[35]

Her attempts at Christianizing were often thwarted or, at least, resisted by those Africans who refused to renounce their beliefs and accept a foreign religion. Two Africans who converted to Christianity under DeLaney's influence were Daniel S. Malekebu and Anna Ruth Malekebu, brother and sister. In both cases, the family objected, and, in both situations, we see not only a conflict between religious beliefs and practices, but also between cultures and ways of life.[36] For one thing, Western Christianity took the convert out of the context of traditional, communal African lifestyles, often disrupting family and village obligations and relationships.

Daniel's family accused him of attempting to "follow the white people's customs." For this reason they opposed his training in the mission. Along with the British government, they also opposed his visit to the United States to get additional training. But, according to DeLaney, Daniel ran away with only a few shillings, walked 200 miles through dangerous forests of "lions, leopards and hyenas," and left with her for the United States on May 1, 1905. In 1906, Daniel urged American Baptists to assist him.

There was even greater resistance to his sister Anna Ruth's conversion and training.[37] Anna had been promised in marriage to a man between forty-five and fifty years old who had eight other wives. She was only eight years old at the time. Her father stated that he would rather cut her throat than allow her to accept a foreign religion. Because their mother refused to give both Anna and Daniel food after their baptism, they subsisted on rats and sometimes suffered from hunger. The children, however, never regretted their decision. When DeLaney left in 1905, Anna had to return to her village. It was DeLaney's hope that the girl would find another mission station to continue training.

During her stay in Africa, facing these ordeals and other challenges, De-Laney undoubtedly drew great strength from her continual communication with Spelman College. The missionary society at the college filled the gulf which a single woman in a strange land must have experienced. The college reminded her of the purpose of her sojourn, helping her to accept the meaning of her hardship and suffering. In her letters, she took pride in speaking of Spelman and "its pioneer workers" in Africa who sought to redeem non-Christians for Christ. From small efforts such as hers may come great things. "Who knows but this very work may grow to be a Spelman in Africa someday."[38] DeLaney hoped that Spelman would encourage others like herself to accept the challenge of African missions.

In 1905, after spending three years in Africa, DeLaney's term was completed and she returned home via the World Baptist Conference meeting that year. But, if entering Africa was difficult, leaving the region proved to be a humiliating experience. According to the NBC minutes of 1905, she was kept aboard ship five days "as a prisoner" and the American diplomatic team seemed to have been more of a hindrance than a help in securing her safe passage.

> The representative of the United States, who should have been her protector, seemed to lead in the plan to humiliate an American woman, traveling alone. The attention of the Secretary of State has been called to it. She was not an immigrant, but a first class passenger, and only transhipping allowing her eight or ten days lay-over in Durban.[39]

By August 2, 1905. DeLaney had arrived in the United States and began activities in support of African missions. Weighing fifty pounds less than she had three years earlier and plagued with "fever," she nevertheless continued to appeal for financial help to evangelize Africa.[40] Her appeals were relatively successful. During the first four years of her return, DeLaney had raised twice the sum needed to pay her salary. Therefore, she aided other prospective missionaries and other mission activities. The 1912 minutes of the NBC stated that "no returned missionary has rendered better service than she."[41]

DELANEY RETURNS TO AFRICA

In June 1912, DeLaney once again embarked upon the African mission field, this time to the hinterland of Liberia, on the West Coast of Africa, about forty miles from the capital city of Monrovia. She was accompanied by Miss Susie

M. Taylor of Camden, South Carolina. Taylor, a graduate of Schofield Seminary in South Carolina, had received missionary training in New York State.[42] Upon arrival in Liberia, Taylor joined another independent woman missionary, Eliza L. Davis of Texas, who was stationed in the Grand Bassa, approximately sixty miles from Monrovia. Together, they began to lay plans for the construction of a school and continued the evangelistic work already started by Davis. By March 1915, however, Taylor was ordered home "because of ill health."[43]

True to character, Emma B. DeLaney traveled alone to the interior, where she founded the mission site, the Seuhn Industrial Mission. Her goals in Liberia, therefore, would not simply be evangelistic, but would also entail training local people along the lines of industrial education, such as cooking and sewing. During the next eight years she encountered many adversities: sickness, theft, isolation, war, resistance to her evangelistic efforts, and, of course, the perennial problem of black missionaries, a lack of funds. She was also concerned because the government seemed unable to control the many indigenous peoples in the interior. According to the missionary, "Things go slow in any part of Africa, but this republic caps the climax."[44]

Missionaries often encountered difficult obstacles, and DeLaney found that her tenure in West Africa met with resistance similar to what she had faced in southern Africa. In 1916, four years into her sojourn there, she wrote that her mission was the first of its type in that area. Perhaps she had received inquiries concerning a perceived lack of missionary success. The likelihood of quick acceptance was not very bright, considering the strong hold Islam had upon people there. DeLaney spoke of an indigenous missionary worker who, with other Christians, when attempting to hold religious services, was chased out of the village. DeLaney and her group had not suffered such forthright antagonism, but had seen people leave during her services.[45]

DeLaney complained about the lack of funds to carry out her work. She needed more food and space to increase the number of children, then sixty-seven in number, in the mission site. Much of DeLaney's financial problem was caused by the disruption in commerce and mail—an effect of World War I. As the missionary herself penned in the same letter:

> The cruel war has almost separated me entirely from my friends. Letters have been sent, but never received. So much mail has been destroyed in this past year.[46]

Later in 1916, DeLaney wrote "We are almost in the midst of a famine." Apparently the ravages of international conflict had taken their toll even in Liberia. Her mission school had increased to eighty-four children but all except twenty-nine were sent away because of the shortages of food. Local traders, she reported, took advantage of the precarious situation by tripling their prices for food. The adverse situation forced the mission to close for two months.

By October 1918, DeLaney had serious concerns that the European war might extend into Liberia. Following the lead of the United States, Liberia broke ties with Germany on May 18, 1917. This was a blow to its economy, since seventy percent of its trade was with Germany. Furthermore, by October 1918, actual conflict in Liberia seemed quite possible; DeLaney prepared for the worst. People began to take their children away from the mission, sometimes without the consent or knowledge of the missionary. Of course DeLaney intended to send the children home in the event of war and was herself ready to leave at a moment's notice. Meanwhile, she made the best of the circumstances, realizing that the people's loyalty fluctuated between the Liberian government, which they undoubtedly still regarded as an imperialist interloper, and the Germans, who probably promised them a return to self-government. Despite the fact that DeLaney presented the image of a tough fighter, a writer in the *Spelman Messenger* noted that "the strain on her is great."[48]

John H. Anderson, a major in the Liberian Frontier Force, later assured her safety in two letters sent to the missionary. The armed forces, according to Anderson, would pay close attention to the region and hold local chiefs responsible for the security of the mission site. At least, DeLaney now had some security. But a combination of "smallpox, war and influenza" and other problems created a paralysis in the work of the mission.[49] Besides her strong faith in God and her devotion to the worth of her missionary task, DeLaney found other ways to bear up under so many adversities. She maintained that part of her strength derived from the enjoyment of the "so-called little things of life."[50]

During these difficult years, DeLaney's relationship and continuous communication with Spelman also provided her with a source of strength and meaning, as it had earlier during her stay in southern Africa. It was the missionary-minded people connected with the College who often aided her financially. But the news of happenings at Spelman appeared to have enheartened her much more than the receipt of monetary contributions. Late in 1914 DeLaney gave the reason for her profound interest in Spelman.

> Although, I cannot write often. I am as deeply interested in Spelman as ever, for she under God, has been the means of making me know that I live not for myself and friends only, but to help others to a higher standard of life.

In 1915, DeLaney wondered if the war had been responsible for the lack of letters from her Spelman friends in African missions. In a letter dated March 12, 1918, she found opportunity to express interest in the progress of her *Alma Mater*. She expressed delight that the enrollment at the college had increased and hoped that such progress would continue. But DeLaney did not permit an opportunity to pass without making a case for a stronger commitment on the part of Spelman to African mission work. "[A]side from the (Spelman's) work that her daughters are doing in the homeland may she send scores of competent workers to Africa, and may the number left behind be able to support a station of her own here!" DeLaney believed that the friends of Spelman had both the numbers and the financial means to carry forth such a project.

> We only need faith to test our strength. I firmly believe that Spelman will some day reproduce herself in Africa through her granddaughters.[52]

Despite her strong religious commitments and moral and financial support from Spelman, the trials of mission work eventually took their toll on DeLaney. In 1920, she returned to the United States for "much needed rest." By October 1920, she arrived in the country and gave speeches on behalf of the NBC Foreign Mission Board. During 1920, she was reunited with Daniel Malekebu, her "son" in African missions, and his wife Flora. After following DeLaney from southern Africa, Daniel was educated in the United States and graduated from Meharry Medical College in Nashville, Tennessee. It must have been a delight and a sense of fulfillment for DeLaney to behold one, who had come to her mission as a boy, now medically trained and returning to Africa with his wife to aid his own people.

It appears that for the next two years DeLaney continued to function as a strong advocate for African missions. After paying her last visit to Spelman in June 1922, DeLaney died of "hematuric fever" on October 7, at her mother's home in Fernandina Beach, Florida. The *Spelman Messenger* observed that DeLaney got very little rest after her return to America. Instead, she kept active, attempting to "realize her dream of a chain of missions round the hinterland of the Negro republic."[53] With her death, the Baptists of the United States lost a courageous and dedicated missionary who served as a vital link between black Baptist educational institutions and African missions.

CONCLUSION

This profile demonstrates the importance of the role of black Baptist women in the African mission movement, particularly as it was manifested through educational institutions. It shows the aggressive involvement of women in evangelical endeavors as promoters, supporters, and missionaries. We have seen that educational institutions founded for blacks in the postwar South had as their intent not only the intellectual development of blacks, but also the active encouragement of evangelistic sentiment both at home and in the African field. Black women, as well as black men, were influenced by the environment found in schools such as Shaw, Virginia Union, and Spelman to such an extent that many embarked on a missionary career in Africa. As such, they influenced the training of Africans both in the field and in American schools.

This short history is but a beginning. More research and study is needed, not only on Emma B. DeLaney, but also on others like Clara Howard, Lula Fleming, Cora Pair Thomas, Lucy Coles, and indeed on schools which sought to bring to pass their interpretation of the prophecy, "Princes shall come out of Egypt; Ethiopia shall soon stretch out her hands unto God." (Psalms 68:31 KJV).

NOTES

1. For an account of the development of African missions among the Afro-American Baptists, see Sandy D. Martin's "The Growth of Christian Missionary Interest in West Africa Among Southeastern Black Baptists, 1880–1915" (Ph.D. diss., Columbia University, 1981). Other valuable works on African missions among black Americans include: Sylvia M. Jacobs, ed., *Black Americans and the Missionary Movement in Africa* (Westport, Conn.: Greenwood Press, 1982); and Walter L. Williams, *Black Americans and the Evangelization of Africa, 1877–1900* (Madison, Wis.: University of Wisconsin Press, 1982).
2. Carter G. Woodson, *History of the Negro Church* (Washington, D.C.: Associated Publishers, 1972), 180–86.
3. E. Franklin Frazier, *The Negro Church in America*, bound with C. Eric Lincoln, *The Black Church Since Frazier* (New York: Schocken Books, 1974). 43–47.
4. For an account of the early history of Spelman, see *The Spelman Messenger*, January 1902, 1–2.
5. Ibid., p. 1.
6. *Spelman Messenger*, April 1902, 3.
7. Ibid., 6.
8. *Spelman Messenger*, March 1918, 7.
9. *Spelman Messenger*, October 1917, 2.

10. *Spelman Messenger,* April 1902, 3.
11. *Spelman Messenger,* October 1919, 2.
12. Ibid.
13. *Spelman Messenger,* January 1916, 1.
14. Ibid., 2.
15. *Spelman Messenger,* November 1916, 8.
16. *Spelman Messenger,* May 1902, 3, 5: December 1902, 1; March 1902, 5: and January 1911, 1.
17. *Spelman Messenger,* November 1915, 1–2.
18. See, *Spelman Messenger,* December 1919, 6: March 1920, 5; and November 1920, 6.
19. *Spelman Messenger,* January 1919, 2.
20. See, *Spelman Messenger,* October 1922, 4.
21. *Spelman Messenger,* February 1902, 5.
22. Minutes, The Baptist General Convention of Florida, p. 9.
23. *Spelman Messenger,* February 1902, 13.
24. Ibid.
25. Ibid.
26. Ibid.
27. *The Mission Herald,* July 1902, 1.
28. Minutes, The National Baptist Convention (NBC). 1903, 40.
29. Minutes, NBC. 1904, 74.
30. *Spelman Messenger,* November 1902, 4.
31. *Spelman Messenger,* March 1903, 5.
32. Minutes, NBC. 1904, 37.
33. *Spelman Messenger,* March 1903, 5.
34. *Spelman Messenger,* January 1904, 7.
35. *The Mission Herald,* March 1903, 7.
36. *Spelman Messenger,* November 1903, 7.
37. Ibid., 1–2.
38. *Spelman Messenger,* May 1905, 1.
39. Minutes, NBC, 1905, 36.
40. *Mission Herald,* August 1905, 1.
41. Minutes, NBC, 1912, 142.
42. Ibid., 141–42.
43. *Mission Herald,* July 1914, 3: September 1914, 3: March 1915, 1.
44. *Spelman Messenger,* May 1913, 6.
45. *Spelman Messenger,* April 1916, 7.
46. Ibid.
47. *Spelman Messenger,* November 1916, 8.
48. *Spelman Messenger,* January 1919, 2.
49. *Spelman Messenger,* March 1919, 4; May 1919, 2.
50. *Spelman Messenger,* May 1919, 2.
51. *Spelman Messenger,* November 1916, 8. A notation of financial contributions from Spelman to DeLaney is also found in the April 1916 issue, 7.
52. *Spelman Messenger,* October 1918, 1.
53. *Spelman Messenger,* October 1922, 4.

PART 4

AFRICAN-AMERICAN WOMEN, RELIGION, AND ACTIVISM

14

JEAN M. HUMEZ

IN SEARCH OF HARRIET TUBMAN'S SPIRITUAL AUTOBIOGRAPHY

Harriet Tubman (1821?–1913) is intensely admired in our era for her anti-slavery work and her daring. Her legend is inspirational for many women searching for models for both antiracist and prowoman activism. Less well known is the religious basis for her activism. She was engaged in what can be viewed as an informal, God-guided ministry, which had both activist and spiritual components. Hers is a spiritual life and ministry many of us would like to know better, but as we attempt to explore it, we are faced with the problem of a "mediated" autobiographical text—Sarah Bradford's *Harriet, the Moses of Her People* (1886), a narrative based on Tubman's own oral testimony as written down by a white woman.

This narrative shares significant features with other postslavery "slave narratives," now acknowledged as important contributions to African-American women's nineteenth-century literary traditions, as well as with the related genre of spiritual autobiography.[1] It has not yet been "discovered" by literary historians, I believe, because of its indeterminate—one might even say "compromised"—status halfway between autobiography (the telling of one's own story) and biography (the telling of someone else's).

The problems associated with using the mediated life story as a source of women's history and as literary text are not unique to this particular work. In our own era, the politics of oral-history text production and usage has begun to receive scrutiny from feminist critics;[2] and in African-American women's literary history in the nineteenth century, issues of mediation are simply not to be avoided.

Except in the relatively small number of cases when the literate author was able to depend primarily on the African-American community—through the churches in particular—for sales, women's life-story texts were frequently produced with greater or lesser degrees of technical and financial assistance from politically allied whites. Such assistance ranged from the relatively light editing and promotion for white audiences that Lydia Maria Child performed for Harriet Jacobs's narrative *Incidents in the Life of a Slave Girl* (1861) through the "ghostwriting" of dictated life stories like Elizabeth's (1863; in Andrews, *Six Women's Slave Narratives*) to the oral historically based biography—the kind of text Bradford produced for Tubman.

Let us begin by acknowledging that such a highly mediated text creates daunting suspicion and resistance, especially for modern readers sensitive to racial power dynamics. Jeffrey C. Stewart, commenting on *The Narrative of Sojourner Truth,* "a dictated autobiography written by Olive Gilbert," a white woman, points out that "Gilbert seizes upon Sojourner's life story as a vehicle for her own indictment of slaveowners." While "Sojourner's narrative . . . provided Gilbert with an opportunity to find her voice," Stewart notes that Gilbert's own voice remained "problematical"—citing editorial comments ranging from the "merely distracting" to the "seriously misleading" (xxxix-xl).

In my own experience, on the one occasion I used the Tubman biography in a course on spiritual autobiography, I found that most students were so offended by Sarah Bradford's position as an interpretive narrator between us and Tubman's experience—and particularly by her use of a nineteenth-century language they could only read as racist—that they were unable to discern much value in the book. I maintained to my students a rather defensive, pragmatic position: that since this text is among the fullest repositories of Tubman's own speech to survive, if we are interested in the historical Tubman, we need to make it yield as much as it can. One of my purposes in this essay is to demonstrate a "triangulation" method for using other surviving sources to shed strong light on the process of mediation and in the process, I hope, to undo some of the distorting effects of that mediation on Tubman's original spoken narrative(s).

In the process of working with the text to make it yield as much of Tubman's original meaning as it can, I have also begun to see the text in another light. I now believe that with the aid of other surviving sources, we can find within Bradford's biography the skeleton of a spiritual autobiography Tubman might have written herself, had she had access to writing through literacy. Tubman used Bradford—the medium at hand—to make public some important insights into the connections she made between her politics and her spiritual life. While it is true that Bradford controlled the final form of the narrative as it was translated from talk to text, Tubman's own agency in the collaborative process of creating meaning can be and should be stressed. Tubman's mediated life story contains, I believe, an essential spiritual transformation "plot" that illuminates the inner sources of her activist life.

As a first step in constructing the outline of this hypothetical plot from within the text of the Bradford biography and other oral-historical sources that remain, we need to envision something of the complex dynamic that existed between Tubman and her white biographical mediator, Sarah Bradford.

THE GENESIS OF THE TUBMAN BIOGRAPHY

In an unsigned article on Tubman published in the abolitionist newspaper the *Freedman's Record* in 1865, the writer asserted: "She says, when the war is over she will learn to read and write, and then will write her own life. . . . It is the strong desire of her friends that she should tell her story in her own way at some future time" ("Moses," 38). Yet soon after the Civil War's end Tubman decided instead to find a sympathetic and willing writer to take down her narrative.

The project of acquiring sufficient literacy may have proved more daunting than she had anticipated, given her other urgent responsibilities. In the immediate postwar years, Tubman lived in Auburn, New York, and was attempting to support her aged parents and a community of former slaves who were now her dependents. She had received no government pension for her work for the Union Army as spy, scout, and nurse, and so looked to the sale of copies of her life story as a source of desperately needed funds.

Tubman's partner in the life-history project, Sarah Hopkins Bradford (1818–1912), of Geneva, New York, was a white woman with clear antislavery politics, whom Tubman met through her parents. Tubman's parents, Benjamin Ross and Harriet Green, had been rescued from slavery by Tubman in 1857 and resettled on a farm in Auburn in 1858. Their Sunday school was taught by Sarah Bradford when she was in Auburn on an extended visit to the family of her brother, Samual Miles Hopkins, a professor at the Auburn Theological Seminary. Bradford helped Tubman's parents correspond with Union Army officers about Tubman's war work, and in this way she first learned of Tubman's exploits and reputation (Bradford, *Scenes* 3). Bradford had published several books of moral tales, history, and biography for young adults by the mid-1860s, and she probably seemed an especially appropriate choice to Tubman because of her publication of an an-tislavery story, "Poor Nina, the Fugitive," in 1855.[3]

Tubman was already an experienced life-story teller at the time she initi-ated the biography project with Sarah Bradford. By the end of the Civil War, two biographical sketches based on interviews had already appeared in print in the abolitionist press, one in 1863[4] and the other in 1865.[5] Brad-ford's interviews with Tubman probably took place both in Tubman's home in Auburn and in her own home in Geneva.[6] The first version of the biog-raphy was assembled very quickly, in 1868, while Bradford was getting ready for a European trip. It was published under the title *Scenes in the Life of Harriet Tubman* in 1869. The sale of the first edition was fully supported by subscribers, including prominent abolitionists Gerrit Smith and Wendell Phillips, and it raised $1200 to pay off a mortgage on Tubman's parents' farm in Auburn. The haste with which Bradford wrote out the manuscript of the 1869 text, apparently without revision, is a lucky circumstance for the historian, of course, because it makes it very likely that the order in which anecdotes are recorded is roughly that in which they came to her attention.[7]

Almost twenty years later, in 1886, Bradford prepared a much rewritten enlargement of the book, under the title *Harriet, the Moses of her People*, again at Tubman's urging, and again to raise funds. This time Tubman needed money to support "the building of a hospital for old and disabled colored people" (Bradford, *Harriet* 78). Bradford seems to have maintained some contact with Tubman in the years between the two publications. Whereas in the first biography she admits to not knowing Tubman very long or well, she refers in the revision to having heard one of Tubman's stories "often" (*Harriet* 73). However, I have only been able to identify one new story told by Tubman in the revision: the account of the escape of "Tilly" (Bradford, *Harriet* 60). In preparation for the revision, then, Bradford does not seem to have reinterviewed Tubman. However, she did go to New York City to interview Tubman's aging abolitionist associate Oliver Johnson (*Har-riet* 90), and she also included new material taken from F. B. Sanborn's *Life and Letters of John Brown* (*Harriet* 96).

It is the later, revised version of Bradford's biography of Tubman that has come down to modern readers in repeated editions. In some ways this is unfortunate, for a comparison of the two versions clearly shows that the ear-lier text brings us closer to Tubman's own view of her experience.

Bradford's control over the narrative of Tubman's life story increased substantially in the revision. With more leisure than she had had in produc-ing the first book, Bradford reorganized the material considerably, and brought into play her habits as a writer of moralistic children's literature, enhancing the "literary" quality of her revised narrative by adding dramatic scenes and rhetorical asides to the reader. Most significantly, in revising, Bradford frequently renarrated in the third person what had once been a first-person account. We lose important detail as a result, along with much of what is represented in the first version in quotation marks as Tubman's own language (in inconsistently rendered dialect supplied by Bradford).

Bradford's revisions have the effect of censoring aspects of Tubman's personality and politics. Individual stories are altered in the revision, frequently with the effect of making Tubman's personality less salty and more saintly. A good example is an extended story about an escaping slave named Joe whom Tubman took to Canada, crossing the border at Niagara Falls by train. In both versions, he comes out of a deep depression when he hears he has reached freedom, and he cannot be distracted from his rapturous religious singing by Tubman's repeated invitation to look out the train window at the waterfall. In the original version as recorded in 1868, Tubman makes a joke about the way Joe's excessive emotional display is cutting him off from the real world: she jestingly says he could have looked at the falls first, and gone to heaven afterward. In the 1886 version, however, Tubman's witticism is dropped and the story ends with the high sentimentality Bradford probably thought more likely to appeal to her white readers (*Harriet* 52–53).

Even more serious is Bradford's censorship of Tubman's pride in her own cleverness, when in the original narrative she spars with and frequently deceives her white oppressors. A notable example is Tubman's story of her clever teasing of the unwitting master on the eve of her escape. In order to say goodbye to her friends without alerting her master about her imminent departure, she boldly passed by him singing verses in the code of a "spiritual song," knowing that he would be unable to interpret the hidden meaning of lines like "I'm bound for the promised land" (Bradford, *Scenes* 17–18). This making a fool of the master disappears in the revised escape story Bradford published in 1886. In another instance, Bradford felt the need in the revision to interrupt a dramatic story of Tubman's rescuing her brothers with two gratuitous and defensive passages on how the duplicity of the slaves may be morally justified (*Harriet* 68–69, 71–72).

Bradford also systematically took out all references to Tubman's racial politics. She omitted a revealing anecdote Tubman had told of refusing to see the stage version of *Uncle Tom's Cabin*, which was playing in Philadelphia in the early 1850s, because she had no heart to "go and see the sufferings of my people played" on stage. "I've heard *Uncle Tom's Cabin* read, and I tell you Mrs. Stowe's pen hasn't begun to paint what slavery is as I have seen it at the far South," she said (Bradford, *Scenes* 22). Also omitted was an anecdote about gross racial discrimination on a railroad as she was returning home from the war, which had led Tubman to contemplate taking legal action (Bradford, *Scenes* 46–47). Bradford also dropped from the later version Tubman's letter from the front during the Civil War (first printed in the *Commonwealth* (Boston) on 30 June 1863), in which she had asked to be sent bloomers to wear on her scouting expeditions and had proudly referred to the heroism of the African-American soldiers who had taken part in the Combahee River raid of 2 June 1863.

In fairness to Bradford, it seems likely that she censored Tubman's life story in the revision at least in part for fear of marring the image of a saintly African-American heroine that she was trying to construct for white readers, in a post-Reconstruction era of virulent white racism. In 1886, Bradford seems to have anticipated white supremacist attitudes on the part of her readers, and to have adopted some of her editorial strategies with these readers in mind. Some of Bradford's omissions seem clearly to have resulted from her racial defensiveness. For example, the omission of two anecdotes dealing with Tubman's asking her friends for money probably reflects Bradford's desire to protect Tubman from the charge of being a "beggar" (*Scenes* 111 and 112). One of these stories may also have been omitted because it shows Tubman feeling shame at her need to ask for money, and Bradford was attempting to create a historical "heroine" who need never feel shame.

As narrator in the 1886 text, Bradford adopts a defensive posture, emphasizing the *contrast* between Tubman's heroism and the degraded condition of other former slaves:

> I am quite willing to acknowledge that she was almost an anomaly among her people, but I have known many of her family, and so far as I can judge they all seem to be peculiarly intelligent, upright and religious people, and to have a strong feeling of family affection. There may be many among the colored race like them; certainly all should not be judged by the idle, miserable darkies who have swarmed about Washington and other cities since the War. (*Harriet* 69)[8]

From a modern perspective, of course, we can see this strategy as feeding into the racism she probably believed she was fighting.

Despite—or perhaps more accurately because of—Bradford's editorial interventions in the story, the later book is an indispensable tool for reconstructing a plausible version of Tubman's spiritual autobiography. By contrasting other versions of some of the key stories Tubman told Bradford with the controlling narrative Bradford created, we can establish with some confidence crucial differences between the emphasis contained in Tubman's own statements about her experience, and those meanings imposed later by Bradford. We will be attempting, in short, to identify Bradford's agenda as Tubman's biographer, and, with the help of other sources, to remove as much of Bradford's editorial intervention as we can identify.

As we try to get closer to what we hypothesize is "Tubman's own perspective" on experience in these sources, however, we must remind ourselves of another layer of difficulty, related to Tubman's own agency, as both giver and withholder of truths about her life. All of these texts derive from particular, historically situated interview sessions in which Tubman was speaking with a "sympathetic" but white interviewer. We would be naive in the extreme, of course, to assume that any one of her self-presentations, even if a tape-recorded text had come down to us, was somehow a representation of the "real" Tubman. This is particularly important to remember in Tubman's case, because of her experience as underground railroad operator and, later, Union Army spy.

All of Tubman's several interviewers emphasize their impressions of her utter truthfulness and integrity, yet without appearing to notice the possible contradiction, they also indicate that she was a skillful strategist of self-presentation, who could and did present herself in a variety of disguises as the situation demanded. Her 1863 interviewer, for example, commented on the way she carefully tested the politics of a new white acquaintance before revealing who she was. Calling on her at her boardinghouse in Boston during the winter of 1858–59, he noted that "One of her means of security was to carry with her the daguerreotypes of her friends; and show them to each new person. If they recognized the likeness, then it was all right" (Bradford, *Scenes* 81). Her antislavery associate Oliver Johnson commented on both her "truthfulness" and her "shrewdness"; while her 1865 interviewer was impressed with her ability to conceal her real emotions behind an expressionless mask ("Moses" 37).

We must also acknowledge the inherent limitations of a collaborative effort like this one in regard to spiritual autobiography. It would be difficult for even the most well-meaning interviewer to convey with complete accuracy the story of another person's inner religious experience, especially when the two are situated in different religious cultures. In Tubman's case, for example, the stories of her spiritual experience were collected by white interviewers who found her religiosity powerful and unsettling and described it as foreign to their own experience. The 1863 interviewer commented on "the strange familiarity of communion with God which seems natural to these people" (Bradford, *Scenes* 77). The 1865 interviewer praised Tubman's "great dramatic power" in describing her religious experience, yet failed to record more than a few circumstances surrounding one such visionary experience Tubman recounted—and nothing of the content of the vision itself was captured ("Moses" 36).

One distinct strength of the Bradford texts, in contrast to the other sources, is the interest in (and respect for) Tubman's visionary experience that they convey. On the one hand, Bradford expressed some fear in both texts that to retell Tubman's spiritual experience, because it was so foreign to many potential readers, "might bring discredit upon the story." She allowed herself a sarcastic reference to the double standard used by those "advocates of human slavery" who have cast "ridicule" on Tubman's accounts of divine guidance, yet themselves "would tell with awe-struck countenance some tale of ghostly visitation, or spiritual manifestation, at a dimly lighted 'seance' " (*Harriet* 75). On the other hand, Bradford let the reader know how impressed she herself was with Tubman's accounts of her spirit leaving the body to visit "other scenes and places, not only in this world, but in the world of spirits." Bradford recorded her own experience with reading the last two chapters of *Revelations* to Tubman, after which Tubman told her of things "which no human imagination could have conceived . . . unless in dream or vision" (*Scenes* 56).

However flawed the Bradford texts may be, then, in my own view they are the best surviving sources for reconstructing at least in outline Tubman's account of her spiritual growth, transformation, and continuing divine guidance.

RECONSTRUCTING TUBMAN'S OWN INTERPRETATION OF HER EXPERIENCES IN SLAVERY

Before turning to an analysis of the central plot of what I take to be Tubman's spiritual autobiography, it is instructive to contrast Bradford's view of Tubman's life in slavery with Tubman's own emphasis—as best it can be reconstructed through looking at the other interview sources as well as differences between the two Tubman texts. Bradford and Tubman differed sharply on the meaning of Tubman's oppression in slavery, and in their views of God. Understanding these differences will help us appreciate more clearly how Bradford intervened in Tubman's central narrative of escape and spiritual transformation.

Bradford's revised narrative presents Tubman's childhood and young womanhood as a story of unmitigated cruelty visited on a passive victim, while Tubman's own stories emphasize her ability to thwart the ends of the oppressive employers to whom her owner hired her out. In increasing the emphasis on victimization in the revised narrative, Bradford undermined a crucial theme in Tubman's storytelling—how she learned and practiced clever techniques of covert resistance as a child, practice that served her well later as a conductor on the underground railroad.

Tubman's emphasis on the control she could exercise through resistance of various kinds is brought out starkly in the 1863 and 1865 interviews. For example, the 1863 account tells of her being taken at the age of six "to live with James Cook, whose wife was a weaver, to learn the trade of weaving. . . . But she would not learn, for she hated her mistress, and did not want to live at home, as she would have done as a weaver" (Bradford, *Scenes* 73–74). Or again, the 1865 interview text gives a nice account of how she outwitted the "very pious mistress" who whipped her "for every slight or fancied fault":

> [She] found that this was usually a morning exercise; so she prepared for it by putting on all the thick clothes she could procure to protect her skin. She made sufficient outcry, however, to convince her mistress that her blows had full effect. ("Moses" 34)

A particularly interesting example of Bradford's overemphasis on victimization occurs in the later text's treatment of Tubman's head injury and resulting condition of "somnolence." Here we hear that Tubman's lifelong susceptibility to sleeping fits was caused by "her master, who in an ungovernable fit of rage threw a heavy weight at the unoffending child, breaking in her skull, and causing a pressure upon her brain, from which in her old age she is suffering still" (Bradford, *Harriet* 15). In strong contrast, the 1863 interviewer's account tells us that Tubman received her injury accidentally, from an overseer, during an incident when she stood up for a fellow field hand, refusing to help tie him up for punishment.[9] Thus Bradford's account increases the malevolence of the slaveowner, and seeks to arouse our pity for the child injured by the "brute," rather than to awaken our respect for the brave young woman who assertively defends another slave from unjust treatment.

Bradford persistently presents Tubman's sleeping fits or "somnolence" as a lifelong disability caused by the injury. Yet two of the embedded stories by

Tubman may be read to suggest a different meaning—that her somnolence was to some degree under her control, and could be used as a weapon against oppression. In one story Tubman, as a young woman, was sent back to her owner when an abusive employer was unable to rouse her from sleep with whipping (Bradford, *Harriet* 22–23). She also told Bradford about a time she staged what sounds like a nineteenth-century "sit-in" in the office of a New York antislavery gentleman who resisted giving her the funds she needed to finance a rescue mission. She promptly fell asleep in his waiting room, and when she finally woke up, received sixty dollars in contributions from sympathetic strangers (*Harriet* 81–82).

Bradford and Tubman also see different meanings in Tubman's experience of hard outdoor physical labor in slavery. Bradford's revised narrative emphasizes the "cruelty" of putting a young woman to strenuous outdoor work (*Harriet* 22). But without whitewashing the oppressive conditions of slavery, Tubman's own prideful emphasis is frequently on her unusual physical strength. I have already noted above that she told her interviewer in 1863 that she rejected training as a weaver in her childhood in part because "she . . . did not want to live at home, as she would have done as a weaver." The same interview suggests her preferring outdoor work to indoor when she had some limited choice—it also strongly suggests her consciousness of the unequal compensation of female and male slaves when they did comparable work. The interviewer records that in her teens she was at first hired out as a field hand, and later after some indoor work "hired her time" from her master, and

> drove oxen, carted, plowed, and did all the work of a man,—sometimes earning money enough in a year, beyond what she paid her master, "to buy a pair of steers," worth forty dollars. The amount exacted of a woman for her time was fifty or sixty dollars,—of a man, one hundred to one hundred and fifty dollars. Frequently Harriet worked for her father, who was a timber inspector, and superintended the cutting and hauling of great quantities of timber for the Baltimore shipyards. . . . While engaged with her father, she would cut wood, haul logs, etc. Her usual "stint" was half a cord of wood in a day. (Bradford, *Scenes* 75–76)

Tubman may also have felt that her sleeping disorder had providentially led her to seek and enjoy outdoor work, and thus indirectly contributed to her acquisition of the unusual physical strength in which she took pride. Her 1865 interviewer reported:

She cannot remain quiet fifteen minutes without appearing to fall asleep. It is not refreshing slumber; but a heavy, weary condition which exhausts her. She therefore loves great physical activity, and direct heat of the sun, which keeps her blood actively circulating. ("Moses" 35)

Given how slavery broke down the gender-based division of labor in nineteenth-century America by which white middle-class women were "protected" from heavy physical labor out of doors, the slave woman field hand would almost inevitably appear degenderized or "masculinized" to a white northern observer. We should therefore be wary of how Tubman's white nineteenth-century interviewers—no matter how strongly politically allied with antislavery—might view and report on her ideas and feelings about her womanhood. Yet the interview passages cited above seem relatively free of editorial insertions, and to the extent we can read them as faithful to her own expressed attitudes, they suggest that Tubman, like Sojourner Truth, had some interest in exploding sexist myths about womanly weakness, as well as racist myths.[10]

Tubman's stories of hardships suffered during her life in slavery seem uniformly designed to emphasize the special providential guidance that was preparing her for her later role as liberator. Bradford dutifully reports on this interpretation, and tries to adopt it herself in several passages of her narrative.[11] But we can see, in an editorial aside, the difficulty Bradford has in accepting Tubman's view: "This cruelty she looks upon as a blessing in disguise (a very questionable shape the blessing took, methinks) . . ." (*Harriet* 22).

The issue for Bradford, it appears, was how one should understand divine providence in relation to slavery. Bradford herself had wondered in the years leading up to the Civil War about how a good God could continue to let slavery exist. As a white northern abolitionist probably in the camp of William Lloyd Garrison, Bradford appears to have looked forward to fearsome punishment of the sins of slaveholders, both in the form of divine intervention in human affairs, and in judgments on individual sinners in the afterlife. This is suggested in her own antislavery tale, "Poor Nina, the Fugitive," published in 1855, in which she has a white southern woman think critically about the abuse of slaves by slaveholders, and "of the vast changes which would take place in the condition of some of those who occupy the relation of master and slave here."

While the man of intelligence, and light, and privileges, who knew his Lord's will and did it not, will be beaten with many stripes, the humblest

> and most ignorant disciple of Jesus, even though his portion here may
> have been stripes and bondage, will be welcomed to the arms of the Sav-
> iour, and greeted as a friend and brother. ("Poor Nina" 175)

In this moral tale, Bradford also interpreted as divine "vengeance" an
epidemic visited on the city where the debauched slaveholder oppressed
the beautiful and pious female slave Nina ("Poor Nina" 283–34).[12]

Tubman herself, at least in the post-Emancipation period, may have
been less concerned with the question of how God planned to punish sinning white slaveholders. Bradford tells us that Tubman said in 1868 that she
believed many slaveholders would go to heaven, forgiven because their participation in slavery was based on ignorance. After all, "Dey don't know no
better. Dey acts up to de light dey hab" (*Scenes* 113).

Was Tubman a churchgoing Christian in the pre-Emancipation period?
None of the recorded stories about her religious life from the 1863, 1865,
or 1868 interviews make any explicit reference to church attendance on her
part, either in childhood or in adulthood.[13] We learn in the 1869 Bradford
text that her aged parents, once established on their farm in Auburn, were
devout churchgoers, attending both Central Church (Presbyterian?) and
Methodist class meetings. We also have Tubman's account of her parents
observing a religious fast twice a week, a practice she says "we" were taught
in the South (Bradford, *Scenes* 108–09). As a Sunday school teacher and
writer, and as the sister of a Presbyterian clergyman and professor at a theological seminary, Bradford would have had a strong interest in Tubman's
religious training in childhood.[14] Yet all Bradford can tell us in 1886 is that
Tubman was "brought up by parents possessed of strong faith in God," and
even then she must *speculate* about Tubman's religious feelings:

> She had never known the time, *I imagine*, when she did not trust Him. . . .
> She seemed ever to feel the Divine Presence near, and she talked with
> God "as a man talketh with his friend." Hers was not the religion of a
> morning and evening prayer at stated times, but when she felt a need, she
> simply told God of it, and trusted Him to set the matter right. (*Harriet* 23)
> [italics mine]

It would not be surprising to learn that Tubman was not a church-affili-
ated Christian during her childhood and young womanhood. Like Harriet
Jacobs, who includes a scathing attack on the southern slavery-justifying
churches in her autobiography, Tubman had probably learned to be suspi-

cious of the religion of slaveholders. One story from her 1865 interview even suggests her early rebellion against the religion of the owner class: "When invited into family prayers, she preferred to stay on the landing, and pray for herself; 'and I prayed to God,' she says, 'to make me strong and able to fight, and that's what I've always prayed for ever since' " ("Moses" 34).

Though silent on her relationship to the formal Christianity of the churches, Tubman did have much to tell her interviewers about her special spiritual gifts, some of which she seems to have been aware of from childhood. For example, she specifically told her 1863 interviewer that she had the spiritual gift of protective foresight, which she believed was inherited from her father, who "could always predict the weather," and "foretold the Mexican war":

> She always knows when there is danger near her—she does not know how, exactly, but " 'pears like my heart go flutter, flutter, and den dey may say 'Peace, peace,' as much as dey likes, *I know its gwine to be war!*" She is very firm on this point, and ascribes to this her great impunity. . . .
> (Bradford, *Scenes* 79–80)

Tubman's stories of her activist antislavery life clearly emphasize guidance by direct unmediated contact with the divine—both through spontaneous gifts of prophetic foresight (often occurring in dreams and waking visions), and through miraculous protection in response to prayer. These are gifts she shared with other nineteenth-century African-American religious visionaries, including the "prophet" and leader of the famous slave rebellion, Nat Turner.[15]

Many stories of how she avoided arrest while she was engaged in rescuing slaves turn on the miraculous answer of her urgent personalized prayers. For example, in one story she must escort a young woman fugitive by boat, but they are put in unexpected danger when the friend they expected to give them tickets is not at the dock. Tubman repeatedly chants "Oh, Lord! You've been wid me in six troubles, *don't* desert me in the seventh!" and she receives the wished-for tickets of passage by divine intervention (Bradford, *Harriet* 60).

The surviving sources strongly suggest that Tubman's view of the relationship of human beings to God was very different from Bradford's. Bradford seems to have seen God as being relatively remote, and possessing two faces or aspects: the kind savior who welcomed the good into heaven, and the stern, intimidating judge who would ultimately punish evildoers. In contrast, Tubman's God emerges from the words attributed to her by her interviewers as a single figure, an approachable partner and unfailing supporter for those who were righting wrongs. God was her name for the source of visionary guidance for her antislavery action. Prayer enabled her to tap directly into the source of such guidance.

We are now in a better position to uncover Tubman's central story of self-liberation and spiritual transformation, a plot comprised of several successive stages. While Bradford's rendition of it in the revised text is both incomplete and reflective of her own agenda, we now know enough about her agenda to correct and supplement Bradford's mythologizing narrative, again with the aid of the other interviews.

TUBMAN'S FUSED EXPERIENCES OF ESCAPE AND TRANSFORMATION

The heart of most spiritual autobiographies is the transformation story, but Tubman's transformation story represents a significant variation on the classical conversion narrative that proved so compelling for many nineteenth-century African-American women, as well as their white counterparts.[16] Like *The Confessions of Nat Turner*—another mediated text of vital significance to modern students of spirituality and liberation—Tubman's spiritual transformation story is inextricably interwoven with a story of external liberation. This sets it strikingly apart from those spiritual autobiographies that follow the standard plot of seeking and finding liberation from sin only.

All four sources I am using contain a version of Tubman's escape story, but only Bradford's two texts present the religious significance of her decision to escape.[17] Two issues are particularly difficult for Bradford, it seems, judging by her interventions: how to present as acceptable in Christian terms Tubman's prayer for her master's death; and how to present the role of Tubman's husband in the escape and transformation story.

Though Bradford herself had apparently wished for divine vengeance to be visited on the slaveholder in 1855, it is not surprising that she had trouble with Tubman's matter-of-fact account of her prayer for the master's death. It is one thing for a nineteenth-century Christian white abolitionist to assign to God the punishment of those responsible for the sin of slavery, and quite another for her to acknowledge that the African-American heroine of her book took responsibility for murderous anger herself. Thus Bradford seems to have done all she could, within the limits of what Tubman must actually have told her, to soften the impact of Tubman's prayer for the master's death.

In the revision, Bradford tells us that when Tubman heard of her master's intent to sell her into southern slavery, she first spent a three-month period praying for a change in his heart before finally deciding to pray for his death. When he died shortly thereafter, we are told she began to pray for the purification of her *own* heart. The clear implication is that Tubman felt deep guilt for wishing him dead, and this guilt touched off the beginning of her own spiritual transformation process.

This effort to assimilate Tubman's feelings to those of the classical guilty candidate for conversion required Bradford to make a crucial change in the original story recorded in 1869. There Tubman represented herself as *simultaneously* praying for her master's ethical transformation and her own purification:

> And so . . . from Christmas till March I worked as I could, and I *prayed* through all the long nights. . . . "Oh Lord change dat man's heart!" . . . When I went to de horse-trough to wash my face, I took up de water in my han' an' I said, "Oh Lord, wash me, make me clean!" Den I take up something to wipe my face, an' I say, "Oh Lord, wipe away all my sin!" When I took de broom and began to sweep, I groaned, "Oh Lord, wha' so ebber sin dere be in my heart, sweep it out, Lord, clar an' clean!" (Bradford, *Scenes* 14)

When her prayer for her own purification happens this way *before* she wishes the master dead, it completely alters the meaning of the prayer. Perhaps, like a shaman in some traditional non-Western religions, she was performing self-purification in order to ensure her worthiness as a recipient of spiritual power. Perhaps her prayer for her own purification was a perceived prerequisite to having her prayer for the transformation of the master heard. Whatever the case, when she realized after three months that her prayer for the transformation of the master was inefficacious, she discarded it. "Den I changed my prayer. Fust of March I began to pray, 'Oh Lord, if you ant nebber gwine to change dat man's heart, kill him, Lord, an' take him out ob de way.' Nex' ting I heard old master was dead, an' he died jus' as he libed" (Bradford, *Scenes* 14–15).

For me, this story suggests that though nominally "Christian," Tubman believed it was no sin to kill one's enemies. It sounds as though after the first three months were over, she realized that the master's *reform* was not according to God's will. Perhaps she had come to believe that God had purposely "hardened his heart"—just as the Lord in Exodus had hardened the hearts of the Egyptians before killing them in a display of power and solidarity with the chosen people. At any rate, she then took the next obvious step for her own self-defense, which was to pray for his death. This prayer, of course, was immediately efficacious.

In the revision, Bradford makes several minor verbal additions at this point, in order to make Tubman appear to be devastated by remorse. For example, while in the original version of the story Tubman did say that she wished for the power to "bring dat pore soul back" and would give money if she had it, Bradford has her say in the revision, "I would give *myself*; I would give eberyting! But he was gone, I couldn't pray for him no more" (Bradford, *Harriet* 24). Bradford stretches Tubman's original narrative as much as she can to convey that Tubman felt she had failed in her duty as a Christian to pray for the sinner's soul while he was alive. Yet if Tubman had really said she felt enormous guilt, surely Bradford could have included more detail about her spiritual anguish. Instead of a traditional "dark night of the soul," in which the sinner's sense of guilt leads to a grace experience, the story of Tubman's reaction to the master's death is curiously truncated in both the original and the revised versions.

To her credit, Bradford does recognize and emphasize in her narration the interpenetration of the external and internal aspects of Tubman's liberation experience. She makes it clear, for example, when the death of the master did not remove the threat that Tubman and her family would be sold, that Tubman experienced divine guidance for her escape, beginning with prophetic visions:

> Already the inward monitor was whispering to her, "Arise, flee for your life!" and in the visions of the night she saw the horsemen coming, and heard the shrieks of women and children, as they were being torn from each other, and hurried off no one knew whither. (*Harriet* 25–26)

The escape narrative assimilates Tubman's journey out of slavery to that of Moses in Exodus. Bradford tells us that, Moseslike, Tubman traveled "always conscious of an invisible pillar of cloud by day, and of fire by night, under the guidance of which she journeyed or rested" (*Harriet*, 27). Tubman had been called by the code name "Moses" for many years before she and Bradford began work together on the life story, and so it seems likely that it was Tubman who proposed the Exodus story as the paradigm for her own escape from slavery. While the 1863 interview included a reference to "a white lady, who knew her story and helped her on her way" (Bradford, *Scenes* 76), the Bradford texts give credit for the escape only to Tubman and God.

At the point in the narrative when Tubman stepped over the line separating southern and northern states, Bradford's text renders her experience in language that clearly fuses spiritual rebirth with liberation from slavery. The description of her sensations is highly reminiscent of other nineteenth-century spiritual autobiographers' accounts of the moment of release from sin through sanctifying grace:

> "I looked at my hands," she said, "to see if I was de same person now I was free. Dere was such a glory ober eberything, de sun came like gold trou de trees, and ober de fields, and I felt like I was in heaven." (Bradford, *Harriet* 30)[18]

Bradford's revised text gives us a three-part spiritual transformation process, then. It begins with Tubman's righteous prayers to remove the master's evil intent. It proceeds with her guilt and remorse for wishing the master dead. It culminates only when, following divine guidance, she has escaped from bondage. At this point Tubman understands that she cannot be truly free alone. Realizing that she has become "a stranger in a strange land" by leaving her family behind, she makes a "solemn resolution": "I was free, and dey should be free also" (Bradford, *Harriet* 32). This final stage goes beyond the conventional Christian spiritual-awakening plots, as the liberated person immediately takes up a mission as a liberator.[19] She makes an immediate vow to bring her whole family north and make a home for them. This is a touching and inspiring moment, and I have no doubt that it actually happened. Yet there was almost certainly a further stage in Tubman's understanding of her spiritual transformation process—a stage that does not appear in either of the Bradford texts, but that can be pieced together from the earlier interview material.

Bradford directs our attention in the preface of the revision not only to Tubman's own chosen Moses model, but also to female models of heroism, citing Joan of Arc and Florence Nightingale as other women who had displayed extraordinary "courage, and power of endurance, in facing danger and death to relieve human suffering" (Bradford, *Harriet* 4). As befits a pious narrative intended to associate its heroine with such a figure as the visionary martial virgin Joan of Arc, Bradford's story naturally emphasizes Tubman's complete selflessness at the moment of her own liberation. However, Tubman was still emotionally bound to her relationship to her husband, and her self-liberation from this tie was a crucial part of this last phase of her transformation story—some of which she told her other interviewers.

Tubman did refer to her husband when telling Bradford her stories in 1868. In the first Bradford text he is briefly mentioned as "a free negro, who not only did not trouble himself about her fears, but did his best to betray her, and bring her back after she escaped" (Bradford, *Scenes* 15). In the escape story, he figures as an antagonist, making fun of her prophetic fears of danger, and calling her a "fool" (Bradford, *Scenes* 15). But Bradford's revised narrative simply omits the role of the husband entirely from the story of Tubman's escape and spiritual transformation. The effect is to censor perhaps the most difficult stage of the process Tubman went through, in giving up worldly and personal satisfactions—including her life as a sexual woman—for the sake of her divinely guided liberator role.[20]

In contrast, the 1865 interview gives us a clear picture of a woman struggling with strong feelings, first of loyalty and love, and then of jealousy and anger at rejection. Tubman told her interviewer that she spent her first two years of freedom working in Philadelphia to earn enough money to hire and furnish a room, and buy clothing for her husband. When she returned to Maryland for him she found him "faithless," living with another wife. He even refused to see her when she sent word to him that she had returned.

It was at this moment that she completed the process of self-transformation and assumed the mantle of the liberator. At first her grief and anger were excessive. She said, "she did not care what master did to her, she would go right in and make all the trouble she could, she was determined to see her old man once more" ("Moses" 35). Only when she realized that there was no point in risking her freedom in order to struggle against him, did her final spiritual change occur. She gave up her anger and decided, in the summary of the 1865 interviewer, "to give her life to bravery. Thus all personal aims died out of her heart; and with her simple brave motto, 'I can't die but once,' she began the work which has made her Moses,—the deliverer of her people" ("Moses" 35).

Thus, in at least one version of her story of escape and transformation, Tubman acknowledged the struggle she had gone through to rid herself of private ties and embodied feelings as a married woman.

Did Bradford hear Tubman tell this story and decide not to record it? This could have happened, either for personal reasons—Bradford's own husband had similarly deserted her for another woman in the late 1850s[21]—

or because she saw it as tarnishing the saintly and self-sacrificing image of Tubman she wanted to project. Or did Tubman herself perhaps decide to omit this part of the story in talking to Bradford three years later? After all, Tubman's interviews with Bradford took place after she had learned of her husband's death—he was killed in Maryland by a white man after defending himself in an argument two years after the end of the Civil War.[22] Tubman may have simply decided to stop telling the story of his betrayal for any one of a number of personal or political reasons.

These open questions remind us again of the fragility of the skeletal spiritual autobiography we have attempted to reconstruct. We certainly do not have the story of transformation and liberation Tubman might have told those closest to her during the underground railroad years. Nor do we have the story she might have told herself privately, at different points in her life, as slavery receded into the past and she worked to support her dependents; as she met and married a new husband; as she spoke for women's rights; as she raised funds for schools and hospitals and the M.E. church in Auburn, New York; and as she created what became the Harriet Tubman Home, a charitable institution for the support of impoverished survivors of slavery.

Instead, we have a partial, mediated spiritual autobiography, whose meaning is contested by two women who, though politically allied and sharing a respect for spiritual life, have clearly different understandings of God, and of the relationship of human and divine in history. I have tried to demonstrate how we may begin to get at the story we can hypothesize Tubman actually told Bradford in 1868—still a story of heroism and religion, but one that does not clearly separate the human from the divine, nor minimize the passions, actions, pleasures, and pains of the embodied Tubman in order to create the spiritual heroine.

NOTES

1. For modern editions of selections from both genres, see Andrews, *Six Women's Slave Narratives* and *Sisters of the Spirit*. There is a growing body of critical work on African-American women's autobiographical narrative traditions. See Braxton, Carby, Foster, and McKay.
2. Claudia Salazar, in "A Third World Woman's Text," and Elizabeth Garrels, in "Rigoberta Menchu's Testimonial," have discussed similar issues in the modern "testimonial genre," using the example of *I . . . Rigoberta Menchu* (1984), a life history of the Guatemalan activist based on interview material gathered and heavily edited by Elisabeth Burgos-Debray.
3. Bradford's publications included three volumes entitled "Silver Lake Sketches" for young people, written under the pseudonym Cousin Cecily; a children's biography of Christopher Columbus (1863); a history of Peter the Great (1858);

The Linton Family (1860); a book for Sunday school classes called *The Chosen People* (1861); and a history of Geneva, New York. Bradford operated a school for girls in the 1860s and later, probably just after preparing the first version of the Tubman biography, in 1868, traveled to Europe with her three daughters. She moved to Rochester in 1895. Her books on Tubman are not among those mentioned in her obituary. I am grateful to Eleanor Clise, archivist at the Geneva Historial Society, and Stephen Erskine, of the Harriet Tubman Collection of the Auburn Library, for aid in locating information about Sarah Bradford and Harriet Tubman.

4. A letter dictated by Tubman, dated 30 June 1863, was printed after the biographical sketch. Earl Conrad attributes the article to the editor of the *Commonwealth,* F. B. Sanborn, whom he characterizes as Tubman's "closest friend" because of their mutual association with John Brown (Conrad 32). Though published in 1863, Sanborn's brief account of Tubman's life may be based on notes made from earlier conversations, perhaps from the summer of 1860 when Tubman made an extensive visit to Sanborn and his Concord associates. Bradford reprinted Sanborn's 1863 *Commonwealth* sketch in her 1869 text. (Page references below will be to this edition.) An account of Tubman's role as scout and leader of an expedition for a guerrilla raid up the Combahee River made by African-American soldiers in June was described in the *Commonwealth* the previous week, 10 July 1863 (Sterling 259–61.)

5. This anonymous article was written by someone associated with the New England Freedmen's Aid Society who probably knew Tubman from the periods she spent in Boston in 1858–59 or 1860. This writer also used information from the 1863 *Commonwealth* piece by Sanborn.

6. Bradford refers to talking with Tubman's sister-in-law Catherine at the "home of the old people" and also to having Tubman stay at her own house (Bradford, *Scenes* 69 and 55). In an appendix, she refers to incidents gathered in further "conversation with Harriet" (107).

7. Bradford apologized in the preface for "the very desultory and hasty manner in which this little book is written," and said she was "obliged to pen down the material to be used in the short and interrupted interviews she can obtain from Harriet, and also to use such letters and accounts as may be sent her, as they come, without being able to work them in, in the order of time" (Bradford, *Scenes* 47). She refers again to the effect of her haste on the first edition in the second version (Bradford, *Harriet* 4–5).

8. In interesting contrast, Samuel Miles Hopkins, Bradford's brother, goes beyond defensiveness in the preface he wrote for the revision, asserting that Tubman's bravery itself is probably a racial characteristic: "She has all the characteristics of the pure African race strongly marked upon her, though from which one of the various tribes that once fed the Barracoons, on the Guinea coast, she derived her indomitable courage and her passionate love of freedom I know not; perhaps from the Fellatas, in whom these traits were predominant" (Bradford, *Harriet* 9).

9. "As the man ran away, she placed herself in the door to stop pursuit. The overseer caught up a two-pound weight from the counter and threw it at the fugitive, but it fell short and struck Harriet a stunning blow on the head" (Bradford,

Scenes 74–75). The 1865 interview has her injury resulting from "a heavy weight thrown by her master at another slave, but which accidentally hit her" ("Moses" 35).

10. Though one would not know it from Bradford, Earl Conrad tells us that Tubman participated in women's rights conventions and speaking as early as 1860, and at one time appeared on the platform with Stanton and Anthony (Conrad 45). Although Shirley Yee also includes Tubman in a small list of African-American women who "bridge" abolitionist and feminist movements "by attending white feminist meetings" (Yee 151), I am not aware of any study exploring in detail Tubman's relationship to the organized women's movement(s) of the nineteenth century.

11. For example: "God had a great work for her to do in the world, and the discipline and hardship through which she passed in her early years, were only preparing her for her after life of adventure and trial; and through these to come out as the Savior and Deliverer of her people, when she came to years of womanhood" (Bradford, *Harriet* 16). Bradford also emphasizes this theme to some extent in the first edition: "Thus was she preparing for the life of hardship and endurance which lay before her, for the deeds of daring she was to do . . ."; and "perhaps her mistress was preparing her, though she did not know it then, by this enforced habit of wakefulness, for the many long nights of travel . . ." (*Scenes* 10 and 13). But elsewhere Bradford hedges on this issue, and says, "*it may be* that she was thus being prepared by the long habit of enforced wakefulness, for the night watches in the woods . . ." (*Harriet* 21; my emphasis).

12. There is a footnote here, and Bradford comments that although "it is not for us . . . to say that special judgments are sent in punishment of particular sins . . . still it does seem to us that signal vengeance is sometimes taken by Jehovah even in this life for crying wickedness . . ." ("Poor Nina" 307).

13. Conrad tells us that she later helped build up African Methodism (44–45), specifically the local A.M.E. church in Auburn.

14. Bradford's brother, Samuel Miles Hopkins, who wrote the preface to the revised Bradford text, was a Presbyterian clergyman and professor of ecclesiastical history and church polity at the Auburn Theological Seminary.

15. Nat Turner also said that, in childhood, he was able to tell things that had happened before he was born, and people said he would be a "prophet" (Turner 41–42). The African-American visionary and Shaker eldress Rebecca Jackson, writing her own much more detailed account of her spiritual life, gives us many examples of her "gifts of power" as well as of "foresight" (Humez 19).

16. See Brereton, *From Sin to Salvation,* for an able discussion of the overt and covert stories of such spiritual narratives as told by pious women.

17. The 1863 account summarizes the escape story itself in a sentence or two. In the slightly more detailed 1865 account, we learn that because Tubman was ill, "a purchaser was not easily found." She "became convinced that she would soon be carried away" and so simply "walked off alone, following the guidance of the brooks, which she had observed to run North" ("Moses" 35). It is, of course, impossible to tell from the surviving sources whether the differences are due to Tubman's telling the story differently on different occasions, or to editorial decisions made by the interviewers.

18. The nineteenth-century African-American Holiness evangelist Amanda Berry Smith recorded a similar impulse at her sanctification: "Then I sprang to my feet, all around was light, I was new. I looked at any hands, they looked new . . . . I went into the dining room; we had a large mirror that went from the floor to the ceiling, and I went and looked in it to see if anything had transpired in my color, because there was something wonderful had taken place inside of me, and it really seemed to me it was outside too" (47).

19. Virginia Brereton has reminded me that some conversion narratives do provide for the converted person taking up a calling as missionary or preacher, however.

20. Bradford does, however, include the full 1863 newspaper account in both editions, and does not actually delete its coverage of the facts of Tubman's marriage and her husband's infidelity.

21. Bradford's own husband, an attorney named John Melancthon Bradford, left their home in Geneva for Chicago sometime in the 1850s, and local rumor has it that he ran off with one of the female household servants. (Archivist Eleanore Clise of the Geneva Historical Society mentioned this rumor to me in a personal communication; it was also mentioned by Stephen Erskine, the librarian in charge of the Harriet Tubman collection at the Auburn public library.)

22. Tubman did ultimately remarry, after word reached her of the death of John Tubman in 1867. According to Earl Conrad (45) she married Nelson Davis in the spring of 1869.

REFERENCES

Andrews, William L. *Sisters of the Spirit: Three Black Women's Autobiographies of the Nineteenth Century*. Bloomington: Indiana University Press, 1986.

_____. *Six Women's Slave Narratives*. New York: Oxford University Press, 1988. Bradford, Sarah Hopkins. *Harriet, the Moses of Her People*. Lockwood and Sons, 1886.

_____. "Poor Nina, the Fugitive." In *Ups and Downs; or, Silver Lake Sketches*. Auburn, NY: Alden, Beardsley and Co., 1855. 269–307.

_____. *Scenes in the Life of Harriet Tubman*. Auburn, NY: W. J. Moses, 1869. Braxton, Joanne M. "Fugitive Slaves and Sanctified Ladies." In *Black Women Writing Autobiography: A Tradition within a Tradition*. Philadelphia: Temple University Press, 1989. 39–79.

Brereton, Virginia. *From Sin to Salvation: American Women's Conversion Narratives, 1800–1980*. Bloomington: Indiana University Press, 1991.

Carby, Hazel V. "Hear My Voice, Ye Careless Daughters: Narratives of Slave and Free Women before Emancipation." In *Reconstructing Womanhood: The Emergence of the Afro-American Woman Novelist*. New York: Oxford University Press, 1987. 40–61.

Conrad, Earl. *Harriet Tubman, Negro Soldier and Abolitionist*. New York: International Publishers, 1942.

Foster, Frances Smith. "Adding Color and Contour to Early American Self-Portraitures: Autobiographical Writings of Afro-American Women." In *Conjuring*:

Black Women, Fiction and Literary Tradition. Marjorie Pryse and Hortense J. Spillers, eds. Bloomington: Indiana University Press, 1985. 25–38.

Garrels, Elizabeth. "Rigoberta Menchu's Testimonal: A Women's Collaborative Text?" Forum on Women in Latin America. Boston, University of Massachusetts, 8 April 1992.

Humez, Jean McMahon, ed. Introduction. *Gifts of Power: The Writings of Rebecca Jackson, Black Visionary, Shaker Eldress*. Amherst: University of Massachusetts Press, 1981.

Jacobs, Harriet A. *Incidents in the Life of a Slave Girl Written by Herself*. Jean Fagan Yellin, ed. Cambridge: Harvard University Press, 1987.

McKay, Nellie Y. "Nineteenth-Century Black Women's Spiritual Autobiographies: Religious Faith and Self-Empowerment." *Interpreting Women's Lives: Feminist Theory and Personal Narratives*. Ed. Personal Narratives Group. Bloomington: Indiana University Press, 1989.

"Moses." *The Freedmen's Record* 1.3 (March 1865): 34–38.

[Sanborn, Franklin B.]. "Harriet Tubman." *Commonwealth* (Boston) 17 July 1863.

Salazar, Claudia. "A Third World Woman's Text: Between the Politics of Criticism and Cultural Politics." In *Women's Words: The Feminist Practice of Oral History*. Sherna Gluck and Daphne Patai, eds. New York: Routledge, 1991. 96-106.

Sanborn, Franklin B. *The Life and Letters of John Brown*. Boston: Roberts, 1885.

Smith, Amanda. *An Autobiography: The Story of the Lord's Dealings with Mrs. Amanda Smith, the Colored Evangelist . . .* Chicago: Meyer, 1893.

Sterling, Dorothy. *We Are Your Sisters: Black Women in the Nineteenth Century*. New York: W. W. Norton, 1984.

Stewart, Jeffrey C. Introduction. *The Narrative of Sojourner Truth*. New York: Oxford University Press, 1991.

Tubman, Harriet. Dictated letter, printed in the *Commonwealth* 30 June 1863. In *Sterling, We Are Your Sisters*. 259–61.

Turner, Nat. *The Confessions of Nat Turner, the Leader of the Late Insurrection in Southhampton, Va. As Fully and Voluntarily Made to Thomas R. Gray . . .* Baltimore, MD: 1831. In *The Confession, Trial, and Execution of Nat Turner, The Negro Insurrectionist . . .* New York: AMS Press, 1975.

Wilson, Harriet E. *Our Nig; or, Sketches from the Life of a Free Black*. Boston: G. C. Rand & Avery, 1859; rpt. New York: Random House, 1983.

Yee, Shirley J. *Black Women Abolitionists: A Study in Activism, 1828–1860*. Knoxville: University of Tennessee, 1992.

15

NELL IRVIN PAINTER

REPRESENTING TRUTH: SOJOURNER TRUTH'S KNOWING AND BECOMING KNOWN

In New York City on the first of June, 1843, a woman known as Isabella Van Wagner changed her name to Sojourner Truth and began an itinerant ministry. The date was momentous, for in 1843, June 1 was Pentecost, the Christian holiday that falls fifty days after Easter and commemorates the day when the Holy Spirit filled Jesus' disciples and gave them the power to preach to strangers. Pentecostals such as Sojourner Truth heed Luke's narration in the biblical book of Acts, in which the Holy Spirit made the disciples speak in tongues, in the foreign languages that let them teach people of all nations of the wonderful works of God. God said through the disciples—already this was mediated knowledge—that he would pour out his spirit upon all flesh, and men and daughters and servants would prophesy.[1]

Born into slavery in New York State, in the Hudson River county of Ulster, about 1797, Isabella took up her ministry in obedience to the Pentecostal imperative that had divided her life between slavery and freedom sixteen years before. The power of the Holy Spirit had struck her first in 1827, when emancipation in New York State, Pentecost, and the attendant slave holiday of Pinkster had virtually coincided. Isabella underwent a cataclysmic religious experience and the Holy Spirit, the power within Pentecost, remained a crucial force throughout her life—a source of inspiration and a means of knowing. To the woman who became Sojourner Truth, knowing and being known were always of both material and epistemological significance.[2]

In this essay, posing questions that previous biographers of Truth have ignored, I will examine how Sojourner Truth used language—spoken and

printed—as self-fashioning, and how others, white women with more education and facility with the culture of the printed word, portrayed her in
published phrases that became the kind of source material most congenial
to historians. My trajectory passes through nineteenth-century information
systems and some encounters related to the construction of the Sojourner
Truth persona by other people, part of the phenomenon that I call invented
greats. I end with the observation that words alone do not encompass
Truth's memory, for she used photography to embody and to empower herself, to present the images of herself that *she* wanted remembered.[3] Working on Sojourner Truth has taught me that if we are to write thoughtful
biographies of people who were not highly educated and who did not leave
generous caches of personal papers in the archives where historians have
traditionally done their work, we will need to develop means of knowing
our subjects, and adapt to our subjects' ways of making themselves known,
that look beyond the written word.

Beginning on that day of Pentecost in 1843, when Sojourner Truth, this
daughter and servant, set out under a new name, she reached many sorts of
people, not strictly speaking in foreign tongues like the disciples, yet using
various verbal and visual means of communication, various languages, so to
speak. Over the course of her career as preacher, abolitionist, and feminist,
Truth (c. 1797–1883) used speech, writing, and photography to convey her
message and satisfy her material needs. "Sojourner Truth," which translates
as itinerant preacher, described her calling rather than the occupation of
household worker through which she gained her livelihood. This haunting
new name expressed two of her three main preoccupations: transitori-
ness/permanence and distrust/credibility. As a working woman who had
been born in slavery, she never became wealthy enough to take her means of
subsistence for granted, and so money remained her third preoccupation.

With near literalness, the name "Truth" expresses her apprehension
about trust. Isabella Van Wagner lived in a world full of people anxious to be
believed, including the self-styled Prophet Matthias in whose Westchester
County commune, called his "kingdom," she lived from 1832 to 1835.[4]
Robert Matthews, who called himself "the Prophet Matthias" and "the
Spirit of Truth" when he proselytized in New York City in the early 1830s,
convinced Isabella and her co-religionists of his holiness. He gathered his
followers around him in a kingdom that quickly disintegrated. By 1835
Matthews/Matthias had been chased out of New York City and gone west;
by 1842 he had died.[5] The ideal of the spirit of truth lived on in his follower.

When Isabella became Sojourner Truth in 1843, she was not merely ap-
propriating the cognomen of her erstwhile spiritual leader, for she had

other, preexisting reasons for her own preoccupation with credibility. As a girl, she had been beaten and sexually abused, and as an enslaved worker, she had found her word doubted. In 1835 she overcame her usual reticence to persuade a New York freethinking journalist, Gilbert Vale, to present her story of the Matthias Kingdom. In a book whose subtitle ended "*Containing the Whole Truth—and Nothing But the Truth,*" Vale conveyed her desire to present "the *Truth,*" "the *truth,*" "the whole truth," "the *whole truth.*"[6] In the 1820s, 1830s, and 1840s, when her concerns about being believed were recorded, she also went to court twice over matters of enormous familial and material importance. In 1828, in order to regain custody of her son Peter, illegally sold into slavery in Alabama, she had to convince a judge in Ulster County, New York, that she was her son's mother. Seven years later, in Westchester County, New York, she sued a couple for libel because they had charged her with poisoning, an accusation ruinous to someone who made her living by cooking for other people. In both court cases, Isabella prevailed, but the experiences surely reinforced her anxiety over the integrity of her word.[7]

As an abused child, oppressed worker, and litigant, she was liable to be doubted in situations of the utmost seriousness. Taken together, these three kinds of experience virtually overdetermined the choice of her new name. "Truth," her self-designation, raises a host of questions related to knowledge, representation, and communication, regarding what I call knowing and being known; those questions are the subject of this essay. I will leave "Sojourner," which speaks to another set of issues regarding impermanence, for another time.

SOJOURNER TRUTH'S KNOWING

Merely asking about the education of "Sojourner Truth" immediately raises the question of the identity of this complex figure. My full-length biography of Truth carries the subtitle "A Life, A Symbol" to accentuate, perhaps to exaggerate, the distinction between the symbolic figure Sojourner Truth, who stands for strong black women, and the historical character Isabella, who was born a slave in the Hudson River valley of New York in about 1797 and who created "Sojourner Truth" at a specific historical juncture.[8]

In good twentieth-century fashion, Truth created a persona that filled a need in American political culture; both the culture and the need still exist today. The image of the mature Sojourner Truth, former slave and emblematic black feminist abolitionist, works metonymically as *the* black woman in American history. The sturdy binary opposite of the debilitated, artificial white lady, Truth is appreciated as straight talking, authentic, unsentimental. She appears to be natural and spontaneous, and in the best tradition of famous Americans, she symbolizes a message worth noting.[9] Truth's persona demands that women who had been enslaved and whose children had been sold be included in the categories of "woman" and "the Negro."

As a symbol of race and gender, Sojourner Truth is usually summed up in a series of public speech acts, the most famous of which is "Ar'n't I a woman?," which Frances Dana Gage reported that Truth uttered at a woman's rights convention in Akron, Ohio, in 1851. This phrase is sometimes rendered more authentically Negro as "*Ain't* I a woman?" Truth is also known for baring her breast before a skeptical audience in Indiana in 1858. In the post-1960s, post-Black Power era of the late twentieth century, a fictive, hybrid cameo of these two actions presents an angry Sojourner Truth, who snarls, "And ain't I a woman?" then defiantly exhibits her breast.[10]

The metonymic Sojourner Truth has knowledge, but no education beyond her experience of slavery. She would seem to have acquired her knowledge in a figurative enslavement, which occurred in a no-time and a no-place located in an abstraction of the antebellum South, as opposed to the Hudson River valley of New York, where Isabella was actually enslaved. What the symbol of Sojourner Truth learned once and for all in slavery enables her to analyze and challenge commonplaces of American race and gender thought. Having been a slave from 1797 to 1827, she needs no further instruction, for it could not affect her opinions or her methods. Of itself, experiencing slavery—not analyzing, representing, or making use of it—primed the figurative Truth to demand, "Ar'n't I a woman?"

Within the figurative construction of Sojourner Truth, the knowledge she took from slavery seems to reach late twentieth-century audiences directly. It would seem that she spoke and automatically entered historical memory permanently, so that we still hear her a century and a quarter later through her own originating force. She would seem to speak to us with a potency that allows her words to endure just as she uttered them, undistorted, unmediated, unedited, unchanging. This Sojourner Truth would not take advantage of technology, nor would she learn techniques of publicity from the people around her. She would not need to learn any skills in order to make herself appealing, for that would have been her birthright. Women with access to print would immediately have seen her as memorable, and they would have recorded her transparently, powerless to shade the image that is now so eagerly consumed. Both her knowledge of the way things were and our knowledge of her would seem to be utterly natural and unvarying. Or so it would seem.

◆ ◆ ◆

Unlike the emblematic Sojourner Truth, the historical figure, whom I am calling Isabella when I speak of her life before 1843, had an education that began in slavery but did not end there. Her first teacher was her mother, Elizabeth, who taught her to say one of the two standard prayers of Christianity, the Pater Noster or Lord's Prayer. (Isabella did not learn the other, the Credo or Apostles' Creed.) From her parents Isabella also learned her family's history of loss through the slave trade that scattered children throughout the North and conveyed thousands of black New Yorkers into perpetual slavery in the South. She was conscious of being a survivor until she reached the age of ten, when her turn to be sold came. Her parents also would have taught her appropriate behavior through corporal punishment, and as a parent she provided the same sort of education by beating her own children.[11]

It was not illegal in New York State to teach slaves to read and write when Isabella was a child, and from the late eighteenth century until slavery was abolished in New York in 1827, a few very fortunate slaves managed to attend missionary schools. The schools, which were located in New York City or other towns such as Albany, lay well beyond Isabella's reach.[12] As a rural person and as a girl, Isabella never went to school. Neither as a child nor as an adult did she ever learn to read or write.

After her emancipation, several people tried to tutor her, for like late twentieth-century people, educated nineteenth-century people took literacy as the signifier of modernity and saw reading as the best means of acquiring knowledge.[13] Then, as now, an inability to read and write seemed the same as ignorance, although often this was not the case. Without direct access to the written word, Isabella/Truth nonetheless used reading along with other means of gathering information. In both regards, she belonged to long-lived epistemological traditions that still have vigor in today's larger worlds. Her ways were those of people who are deeply religious, rural, female, poor, or unschooled. All these categories included Americans who were black and/or unfree, but the correlations were not automatic, as the dissimilar pursuits of Frederick Douglass and Sojourner Truth confirm.

In the mid-1840s, Frederick Douglass and Sojourner Truth, two former slaves of contrasting temperament, got to know each other in the Northampton Association of Education and Industry in Northampton,

Massachusetts, a utopian community, founded in 1841, that engaged in the cooperative production of silk. Douglass, who had escaped from slavery in Maryland in 1838 and become a protégé of William Lloyd Garrison, was teaching himself, in his words, "to speak and act like a person of cultivation and refinement"—an effort in which he succeeded brilliantly. Douglass, like many other fugitive slaves, associated illiteracy with enslavement and strove to complete his emancipation through the acquisition of fluency—elegance, to be more precise—in reading and writing. Marking his distance from Truth, Douglass recalled her as a "strange compound of wit and wisdom, of wild enthusiasm and flint-like common sense. She was a genuine specimen of the uncultured [N]egro. She cared very little for elegance of speech or refinement of manners." While Douglass was trying to acquire the polish of a modern educated man, Truth, he said, "seemed to feel it her duty to trip me up in my speeches and to ridicule [me]." Literacy was the main means Douglass used as he sought to establish himself as a free person, but Truth appeared to disdain the print-based culture he was mastering. She did not need to read in order to know.[14]

From the 1830s until her death, observers commented upon her intelligence. According to Gilbert Vale, the free thought journalist who came to know Truth in the mid-1830s, she had "a peculiar and marked character. Nature has furnished her, not with a beautiful, but with a strong body and mind." He described her as "not exactly bad looking but there is nothing prepossessing or very observant or intelligent in her looks." After long conversations with her, he found her to be a woman of "shrewd, common sense, energetic manners . . . [who] apparently despises artifice," but he inserted a caveat: She was "not exactly what she seems." She was quiet and reflective and had her own private and very wise opinions about everything and everybody. Ever the keen observer, she usually kept those opinions to herself. In 1851, while she was still obscure, Rochester, New York, abolitionists noticed her perspicacity. One warned, "If any one wants to play a bo-peep game with truth, beware of Sojourner," for although she seems "simple and artless . . . her eye will see your heart and apprehend your motives, almost like God's." Another concluded that Truth's illiteracy was "the shield to guard her rare intuitions, her great pure heart and strong individuality from any worldly taint." Obviously, illiteracy did not separate Truth from wisdom.[15]

Isabella / Sojourner Truth employed three main ways of knowing: observation and practice, divine inspiration, and, in a special sense of the word, reading. In none was she unique. First, as the New York journalist recognized in the 1830s, she was a shrewd observer of other people. As a slave, a woman, a black person, and a household worker, Isabella learned to decipher other people as a technique for survival. Once called woman's intuition, this ability to decode others without indicating what one perceives is a sense cultivated by the powerless who seek to survive their encounters with the powerful. Isabella occupied a subaltern subject position, and she kept her eyes open and her mouth closed unless she was in a protected situation or had some pressing motive for speaking out.

Isabella learned the skills she used as a worker and a speaker through apprenticeship and practice, as nonreaders have done over the ages, and as readers still do when faced with difficult maneuvers that are hard to convey in writing, such as techniques in knitting or in the use of a computer. As a free woman in New York City, Isabella worked in the households of the same people over many years; that record is testimony to her competence in performing to a metropolitan standard. These household skills served Truth in her subsequent career. When she first went on the road as a preacher in 1843, she earned subsistence and respect by cooking dishes *à la* New York City for provincials on Long Island. This knowledge proved useful again in the late 1860s, when she was employed as the matron at the Freedmen's Village in Washington, D.C., and taught freedwomen the very same household skills.

As a preacher, Sojourner Truth learned through rehearsal. Even before she left the Hudson River valley, her employer's brother reported that she worked in the kitchen "preaching as she went and kept preaching all day." Her employer "told her she ought to live somewhere in a big place where she would have a good many people to preach to." In the late 1820s and early 1830s, she preached regularly at the camp meetings that convened around New York City, where she became very popular.[16] By the time she joined the antislavery feminist lecture circuit in the late 1840s, Sojourner Truth was a practiced public speaker. She had long since conquered stage fright and doubts about the propriety of speaking in large, mixed gatherings when she stood up to speak to reformers.

Like many people who are very religious, Isabella/Truth learned through a second channel, divine inspiration—the voice of the Holy Spirit—a route to knowledge through faith that many believers, then and now, prefer to formal education. Pentecostals such as Truth prize the voice of the Holy Spirit as the premier means of enlightenment. Methodists and Baptists routinely praise a preacher for having spirit (in the sense of animation or soul), and one who displays abundant book learning without spirit may be dismissed as lacking. The experience of a figure from Methodist history who has much in common with Sojourner Truth may be instructive. In the early nineteenth century, Harry Hosier, a manumitted slave, was the servant and driver of the pioneering Methodist bishop, Francis Asbury, in the New York conference. Called "Black Harry," Hosier was renowned as a preacher. After a fellow Methodist failed in an attempt to teach him to read, Hosier said that when he tried to read, he lost the gift of preaching. He said: "I sing by faith, pray by faith, preach by faith and do everything by faith; without faith in the Lord Jesus I can do nothing."[17]

Like Harry Hosier, Sojourner Truth said that she talked to God, and God talked to her. Such modern scholars as Walter J. Ong believe, with Harry Hosier and perhaps with Sojourner Truth, that literacy stills the voices in one's head that speak divine inspiration. Truth may have distrusted writing, as people bred in oral cultures have over the centuries. In Plato's *Phaedrus*, Socrates tells the story of Thoth, the second-rank Egyptian god who invents writing as a means of improving memory and wisdom and takes it to the paramount god, Amon. Amon is not impressed, and he denigrates Thoth's innovation as no means to wisdom, but a recipe for forgetfulness and ignorance. Socrates warns that writing cannot engage in dialectic and hence lacks the ability to defend itself properly or "give any adequate account of the truth." Writing, for Socrates and for many who came after, portended only "the conceit of wisdom instead of real wisdom."[18]

Isabella / Sojourner Truth did use writing and printing, both as a third means of learning and as a way of communicating with others. What Truth learned from written texts, especially the Bible, came not through the solitary study that academics practice, not through seeing words and reading them silently, but in the traditional manner, through listening to someone read writing aloud. In hearing the Bible, Truth studied it. Analysts of reading and literacy emphasize that her way of using writing has been far more prevalent over the course of human history than literate people acknowledge. She was one of the masses of early nineteenth-century evangelical Protestants who believed that scholarly commentary, indeed, any commentary, obscured the deeper meaning of the Bible, which spoke directly to each believer. She preferred children to adults as readers, she said, because children would read the same passage repeatedly, without interpretation, whereas adults tended to lapse into useless explanation when asked to repeat a verse.[19]

In a system of spoken knowledge, authorship is a more complex matter than when thinker and scribe are one, for the functions of author and writer are disconnected. The author of the text is the knower and speaker, while the person who writes down the words is the amanuensis. Sojourner Truth used writing in this way when she dictated her autobiography to Olive Gilbert in Northampton in the late 1840s. Gilbert interposed her own ear and by dint of having taken down a third-person narrative acquired citation as the author of the *Narrative of Sojourner Truth*.

Bibliographical citation encourages the contrast between Olive Gilbert, the educated manipulator of the pen, and Sojourner Truth, the narrator untouched by literate culture, but such a dichotomy separates their roles too neatly. (As Gayatri Chakravorty Spivak would say, so stark a contrast saturates their identities.) Only the symbolic figure of Sojourner Truth could preserve an uncontaminated ignorance of the power of printed narration after having lived around educated people for decades. The historical person Isabella/Truth was an employee and comrade of wealthy and educated people in New York City, the Matthias commune, and the Northampton Association in the 1830s and 1840s. Though she may have poked fun at young Frederick Douglass, she, like him, absorbed the ideals and practices of people who were more firmly implanted in the metropolitan culture of writing and respectability. One telltale sign is a criticism of her peers in slavery in rural Ulster County: their thoughts, she says in her *Narrative,* were no longer than her little finger. Her photographs (to which I shall return) similarly betray an acceptance of the material culture of the people with whom she lived.[20]

In addition to her narrative, Truth occasionally dictated letters to friends and associates, of which few are extant. Those that survive deal with commodities, with the selling and distributing of her material means of support: her books and photographs. She was looking to sell and promote her narrative when she encountered two of the educated white women who made her widely known in the nineteenth and twentieth centuries: Harriet Beecher Stowe and Frances Dana Gage. Their medium was written language, which the French psychoanalyst Jacques Lacan associates with a psychic system permeated by masculine, normative standards of culture and education.[21] Gage, especially, was keenly sensitive to women's disadvantages vis-à-vis men in American political culture. But compared with Truth, she possessed enormous power within the information network in which they both functioned, and her ability to shape perceptions of Truth far outstripped Truth's own, at least through print. Ironically, perhaps, in her manipulation of the written word, the radical feminist Gage stood for what Lacan calls the paternal metaphor, the symbol of culturally sanctioned authority and power, in relation to Truth. Truth had a magnetic personality, but she was not formally educated, and only through others could she communicate in writing. Hence the meanings of her persona were more subject to other people's interpretation than is usual when a literate person moves onto the public stage.[22] The disjuncture between self-representation and

Truth's representation at the hands of others creates unexpected complications for a biographer trained as an academic historian, for the memory of Truth resides in words that do not render their meaning straightforwardly and in images that we historians are not trained to interpret. Coming to know Sojourner Truth requires familiarity with more than our everyday printed words.

KNOWING SOJOURNER TRUTH

The first thing that strikes a historical biographer of Sojourner Truth is an embarrassment in regard to the rhetorical question, "Ar'n't I a woman?," for which she is famous. A look in volume 4 of the *Black Abolitionists' Papers* shows that, although Truth gave a speech in the famous venue, Akron, Ohio, in the famous year, 1851, the contemporary report (appendix 1 to this essay) does not include the crucial line. Before the *Black Abolitionists' Papers* went to press, the editor and staff passionately debated which version of the speech to publish. Ultimately, they followed their regular editorial policies and published the report of Truth's speech that had appeared in the *Salem* [Ohio] *Anti-Slavery Bugle* in June 1851. According to C. Peter Ripley, editor of the Black Abolitionist Papers Project, it was "the most complete and accurate version" of the event. Further, he adds, the circumstances surrounding the *Bugle's* report—its contemporaneity, its author's familiarity with Truth—reinforced its reliability.[23]

The second thing that strikes a biographer seeking to pierce the mystery of Sojourner Truth's 1851 speech is that other documentation is not to be found where historians normally look. This is true of women's history in general, as Virginia Woolf noted in 1929 in *A Room of One's Own*. There she asks, rhetorically, of research on women: "If truth is not to be found on the shelves of the British Museum, where is . . . truth?"[24] No, Truth is not in the British Museum or in other archives; her sources are mostly periodical reports of her speeches, many of which she gave to encourage sales of the objects that she sold to support herself, themselves valuable sources. These are her *Narrative* and photographic portraits ("shadows") that she paid for and therefore controlled. The answer to the question of how Truth and "Ar'n't I a woman?" became identified lies in what might be termed Sojourner Truth's marketing technique.

Sojourner Truth, the itinerant preacher, created and marketed the persona of a charismatic woman who had been a slave, and it is precisely through her marketing of herself or, as she put it, her selling the shadow to support her substance, that her name is known today. As the principal symbol of strength and blackness in the iconography of women's culture, Truth has been bought and sold for more than a century. She had dozens of colleagues among feminist abolitionists, such as Frances Dana Gage, and itinerant preachers, such as Harriet Livermore, whose names have been almost totally forgotten. Truth's black female peers—the abolitionists Maria Stewart, Sarah Douglass, Sarah Remond, and Frances Ellen Watkins Harper and the preachers Jarena Lee, Zilpha Elaw, Julia Foote, and Rebecca Cox Jackson—are just as obscure.

The difference is that Truth, though illiterate, utilized the information systems of her time with phenomenal success. To recover her traces, a biographer must consult her preferred, visual medium of photography, as well as the biographer's own, which is language in print. What is known of Sojourner Truth in print comes mainly from the pens of four educated white women (Olive Gilbert, Harriet Beecher Stowe, Frances Dana Gage, and Frances Titus) who were fascinated by Truth and sought to capture her in writing. Titus, who was Truth's neighbor and publicist in Battle Creek, Michigan, accompanied Truth on speaking trips in the 1870s and arranged for the republication of her *Narrative* in the 1870s and 1880s. There Titus listed herself as author.[25] Titus's work has a place in a comprehensive analysis of the making of the figure of Sojourner Truth, but by the time she joined Truth's enterprise, the persona and the epistemology of Sojourner Truth had already taken shape.

Narratives of Sojourner Truth

The first of Truth's amanuenses was Olive Gilbert, to whom Truth dictated her life story, which Truth published in 1850 in Boston as the *Narrative of Sojourner Truth*. This 128-page pamphlet narrates Isabella's life as a slave, her conversion in 1827, and her experiences with New York Pentecostals (then called Perfectionists), including her time in the kingdom of the Prophet Matthias. The *Narrative* ends on a pathetic note, with Truth disillusioned by her experiences in intentional communities: the Matthias Kingdom and the Northampton Association. In a tone innocent of bitterness or anger, she expresses satisfaction that her old owner, John J. Dumont, has come to see the evil inherent in slavery. Truth emerges from the first edition of her *Narrative* as a slightly piteous figure, an object of charity whose life story is first and foremost for sale. That tale is bound to disappoint anyone seeking the powerful feminist abolitionist of the 1850s or the dignified figure of the photographs from the 1860s and 1870s.

When Sojourner Truth and Olive Gilbert collaborated on the manuscript that would become the *Narrative,* both were resident in the Northampton Association of Education and Industry. Truth had arrived at Northampton in the late fall of 1843, after her first half year as "Sojourner Truth." Olive Gilbert belonged to the Northampton Association in 1845 and 1846.[26]

Little is known of Gilbert: She was born in 1801 and was from Brooklyn, Connecticut. Relatively well educated and well read, Gilbert was of a utopian and spiritualist turn of mind. She spent almost two years between 1846 and 1849 in Daviess County in northern Kentucky, probably as a governess, which interrupted her work with Truth. After stints back in her Connecticut hometown at midcentury, Gilbert returned to Leeds, in the Northampton environs, and she still belonged to reform-minded circles in the early 1870s.[27]

Americans with antislavery and feminist convictions seem to have been unusually predisposed to purchase information conveyed in print. Reflecting this predilection, the ex-slave narrative as a genre came of age in the 1840s. Slave narratives had appeared since 1760, but in the 1840s several— by Frederick Douglass, William Wells Brown, and Henry Bibb—became best sellers. The "great enabling text" was the *Narrative of the Life of Frederick Douglass, An American Slave,* which appeared in 1845 and sold forty-five hundred copies in less than six months. It was reprinted six times in four years.[28] As a publishing phenomenon and as the autobiography of a man whom Truth had encountered at the Northampton Association, the *Narrative of the Life of Frederick Douglass* would have inspired Sojourner Truth. The genesis of the project that became the *Narrative of Sojourner Truth* is unclear, but the mid-1840s were auspicious culturally and technologically.

In the early nineteenth century, with the deployment of new papermaking and typesetting technology, publishing passed its first great developmental watershed since the fifteenth century and changed from an art to an industry.[29] After the conjunction of stereotyping and electroplating in the 1840s, each edition of a book no longer needed to be composed entirely anew. Henry Wadsworth Longfellow and James Fenimore Cooper had created the paying occupation of American author in the 1820s, and there followed a small but important cohort of women novelists who supported themselves through their writing. By the time of Sojourner Truth's collaboration with Olive Gilbert, the American reading public and the market for books had grown tremendously, yet books still reached a tiny proportion of Americans. Even in paper covers, books usually cost between thirty-eight and sixty-three cents, which represented between a sixth and more than a

274 half of the weekly earnings of people who were paid wages for their labor. Slaves, who were not paid for their labor, lacked the resources to purchase books and papers, even if they had broken the laws and learned to read.

A distribution network was also newly in place, along which printed media moved with relative ease and speed, for the railroad network and postal system regularly served the Northampton Association with pickups and delivery of mail and newspapers. Truth had access to the primary means of distribution of objects and information, packages, letter mail, and newspapers, the last of which numbered in the tens of thousands nationally.[30]

◆ ◆ ◆

After Gilbert and Truth completed their work in 1849, Truth's Northampton connections paid off again, this time through her contact with William Lloyd Garrison, the editor of the Boston-based *Liberator*. Garrison's American Anti-Slavery Society had published Douglass's narrative, and both Garrison and Douglass treated the Northampton Association as a sort of progressive summer camp. Garrison had family there, for he had married the sister of George Benson, one of the association's founders. Through Benson and Garrison, Truth contacted George Brown Yerrinton, the printer of the *Liberator*, a freethinker whose ties to progressive causes and publications dated back to the 1820s. Thus the Northampton Association not only helped Truth ease herself out of preaching and into antislavery and woman's rights advocacy, it also located her printer.[31]

From an otherwise unknown James Boyle, Truth obtained the money to have her *Narrative* printed.[32] Because Truth paid for the printing, Yerrinton cannot be called the publisher of her book, though he later sold her the stereotyped plates. That Truth published herself was not unusual at the time, for the line between publisher and printer was only becoming established in the 1850s, and the functions of printing, distributing, and selling books were not always distinct. Sojourner Truth, acting as her own distributor and bookseller, was well within the bounds of ordinary practice. What was unusual was the book's price, kept low, perhaps, to facilitate purchase. At twenty-five cents per copy, her 128-page, 7¾-by-5-inch, soft-covered *Narrative* represented a bargain.

Sojourner Truth's *Narrative*, which is seldom cited as a source of information on slavery in New York or in general, seems to have been appreciated by its purchasers more as an object than as a text. Any book straddles the blurry boundary between text and object, but Truth's *Narrative* is particularly difficult to classify. It is the autobiography of a woman who neither read nor wrote, and it was made to provide her material support. The *Narrative* seems to have been little read—it was not discussed as a text, and it may have represented less a text that conveyed meaning than an artifact, a commodity. As a work composed to raise money, Truth's *Narrative* belonged to a recognizable subgenre of black autobiography.[33] In this regard, it resembled the tokens that recipients of charity still offer to givers. It functioned as do the little flags that deaf-mutes sell in airports or the book by one's colleague that one buys but never reads, having heard the colleague speak about the subject for years. Well-intentioned reformers went to hear Sojourner Truth present herself as a slave mother and bought copies of her little book to express solidarity, to contribute to her well-being, and to indicate their own relative position and status in society. As Truth sold her being as a slave woman, her customers bought the proof of their social difference from her.[34]

Although they hardly belonged to a postindustrial society in which patterns of consumption are seen as markers of identity, abolitionists and feminists, among other self-conscious communities, nonetheless placed great importance on how they spent their money. Abolitionists boycotted slave-grown produce and held antislavery fairs to sell virtuous objects and to raise money for the cause. As Jean Fagan Yellin has shown, the feminist antislavery community generated an iconography and a world of goods that attested to the vigor of their convictions. The conjunction between money and morals worked to the advantage of Sojourner Truth, who embodied the linked causes of feminism and antislavery and had something to sell. The *Narrative of Sojourner Truth* promised its reader the story of one woman who had been a slave; it immediately assured its purchaser that information about her own virtue had been conveyed.[35]

Tending to their habits of consuming, in the literal as well as the figurative sense, many feminist abolitionists went beyond patronizing antislavery fairs and boycotting slave produce. Their morals encompassed what they ate and did not drink and their preferred means of avoiding and combating disease. Abby Foster Kelley followed the Graham whole-grain, vegetarian diet, and other feminist abolitionists believed in drinking cold water, eating whole grains and vegetables, taking water cures, and pursuing unorthodox methods of healing. In the reform culture in which Sojourner Truth moved and offered her *Narrative* for sale in the 1850s, what one bought signified what one believed or what one was. Meaning might emerge from one's purchases as well as from the printed page.

More than a century and a quarter after its publication, the *Narrative of Sojourner Truth* still has not found its niche in the literature of ex-slaves. Although Truth's images often figure as symbols of black womanhood, she is never discussed as a slave narrator and her account is rarely quarried for information on enslaved blacks in New York State. Compared with Douglass's three autobiographies—particularly the first, which has continually been republished in popular editions—Truth's *Narrative* until recently remained expensive and inaccessible.[36]

Truth's strategy for publicizing her book and increasing its sales has served authors for centuries. Like authors then and now, Truth went on the lecture circuit after she published her book in 1850, speaking and selling copies to audiences who were intrigued by her personal appearance. Among the meetings she attended to sell her book was the 1851 woman's rights convention in Akron.

Personal appearances worked well in the market that Truth could reach personally, but her obscurity militated against her with people she could not address. To communicate with a broader range of potential buyers, she needed the endorsement of those better known than she. Although Garrison had introduced the first edition of her book in 1850, authenticating her standing as an ex-slave and attesting to the virtue of the purchase, in 1853 Truth seized the initiative when she realized that a profitable endorsement was within her reach. Joining the legions of authors and publishers seeking advantageous "puffs"—now called blurbs—Truth approached the world's best-selling author for a puff, which she received. It began:

> The following narrative may be relied upon as in all respects true & faithful, & it is in some points more remarkable & interesting than many narratives of the kind which have abounded in late years.
>
> It is the history of a mind of no common energy & power whose struggles with the darkness & ignorance of slavery have a peculiar interest. The truths of Christianity seem to have come to her almost by a separate revelation & seem to verify the beautiful words of scripture "I will bring the blind by a way that they knew not, I will make darkness light before them & crooked things straight."

There is no way of knowing whether Stowe's puff boosted Truth's sales, but it certainly began a discursive relationship between Sojourner Truth and Harriet Beecher Stowe that extended into the following decade.[37]

◆ ◆ ◆

The 1851 publication of *Uncle Tom's Cabin* as a serial in Gamaliel Bailey's moderate, antislavery Washington *National Era* had proved wildly successful, and when the book appeared in 1852, it became a sensation that transformed its author's career. Stowe had been writing since the mid-1830s, but the shocking revision of the Fugitive Slave Act in the Compromise of 1850 galvanized her into writing the book that broke records throughout the world. The first year's sales of *Uncle Tom's Cabin* reached a phenomenal three hundred thousand, bringing Stowe ten thousand dollars in royalties, a fortune at the time. She built Oakholm, a huge Italianate-Tudor mansion in Hartford, Connecticut; took trips to Europe, basked in adoration on both sides of the Atlantic, and turned her talents to the defense of her new friend, Lady Byron, and glorification of her native New England.[38]

Uncle Tom's Cabin made Stowe a highly sought-after author. Her work appeared in the *Independent*, her brother Henry Ward Beecher's prestigious national religious newspaper, but soon she wrote less for the *Independent* and more for the even more sophisticated and less political *Atlantic Monthly*, where she was paid about two hundred dollars per article. In 1863, ten years after Sojourner Truth had come soliciting a blurb, Stowe reworked a short piece she had written in 1860 and published it in the *Atlantic Monthly* as "Sojourner Truth, the Libyan Sibyl."[39]

Having adjusted her life-style to a prosperity that could be maintained only by a constant influx of additional funds, Stowe was writing quickly about a marketable subject.[40] She had never been a radical abolitionist—and she was only a moderate advocate of woman's rights—but in the early 1860s material on the Negro was very much in demand. With the Emancipation Proclamation and the acceptance of black men into the Union army, northern newspapers and magazines were full of articles on blacks. Writing to the market, Stowe presented a tableau in which she and her family appeared as people of culture who appreciated Sojourner Truth as a primitive *objet d'art* and source of entertainment. In her use of the name *sibyl*, Stowe captured Truth's prophetic side. Above all, however, Stowe emphasized Truth's Africanness and otherness, tendering her speech in Negro dialect and praising her naïveté. Mining the vein that had produced her black characters in *Uncle Tom's Cabin*, Stowe made Truth into a quaint and innocent exotic who disdained feminism.

Stowe presents Truth as telling of becoming a Methodist in Ulster County in about 1827. The quote, in dialect, is framed by Stowe's comments, in standard English. Stowe quotes herself as asking: "But, Sojourner, had you never been told about Jesus Christ?" To which Truth answers:

> No, honey. I had n't heerd no preachin'—been to no meetin'. Nobody had n't told me. I'd kind o' heerd of Jesus, but thought he was like Gineral Lafayette, or some o' them. But one night there was a Methodist meetin'

somewhere in our parts, an' I went; an' they got up an' begun for to tell der'speriences: an' de fust one begun to speak. I started, 'cause he told about Jesus.... An' finally I said, "Why they all know him!" I was so happy! an' then they sung this hymn.

Stowe then adds, again in contrasting standard English: "(Here Sojourner sang, in a strange, cracked voice, but evidently with all her soul and might, mispronouncing the English, but seeming to derive as much elevation and comfort from bad English as from good)." After quoting Truth's hymn, "There Is a Holy City," Stowe explains that Truth "sang with the strong barbaric accent of the native African . . . Sojourner, singing this hymn, seemed to impersonate the fervor of Ethiopia, wild, savage, hunted of all nations, but burning after God in her tropic heart."[41]

In "Sojourner Truth, the Libyan Sibyl," Stowe made mistakes, some careless, some contrived: She wrote, for instance, that Truth had come from Africa, and, even though Truth was very much alive and active in Washington, D.C., at the time, that she was dead. (Truth did not die until 1883.) For all her misstatements, Stowe provided Truth with the identity that would cling to her until late in the nineteenth century.

A more obscure person who was still in the thick of the woman's rights and antislavery movements might well be chagrined by Stowe's commercialism, particularly if there was an element of rivalry. Stowe's article thus roused another woman writer with far stronger reform credentials, Frances Dana Gage, to write.

◆ ◆ ◆

An Ohio radical, Frances Dana Gage (1808–1884) was known as a woman's rights woman whose writing appeared occasionally in the *Independent*. Largely self-educated, Gage contributed to feminist and agricultural newspapers in the 1850s and 1860s under the pen name Aunt Fanny and became a popular public speaker. She corresponded familiarly with Susan B. Anthony, with whom she toured in 1856.[42] As an antislavery feminist, Gage was both a sharp critic of the patriarchial family and a folksy character who wrapped her critique of conventional society in the commonplaces of her role as wife and mother of eight. Although recognized as a talented speaker and writer within temperance, antislavery, and feminist circles, Gage never took the step up to the *Atlantic Monthly* or other widely read, fashionable magazines. Throughout her life she remained with the religious and feminist press, and among her eleven books of fiction, those published for temperance organizations predominate.

Gage was unusual, though not unique, in focusing her woman's rights rhetoric on working-class women. From the 1850s through the 1870s, she constantly subverted antisuffrage argument by describing women who did taxing labor, such as a woman in rags who walked along a canal in Cincinnati with "half a cart load of old fence-rails set into a big sack that was strapped round her neck ... half bent to the earth with a burden that few men could have carried" and a woman in St. Louis who walked two miles "with a child six months old—a large fat boy on her left shoulder, while on her head she is holding some thirty, forty, or fifty pounds of flour. She walks with a firm step, and carries her burden with apparent ease."[43] When antifeminists protested that equal rights would expose women to the rough-and-tumble of economic and political strife, Gage pointed to poor women who were already immersed in an acute struggle for existence, working as hard as men in thoroughly unpleasant circumstances but handicapped by their lack of civil rights and equal pay.

Gage had chaired the 1851 woman's rights convention in Akron where Truth had come to sell her newly published *Narrative*. She did not write an essay dedicated entirely to Truth immediately, but Gage recognized the attractiveness of Truth's persona and used her as the model for an October 1851 episode of a series she was publishing in Jane Swisshelm's *Pittsburgh Saturday Visiter*. In "Aunt Hanna's Quilt: Or the Record of the West. 'A Tale of the Apple Cellar,' " Gage drew the fictional word portrait of a fugitive slave whom she called Winna:

> She was black—black as November night itself—tall, straight and muscular. Her wool was sprinkled with grey, that showed her years and sorrows, and her countenance was strikingly interesting. Her features once must have been fine, and even yet beamed with more than ordinary intelligence; her language was a mixture of the African lingo and the manner of the whites among whom she lived.

Winna lamented that all her children had been lost to the slave trade: "I'se had thirteen of 'em. They are all gone—all gone, Miss, I don't know where's one [of them]."[44]

In 1862 and 1863 Gage was in the South Carolina Sea Islands working with freed people in the "rehearsal for Reconstruction," and after her return to the North, she undertook an interstate tour to solicit support for freedmen's relief. Reading Stowe's article twelve years after the meeting in Akron, Gage may well have realized that she could produce a more riveting and true-to-life version of Sojourner Truth than Stowe's quaint little character.

Less than a month after the appearance of Stowe's "Libyan Sibyl," Gage published in the *Independent* the account of Truth that we recognize today (it appears here as appendix 2). Gage quoted Sojourner Truth as saying that she had had thirteen children, all of whom had been sold away from her (although Truth had five children and said so in her *Narrative*). In this letter these famous lines appeared for the first time: "And ar'n't I a woman? Look at me. Look at my arm. . . . I have plowed and planted and gathered into barns, and no man could head me—and ar'n't I a woman?"[45]

◆ ◆ ◆

Stowe and Gage let many years intervene between meeting Truth and writing about her by name. But while Stowe drew Truth as a quaint, minstrel-like, nineteenth-century Negro, Gage made her into a tough-minded, feminist emblem by stressing Truth's strength and the clash of conventions of race and gender and by inventing the riveting refrain, "And ar'n't I a woman?" During the mid-nineteenth century, Stowe's rendition of Truth captured American imaginations, and the phrase "Libyan Sibyl" was endlessly reworked, even by Gage, who termed Truth the "Libyan Statue" in her letter to the *Independent,* and Olive Gilbert, who in a letter to Truth written in the 1870s spoke of Truth as the "American Sibyl."[46]

Along with another phrase that had appeared in Stowe's piece—Truth's rhetorical and possibly apocryphal question to Douglass, "Frederick, is God dead?"—versions of the "Libyan Sibyl" personified Truth until the end of the nineteenth century.[47] As an expression of enduring Christian faith, she became the authentic Negro woman, the native, the genius of spiritual inspiration uncorrupted by formal education. Toward the end of the century, however, Gage's version of Truth began to overtake Stowe's, as woman suffragists advanced Gage's Truth.

Although Frances Titus had reprinted Gage's letter as well as Stowe's article in the 1878 edition of *The Narrative of Sojourner Truth,* the primary means of popularizing "And ar'n't I a woman?" was the publication of the *History of Woman Suffrage* in 1881.[48] As for the antislavery movement, so for woman suffrage: those nineteenth-century Americans who were attuned to the power of the published record have profoundly influenced subsequent representations of the past. Nineteenth-century evangelicals outside the mainline denominations—who were far more likely to hear, comprehend, and appreciate Sojourner Truth in her own self-definition as a preacher—were less solicitous than reformers about preserving and publishing their records. Practically by default, the feminists and abolitionists, who published copiously, fashioned the historic Sojourner Truth in their own image, the one created by the feminist Frances Dana Gage.

◆ ◆ ◆

As the woman suffrage pioneers Susan B. Anthony and Elizabeth Cady Stanton were growing old in the late 1870s, they recognized a need to gather and publish the papers of the movement they had inspired in 1848 and organized in the succeeding thirty years. They wrote surviving activists to request documents, which they combined with newspaper reports and published in three volumes between 1881 and 1886. Stanton was living in Tenafly, in northern New Jersey, as she carried out most of the work; Anthony came from Rochester, New York, from time to time to visit and assist. Gage, who in the years since 1851 had moved from McConnellsville, Ohio, to St. Louis, was then living in Vineland, in southern New Jersey, a center of temperance and woman's rights enthusiasm. Having corresponded with Anthony and Stanton since the 1850s, Gage would have welcomed a request to contribute material for the *History of Woman Suffrage*. In 1879 she wrote that she was looking over her old papers and manuscripts.[49]

The feminist press of the 1880s testifies to Gage's enduring reputation as an ardent feminist. Although in wretched health, she continued to contribute to women's newspapers. After Sojourner Truth's death in 1883, the Boston *Woman's Journal* reprinted Gage's report of Truth's Akron speech. Through letters to feminist gatherings and published utterances, Gage spoke for temperance and woman suffrage right up to her death in 1884.[50] Stowe, in contrast, had turned away from reform entirely. From the early 1860s through the mid-1880s she was still writing a book a year, but she did not return to political themes. In her old age Stowe lived in Florida and became increasingly childlike, and her writing was of local color and quaint New England characters.

By the end of the century, Gage's Truth was doing feminist work for woman suffragists all around the country, though sometimes in turn-of-the-century fashion. A Memphis suffragist who imagined Truth as an "old negro mammy" nevertheless quoted Gage's report of the 1851 speech as a stick with which to beat antisuffragists, in this instance, the Reverend Thomas Dixon.[51] No longer the symbol of Christian trust, the uncorrupted Negro, or African genius, Truth was now the embodiment of women's strength that Gage had crafted. Stowe's 1863 portrait of Truth, written by a best-selling author whose religious sensibility was stronger than her feminism, expressed Victorian sentimentality. Gage's 1863 portrait of Truth, written by a woman whose radicalism had kept her at the far margins of American letters during her lifetime, has worn-and sold-well during the twentieth century.

Invention and History

It may seem ironic that Sojourner Truth is known for words she did not say, but American history is full of symbols that do their work without a basis in life. As a black and feminist talisman rather than a text, Sojourner Truth is still selling. She remains more sign than lived existence, like Betsy Ross, Chief Seattle, and Mason ("Parson") Weems's George Washington, who are also best remembered for deeds they did not perform and words they did not utter. Like other invented greats, Truth is consumed as a signifier and beloved for what we need her to have said. It is no accident that other people writing well after the fact made up what we see as most meaningful about each of those greats.

Parson Weems, who was, incidentally, a book distributor, invented the story of young George Washington's chopping down a cherry tree and being unable to tell a lie about his deed. The story played a major role in Weems's biography of Washington, which was, of course, for sale. It is perhaps not so well known that the legend of Betsy Ross, the woman celebrated for sewing the first American flag, is also fiction. Elizabeth Griscom Ross Ashburn Claypoole was a seamstress who lived in Philadelphia when the Declaration of Independence was being drafted, but her tale is the invention of her grandson, William Canby, who made it all up in 1870. During the mid-1770s the house that the city of Philadelphia has designated a historical place, where the Betsy Ross doll is for sale for $19.95, was a tavern. The bones in her grave are unidentified. Canby's Betsy Ross fills the need for a Founding Mother among the parade of men who personify the birth of the United States of America.[52]

The practice of inventing great people endures, as in the legend of *Brother Eagle, Sister Sky*, a best-selling volume said to be an 1854 speech by wise old Chief Seattle, a Native American and environmental prophet. This book, which the Earth Day U.S.A. Committee sends out as a fund raiser, is the creation of a screenwriter from Texas named Ted Perry. He wrote the text in 1971 and is horrified that it has been attributed to Chief Seattle. As in the case of Sojourner Truth's "Ar'n't I a woman?" and Betsy Ross's American flag, what makes Chief Seattle's speech work in American culture has little to do with the historical person.[53]

Today Americans who love Sojourner Truth cherish her for what they need her to have said and buy her images to invest in the idea of strong women, whether or not they are black. As in the nineteenth century, Americans consume Sojourner Truth as the embodiment of a meaning necessary for their own cultural formations, even though that meaning has changed radically since Harriet Beecher Stowe first presented it. The market for historical symbols is not limited to words, however, and Sojourner Truth images, now distributed mostly through outlets catering to feminists, have also sold briskly. This is as it was in the mid-nineteenth century.

As a person whose depiction in print depended upon the imagination of other people, Sojourner Truth was able to influence those representations only marginally. Although she never distanced herself from the texts through which Gilbert and Gage portrayed her, she attempted to correct Stowe's article within three months of its publication, protesting in a letter to the *Boston Commonwealth* that she was not African and that she never called people "Honey." She sent the editor, James Redpath, six copies of her *Narrative,* suggesting that her correct history was to be between its covers. She also asked readers to purchase her photograph, for she was in ill health and restricted to her home in Battle Creek, Michigan. "I am," she said, "living on my shadow."[54] As though surrendering language to women who were initiated into the esoteric practices of writing and publishing, she sought self-representation in a medium that many Americans, even the highly educated, regarded as transparent and whose etymology came from the Greek words meaning "light writing": photography.

Truth in Photography

After the Stowe and Gage essays increased her visibility in 1863, Sojourner Truth found a new means of reaching supporters and raising money in the rage for the new *cartes de visite* from France. Between 1863 and about 1875, Sojourner Truth had at least fourteen photographic portraits made of herself in two formats, *carte de visite* (4-by-2½ inches) and cabinet card (6½-by-4½ inches), in at least seven sittings. In the 1860s and 1870s, Truth stocked copies of these photographs and the *Narrative of Sojourner Truth* to sell through the mail and wherever she made personal appearances. While donations of any size were welcome, Truth seems to have asked about $.33 for each *carte de visite* and $.50 for the larger cabinet cards, in line with the prices that photographers and publishers charged in the early 1860s, $2.00 to $3.00 per dozen.[55]

Photographic portraiture spread as soon as photography was invented in 1839. Daguerreotypes made portraits commonplace in the 1840s, and Douglass and Gage both sat for daguerreotype likenesses. Two subsequent developments—the 1851 invention of collodion wet-plate negative technology, which made it possible to print an indefinite number of prints from a single negative, and the 1854 patenting of the multilens camera—ushered in the era of popular portrait photography. *Cartes de visite*, the invention of André Adolphe Eugène Disdéri of Paris in the mid-1850s, were made with a camera with four, six, eight, or twelve lenses exposing different portions of a single large plate. If the lenses were opened simultaneously, several small photos of the same pose were produced. If the lenses were opened sequentially, the sitter could adjust her pose from one exposure to another. Once the negative was developed, the photos would be mounted and cut apart, and the four, eight, or more photographs the size of a visiting card would be cheap, having been developed and printed all at once. Because *cartes de visite* were so small, they did not permit much background or detail, but they became the most popular form of portrait in the early 1860s. In their ubiquity, *cartes de visite* began to make photographic images a means of communication as familiar and accepted as the printed word.[56]

During the Civil War, *cartes de visite* filled a multitude of purposes. *Cartes de visite* of great men were sold as inspiration to the masses; authors (such as Stowe), politicians (such as Abraham Lincoln, whose 1860 *carte* by Mathew Brady was a campaign token), actors, and lecturers (such as Gage) carried them about and sold them at personal appearances and through other outlets as handy forms of publicity, like twentieth-century baseball cards. More to the point for Sojourner Truth, some circulated within the Union as anti-Confederate propaganda-images of starved prisoners of war from the Confederate prison at Andersonville, Georgia, the scourged back of the fugitive slave volunteer Gordon, and white-looking children whose whiteness had not protected them from enslavement.[57] These fund-raising *cartes* may well have inspired Truth, for her portraits would also have served to remind purchasers that she symbolized the woman who had been a slave.

Had Truth's *cartes de visite* served only as abolitionist fund raising, Truth might have chosen to pose in settings or costumes that evoked the tragedy of her origins. Like Gordon of the whip-scarred back, she might have prominently exhibited some image of suffering or toil, such as her right hand, injured during her last year in slavery. Or she might have circulated the only image of Sojourner Truth other than her photographs (or engravings made from them), a sketch made of her in Northampton, probably in the 1860s. In this drawing, she is doing laundry, her arms plunged deep into wash water. That was not the kind of image in her photographs, and she did the choosing.[58]

The portrait, one of her favorites, was taken in Detroit in 1864. This *carte de visite* is in the vernacular style that became widespread in the 1850s, as daguerreotypes grew more popular than painted portraits with elaborate backdrops. This photo shows no landscape or interior, and the props—knitting, a book, and a vase full of flowers on a table—are simplified into tokens of leisure and feminine gentility. As in all of the other photographs of Sojourner Truth, she wears expertly tailored clothing made of handsome, substantial material, the black and white she favored for public speaking. In several portraits she is dressed in the Quaker-style clothing that feminist and antislavery lecturers wore to distinguish themselves from showily dressed actresses, who were not respectable figures. Her hair is wrapped plainly, but not in the madras handkerchief that Harriet Beecher Stowe characterized as in the "manner of her race."[59] In other photographs, Truth wears fashionable clothing, again very well tailored, and she presents the image of a respectable, middle-class matron but, perhaps, also that of a woman advertising her suitability as a model of civilized comportment for the freedwomen refugees in Washington, D.C.

She is sitting in a studio (in other portraits, also taken in studios, she stands with a cane or sits holding a book or portrait), with knitting in her hands and a book on the table. Truth knitted, but this yarn, held in only one hand, conveys mainly the motherliness that was central to her self-fashioning. According to the conventions of the genre of celebrity portraiture, she looks past the camera, which lends an air of weighty seriousness.[60] Her posture is relaxed but upright, communicating an impression of easy composure. For a woman of at least sixty-five, she looks remarkably young, but the relative youthfulness of her appearance takes nothing from the overall gravity of the persona. She is mature and intelligent, not reading, but wearing eyeglasses that might have helped her knit and that certainly, like the book on the table, gave her an educated air. In none of these portraits is there anything beyond blackness that would inspite charity, nothing of the piteous slave mother, chest-baring insolent, grinning minstrel, or amusing naïf.

The original caption, "I Sell the Shadow to Support the Substance. SOJOURNER TRUTH," explains the photograph's fund-raising function and is as much a part of the rhetoric of the image as the portrait itself. That caption rarely appears in late twentieth-century representations, although the image is for sale today from several feminist mail-order houses. Sojourner Truth photographs still bear a caption; however, sentences from Gage's "Ar'n't I a woman?" report replace "I sell the shadow to support the substance," because the market has changed, in its tastes and in its relation to Truth herself. Current consumers purchase images of Truth to embody strength, not dependence, no matter how dignified its composition. More to the point, it is no longer possible to contribute to Truth through purchase of her book or *carte de visite*. "I sell the shadow to support the substance" exhorted its original purchasers and today remains authentic, but in today's context, with Truth long dead and without heirs who claim her estate, it means very little.[61]

Like legions of other *cartes de visite*, Sojourner Truth's portraits show a solid bourgeoise, even to the eyeglasses. The image does not capture the woman who belonged to the weird Matthias Kingdom in the 1830s or who reportedly rolled up her sleeve to bare her arm or took down her bodice to show her breast in the 1850s. The woman sitting here does not look as though she would speak in dialect, and hers is the antithesis of a naked body. Blackness, of course, conveyed its own messages.

Although prosperous African Americans had their photographs taken for their own use, bourgeois portraiture was as uncommon as bourgeois blacks. In the 1860s images of black people were rare, and most of them had not been taken at the instigation of the subjects. Photographs of black men were most often found in the files of city police, where photography had taken its place as a tool of law enforcement two decades earlier.[62]

Another genre of photography also took people of color as its subject matter: the anthropological specimen photographs that displayed "types" of native peoples to educated metropolitans. In anthropological photographs, captive individuals, usually stripped of their clothing and staring straight into the camera, were displayed as examples of otherness, like insects pinned in cases or stuffed mammals in museums. British and French explorers specialized in this genre of natural history photography, but the American biologist Louis Agassiz had specimen photographs of enslaved African Americans taken in the 1850s.[63] Sojourner Truth's posture, clothing, and stance distinguish her from the criminals or native types who shared her color, for she is well groomed, well clothed, and posed so as not to look directly into the camera's lens. Nevertheless, the same underlying assumption may have made all three sorts of photographs serviceable: the widespread nineteenth-century belief that the camera captured reality.

Henry David Thoreau, Ralph Waldo Emerson, and Oliver Wendell Holmes, among others (perhaps including Sojourner Truth), thought that the photograph was, in Thoreau's words, "an exact and accurate description of facts."[64] The transparency that many saw as the identifying characteristic of photography would seem to allow an unmediated view of the subject, and that characteristic may have made photography all the more attractive to Sojourner Truth. But while theorists of photography hailed it as reality, portrait photography was thoroughly commercialized; set poses and formulaic presentations were its stock-in-trade. The poses were meant to convey two different and ultimately incompatible messages; the metonymic, through which the sitter stood for respectable social standing, and the individual, through which the image revealed the sitter's unique inner character.

Even as her *cartes de visite* portrayed Sojourner Truth—the woman who had been a slave, the subject of the *Narrative of Sojourner Truth,* the advocate of black emancipation and woman's rights—they also appealed to the preconditioned sight of her clientele, which transformed the palm-sized image of a woman in a studio into the simulacrum of a well-dressed Victorian in a tasteful parlor. These inherently discrepant meanings, like the tongues in which Jesus' disciples spoke to the people of many nations when the Holy Spirit filled them, were subject to reinterpretation. Photography may be writing with light, but like writing with words, it is a sign system and has its own rhetorics of representation.[65] Sojourner Truth was seizing control of her replicas: shaping the meaning of the images that she sold by deciding when to have her photograph taken, what to wear, what expression to adopt, which props to hold, and which photographer to patronize, while her photographer adjusted the framing, focus, and distance. Because she sold her *cartes de visite* to people whose possessions were likely to end up in repositories, she still exercises that control.

Sojourner Truth's photographic portraits are not transparent representations of her authentic being, nor do they convey a simple truth. In her *cartes de visite,* as in other photographs, the sense of reality is enigmatic. As one critic notes, photographic images are a place of "resistance to meaning."[66] If there is no unmediated access to Sojourner Truth, no means of knowing her with certainty, nonetheless some conclusions can be drawn about how she wanted to be known.

Sojourner Truth was willing to use the resources offered by popular culture to replicate and distribute representations of herself for her material support, and she did need the money. A slave until she was thirty, Isabella was destitute when she entered life as a free woman in 1827. She worked at ill-paid household labor in New York City until she became Sojourner Truth in 1843. Yet after the 1850 publication of her *Narrative,* she managed to buy a house in Northampton in 1850, a house in Harmonia, Michigan, in 1856, and a house in Battle Creek, Michigan, in the 1860s, in which she died in 1883. With the exception of $390 that the Freedmen's Bureau paid her for relief work in Washington after the Civil War, her means of support were the proceeds from the sale of her book and her "shadows" and donations from her reform-minded audiences and supporters. Considering the poverty in which masses of freed people and working women remained in the nineteenth century, her persona—as embodied in these objects— proved remunerative. By contrast, her husband had died in an Ulster

County, New York poorhouse before the Civil War, and her daughters died destitute in Battle Creek in the late nineteenth and early twentieth centuries. They lacked marketable personas and a supply of commodities with which to memorialize them.

◆ ◆ ◆

As though filled with the Holy Spirit, but adapting to the nineteenth century disciples' speaking in tongues, Sojourner Truth employed photographs as a means to communicate without writing. *Cartes de visite* might seem to circumvent the whole system of learned culture and racial stereotype that is embedded in language, so as to allow her to reach others directly. Her images, apparently unmediated, seemed to be truthful replications that communicated the essence of her real self. In photographs that she arranged and paid for, Sojourner Truth embodied herself for herself, but not in words, which would have been more convenient for her biographer. As in the 1840s, when demand for slave narratives made her own venture into that product line profitable, Truth seized upon new technology to do her work of self-representation.

As a woman whose person had been the property of others and who remembered being despised and abused, Truth may well have cherished her portraits as her own literal embodiment: as a refutation of her having deserved the abuse that she had received, as a rendering visible of the spirit otherwise trapped within. Images like hers were largely missing from American culture, even from the feminist and antislavery subcultures. Through her images, created by modern means, Truth earned money, ensured her physical survival, and, more, inserted herself into historical memory.[67] Sojourner Truth sold the shadow to support the substance when the substance was her own bodily subsistence and when the substance was her place in history. She appropriated the power of the American gaze and used it in her own mimesis.

Truth's widely circulated photographs traveled in broad currents of American culture, for by popularizing the photographic image, *cartes de visite* such as hers contributed to the simplification of experience, easing individuality into directly grasped symbol.[68] In the nineteenth century this process made Sojourner Truth = "the Libyan Sibyl" = black exotic, and in the twentieth century, it made Sojourner Truth = "Ar'n't I a woman?" = strong (black) woman. In exchange for handy symbolism, however, something less predictable is lost: the complicated and unexpected experience of a northern ex-slave and itinerant preacher who invented Sojourner Truth in New York City in 1843 and who made herself into a familiar figure among feminist abolitionists through the sale of endlessly reproducible objects. Her little photographs could speak to people of all nations (feminists and nonfeminists), but like the voice of the Holy Spirit, their meaning remains powerful and ambiguous.

APPENDIX 1

This is the report of Sojourner Truth's speech in Akron, Ohio, in 1851 as it appears in the *Salem* [Ohio] *Anti-Slavery Bugle,* June 21, 1851, reported by Marius Robinson. The newspaper is held by the American Antiquarian Society, Worcester, Massachusetts.

One of the most unique and interesting speeches of the Convention was made by Sojourner Truth, an emancipated slave. It is impossible to transfer it to paper, or convey any adequate idea of the effect it produced upon the audience. Those only can appreciate it who saw her powerful form, her whole-souled, earnest gestures, and listened to her strong and truthful tones. She came forward to the platform and addressing the President said with great simplicity:

May I say a few words? Receiving an affirmative answer, she proceeded; I want to say a few words about this matter. I am a woman's rights [*sic*]. I have as much muscle as any man, and can do as much work as any man. I have plowed and reaped and husked and chopped and mowed, and can any man do more than that? I have heard much about the sexes being equal; I can carry as much as any man, and can eat as much too, if I can get it. I am as strong as any man that is now. As for intellect, all I can say is, if a woman have a pint and a man a quart—why cant she have her little pint full? You need not be afraid to give us our rights for fear we will take too much,—for we cant take more than our pint'll hold. The poor men seem to be all in confusion, and dont know what to do. Why children, if you have woman's rights give it to her and you will feel better. You will have your own rights, and they wont be so much trouble. I cant read, but I can hear. I have heard the bible and have learned that Eve caused man to sin. Well if woman upset the world, do give her a chance to set it right side up again. The Lady has spoken about Jesus, how he never spurned woman from him, and she was right. When Lazarus died, Mary and Martha came to him with faith and love and besought him to raise their brother. And Jesus wept—and Lazarus came forth. And how came Jesus into the world? Through God who created him and woman who bore him. Man, where is your part? But the women are coming up blessed be God and a few of the men are coming up with them. But man is in a tight place, the poor slave is on him, woman is coming on him, and he is surely between a hawk and a buzzard.

This report also appears with commentary in C. Peter Ripley, ed., *The Black Abolitionist Papers* (5 vols., Chapel Hill, 1985–1992), IV, 81–83.

APPENDIX 2

This is the letter that Frances Dana Gage published in the *Independent*, April 23, 1863. The letter was soon reprinted and edited by various newspapers, including the *Boston Commonwealth,* May 1, 1863, which cut the lines about being whipped. Both newspapers are in the collections of the American Antiquarian Society, Worcester, Massachusetts.

"SOJOURNER TRUTH" BY MRS. F. D. GAGE.

The story of "Sojourner Truth," by Mrs. H. B. Stowe, in the April number of *The Atlantic* will be read by thousands in the East and West with intense interest; and as those who knew this remarkable woman will lay down this periodical, there will be heard in home-circles throughout Ohio, Michigan, Wisconsin, and Illinois many an anecdote of the weird, wonderful creature, who was at once a marvel and a mystery.

Mrs. Stowe's remarks on Sojourner's opinion of Woman's Rights, bring vividly to my mind a scene in Ohio, never to be forgotten by those who witnessed it. In the spring of 1851, a Woman's Rights Convention was called in Akron, Ohio, by the friends of that then wondrously unpopular cause. I attended that Convention. No one at this day can conceive of the state of feeling of the multitude that came together on that occasion.

The Convention in the spring of 1850, in Salem, Ohio, reported at length in *The New York Tribune* by that staunch friend of Human rights, Oliver Johnson, followed in October of the same year by another convention at Worcester, Mass., well reported and well abused, with divers minor conventions, each amply vilified and caricatured, had set the world all agog, and the people, finding the women *in earnest,* turned out in large numbers to see and hear.

The leaders of the movement, staggering under the weight of disapprobation already laid upon them, and tremblingly alive to every appearance of evil that might spring up in their midst, were many of them almost thrown into panics on the first day of the meeting, by seeing a tall, gaunt black woman in a gray dress and white turban, surmounted by an uncouth sun-bonnet, march deliberately into the church, walk with the air of a queen up the aisle, and take her seat upon the pulpit steps: A buzz of dis-

approbation was heard all over the house, and such words as these fall upon
listening ears:

"An abolition affair!" "Women's Rights and niggers!" "We told you so. Go it, old darky!"

I chanced upon that occasion to wear my first laurels in public life, as president of the meeting. At my request, order was restored, and the business of the hour went on. The morning session closed; the afternoon session was held; the evening exercises came and went; old Sojourner, quiet and reticent as the "Libyan Statue," sat crouched against the wall on a corner of the pulpit stairs, her sun-bonnet shading her eyes, her elbow on her knee, and her chin resting on her broad, hard palm.

At intermissions she was busy selling the "Life of Sojourner Truth," a narrative of her own strange and adventurous life.

Again and again timorous and trembling ones came to me and said with earnestness, "Don't let her speak, Mrs. G. It will ruin us. Every newspaper in the land will have our cause mixed with abolition and niggers, and we shall be utterly denounced." My only answer was, "We shall see when the time comes."

The second day the work waxed warm. Methodist, Baptist, Episcopal, Presbyterian, and Universalist ministers came in to hear and discuss the resolutions brought forth. One claimed superior rights and privileges for man because of superior intellect; another because of the manhood of Christ. If God had desired the equality of woman, he would have given some token of his will through the birth, life, and death of the Savior. Another gave us a theological view of the awful sin of our first mother. There were few women in those days that dared to "speak in meeting," and the august teachers of the people, with long-winded bombast, were seeming to get the better of us, while the boys in the galleries and sneerers among the pews were enjoying hugely the discomfiture, as they supposed, of the strong-minded. Some of the tender-skinned friends were growing indignant and on the point of losing dignity, and the atmosphere of the convention betokened a storm.

Slowly from her seat in the corner rose Sojourner Truth, who, till now, had hardly lifted her head. "Don't let her speak," gasped a half-dozen in my ear. She moved slowly and solemnly to the front; laid her old bonnet at her feet, and turned her great speaking eyes to me:

There was a hissing sound of disapprobation above and below. I rose and announced "Sojourner Truth," and begged the audience to keep silence for a few moments. The tumult subsided at once, and every eye was fixed on this almost Amazon form, which stood nearly six feet high, head erect, an eye piercing the upper air like one in a dream. At her first word there was a profound hush. She spoke in deep tones, which, though not loud, reached every ear in the house, and away through the throng at the doors and windows.

"Well, chillen, whar dar's so much racket dar must be som'ting out o' kilter. I tink dat, 'twixt the niggers of de Souf and de women at de Norf, all a-talking 'bout rights, de white men will be in a fix pretty soon. But what's all this here talking 'bout? Dat man over dar say dat woman needs to be helped into carriages, and lifted ober ditches, and to have de best place eberywhar. Nobody eber helps me into carriages, or ober mud-puddles, or gives me any best place;" and, raising herself to her full height, and her voice to a pitch like rolling thunder, she asked, "And ar'n't I a woman? Look at me. Look at my arm," and she bared her right arm to the shoulder, showing its tremendous muscular power. "I have plowed and planted and gathered into barns, and no man could head me—and ar'n't I a woman? I could work as much and eat as much as a man, (when I could get it,) and bear de lash as well—and ar'n't I a woman? I have borne thirteen chillen, and seen 'em mos' all sold off into slavery, and when I cried out with a mother's grief, none but Jesus heard—and ar'n't I a woman? When dey talks 'bout dis ting in de head. What dis dey call it?" "Intellect," whispered some one near. "Dat's it, honey. What's dat got to do with woman's rights or niggers' rights? If my cup won't hold but a pint and yourn holds a quart, wouldn't ye be mean not to let me have my little half-measure full?" and she pointed her significant finger and sent a keen glance at the minister who had made the argument. The cheering was long and loud. "Den dat little man in black dar, he say woman can't have as much right as man 'cause Christ wa'n't a woman. *Whar did your Christ come from?*"

Rolling thunder could not have stilled that crowd as did those deep wonderful tones, as she stood there with outstretched arms and eye of fire. Raising her voice still louder, she repeated,

"Whar did you Christ come from? From God and a woman. Man had noting to do with him." Oh! what a rebuke she gave the little man. Turning again to another objector, she took up the defense of Mother Eve. I cannot follow her through it all. It was pointed and witty and solemn; eliciting at almost every sentence deafening applause; and she ended by asserting "that if de fust woman God ever made was strong enough to turn de world upside down all her one lone, all dese togeder," and she glanced her eye over us, "ought to be able to turn it back an git it right side up again, and now dey is asking to, de men better let 'em." (Long continuous cheering.) " 'Bleeged to ye for hearin' on me, and now old Sojourner ha'n't got nothin' more to say."

Amid roars of applause she turned to her corner, leaving more than one of us with streaming eyes and hearts beating with gratitude. She had taken us up in her great strong arms and carried us safely over the slough of difficulty, turning the whole tide in our favor.

I have given but a faint sketch of her speech. I have never in my life seen anything like the magical influence that subdued the mobbish spirit of the day, and turned the jibes and sneers of an excited crowd into notes of respect and admiration. Hundreds rushed up to shake hands and congratulate the glorious old mother, and bid her "God-speed" on her mission of "testifying agin concernin' the wickedness of this here people."

Once upon a Sabbath in Michigan an abolition meeting was held. Parker Pillsbury was speaker, and expressed himself freely upon the conduct of the churches regarding slavery. While he spoke, there came up a fearful thunder-storm. A young Methodist rose and, interrupting him, said he felt alarmed; he felt as if God's judgment was about to fall upon him for daring to sit and hear such blasphemy; that it made his hair almost rise with terror. Here a voice sounding above the rain that beat upon the roof, the sweeping surge of the winds, the crashing of the limbs of trees, swaying of branches, and the rolling of thunder, spoke out: "Chile, don't be skeered; you're not goin' to be harmed. I don't speck God's ever heern tell on ye!"

It was all she said, but it was enough. I might multiply anecdotes (and some of the best cannot be told) till your pages would not contain them, and yet the fund not be exhausted. Therefore, I will close, only saying to those who think public opinion does not change, that they have only to look at the progress of ideas from the standpoint of old Sojourner Truth twelve years ago.

The despised and mobbed African is now the heroine of an article in the most popular periodical in the United States. Then Sojourner could say, "If woman wants rights, let her take 'em." Now, women do take them, and public opinion sustains them.

Sojourner Truth is not dead; but, old and feeble, she rests from her labors near Battle Creek, Michigan.

NOTES

Nell Irvin Painter is the Edwards Professor of American History at Princeton University. She wishes to thank the National Endowment for the Humanities (grant FA-30715-92), the staffs of the American Antiquarian Society and the Schlesinger Library of Radcliffe College, Thadious Davis, Joan Hedrick, Patricia Hill, Dona Irvin, Mary Kelley, Ray Matthews, Nellie McKay, Richard Newman, Lyde Cullen

Sizer, Elaine Wise, Jean Fagan Yellin, Ronald Zboray, Nancy Hewitt, David Blight, and David Thelen.

1. Isabella's name, like the names of many African Americans, changed over the course of her lifetime. Her father was known as James Bomefree, but as a slave, Isabella was known only by her first name. Her last employers in Ulster County, New York, were named Van Wagenen, the name she used until 1843; biographers have generally used that name. However, reports in New York City and records of the Northampton Association of Education and Industry indicate that in the mid-1840s, she was known there as "Isabel or Isabella Vanwagner," "Isabel or Isabella Vanwagnen," as well as "Sojourner" and "Mrs. Sojourner." See vol. 5, Accounts, pp. 245, 251, Northampton Association of Education and Industry Records, 1836–1853 (American Antiquarian Society, Worcester, Mass.); vol. 7, Day Book No. 4, pp. 24, 246, 149, 183, 209, 210, *ibid.* Acts 2:1–18.
2. [Olive Gilbert and Frances Titus], *Narrative of Sojourner Truth; A Bondswoman of Olden Times, Emancipated by the New York Legislature in the Early Part of the Present Century; With a History of Her Labors and Correspondence Drawn From Her "Book of Life"* (1878; Salem, N.H., 1990), 62–71.
3. The association of photography with power comes from Susan Sontag, *On Photography* (New York, 1977), 4, 9.
4. See Karen Halttunen, *Confidence Men and Painted Women: A Study of Middle-Class Culture in America, 1830–1870* (New Haven, 1982); and John F. Kasson, *Rudeness and Civility: Manners in Nineteenth-Century Urban America* (New York, 1990).
5. *New York Journal of Commerce*, Sept. 26, 1834; *New York Commercial Advertiser*, Sept. 26, 1834; *New York Courier and Enquirer*, Oct. 2, 1834, April 17, 1835. For a full-length treatment of Matthias, see Paul E. Johnson and Sean Wilentz, *The Kingdom of Matthias* (New York, 1994).
6. G[ilbert] Vale, *Fanaticism; Its Source and Influence, Illustrated by the Simple Narrative of Isabella in the Case of Matthias, Mr. and Mrs. B. Folger, Mr. Pierson, Mr. Mills, Catherine, Isabella, &c. &c. A Reply to W. I., Stone, with Descriptive Portraits of All the Parties, While at Sing-Sing and at Third Street.—Containing the Whole Truth—and Nothing But the Truth* (New York, 1835), pt. I, 3–6, 63.
7. On beatings, see [Gilbert and Titus], *Narrative of Sojourner Truth*, 26–27, 33. On sexual abuse, see *ibid.*, 29–31, 81–82. The use of corporal punishment to discipline slaves has been widely acknowledged. On the sale of Truth's son, following a practice that was illegal but nonetheless common, see *ibid.*, 44–54. Although his mother had the law on her side, she was rare among the poor and uneducated in being able to exercise her legal rights. For the most famous case of a New Yorker kidnapped and sold South, see Solomon Northup, *Twelve Years a Slave*, ed. Sue Eakin and Joseph Logsdon (Baton Rouge, 1968). The slander case grew out of the breakup of the Matthias Kingdom. Benjamin and Ann Folger accused Isabella of having attempted to poison them; she countersued and won a $125 settlement. See Vale, *Fanaticism*, pt. II, 3, 116; and Johnson and Wilentz, *Kingdom of Matthias*, 167–68.

8. Nell Irvin Painter, *Sojourner Truth: A Life, A Symbol* (forthcoming). This biography will be published in 1995 by W. W. Norton & Co.

9. See Jean Fagan Yellin, *Women and Sisters: The Antislavery Feminists in American Culture* (New Haven, 1989), 77–87; and Leo Braudy, *The Frenzy of Renown: Fame and Its History* (New York, 1986), 450–583.

10. See Nell Irvin Painter, "Sojourner Truth in Life and Memory: Writing the Biography of an American Exotic," *Gender and History*, 2 (Spring 1990), 3–16.

11. Isabella married Thomas, a fellow slave of John J. Dumont, in about 1814. Her *Narrative* provides a few clues as to the nature of their relationship, though it indicates that Isabella left Thomas as soon as she was free. Between about 1815 and about 1826, Isabella had five children, the names and birth dates of only four of whom are known: Diana, born c, 1815; Peter, c. 1821; Elizabeth, c. 1825; and Sophia, c. 1826. These dates are from the Berenice Bryant Lowe Collection (Bentley Historical Library, University of Michigan, Ann Arbor).

12. Edgar J. McManus, *A History of Negro Slavery in New York* (Syracuse, 1966), 70, 173.

13. See Carleton Mabee, *Sojourner Truth: Slave, Prophet, Legend* (New York, 1993), 60–66, 217–18; and Carleton Mabee, "Sojourner Truth, Bold Prophet: Why Did She Never Learn to Read," *New York History*, 69 (Jan. 1988), 55–77. Mabee's approach to Truth epistemology is very different from mine, in that he sees literacy as the single conduit to knowledge. His definition of truth is more rigid, for he does not discuss issues of representation.

14. Frederick Douglass, "What I Found at the Northampton Association," in *History of Florence, Massachusetts. Including a Complete Account of the Northampton Association of Education and Industry*, ed. Charles A. Sheffeld (Florence, 1895), 131–32. Douglass's first wife, Anna, like Truth, did not read or write. Their children, however, were all carefully educated, the daughter in the arts, the sons in the printing trade. See William S. McFeely, *Frederick Douglass* (New York, 1991), 92, 154, 160–61, 239, 248–49, 258.

15. Vale, *Fanaticism*, pt. II, 126, pt. I, 61–63; E[lizabeth] A. Lukins, "George Thompson in Rochester," *Salem* [Ohio] *Anti-Slavery Bugle*, May 17, 1851.

16. Carl Van Wagenen, memoir and genealogy, March 8, 1991, quoting a letter of Jan. 29, 1884, found in the home of Beatrice Jordan of St. Remy, N.Y. (in Nell Irvin Painter's possession).

17. C. W. Christman, Jr., *The Onward Way: The Story of the New York Annual Conference of the Methodist Church, Commemorating the 150th Session of the Conference, June 16, 1800-May 12, 1949* (Saugerties, 1949), 79–81.

18. Walter J. Ong, *Orality and Literacy: The Technologizing of the Word* (London, 1982), 78–116; Plato, *Phaedrus and the Seventh and Eighth Letters*, trans. Walter Hamilton (London, 1973), 96–99. A study of nineteenth-century black Canadians finds that literacy was often of more symbolic than material use, for it brought little advantage or disadvantage in everyday life to people so subject to racial prejudice. See Harvey Graff, *The Literacy Myth: Literacy and Social Structure in the Nineteenth-Century City* (New York, 1979), 51–91.

19. Richard D. Brown, *Knowledge Is Power: The Diffusion of Information in Early America, 1700–1865* (New York, 1989), 125–35, 184–85, 244, 283; [Gilbert and Titus], *Narrative of Sojourner Truth*, 108.

20. Gayatri Chakravorty Spivak, "Once Again into the Postcolonial Banal." paper presented at the Davis Center for Historical Studies, Princeton University, March 1. 1991 (in Painter's possession). Spivak uses the concept of overstated differences in several essays, including Gayatri Chakravorty Spivak, "Three Women's Texts and a Critique of Imperialism," in *"Race," Writing, and Difference,* ed. Henry Louis Gates, Jr. (Chicago, 1986), 262–80, and in Gayatri Chakravorty Spivak, *In Other Worlds: Essays in Cultural Politics* (New York, 1988). [Gilbert and Titus]. *Narrative of Sojourner Truth,* 24.

21. Jacques Lacan writes often of the "symbolic" system, but because in this essay I use "symbolic" in its usual sense, I am avoiding Lacan's terminology. The contrast between the "symbolic" and "imaginary" realms runs throughout his work. For a brief treatment, see Jacques Lacan, *The Seminar of Jacques Lacan,* bk. I: *Freud's Papers on Technique,* ed. Jacques Alain Miller, trans. John Forrester (New York, 1988), 208–49, esp. 233–44.

22. Leo Braudy points out that the meaning of any performer is what her audiences want her to mean, for "to be talked about is to be part of a story, and to be part of a story is to be at the mercy of storytellers—the media and their audience." Braudy, *Frenzy of Renown,* 583, 592.

23. C. Peter Ripley to Nell Irvin Painter, Oct. 8, 1992 (in Painter's possession). C. Peter Ripley, ed., *The Black Abolitionist Papers* (5 vols., Chapel Hill, 1985–1992), IV, 81–83.

24. Virginia Woolf, *A Room of One's Own* (1929; San Diego, 1981), 26.

25. [Gilbert and Titus], *Narrative of Sojourner Truth,* xii.

26. Vol. 3, p. 229; vol. 7, pp. 304–27, Northampton Association of Education and Industry Records.

27. *International Genealogical Index* (microfiche, 9,231 fiche, Salt Lake City, 1988); [Gilbert and Titus], *Narrative of Sojourner Truth,* 276–78. Olive Gilbert may well have been associated with her Connecticut neighbor, Prudence Crandall, who lived in a nearby town and was prosecuted in 1833–1834 for her willingness to educate black as well as white girls. George Benson, a founder of the Northampton Association, was proud of his part in Crandall's defense.

28. William L. Andrews, *To Tell a Free Story: The First Century of Afro American Autobiography, 1760–1865* (Urbana, 1986), 97, 138.

29. Hellmut Lehmann-Haupt, *The Book in America: A History of the Making, the Selling, and the Collecting of Books in the United States* (New York, 1939), 63–64; Ronald J. Zboray, "Antebellum Reading and the Ironies of Technological Innovation," in *Reading in America: Literature and Social History,* ed. Cathy N. Davidson (Baltimore, 1989), 188–89.

30. Mary Kelley, *Private Woman, Public Stage: Literary Domesticity in Nineteenth Century America* (New York, 1984), 10–11; Zboray, "Antebellum Reading." 190; Brown, *Knowledge Is Power,* 218, 19, 282. See also Raymond Williams, *The Long Revolution* (1961, Harmondsworth, 1965), 186–88.

31. Printers' file (American Antiquarian Society).

32. Victoria Ortiz, *Sojourner Truth: A Self Made Woman* (Philadelphia, 1974), 92 Ortiz says that Truth's *Narrative* went through six editions, but seven appear in *The National Union Catalog, Pre 1956 Imprints* (754 vols. London, 1968–), CX–CIX, 469.

33. Andrews, *To Tell a Free Story*, 108.
34. See, for example, Jean Baudrillard, *Le systeme des objects: Les essais CXXXVII* (The object system) (Paris, 1968), 14–16, 116–21; Claude Levi-Strauss, *Conversations with Claude Levi-Strauss*, ed. G. Charbonnier, trans. John Weightman and Doreen Weightman (London, 1969); and Nell Irvin Painter, "Difference, Slavery, and Memory: Sojourner Truth in Feminist Abolitionism," in *The Abolitionist Sisterhood: Women's Political Culture in Antebellum America*, ed. Jean Fagan Yellin and John C. Van Horne (Ithaca, 1994), 140–59.
35. Yellin, *Women and Sisters*, 23–26; Lee Chambers-Schiller, " 'A Good Work Among the People': The Political Culture of the Boston Antislavery Fair," in *Abolitionist Sisterhood*, ed. Yellin and Van Horne. See Mary Douglas and Baron Isherwood, *The World of Goods* (New York, 1979), 59–70, 76–84.
36. This situation will presently change. Truth's 1878 *Narrative* is currently available in paperback through Oxford University Press: [Olive Gilbert], *Narrative of Sojourner Truth, A Bondswoman of Olden Time: With a History of Her Labors & Correspondence Drawn from Her "Book of Life"* (New York, 1991). A new Vintage edition of the original, 128-page, 1850 work has appeared: Margaret Washington, ed., *The Narrative of Sojourner Truth* (New York, 1993). I will republish the whole 1884 edition with a full introduction in 1995.
37. For a discussion of "puffing," often a more commercial transaction than today's "blurbing," which is not done for money, see Kelley, *Private Woman, Public Stage*, 9. Stowe's puff became the introduction to the late 1853 edition of *The Narrative of Sojourner Truth*. The original, in Stowe's hand, is in the possession of Lisa Baskin of Leeds, Massachusetts, and is used here with permission.
38. Susan Coultrap-McQuin, *Doing Literary Business: American Women Writers in the Nineteenth Century* (Chapel Hill, 1990), 86–90, 94–99.
39. *Ibid.*, 97–98; Harriet Beecher Stowe, "Sojourner Truth, the Libyan Sibyl," *Atlantic Monthly*, 11 (April 1863), 473–81. On Stowe's "Libyan Sibyl," see Painter, "Sojourner Truth in Life and Memory"; and Patricia Hill, "Writing Out the War: Harriet Beecher Stowe's Averted Gaze," in *Divided Houses: Gender and the Civil War*, ed. Catherine Clinton and Nina Silber (New York, 1992), 260–78.
40. I am indebted to Stowe's most recent scholarly biographer, Joan Hedrick, for this information. Joan Hedrick to Painter, Sept. 30, 1989 (in Painter's possession). See Joan Hedrick, *Harriet Beecher Stowe: A Life* (New York, 1994).
41. Stowe, "Sojourner Truth, the Libyan Sibyl," 476–77, 480. My analysis differs from that of Margaret Washington, who says that "the immediate impression of Sojourner that [Stowe] advanced was candid and memorable." Margaret Washington, "Introduction: The Enduring Legacy of Sojourner Truth," in *Narrative of Sojourner Truth*, ed. Washington, xi.
42. See *Philadelphia Woman's Advocate*, Feb. 26, 1856; Frances Dana Gage to Susan B. Anthony, [c. 1856], Papers of Frances Dana Barker Gage, 1808–1884 (Schlesinger Library, Radcliffe College, Cambridge, Mass.).
43. *Pittsburgh Saturday Visiter*, Nov. 16, 1850; Philadelphia Woman's Advocate, June 21, 1856.
44. *Pittsburgh Saturday Visiter*, Oct. 18, 1851.
45. Frances Dana Gage, "Sojourner Truth," *Independent*, April 23, 1863.

46. *Ibid.;* Olive Gilbert to Sojourner Truth, Jan. 17, 1870, [c. 1870], in [Gilbert and Titus], *Narrative of Sojourner Truth,* 276–78.

47. The "Frederick, is God dead?" anecdote appears in Harriet Beecher Stowe, "The President's Message," *Independent,* Dec. 20, 1860. On it, see Mabee, *Sojourner Truth,* 83–84

48. Elizabeth Cady Stanton, Susan B. Anthony, and Matilda Joslyn Gage, *History of Woman Suffrage* (3 vols. New York, 1881–1886), 1, 110–13.

49. Matilda Joslyn Gage (no relation to Frances Dana Gage) aided Elizabeth Cady Stanton and Susan B. Anthony in preparing the *History of Woman Suffrage.* Three later volumes, edited by Ida Husted Harper, took the story up to the passage of the Nineteenth Amendment giving women the vote nationwide. *Boston Woman's Journal, Aug. 30, 1879; Elizabeth Griffith. In Her Own Right: The Life of Elizabeth Cady Stanton* (New York, 1984), 176–83; Ellen Carol DuBois, "Making Women's History: Activist Historians of Women's Rights, 1880–1940," *Radical History Review,* 49 (Winter 1991), 61–84.

50. *Boston Woman's Journal,* Dec. 1, 1883, Nov. 15, Dec. 27, 1884.

51. Folder 1, Lide Parker (Smith) Meriwether Papers (Schlesinger Library).

52. Barry Schwartz, *George Washington: The Making of an American Symbol* (Ithaca, 1987); *Wall Street Journal.* June 12, 1992, p. 1.

53. *New York Times,* April 21, 1992. p. 1. See Chief Seattle, *Brother Eagle, Sister Sky: A Message from Chief Seattle* (New York, 1991).

54. "Letter from Sojourner Truth:" *Boston Commonwealth,* July 3, 1863.

55. Kathleen Collins, "Shadow and Substance: Sojourner Truth," *History of Photography,* 7 (July–Sept. 1983). 183–205, esp. 199; William C. Darrah, *Cartes de Visite in Nineteenth Century Photography* (Gettysburg, 1981). 19. The *carte de visite* appeared in the United States in 186 and quickly gained enormous popularity.

56. The Frederick Douglass daguerreotype (8; 6.9 c.), c. 1847, is held by the National Portrait Gallery. Washington, D.C. See *History of Photography,* 4 (July 1980), frontispiece. The Frances Dana Gage daguerreotype undated, is in the possession of Jerry Barker Devol, Devola, Ohio. André Rouille, "The Rise of Photography (1851–70)," in *A History of Photography: Social and Cultural Perspectives,* ed. Jean-Claude Lemagny and André Rouille, trans. Janet Lloyd (Cambridge. Eng., 1987). 40; Darrah. *Cartes de Visite in Nineteenth Century Photography,* 1–22, 10–12, 19, 24.

57. See Kathleen Collins. "The Scourged Back," *History of Photography,* 9 (Jan.–March 1985), 43–45; Kathleen Collins, "Portraits of Slave Children," *ibid.* (July–Sept. 1985), 187–210; and Kathleen Collins, "Photographic Fund-raising: Civil War Philanthropy:" *ibid.,* II (July–Sept. 1987), 173–87.

58. The drawing is by Charles C. Burleigh, Jr., who was a child in the late 1840s, after the breakup of the North-Hampton Association of Education and Industry, when Sojourner Truth still lived in Northampton. He probably drew from memory and imagination, inspired by Stowe's "Sojourner Truth, the Libyan Sibyl," Charles C. Burleigh. Jr., *Sojourner Truth,* [1860s], drawing (Historic Northampton, Northampton, Mass.)

59. Stowe, "Sojourner Truth, the Libyan Sibyl," 473.

60. Susan Sontag speaks of the three-quarters gaze as conveying an "ennobling abstract relation to the future." Sontag, *On Photography,* 38.

61. On captions and viewers, see Victory Burgin, "Looking at Photographs," in *Thinking Photography,* ed. Victor Burgin (Houdmills, 1982), 144–46. The Historical Society of Battle Creek, Michigan, sells Sojourner Truth postcards to raise funds. These photographs retain the original caption, but below "SOJOURNER TRUTH" they add "Historical Society of Battle Creek, Michigan."

62. Joel Snyder, "Inventing Photography," in *On the Art of Fixing a Shadow: One Hundred and Fifty Years of Photography,* ed. Sarah Greenough et al. (Washington, 1989).

63. Allan Sekula, "The Body and the Archive," in *The Contest of Meaning: Critical Histories of Photography,* ed. Richard Bolton (Cambridge, Mass., 1989), 343–46; Alan Trachtenberg, *Reading American Photographs: Images as History: Mathew Brady to Walker Evans* (New York, 1989), 53–54.

64. Alan Trachtenberg, "Photography: The Emergence of a Keyword" in *Photography in Nineteenth Century America,* ed. Martha A. Sandweiss (Fort Worth, 1991), 22.

65. André Rouille and Bernard Marbot, *Le corps et son image: Photographies du dix neuvieme siecle* (The body and its image: Photographs from the nineteenth century) (LaRochelle, 1986), 13–19, 30; Trachtenberg, *Reading American Photographs,* 28, 40; Miles Orvell, *The Real Thing: Imitation and Authenticity in American Culture, 1880–1940* (Chapel Hill, 1989), 77–78, 88–89; Snyder, "Inventing Photography," 21–22; John X. Berger and Oliver Richon, eds., *Other than Itself: Writing Photography* (Manchester, 1989), n.p.

66. Françoise Heilbrun, *L'invention d'un regard (1839–1918)* (The invention of a gaze, 1839 1918) (Paris, 1989), 16. For the quoted phrase, see Roland Barthes, "Rhetoric of the Image," in *Classic Essays on Photography,* ed. Alan Trachtenberg (New Haven, 1980), 269 Sigfried Kracauer adds that photographs are "surrounded with a fringe of indistinct multiple meanings" See Sigfried Kracauer, "Photography," *ibid.,* 265.

67. Truth's attempt to embody herself through her photographs has not prevented critics from writing about her as though her existential and historic dimensions and her physical body were attenuated. Denise Riley uses Truth to interrogate the category "women," suggesting playfully that Truth might now ask, "Ain't I a fluctuating identity?" See Denise Riley, *"Am I That Name?" Feminism and the Category of 'Women' in History* (Minneapolis, 1988), 1. Donna Haraway reads Truth as a trickster figure, "a shape changer." See Donna Haraway, "Ecce Homo, Ain't (Ar'n't) I a Woman, and Inappropriate/d Others: The Human in a Post-Humanist Landscape," in *Feminists Theorize the Political,* ed. Judith Butler and Joan W. Scott (New York, 1992), 86–100. For an analysis more kindred to my own, see Richard Powell, "Sojourner Truth and the Invention of Genteel Domesticity in Her Photographic 'Self-Portraiture,'" paper delivered at the meeting of the College Art Association, New York, January 1994 (in Painter's possession).

68. Elizabeth Anne McCauley, *A. A. E. Disdéri and the Carte de Visite Portrait Photograph* (New Haven, 1985).

16

GRACE JORDAN MCFADDEN

SEPTIMA P. CLARK AND THE STRUGGLE FOR HUMAN RIGHTS

Septima Poinsette Clark's death on December 15, 1987, ended her struggle for human rights for her people within the framework of the United States' political, social, and economic system. Referred to as the "Mother of the Movement," by Martin Luther King, Jr., she had been at the vanguard of the human rights quest.[1]

A native of Charleston, South Carolina, she was born on May 3, 1898. Her father, Peter Poinsette, was born a slave on the Joel Poinsette farm between the Waccamaw River and Georgetown. Her mother, Victoria Warren Anderson Poinsette, was born in Charleston and was taken to Haiti by her uncle in 1864, along with her two sisters, Martha and Maseline.[2]

> My father was very gentle and my mother was very haughty. The English did a better job in Haiti teaching them to read and write, so she [Victoria Poinsette] boasted of being a free issue. She often said, "I never gave a white woman a drink of water." My father was such a gentle, very wonderful guy. It was good for those two to be together because my mother, with her haughtiness, and my father, with his gentleness, I felt that I stood on a platform that was built by both. And when I went to Mississippi and Texas and places like that, I had a feeling that his nonviolence helped me to work with the people there and her haughtiness helped me to stay. . . . I got into many places where we had a lot of harassment from the Ku Klux Klan and the White Citizen's Council in Tuscaloosa, Alabama, and Grenada, Mississippi, and Natchez, Mississippi. I stood on a platform built by my mother and father.[3]

Septima Poinsette's father worked as a caterer following the Civil War. Her mother took in laundry. Since teaching was one of the few professions available to black women at the beginning of the twentieth century, Septima took the state examination in 1916 after having completed twelfth grade at Avery Normal Institute in Charleston, South Carolina.[4] Teaching would enable her to have a career and help her family financially.

> I had to take an examination of eleven subjects in order to teach. . . . I received the licientiate of instruction and went over to John's Island to teach in a two-teacher school there. In that two-teacher school we had 132 children and a building that was creosoted black. We were all black together. Across the road from where I worked was a white schoolhouse that was whitewashed and three children attending that with one teacher. That teacher received $85 a month for her teaching and living. And the rest of us, the two teachers who taught across the street—I was the teaching principal so I got $35 and the assistant $25. Both of us made $60 to the one teacher who made $85 for three children. And there we were working for $60 a month with 132 children.[5]

Poinsette remained on John's Island for three years, during which time she became a crusader for the equalization of teachers' salaries as well as an active proponent for black teachers being allowed to teach in Charleston's public schools and becoming public school principals. In 1919, she returned to Charleston to teach sixth grade at Avery Normal Institute. It was then that her civil rights work commenced. She attended NAACP meetings in Charleston and heard Edwin Halston, a prominent artist and civil rights advocate, discuss the conditions facing black people during that historic epoch. She was inspired by Halston as well as by Thomas Ezekiel Miller, who had served as a congressman from South Carolina during Reconstruction and later became president of South Carolina State College. Miller and Halston addressed mass meetings in order to generate support for black teachers to teach in the public schools of Charleston. Poinsette began her civil rights work by going door-to-door, asking people to sign petitions.

> Now, a lot of people in downtown Charleston said that only the mulattoes wanted their daughters to work in the schools, but that the chauffeurs and cooks didn't mind whatsoever. They were satisfied for their daughters to come to us as they had. And that's when we put on the door-to-door campaign. Some people wrote their names on pieces of paper bags to say that

they wanted their daughters to work in the public schools as well. I was teaching at Avery then. I was teaching the sixth grade. So I took my class one day, with the permission of the principal, and we walked the streets from one door to another and received those signatures. And those signatures Mr. Halston gave to Tom E. Miller who was at State College in Orangeburg. And Tom E. Miller wanted 10,000 signatures. We put them in a croaker sack and he took them up to the legislature to let them know that there were blacks who were cooks and maids and chauffeurs who wanted their children to teach black children in the public schools of Charleston. And in 1920, well, the end of 1919, when the legislature closed, that thing became a law.[6]

And the following year we had Negro principals. We had been victorious in this my first effort to establish for Negro citizens what I sincerely believed to be their God given right.[7]

As a youngster she enhanced her social and racial consciousness while watching ships from Marcus Garvey's Black Star Shipping Line dock at Charleston Harbor and seeing passengers embark and disembark. This venture filled her with racial pride and dignity. Marcus Garvey, a Jamaican immigrant, had founded the Universal Negro Improvement Association in 1916. The UNIA was a worldwide racial and economic program among people of African descent. Later, as a student at Atlanta University in 1937, Clark would take a course from Dr. W. E. B. Du Bois whom she described as "an aloof professor" but a thorough scholar. Du Bois, an eminent scholar and author, founder of the Niagara Movement, co-founder of the NAACP and editor of its *Crisis* magazine, would influence Clark's documentation of events as well as her commitment to writing.

Septima Poinsette married seaman Nerie Clark in May 1920. Two children were born to the marriage, a daughter who died a month after her birth and a son, Nerie Clark, Jr. Nerie Clark was at sea during the early years of the marriage. Following his discharge from the navy, the family moved to Dayton, Ohio. The marriage was short-lived, however. Nerie died of kidney ailment in December 1925 shortly before his thirty-sixth birthday. Having to support her young son, Septima Clark lived with her husband's relatives in Dayton and Hickory, North Carolina, before finally settling in Columbia, South Carolina, in 1929, where she remained until 1947. During her time in Columbia she received her B.A. from Benedict College and her M.A. from Hampton Institute. In 1935, she sent her son back to Hickory to live with his paternal grandparents. Nerie, Jr. remained there through high school. Clark explained that the move was necessary because she didn't earn enough money to support her son and most boarding houses would not allow children.[8] A benefit of this separation from her child was that Clark now had the freedom necessary for social and political action.

The move to Columbia had increased her consciousness.

> I hadn't been in Columbia long, in fact, before I discovered that upcountry Columbia, in the center of the state, was different from my native low country Charleston. In Charleston, both white and Negro were rooted in tradition. Columbia was more democratic. . . . In Columbia everyone mixed, and the schoolteachers were considered rather high up in the social ladder and the doctor's wife and the schoolteacher and the woman working as a domestic sat down at the bridge table. In fact, when Negro doctors in Columbia had their meetings, they would invite not only their wives and their more elite friends to the social functions but also their patients. They left no one out.[9]

During her years in Columbia, South Carolina, Clark began her work in citizenship education. Wil Lou Gray, head of the South Carolina Adult Education Program in 1935, had been asked by the army to establish a program to help educate black illiterate soldiers stationed at Camp Jackson (now Fort Jackson) following World War I. Approximately 50 percent of South Carolina's men who sought military service were not accepted because of illiteracy.[10] This introduction to citizenship education trained soldiers to sign their names to pay slips, read bus routes and learn to count. The Camp Jackson program later became the basis for the citizenship schools Septima Clark designed at Highlander Folk School and SCLC. Clark's ability to link social reform with educational advancement began with her teaching on John's Island in 1916. It would continue throughout her life as a proponent of citizenship education.

It was in Columbia that Septima Poinsette Clark became actively involved in the teachers' salary equalization campaign. She worked with Booker T. Washington High School principal J. Andrew Simmons; NAACP lawyer Thurgood Marshall, South Carolina civil rights lawyer Harold R. Boulware, and others in preparing a court case. Proclaimed Clark: "My participation in this fight to force equalization of white and Negro teachers' salaries on the basis of certification, of course, was what might be described by some no doubt, as my first radical job. I, however, would call it my first effort in a social action, challenging the status quo. It was the first time I had worked against people directing a system for which I was working."[11]

The hearings were held in the South Carolina State House. The black people who attended were not allowed to sit on the main floor. Clark recalls:

> When we were having the hearings for the teachers' salaries equalization, we had to sit in the balcony. We couldn't sit on the main floor. Segregation was still in '35 and '36. But, I went and stayed from around 3:00 p.m. in the afternoon until around nine o'clock at night. And, I was hearing this thing through. And, finally they decided that we would have to take an examination. . . . I took the examination and made an A on it. Immediately my salary tripled. I thought I was wealthy then. . . . Now the principal who worked on the equalization, J. A. Simmons, he resigned after we met because he felt they were going to dismiss him. But, I worked on until 1947, from '36 until '47, when my mother took sick and she had a stroke and then I came home because I wanted to be with her. I had been in Columbia for eighteen years. Following that court decision my salary had advanced to almost $4,000 a year.[12]

In 1945 Federal District Judge J. Waties Waring of South Carolina, who later became a friend of Septima Clark, ruled in Viola Duvall's class action suit on behalf of Charleston, South Carolina's black teachers that teachers with equal education should receive equal pay.[13]

Clark worked in the Charleston public schools from 1947 to 1956. During this time, she was active with the YWCA, attended workshops on desegregation at Highlander Folk School in Tennessee, and supported civil rights efforts. She was also a member of the Charleston NAACP, serving as its membership chairperson. On April 19, 1956, the South Carolina legislature passed a law stipulating that no city or state employee could be affiliated with any civil rights organization. But Clark refused to conceal her membership: "I couldn't refuse them, and I was dismissed." Clark's political action was well grounded by now. She had signed her name to 726 letters that were sent to black teachers requesting that they protest the law. Only 26 answered, and when Clark urged them to talk to the superintendent of schools, only 11 agreed to go and only 5 actually showed up. (The superintendent told them that they were years ahead of their time.) Shortly thereafter, Clark was fired. She was 58 years old and had been teaching for forty years. She not only lost her job, but also her state retirement benefits. In 1976 Governor James Edwards, the first Republican governor of South Carolina, wrote Clark to acknowledge that she had been unjustly terminated and thus was entitled to her pension.[14]

Once again Clark turned adversity to her advantage. She now had more time for social activism, and Myles Horton, director of Highlander Folk School in Monteagle, Tennessee, recruited her as director of workshops. Highlander was an authentic proponent of social change: the school advocated human brotherhood and sought to eliminate stereotypes, break down racial barriers, and develop leaders. Beneficiaries of its programs spanned a wide gulf, from Esau Jenkins of John's Island who gained social welfare skills to aid his fellow islanders to Rosa Parks who gained knowledge of civil disobedience and, as a consequence, sparked the Montgomery bus boycott.

> [Rosa Parks] came to Highlander Folk School while I was directing the education program in 1955. She was working with a youth group in Montgomery and she said, "I want to come and see if I can do something for my people." So she came. We sent money and gave her a scholarship. And when she went home, she had gained enough courage, enough strength to feel that she could stand firm and decide not to move when that man asked for her seat.[15]

Highlander Folk School prepared Clark for her subsequent work with the Southern Christian Leadership Conference (SCLC).

> Highlander workshops were planned and conducted to emphasize a cooperative rather than a competitive use of learning. They hoped through the teaching of leaders to advance a community, rather than individuals, though the advancement of the community always advanced the individuals in it. People came to Highlander to seek enlightenment on issues whose proper solution, followed by adequate social action, would promote the advancement of all. Highlander Folk School's workshops included persons of all races and levels of economic and education success.[16]

Clark sought the assistance of many outstanding black leaders to assist her at Highlander. In July 1960 she wrote to Ella Baker: "We are attempting to help these people [the young people in the sit-in movement] by bringing them to the school for a workshop on the tactics and techniques of follow-through in school desegregation, voter registration, leadership education. Won't you come to this workshop and show your experiences in the current problems?"[17] Baker came to Highlander in 1960 and worked with Clark training young people for leadership roles and responsibilities in the civil rights movement.

In the spring of 1961, Septima Clark departed from her position at High-lander Folk School, though she remained on the staff as an educational con-sultant. She was recruited by Martin Luther King, Jr. and joined the staff of SCLC as director of education and teaching. This affiliation paralleled her work at Highlander, focusing on citizenship training, voting, and liter-acy. At the age of sixty-three, Clark traveled throughout the Southern states directing workshops for SCLC. She instilled in the minds of her workshop participants that they must become cognizant of "the non-partisan basis of the American system. They are taught their constitutional rights and how to organize to obtain the political power to get streetlights or better roads and schools in their part of town. The right to peaceful assembly and to petition for redress of grievances is related to how they can organize their own com-munity for change."[18] She was the first woman elected to the Executive Board of SCLC.

Clark's involvement with SCLC fully tested the qualities of patience, en-durance, and strength of mind that had been instilled in her by her parents. Of her years with SCLC, she stated:

> I went to SCLC and worked with Dr. King as director of education and di-rector of teaching. And there traveled from place to place getting people to realize that they wanted to eliminate illiteracy. We had to eliminate illiter-acy first! And then after eliminating illiteracy, then we went into registra-tion and voting and getting them to want to register and vote. And of course, you know we had a terrible struggle because thirty or more per-sons were killed in the registration and voting drive. But we didn't stop! We went on! And in '64 we got the Civil Rights Bill and they couldn't ha-rass us as we worked in the lines.[19]
>
> I first started holding workshops in a place called Liberty County, Geor-gia. People in Liberty learned how to write their names and read and write under trees, in beauty parlors. Then we would go down with them to the registration office. The people were eager to go there. A man in Liberty County, Georgia said to me, "Its a dangerous thing to do. Why do you live dangerous?" And I replied, "It's something that I have to do!" And it was. We were often harassed by the White Citizen's Council. Following one of our meetings in Grenada, Mississippi, just about five minutes after we got out of the church, it was set afire. I don't know how they got in to put those things around the church.[20]

Clark's work with SCLC required that she travel throughout the South-eastern United States directing workshops in citizenship, education, and voting. In southern Georgia, she conducted workshops on how to make out a bank check.

> We brought in a banker from a little town outside of Savannah. McRae, I think it was, and he put the whole form up on the board and showed them how to write this thing out and how to put your date and how to write it out. He told them, "Don't leave a space to the end of the check. Someone else could write your number in there and you'd get out more than you expected, and then when you finish putting down the amount, take a line and carry it all the way to that dollar, to the thing that says dollar."[21]

The white citizens started to harass black people who were learning proper banking methods.

> The Black people had been in the habit of having them make out the check for them, and they'd just sign with a "X." One fellow said though, that he went to the bank and the White man said to him, "Just bring it over here, and I'll fix it for you." The Black man said, "No, I can write my name." The White man said, "Oh, God, these niggers done learned to write their names."[22]

The goal of the Citizenship Schools was to provide full citizenship through education. Clark sought to place non-traditional teachers at her schools. Communities which sought her teachers desired individuals who by their backgrounds would make good teachers, such as beauticians, farmers, tradesmen, etc. Clark wanted those who offered "a 'folk' approach to learning rather than a classical one."[23]

Septima Clark's recollections of SCLC provide insight into the role of women in the organization as well as the reluctance of some black ministers to have their parishioners involved in her program.

> I found Dr. King to be a very, very nonviolent man. He proved to us all that nonviolence would work. He also made black people aware of their blackness and not ashamed of being black. The thing that I think stands out a whole lot was the fact that women could never be accorded their rightful place even in the southern Christian Leadership Conference. I can't ever forget Reverend Abernathy saying, "Why is Mrs. Clark on the Executive Board?" And Dr. King saying, "Why, she designed a whole program." "Well, I just can't see why you got to have her on the Board!" They just

didn't feel as if a woman, you know, had any sense. See, Mrs. King has come into her own since Dr. King's death. Because most of them felt that a woman couldn't say much or do much. I don't know if you know Ella Baker who lives in New York now. She had a brilliant mind in the beginning of the Southern Christian Leadership Conference. But the men never would feel, you know, she had a rightful place there. I think that up to the time that Dr. King was nearing the end that he really felt that black women had a place in the movement and in the whole world. The men didn't, though! The men who worked with him didn't have that kind of idea.[24]

According to Clark, Rosa Parks never managed to achieve her rightful place in the civil rights movement.

If you notice the movie, *From Montgomery to Memphis,* not even Rosa Parks was accorded her rightful place in the whole movie. We talked about it, she and I. She gave Dr. King the right to practice his nonviolence. Because by refusing to get up out of that seat was the real fact that he could organize the boycott and work with people all through. And it went into many countries. People from China sent money for station wagons and from India and other places. And it was Rosa Parks who started the whole thing.[25]

Septima Clark, too, has been an outspoken advocate of nonviolence. Her Christmas message in December 1967 articulated her convictions.

The way I see it, the test is on us now, those who believe in nonviolence and brotherhood. Things which I hear labeled out-of-date and unrealistic, we must make it work. We must build a foundation throughout the long hot summers and long cold winters. This foundation, whether rooted in Christianity or single person-to-person contact must achieve what has not been done before, and it must be solidly rooted in truth and love. This must be done more quickly than ever before, because time is running out and may have already run out.[26]

As a social activist, Clark was committed to leadership training and follow-through. In December 1963, she wrote Martin Luther King, Jr., concerning her frustrations with those who she felt were more interested in glamour of the movement than the daily work with the people.

Many states are losing their citizenship schools because there is no one to do follow-up work. I have done as much as I could. In fact, I'm the only paid staff worker doing field visitation. I think that the staff of the SCLC working with me in the Citizenship Education Program feels that the work is not dramatic enough to warrant their time. Direct action is so glamorous and packed with emotion that most young people prefer demonstration over genuine education.

It seems to me as if Citizenship Education is all mine, except when it comes time to pick up the checks.[27]

Reflecting on her years with SCLC, Clark believed that training in citizenship education helped women to realize their worth in society. Of course, she stressed that this was not a goal of the training schools. However, Clark contended that women who participated in citizenship education became aroused citizens and assumed positive roles in the quest for civil as well as women's rights. Their gaining the right to vote freed the individual as well as the group.

Women, ninety-one, eighty-one years of age, we could teach them in twenty minutes and we had cars outside waiting to take them right to the courthouse. They signed their names and they got a number that said that they could register and vote in August [1965]. Well, I stayed there from May until August and by the time we left, 7,002 of them had signed their names and had received a number. That's why we have a large number of our people in Alabama voting today.[28]

The SCLC Citizenship Education Program that Clark directed went into eleven deep South states. Her efforts resulted in black people achieving the right to vote and, thus, becoming active participants in the body politic.

After her departure from SCLC, Clark still remained a social activist. She conducted workshops for the American Field Service, helped raise scholarships for deserving young people, organized day-care facilities, and remained an advocate for civil rights. In 1975 she was elected a member of the Charleston, South Carolina, School Board. The College of Charleston awarded her an Honorary Doctorate of Humane Letters in 1978. (The home where she was born is now owned by the college.) In February 1979, President Jimmy Carter recognized her work by presenting her with a Living the Legacy Award. Since then, a section of the Charleston Highway has been named in her honor.

Clark maintained that her greatest honor was serving humanity. From collecting signatures in a croaker sack to her productive citizenship education program, she never wavered in her conviction that if you put forth the effort, change would eventually come.

> The only reason why I thought the Citizenship School Program was right was because when they went down to register and vote, they were able to register and vote. They received their registration certificate. Then I knew that what I did must have been right. . . . It was an experiment that I was trying. When I went into communities and talked to people, I couldn't say that I was saying the right thing. But as I see people work in these communities and decide that they were going to attempt to do some of the things that were recommended and after attempting to do some of the things that were recommended they were able to be successful, like housing, and being able to get checks signed at banks, getting able to be recognized in the community among their own people and in their churches, then I knew that that experiment had worked out. But I couldn't be sure that the experiment was going to work. I don't think anybody can be sure. You just try and see if it's coming.[29]

Clark's Christmas message in 1965, "A Look to the Future," articulated the essence of her political and social philosophy.

> The greatest evil in our country today is not racism but ignorance. . . . This is the great challenge to black and white leadership. Our basic philosophy is clear. We do not need a new one. We are committed to an integrated society—for a truly democratic society, there can be no freedom without integration. Our task then is to nurture and strengthen the newly developing political strength among both young Blacks and young Whites, who have already made a magnificent contribution to the struggle for a more humane and just society. But further, we must try harder than ever to reach the great mass of the uninformed, whose basic interests are no different from our own—if they but knew it.[30]

Clark nurtured her social and political philosophy with her strong beliefs. One had a moral obligation, she asserted, to serve God via his or her service to humanity. In 1971, she proclaimed:

SEPTIMA P. CLARK

311

We are young at heart when we have a tremendous faith in God and in the
future, when we have a sense of exaltation in the sweeping movements
of a rapidly changing society and world.
We are old when we rise against our times, when we resist all change.
We are young as our dreams, our hopes and our enthusiasm.
We are as old as our fears, our frustrations, our doubts.
We need to feel wanted and to find the joy that grows out of service
to others if the last of life for which the first was made is to be a time of
happiness for those of us who are growing older.[31]

On the occasion of Dr. Martin Luther King, Jr.'s death in 1968, Clark
proclaimed, "His was no middle-class write-in campaign for Civil Rights, it
was a movement that took the people into the streets to confront clubs,
hoses, horses, and dogs; to face the oppressors while armed only with the
almighty power of love; to turn the cheek not to avoid the present pain, but
to see the true nation and new order of the future that God was already
making. His peace was not in a cozy rally, but in a reordering of our national
priorities from military power to that of human empowerment."[32] Her tribute to King could easily be extended to her. The depth of her commitment,
the magnitude of her faith, her power of endurance, and her unrelenting
crusade for justice allowed her to put into operation a program of citizen
participation that transformed American society. Myles Horton, who died
in January 1990, gave Clark the framework at Highlander Folk School to
develop her program of citizenship education. Clark, he proclaimed, was a
committed public servant and dedicated advocate of social change.[33]

NOTES

1. *State Newspaper,* Columbia, South Carolina, December 15, 1987.
2. Grace Jordan McFadden, *Oral Recollections of Septima Poinsette Clark* (Columbia: USC Instructional Services Center, 1980).
3. *Ibid.*
4. Septima P. Clark, personal interview, February 1, 1975.
5. *Ibid.*
6. *Ibid.*
7. Septima Clark, *Echo in My Soul* (New York: E.P. Dutton, 1962), p. 61.
8. Clark, interview, February 20, 1987.
9. Clark, *Echo in My Soul,* p. 80.
10. DaMaris E. Ayres, *Let My People Go, The Biography of Wil Lou Gray* (South
Carolina: The Attic Press, 1988), p. 76.
11. Clark, *Echo My Soul,* p. 82.
12. McFadden, *Oral Recollections of Septima P. Clark.*

13. Tinsley E. Yarbrough, *A Passion for Justice: J. Waties Waring and Civil Rights* (New York: Oxford University Press, 1987), pp. 44–46.

14. James E. Edwards to Septima P. Clark, Septima P. Clark Collection, Robert Scott Small Library.

15. Clark interview, February 1, 1975.

16. Clark, *Echo in My Soul*, p. 178.

17. Septima Clark to Ella Baker, July 11, 1960, Septima P. Clark Collection.

18. Septima P. Clark, *Nature of the Citizenship Education Program*, private collection of Septima P. Clark, Charleston, SC.

19. McFadden, *Oral Recollections of Septima P. Clark*.

20. Clark, interviews, 1975 and 1980.

21. Septima P. Clark with Cynthia S. Brown, *Ready Within: The Story of Septima P. Clark*, p. 75, private collection of Septima P. Clark.

22. *Ibid.*, p. 76.

23. Clark, *Echo in My Soul*, p. 466.

24. McFadden, *Oral Recollections of Septima P. Clark*.

25. *Ibid.*

26. Septima P. Clark, *Christmas Message 1967*, Robert Scott Small Library.

27. Septima P. Clark to Martin L. King, Jr., December 1963, Septima P. Clark Collection.

28. Clark, interviews 1975 and 1980.

29. Clark, *Ready Within*, p. 101.

30. Septima P. Clark, *Christmas Message 1965*, Robert Scott Small Library.

31. Septima P. Clark, *Christmas Message 1971*, Robert Scott Small Library.

32. Septima P. Clark, *The Occasion—Martin Luther King, Jr.*, private collection of Septima Poinsette Clark.

33. Grace Jordan McFadden, conversation with Myles Horton, October 17, 1988, Atlanta, Georgia.

SELECTED BIBLIOGRAPHY FOR FURTHER READING

BIOGRAPHICAL ESSAYS AND BOOKS

Albert, Mimi. "Out of Africa [Luisah Teish]." *Yoga Journal* (January/February 1987): 32–66.

Allen-Sommerville, Lenola. "Sojourner Truth: 'The Preacher'." *Religion and Public Education* 14 (Fall 1987): 396–400.

Baker-Fletcher, Karen. *A Singing Something: Womanist Reflections on Anna Julia Cooper*. New York: Crossroads Press, 1994.

Brent, Peggy. "Remembering Sister Thea." *Teaching English in the Two-Year College* 19 (February 1992): 15–17.

Brown, Elsa Barley. "Womanist Consciousness: Maggie Lena Walker and the Independent Order of Saint Luke." *Signs: Journal of Women in Culture and Society* 14 (Spring 1989): 610–633.

Bryan, Violet Harrington. "Frances Joseph-Gaudet: Black Philanthropist." *SAGE* III, No. 1 (Spring 1986): 46–49.

Code, J. B. "Colored Catholic Educator Before the Civil War: Mother Mary Lange of the Oblates of Providence." *Catholic World* 146 (January 1938): 437–443.

Corruthers, Thomasine. "Lucy Ellen Moten." *Journal of Negro History* 19 (January 1934): 102–106.

Detiege, Sister Audrey Marie. *Henriette Delille, Free Woman of Color: Foundress of the Sisters of the Holy Family*. Sisters of the Holy Family, 1976.

Diamondstein, Barbaralee. "Pauli Murray." In *Open Secrets: Ninety-Four Women in Touch With Our Time*. New York: Viking Press, 1972.

Edson, Lee. "Mother Waddles: Black Angel of the Poor." *Reader's Digest* (October 1972): 175–178.

Fichter, S.J., Joseph H. "The White Church and the Black Sisters." *U.S. Catholic Historian* 12 (Winter 1994): 31–48.

314

Fitzgerald, Sharon. "The Glorious Walk of Marion Williams." *American Visions* 8 (December 1993): 48–51.

Foster, Frances Smith. " 'Neither Auction Block Nor Pedestal:' The Life and Religious Experiences of Jarena Lee, A Coloured Lady." *New York Literary Forum* (1984): 143–147.

Fry, Gladys-Marie. "Harriet Powers: Portrait of a Black Quilter." *SAGE* IV (Spring 1987): 11–15.

George, Luvenia A. "Lucie E. Campbell: Her Nurturing and Expansion of Gospel Music in the National Baptist Convention, U.S.A., Inc." In *We'll Understand It Better By and By*, edited by Bernice Johnson Reagon. Washington: Smithsonian Institution Press, 1992.

Griggs, A.C. "Lucy Craft Laney." *Journal of Negro History* 19 (January 1934): 97–102.

Haley, Alex. "She Makes a Joyful Music [Mahalia Jackson]." *Reader's Digest* (November 1991): 196–202.

Haney, Elly. "Pauli Murray: Acting and Remembering." *Journal of Feminist Studies in Religion* 4 (Fall 1988): 77–79.

Hardesty, Nancy A. "Amanda Smith, Touring Evangelist." In *Great Women of Faith: The Strength and Influence of Christian Women*. Grand Rapids, Michigan: Baker Book House, 1980.

Hartvik, Allen. "Catherine Ferguson, Black Founder of a Sunday School." *Negro History Bulletin* (December 1972): 176–177.

Hubbard, Kim. "Shirley Caesar Belts the Gospel According to God and Grammy." *People Weekly* Vol. 28, No. 19 (November 19, 1987): 85–86.

Jacobs, Sylvia. "Three Afro-American Women [Fanny Jackson Coppin, Amanda Berry Smith, Sarah Gorham]." In *Women in New Worlds*, edited by H.F. Thomas and R.S. Keller. Nashville: Abingdon Press, 1981.

Jennings, Willie J. "When Mahalia Sings: The Black Singer of Sacred Song as Icon." *Journal of Black Sacred Music* 3 (Spring 1989): 6–13.

Jones, Adrienne Lash. *Jane Edna Hunter: A Case Study of Black Leadership, 1910–1950*. Brooklyn: Carlson Publishing, 1990.

Lawson, Ellen N. "Sarah Woodson Early: 19th Century Black Nationalist 'Sister'." *UMOJA* 2 (Summer 1981): 15–26.

Paradin, Victor. "Mahalia Jackson." *American History* (September 1994): 42–43.

Peebles-Wilkins, Wilma. "Black Women and American Social Welfare: The Life of Frederica Douglass Sprague Perry." *Affilia* 4 (Spring 1989): 33–44.

Perkins, Linda M. "Heed Life's Demands: The Educational Philosophy of Fanny Jackson Coppin." *Journal of Negro Education* 51 (1982): 181–190.

Reitz, Rosetta. "Sister Rosetta Tharpe." *Hot Wire* Vol. 7, No. 2 (May 1, 1991):16.

Schwerin, Jules Victor. *Got to Tell It: Mahalia Jackson, Queen of Gospel*. New York: Oxford University Press, 1992.

Simson, Renate Maria. "Whoever Heard of Josephine Heard?" *College Language Association Journal* (December 1982): 256–261.

Townes, Emilie M. *Womanist Justice, Womanist Hope* [Ida B. Wells-Barnett]. Atlanta, GA: Scholars Press, 1993.

Williams, Richard E. "Mother Rebecca Jackson: One of the Black Shakers in Philadelphia." *The Shaker Messenger* 1 (Spring 1979): 3–5.

AUTOBIOGRAPHIES, DIARIES, AND ORAL HISTORIES

Amber, Jeannine. "I'm Black and Jewish." *Glamour* 92 (August 1994): 132.

Andrews, William. *Sisters of the Spirit: Three Black Women's Autobiographies of the Nineteenth Century* [Jarena Lee, Julia Foote, Zilpha Elaw]. Bloomington: Indiana University Press, 1986.

Fields, Mamie Garvin. *Lemon Swamp and Other Places: A Carolina Memoir*. New York: Free Press, 1983.

Georgia Writers' Project. *Drums and Shadows: Survival Studies Among the Georgia Coastal Negroes*. Athens: University of Georgia Press, 1940.

Hull, Gloria T., ed. *Give Us Each Day: The Diary of Alice Dunbar-Nelson*. New York: W. W. Norton and Co., 1984.

Ione, Carol. *Pride of Family: Four Generations of American Women of Color*. New York: Summit Books, 1991.

Jackson, Mahalia with Evan McLeod Wylie. *Movin' on Up*. New York: Hawthorn Books, 1966.

Jackson, Rebecca Cox. *Gifts of Power: The Writings of Rebecca Cox Jackson, Black Visionary, Shaker Eldress*. Amherst: University of Massachusetts Press, 1987.

Jacobs, Harriet. *Incidents in the Life of a Slave Girl Written By Herself*. 1861; revised edition edited by Jean Fagan Yellin. Cambridge: Harvard University Press, 1987.

Logan, Onnie Lee. *Motherwit: An Alabama Midwife's Story*, as told to Katherine Clark. New York: Plume, 1989.

Murray, Pauli. *Proud Shoes: The Story of An American Family*. New York: Harper and Row, 1956.

———. *Song in a Weary Throat: An American Pilgrimage*. New York: Harper and Row, 1987.

———. *Autobiography of a Black Activist, Feminist, Lawyer, Priest, and Poet*. Knoxville: University of Tennessee Press, 1987.

Rice, Sarah. *He Included Me: The Autobiography of Sarah Rice*, transcribed and edited by Louise Westling. Athens: University of Georgia Press, 1989.

Simonsen, Thordis, ed. *You May Plow Here: The Narrative of Sara Brooks*. New York: W. W. Norton and Co., 1986.

Smith, Amanda. *An Autobiography: The Story of the Lord's Dealings With Mrs. Amanda Smith, the Colored Evangelist*. 1893, Reprint New York: Oxford University Press, 1988.

Spiritual Narratives [Susan Houchins, ed., Maria W. Stewart, Jarena Lee, Julia A. J. Foote, Virginia W. Broughton]. New York: Oxford University Press, 1988.

Taylor, Susie King. *Reminiscences of my Life in Camp with the 33rd U. S. Colored Troops, Late 1st South Carolina Volunteers*. 1902; revised edition, edited by Patricia W. Romero and Willie Lee Rose. New York: Markus Wiener Publishing, 1988.

Taylor, Susan L. *In the Spirit: Inspirational Writings of Susan L. Taylor*. New York: Amistad, 1993.

Teish, Luisah. *Jambalaya: The Natural Woman's Book of Personal Charms and Practical Rituals*. New York: Harper and Row, 1985.

OTHER SOURCES

Anderson, *Burning Down the House: MOVE and the Tragedy of Philadelphia* [Ramona Africa]. New York: Norton, 1987.

Baer, Hans A. "The Limited Empowerment of Women in Black Spiritual Churches: An Alternative Vehicle to Religious Leadership." *Sociology of Religion* 54 (Spring 1993): 65–82.

Baldwin, Lewis. "Black Women and African Union Methodism, 1813–1983." *Methodist History* 21 (July 1983): 225–237.

Bambara, Toni Cade. *The Black Woman: An Anthology.* New York: New American Library, 1970.

Bassard, Katherine Clay. "Spiritual Interrogations: Conversion, Community and Authorship in the Writings of Phillis Wheatley, Ann Plato, Jarena Lee, and Rebecca Cox Jackson." Ph.D. diss., Rutgers The State University of New Jersey-New Brunswick, 1992.

Cannon, Katie G. *Black Womanist Ethics.* Atlanta, GA: Scholars Press, 1988.

Carby, Hazel V. *Reconstructing Womanhood: The Emergence of the Afro-American Woman Novelist.* New York: Oxford University Press, 1987.

Carpenter, Delores C. "Black Women in Religious Institutions: A Historical Summary From Slavery to the 1960s." *Journal of Religious Thought* 46 (Winter-Spring 1989–1990): 7–27.

Dash, Julie. *Daughters of the Dust: The Making of an African-American Woman's Film.* New York: New Press, 1992

———. *Daughters of the Dust.* Geechee Girls Production, 1992.

Davis, Lenwood G. "The Black Woman in America: Autobiographical and Biographical Material." *Northwestern Journal of African and Black American Studies* 2 (Winter 1974): 27–29.

Dupree, Sherry Sherrod, ed. *Biographical Dictionary of African-American Holiness-Pentecostals, 1880–1990.* Washington, D.C.: Middle Atlantic Regional Press, 1989.

Giddings, Paula. *When and Where I Enter: The Impact of Black Women on Race and Sex in America.* New York: Bantam Books, 1984.

Gilkes, Cheryl Townsend. "Womanist Ideals and the Sociological Imagination." *Journal of Feminist Studies in Religion* 8 (Fall 1992): 147–151.

———. "Christian Ethics and Theology in Womanist Perspective." *Journal of Feminist Studies in Religion* 5 (Fall 1989): 105–109.

Goldsmith, Peter. "A Woman's Place is in the Church: Black Pentecostalism on the Georgia Coast." *Journal of Religious Thought* 46 (Winter-Spring 1989–1990): 53–69.

Harris, Barbara C. "A Cloud of Witnesses: Black Women in the Anglican Communion." In Carter Heyward and Sue Phillips, ed. *No Easy Peace: Liberating Anglicanism.* Lanham, MD: University Press of America, 1992.

Height, Dorothy I. "The New Black Woman." *Journal of Ecumenical Studies* 16 (Winter 1979): 166–169.

Higginbotham, Evelyn Brooks. *Righteous Discontent: The Women's Movement in the Black Baptist Church.* Cambridge: Harvard University Press, 1993.

———. "En-Gendering Leadership in the Home Mission Schools." *American Baptist Quarterly* 12 (March 1993): 10–25.

Hine, Darlene Clark. *Black Women in America: An Historical Encyclopedia*. Brooklyn, NY: Carlson Publishing, 1993.

———. *Hine Sight: Black Women and the Reconstruction of American History*. Brooklyn, NY: Carlson Publishing, 1994.

Jones, Lisa C. "Preachers Married to Preachers." *Ebony* 49 (September 94): 80–82.

Moore, Irene, ed. "The Intersection of Racism and Sexism: Theological Perspectives of Afro-American Women." *Journal of Women and Religion* 9–10 (1990–1991): 7–101.

Murray, Pauli. "Minority Women and Feminist Spirituality." *Witness* 67 (Fall 1984): 5–9.

Myers, William H. *God's Yes Was Louder Than My No: Rethinking the African-American Call to Ministry*. Grand Rapids, MI: W.B. Eerdmans, 1994.

Noble, Jeanne. *Beautiful, Also, Are the Souls of My Black Sisters: A History of the Black Woman in America*. Englewood Cliffs, NJ: Prentice-Hall, 1978.

Perry, Regina A. *Harriet Powers' Bible Quilts*. New York: Rizzoli International, 1994.

Phelps, Jamie. "Choose Life: Reflections of a Black African-American Roman Catholic Woman Religious Theologian." In *Women and Church*. Melanie May, ed., Grand Rapids, MI: W.B. Eerdmans, 1991, 43–48.

Plaskow, Judith and Elizabeth Schussler-Fiorenza, eds. "Metalogues and Dialogues: Teaching the Womanist Idea." *Journal of Feminist Studies in Religion* 8 (Fall 1992): 125–155.

Reuther, Rosemary Radford and Rosemary Skinner Keller, eds. *Women and Religion in America*. San Francisco: Harper and Row, 1981.

Richardson, Marilyn. *Black Women and Religion: A Bibliography*. Boston: G.K. Hall and Co., 1980.

Riggs, Marcia. *Awake, Arise, and Act: A Womanist Call for Black Liberation*. Cleveland: Pilgrim Press, 1994.

Rodgers-Rose, La Frances. *The Black Woman*. Beverly Hills: Sage Publications, 1980.

Salem, Dorothy. *To Better Our World: Black Women in Organized Reform, 1890–1920*. Brooklyn, NY: Carlson Publishing, 1990.

———. *African-American Women: A Biographical Dictionary*. New York: Garland, 1993.

Sanders, Cheryl, ed. *Living the Intersection: Womanism and Afrocentrism in Theology*. Minneapolis: Fortress Press, 1995.

Sawyer, Mary R. "Black Religion and Social Change: Women in Leadership Roles." *Journal of Religious Thought* 47 (Winter-Spring 1991): 16–29.

Saxon, Tina T. "Breaking the Taboo: Black Women as Pastors in the Black Baptist Tradition." Ph.D. dissertation, Andover Newton Theological School, 1991.

Say Amen, Somebody. Pacific Arts Video Records, 1982.

Sims, Janet L. *The Progress of Afro-American Women: A Selected Bibliography and Resource Guide*. Westport, CT: Greenwood Press, 1980.

Smith, Jessie Carney. *Notable Black American Women*. Detroit: Gale Research, Inc., 1992.

————. *Epic Lives: One Hundred Black Women Who Made a Difference*. Detroit: Visible Ink Press, 1993.

Thomas, Kathy A. "Creating a Womanist Theology: Why Feminist Theology is Not Enough for the African-American Woman." *A.M.E. Zion Quarterly Review* 101 (October 1989): 26–34.

Townes, Emilie M., ed. *A Troubling in My Soul: Womanist Perspectives on Evil and Suffering*. Maryknoll: Orbis Books, 1993.

Travis, J. Ruth. "Preaching Styles of Female Pastors in the African Methodist Episcopal Church, Baltimore, Maryland." Ph.D. dissertation, United Theological Seminary, 1992.

Walker, Margaret. *For My People*. New Haven: Yale University Press, 1942.

Williams, Delores S. *Sisters in the Wilderness: The Challenge of Womanist God-Talk*. Maryknoll: Orbis Books, 1993.

————. "Women's Oppression and Lifeline Politics in Black Women's Religious Narratives." *Journal of Feminist Studies in Religion* 1 (Fall 1985): 59–71.

INDEX

Abernathy, Ralph, 307
Addison, Clarence C., 111, 120
African American Islam, 14
African Methodist Episcopal Church, 2, 10–12, 94–108, 129
African Methodist Episcopal Zion Church, 2, 129, 177–185
African Mission School, 189, 191
African Mission School Society, 190
African Orthodox Church, 118
African Universal Church, 2, 110–123
Agassiz, Louis, 286
Ahlstrom, Sydney, 136
Ajaye, Rev., 115
American Anti-Slavery Society, 274
American Baptist Home Missionary Society, 221
American Colonization Society, 190
American Field Service, 309
American Missionary Assocation, 221, 203–219
Amherst College, 191
Anderson, Ebenezer Johnson, 122 n 24
Anderson, John H., 232
Anderson, Marian, 69
Anderson, Victoria Warren, 300
Andrews, Inez, 32
Andrews, William, 83, 240
Angelica, Sister, 86
Angelou, Maya, 1

Anthony, Susan B., 152, 278, 281
Asbury, Francis, 269
Askins, Mrs., 100
Assocation for the Study of Negro Life and History, 184
Asylum for the Deaf and Dumb, 191
Auburn Theological Seminary, 241
"Aunt Hanna's Quilt: Or the Record of the West", 279
Austin, Ann 122, n 18
Avery Normal Institute, 177, 301

Bailey, Gamaliel, 276
Baker, Ella, 305, 308
Balas, Marie, 78, 83
Baldwin, R.R., 179
Baptist Churches, 2, 7, 12, 34, 56–70, 142–57, 220–35
Barmore, Lilly, 165
Bass, Martha, 33
Bassette, M. E., 206
Beecher, Henry Ward, 277
Bell, Michael E., 122 n 18
Benedict College, 222, 302
Benson, George, 274
Bethune, Albertus, 128
Bethune, Mary McLeod, 1, 61, 124–39
Bethune-Cookman College, 124
Bibb, Henry, 273
Biddle, George, 178

Bilbo, Theodore, 120
Binford, John A., 58
Binford, Lloyd T., 58
Black Abolitionist Papers Project, 271
Black Abolitonist Papers, 271
Black Reconstruction in America, 203
Black Star Shipping Line, 302
Blight, David, 294
Boegue, Rosine, 78
Booker T. Washington High School, 303
Boone, Theodore S., 143
Boulware, Harold R., 303
Boyd, Richard H., 144
Boyle, James, 274
Bradford, Alex, 46
Bradford, Sarah, 239–261
Bradley, J. Robert, 69–70
Brady, Matthew, 284
Branch family, 228
Bresi-Ando, Ebenezer, 118, 12 n 24
Brewer, Eileen, 81–82
Brewster, W. Herbert, 46
British Museum, 271
Brooks, Sara, 8
Brother Eagle, Sister Sky, 282
Broughton, Virgina, 142, 143
Brown, John, 207
Brown, John Mifflin, 104
Brown, T.J., 65
Brown, William Wells, 273
Brownell, Thomas C., 192, 194
Bryant, G. W., 101
Bryant, Sylvia C.J., 142
Buchman, Frank, 136–37
Burdick, Mary, 205
Burges, George, 195
Burke, Jack, 160
Burroughs, Nannie H., 61, 140–57
Byron, Lady, 277

Caesar, Elizabeth, 191, 192, 194
Caesar, Gustavus V,. 189, 192, 194, 198
Campbell, Burrell, 57
Campbell, Isabella Wilkerson, 57, 64, 66
Campbell, Jabez, 104, 105
Campbell, Lora, 58–59

Canby, William, 282
Candee, George, 210
Caravaglios, Maria, 80
Caravans, 32
Carter, Jimmy, 309
Cary, Mary Ann Shadd, 80, 219 n 56
Caton, Richard, 86
Catt, Carrie Chapman, 152
Champion, Laura, 110
The Charitable Society in the African Sunday School, 190
Cheek, L.N., 228
Child, Lydia Maria, 240
Chilembwe, John, 228
Christian Science, 9
Clark College, 221
Clark, Lena, 225
Clark, Nerie, 302
Clark, Nerie Jr., 302
Clark, Septima P., 300–312
Claypoole, Elizabeth, 282
Cleveland Museum of Art, 21
Coan, William, 205, 206, 207
Cobb, Clarence, 33
Coles, Lucy, 234
College of Charleston, 309
Colored Methodist Episcopal Church, 129
Colston, James, 135
Columbia University, 63
Compromise of 1850, 277
Cone, James, 75, 140
The Confessions of Nat Turner, 252
Congo Mission Circle, 225
Convention of Gospel Choirs and Choruses, 34
Cook, J.D., 67
Cook, James, 247
Cook, Maxwell, 112
Cook, W. D., 101, 103
Cookman Institute, 133
Cooper, James Fenimore, 273
Cooper, Mrs., 100
Cotton States Exposition, 22
Craft, Ellen, 80
Cresson, Elliott, 191
Crum, Postmaster, 182

Daffin, Sallie, 209
Davage, D.S., 130–31
Davis, Jefferson, 58
Davis, Thadious, 293
Day Dawn in Africa, 196
Dayton Normal and Industrial Institute
   for Negro Girls, 129
Delaney, Emma B., 220–35
Deluol, Louis, 88
DeMontfort, St. Louis, 84
Derrik, Butler, 100
deSoto, Hernando, 57
Dickerson, Dennis, 216
Dickerson, William F., 7, 100, 102
Dillingham, John, 193
Disdéri, Andre, 284
Dixon, Thomas, 281
Domestic and Foreign Missionary Soci-
   ety, 191, 192, 194, 198
Donovan, Mary S., 189
Dorsey, John, 159
Dorsey, Thomas A., 32, 33, 34, 46, 48
Douglass, Frederick, 100, 266–67, 270,
   273, 274, 276, 280, 283
Douglass, Sarah, 272
Drew University, 178
Du Bois, William E.B., 77, 203, 302
Dumont, John J., 272
Dunbar, Paul Lawrence, 9
Dunbar-Nelson, Alice, 9–10
Duncan, Clara, 209
Duncan, Sarah, 106
Duvall, Viola, 304
Dyer Anti-Lynching Bill, 148

Early, Sara Jane Woodson, 204
Edwards, James, 304
Elaw, Zilpha, 94, 272
Elizabeth, 240
Emerson, Ralph Waldo, 286
England, John, 81
Episcopal Church, 129, 189–202, 221
Equal Suffrage League, 151
Ethiopian Movement, 228
"Even a Child Can Open the Gate", 69

Fair, Rogers P., 130

Feichert, Lillian, 184
Felts, Alice S., 104
Fisher, Mary, 122 n 18
Fisk Universtiy, 221
Fleming, Lula, 234
Fletcher, Lucy, 33
Florida Memorial College, 65
Foote, Julia, 272
Ford, Arnold J., 116
Ford, Clarence, 33
Ford, Emma, 33
Ford, Geneva, 33
Ford, Mary, 33
Forten, Charlotte, 204
Fortune, T. Thomas, 180
Foster, Fannie, 33
Foster, Susie S., 142
Franklin, Aretha, 1
Frazier, Doris Fidmont, 36
Freedmen's Bureau, 212
Freedmen's Village, 268
Fry, Gladys-Marie, 22, 26, 28
Fry, J.G., 96, 99
Fugitive Slave Act, 277

Gage, Frances Dana, 265, 270, 272,
   278–80, 290, 284, 283
Gallaudet, Thomas H., 191
Garrison, William Lloyd, 249, 267, 274,
   276
Garvey Marcus, 110–11, 120, 302
Gaskill Street Coloured Infant School,
   191–92
Genovese, Eugene, 140,146
Gentry, Geneva, 33
Gibson, Garretson W., 196, 197
Gilbert, Olive, 240, 269, 272–74, 280,
   283
Giles, Harriet, 222
Gilkes, Cheryl Townsend, 6, 76
Gilliard, Georgia M., 223
Gilmore, Glenda, 216
"Give Me Wings", 38, 44–46, 48
Gleason, Miss, 207, 209
Glenn, Isabel Kelly, 223
"God Be with You Till We Meet Again",
   38

Gordon, Nora A., 224
Gordon, R.C., 224
Gosnell, Harold, 152
Graham, Sylvester, 275
Gray, Wil Lou, 303
Green, Claude, 112
Green, Harriet, 241

Haines Institute, 128
Hall, Charles Cuthbert, 30 n 2
Hall, James, 194, 196
Hall, Mrs., 100
Halston, Edwin, 301–302
Hampton Institute, 302
Harding, Vincent, 73
Harding, Warren G., 184
Harper, Frances Ellen Watkins, 80,
    272, 219 n 56
Harriet, the Moses of Her People, 239,
    242
Harris, Blanche, 208, 209
Hartford Female African Society, 190
Hayes, Rutherford B., 124
Haynes, George, 149
Heard, Josephine, 11–13
Hedrick, Joan, 293
Heilbut, Anthony, 32
"He Understands; He'll Say, 'Well
    Done' ", 67
Hewitt, Nancy, 294
Higginbotham, Evelyn Brooks, 7
Higgins, Elizabeth, 33
Higgins, Fletcher, 33
Highgate, Edmonia, 206, 207, 208, 209
Highlander Folk School, 303, 304, 305,
    396, 311
Hill, Patricia, 293
Hill, Robert A., 121, 122 n 6
Hine, Darlene Clark, 159
History of Woman Suffrage, 280–81
Hitler, Adolf, 137
Hodes, Martha, 216
Hoffman, G., 78
Holmes, Oliver Wendell, 286
Hoover, Herbert, 125
Hopkins, Samuel Miles, 241
Horton, Myles, 305, 311

Hosier, Harry, 268–69
Howard, Clara A., 224, 234, 225
"How the Sisters Are Hindered from
    Helping", 142
Hughes, S.A., 96
Hughes, Sarah Ann, 94–109
Hunter, George, 98
Hutchins, Artelia, 34
Hutchinson, Anne, 94

"If You Just Keep Still", 34
Incidents in the Life of a Slave Girl, 13,
    240
Irvin, Dona, 293
Izell, Norman L., 57

Jackson, Ada, 224
Jackson, Jackie, 32, 35, 37
Jackson, Mahalia, 11–13, 33, 35, 43
Jackson, Rebecca Cox, 272
Jacobs, Harriet, 13–14, 240, 250
Jenkins, Esau, 305
Jeter, Deacon, 65–66
Jimmerson, George D., 98, 101
Joan of Arc, 255–56
Johnson, Clifton H., 4
Johnson, Elisabeth Mars, 189–202
Johnson, J. Francis, 177
Johnson, James H. A., 101
Johnson, Leah R., 177
Johnson, Mordecai, 65
Johnson, Oliver, 242, 245
Johnson, William, 189, 191, 192, 198
Johnson, William, Jr., 192
Jones, Cary Harold, 118, 122 n 24, 123
    n 33
Jones, Edward, 189, 191, 192
Jordan, L.C., 143
Joubert, Jacques, 77, 79, 82, 83, 84, 85,
    86, 87

Karolik, M., 30 n 2
Kelley, Abby Foster, 275
Kelley, Mary, 293
Kemper, Jackson, 191, 198
Kennedy, Charles, 59, 63

Kilson, Marion, 121
King, Coretta Scott, 308
"King of My Life, I Crown Thee Now",
    38
King, Martin Luther Jr., 300, 306, 307,
    308, 311
Knesipi, King, 111, 112
Kofey, Laura Adorkor, 110–23
Ku Klux Klan, 300

Lacan, Jacques, 270
Laney, Lucy Croft, 128
Lange, Elizabeth, 78, 79–80, 82, 83, 84,
    88
Laveau, Marie, 1
Layten, S. Willie, 142, 143, 145, 147,
    149, 151, 152
Leak, R. H. W., 98, 101, 104
"Learning on the Everlasting Arms",
    138
Lee, Benjamin F., 96, 99, 103–104
Lee, Jarena, 5, 6
Lemon, Laura, 106
"Lest I Forget", 38
"Let Me Call You Sweetheart", 138
Lewter, Nicholas, 73
Liberia, 189–202
Liberian Frontier Force, 232
Life and Letters of John Brown, 243,
    277
"The Lifeboat Is Coming", 44, 46–48
*The Life and Religious Experiences of
    Jarena Lee, a Coloured Lady, Giving
    an Account of Her Call to Preach the
    Gospel*, 5
*Life of James Mars, a Slave Born and
    Sold in Connecticut*, 190
Lincoln, Abraham, 284
Livermore, Harriet, 272
Livingstone College, 181
Logan, Onnie Lee, 10–11, 14
Longfellow, Henry Wadsworth, 273
Louise, Gabriel, 86

Malekeba, Anna Ruth, 229
Malekebu, Daniel, 225, 229, 233
Malekebu, Flora, 233

Marcus, Alma, 121
Mars, James, 190, 195
Mars, Jupiter, 190–91
Marshall, Thurgood, 303
Marthews, Ray, 293
Martin-Dow, DeWitt, 115, 118
Maryland State Colonization Society,
    194
Matthews, Robert, 263
Matthias the Prophet, 263, 270, 272,
    286
May, Joe, 33, 43
Mayesville Institute, 126
Mbiti, John, 75
McCarroll, Eugene Preston, 118
McCloud, Aminah Beverly, 14
McIntosh, Patsy, 125
McKay, Nellie, 293
McLeod, Samuel, 125
Meharry Medical College, 233
Methodist Episcopal Church, 2,
    124–39, 221
Methodist Protestant Church, 105, 132
Miller, Thomas E., 302
Mitchell, Henry, 73, 75
Mitchell, Robert, 144
Moman, Rachel, 99, 108 n 25
Moody Bible Institute, 127, 178
Moody, Dwight L., 127
Moore, Richard V., 135
Moore, T.A., 65
Moral Rearmament Movement, 136–37
Morehouse College, 65, 222
Morgan State, 221
Mormonism, 2, 158–76
Morning Glories, 12
Morris, E.C., 151
Morris, Elias Camp, 144
Morrison, Roy T., 68–69

Narrative of Sojourner Truth, 270, 271,
    272, 273, 274, 275, 280, 283
*Narrative of the Life of Frederick
    Douglass, An American Slave*, 273
National Association for the Advance-
    ment of Colored People, 125, 148,
    150, 301, 302, 303, 304

National Association of Colored
Women, 150, 152, 181
National Council of Negro Women,
124, 131, 134–35
National League of Republican Col-
ored Women, 152
National Youth Administration, 124,
131, 134–35
Negro History Week, 184
New Jersey Federation of Colored
Women's Clubs, 181–83
New Jersey Manual Training and Indus-
trial School for Colored Youth, 184
New Jersey State Suffrage Assocation,
183
New Thought, 10
Newman, Richard, 293
Niagara Movement, 302
Nierenberg, George, 32
Nightingale, Florence, 255
Nimmo, James, 112, 122 n 12
Northampton Association of Education
and Industry, 266, 273, 274
The Northern Teacher in the South, 203
Nyombolo, E. M., 114, 118, 119

O'Neal Twins, 33, 36
Oberlin College, 13, 205, 208, 209, 214
Oblate Sisters of Providence, 73–93
Ong, Walter J., 269
Ouaye, Buitiful, 123, n 31
Owens, L.E., 60
Owens, S.A., 65

Palmer, Mrs., 100
Paris, Peter, 140,145
Parkard, Sophia B., 222
Parks, Rosa, 305, 308
Parrish, Mary, 143
Patterson, Orlando, 4
Paul, Alice, 152
Payne, Daniel A., 96,98,99
Peake, Mary, 204
Pearl, Henry, 160
Pearl, Mary Patterson, 160
Pement, Philemon, 167
Pentecostal Movement, 2

Perry, Regina, 27
Perry, Ted, 282
Phaedrus, 269
Phelps, Jamie, 86
Phillips, Wendell, 242
Phillips, William H., 142
Pinkster, 262
Pinney, John B., 194
Plato, 269
Poinsette, Joel, 300–301
Poinsette, Peter, 300–301
Poinsette, Victoria, 300
"Poor Nina, the Fugitive", 241, 249
Powers, Harriet, 21–31
Pratt, Jerry, 35
Presbyterian Church, 2, 125, 128, 213,
250
Preston, Katherine Hall, 30 n 2
Price, Zella Jackson, 37
Putnam, Mr., 212

Quarles, Frank, 222

Raboteau, Albert, 140, 216
Rainey, Ma, 34
Randolph Leah Viola, 178
Randolph, Florence Spearing, 177–85
Randolph, Hugh, 177, 178
Rattray, Margaret, 225
Reddick, Hannah, 151
Redpath, James, 283
Reed, Mary, 206, 207
Reeves, Garth, 121
Remond, Sarah, 272
Reorganized Church of Jesus Christ of
Latter Day Saints, 158–76
Reynolds, Mrs. M.C., 222
Rice Sarah, 7
Rice-Sauer, Edie, 109 n 49
Ripley, C. Peter, 271
Robbins, Amy E., 158–76
Robbins, Arnold, 170
Robbins, Eugene Wentworth, 163
Robbins, Herbert M., 65, 161, 163
Robbins, LaVerne, 171
Robbins, Russell, 165, 169
Roberts, Deotis, 140

Roberts, E.D., 96
Robinson, Marius, 289
Roger Williams College, 65
Rollin, Frances "Frank", 8–9
Roman Catholic Church, 2, 73–93
A Room of One's Own, 271
Roosevelt, Eleanor, 130
Roosevelt, Franklin D., 124, 125
Roosevelt, Theodore, 151
Rosemond, Connie, 69
Ross, Benjamin, 241
Ross, Betsy, 282
Rush, Gertrude, 152
Russwurm, John B., 194
Rust College, 62, 221

Sampson, George D., 101
Sanborn, F.B., 242
Sauls, Scipio, 98
Savage, Thomas S., 194–95, 196
Say Amen, Somebody, 32
Scenes in the Life of Harriet Tubman, 242
Schofield Seminary, 231
Scotia Seminary for Negro Girls, 127
Scott, Anna M., 196
Scott, Emmett J., 149
Sears, Ernest, 118–19, 120
Seattle, Chief, 282
Seuhn Industrial Mission, 224, 225, 231
Shaw University, 222
Shaw, Anna Howard, 105, 109 n 49, 152
Shelby, Thomas, 59, 60
Shillady, John R., 148
Shippy, George, 160
Sigourney, Lydia H., 190
Simmons, J. Andrew, 303–304
Simmons-Akers Singers, 32
Six Women's Slave Narratives, 240
Sizer, Lyde Cullen, 293–94
Smith, Amanda Berry, 5–6, 94, 95, 107 n 9
Smith, Bessie, 33
Smith, E.A., 170
Smith, Frederick M., 168
Smith, Genesser, 3
Smith, Gerrit, 242
Smith, Jacqueline, 34

Smith, James Peter, 34
Smith, Jennie, 21
Smith, William, 160
Smith, Willie James, 34, 35, 36, 37
Smith, Willie Mae Ford, 32–54
Society of Friends, 208
"Sojourner Truth, the Libyan Sibyl",
    277–8
"Something Within", 69
Soul Theology: The Heart of American
    Black Culture, 73
South African Baptist Association, 228
South Carolina State College, 301
Southern Christian Leadership Confer-
    ence, 303, 305
Spearing, Anna Smith, 177
Spearing, John, 177
Spelman College, 220–35
Spivak, Gayatri C., 270
St. Augustine's College, 221
Stanley, Frances Griffith, 213
Stanley, John Carruthers, 213–14
Stanley, John Stewart, 213–14
Stanley, John Wright, 213–14
Stanley, Kitty, 213
Stanley, Sara G., 203–219
Stanton, Elizabeth Cady, 281
Steward, Mamie, 150
Stewart, Emma, 35
Stewart, Jeffrey, 240
Stewart, Lydia Carruthers, 213
Stewart, Maria, 272
Stewart, Violet, 37
Still, Mary, 204, 205
Stokes, Albert, 112
Stokes, Edward C., 183–84
Stowe, Harriet Beecher, 243, 270, 272,
    276, 277, 283, 285, 290, 281
Swint, Henry Lee, 203
Swisshelm, Jane, 279

Taylor, Susie King, 15
Taylor, Susie M., 231
Taylor-Greenfield, Elizabeth, 80
Teish, Luisah, 11
Temperence Union League, 181
Tennessee State University, 62

Tharpe, Rosetta 50, n 4
Thelen, David, 294
"There Is a Holy City", 278
Thomas, Catherine Ann, 159
Thomas, Charles Edward, 159
Thomas, Charles W., 164
Thomas, Cora Pair, 234
Thomas, Eliza Jane Pearl, 159
Thomas, Marie Helen, 84
Thompson, James Madison, 193, 194, 195
Thompson, James Madison Jr., 195
Thompson, Mary Agnes, 196
Thoreau, Henry David, 286
Thurman, Howard, 65
Tilden, Samuel J., 124
Titus, Frances, 272
Topp, E. B., 226
"Touch Me, Lord Jesus", 69
Tougaloo College, 221
Townsend, A.M., 64–65
Truman, Harry S., 125
Truth, Sojourner, 1, 80, 262–99
Tubman, Harriet, 3, 239–61
Tucker, Thomas, 205
Turner, Henry McNeal, 102–103, 105, 106, 108 n 25, 109 n 42
Turner, Martha, 106
Turner, Nat, 251

Uncle Tom's Cabin, 243, 276, 281
Unity Movement, 9
Universal Negro Improvement Association, 302
Upton, Lucy Houghton, 224

Vale, Gilbert, 264, 267
Van Wagner, Isabella, 262–67, 287
Van Wagner, Peter, 264
VanPelt, Peter Jr., 191
Vesey, Deacon, 68
Victoria, Queen, 80
Vlach, John, 28

Walker, Margaret, 1
Walker, Samuel, 206, 209–210
Ward Singers, 32

Ward, Mary, 81
Waring, J. Waties, 304
Washington College, 189
Washington, Booker T., 59–60, 143, 151
Washington, Ernestine B., 50 n 4
Washington, George, 282
Weems, Mason, 282
West, Cornel, 140
"We've Fought Every Race's Battle But Our Own", 150
Whipple, George, 205, 206, 207, 209
White Citizen's Council, 300, 306
Whitfield, James, 79, 81
Whitman, Lena Clark, 225
Whittier, John G., 219 n 56
Williams, Floyd, 67–68
Williams, L.K., 69
Williams, Lucie E., Campbell 56–70
Williams, Mary, 33
Williams, Mrs., 100
Williams, Peter Jr., 193
Willigman, Charity, 84
Willigman, Sarah, 84
Wilson, Emma, 125
Wilson, John F., 216
Wilson, Lillie Belle, 223
Wilson, Margaret, 94, 95, 96, 97, 100, 101, 104
Wilson, Woodrow, 149, 183
Winholtz, Wilford G., 171
Wise, Elaine, 294
Wolfe, Millie, 106
Women's Christian Temperence Union, 179, 180, 181
Woodburg, Prof., 205, 206, 207
Woodward, Charles, 212
Woolf, Virginia, 271
World Baptist Conference, 230

Yellin, Jean Fagan, 275, 294
Young Women's Christian Associaton, 304
Young, Brigham, 158
Young, Roy M., 162

Zboray, Ronald, 294
Zero, Flora, 225